*This world that we
live in is gentle yet sad,
fun yet sorrowful,
strong yet ephemeral...*

# WHAT a WONDERFUL WORLD!

STORY & ART BY
**Inio Asano**      volume
**two**

VIZ Signature Edition

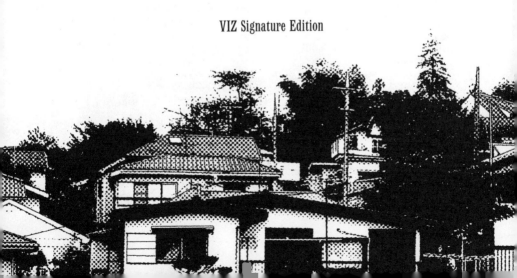

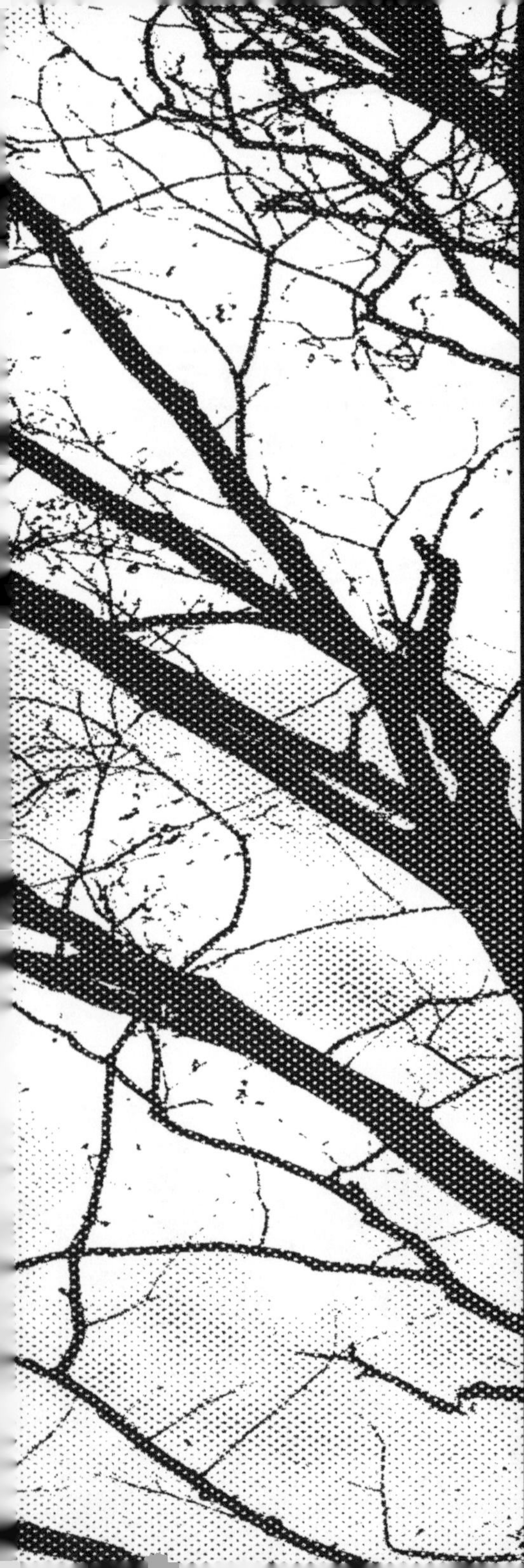

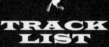

# TRACK LIST

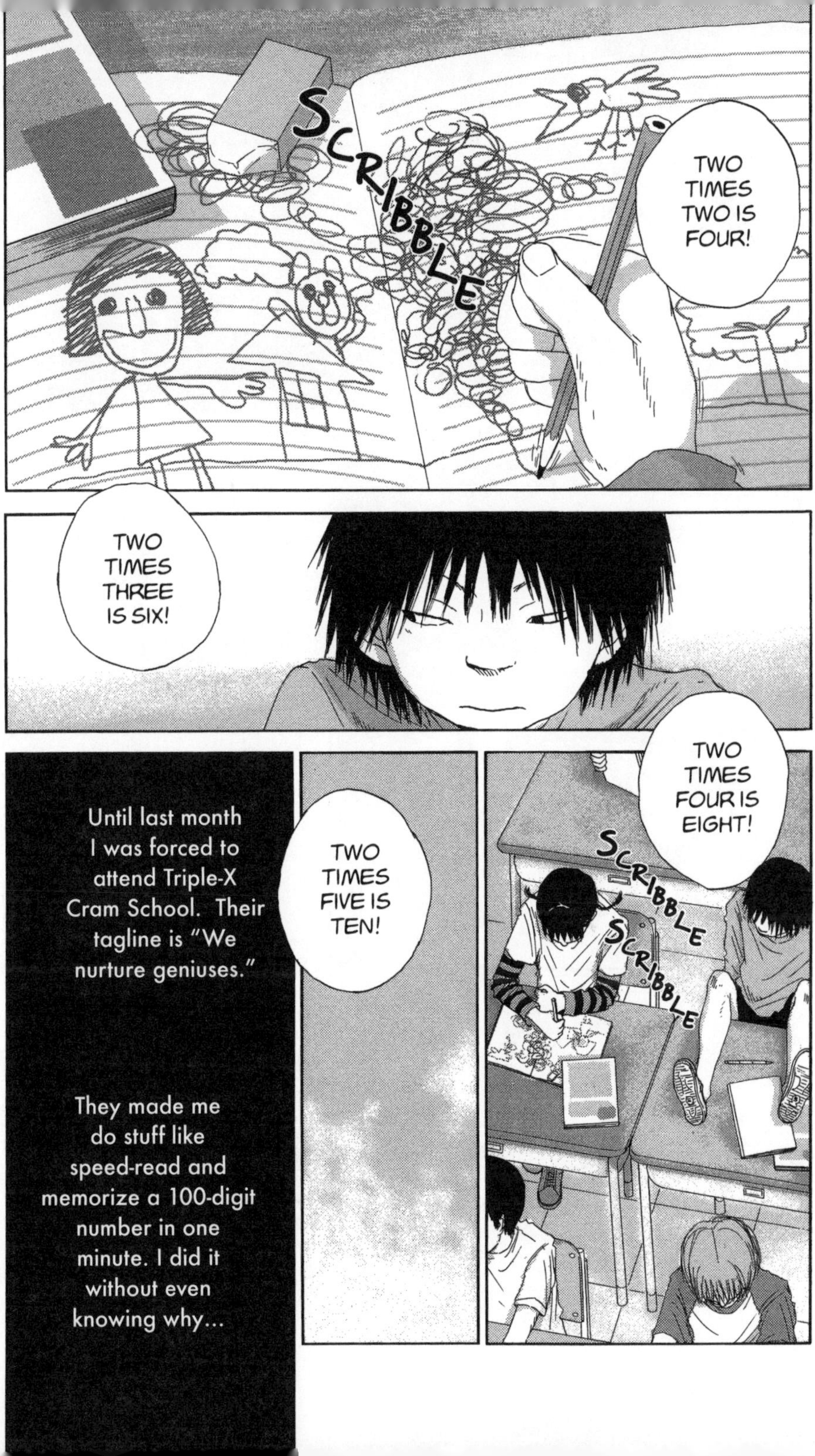
SCRIBBLE
TWO TIMES TWO IS FOUR!
TWO TIMES THREE IS SIX!
TWO TIMES FOUR IS EIGHT!
SCRIBBLE
SCRIBBLE
TWO TIMES FIVE IS TEN!
Until last month I was forced to attend Triple-X Cram School. Their tagline is "We nurture geniuses."
They made me do stuff like speed-read and memorize a 100-digit number in one minute. I did it without even knowing why...

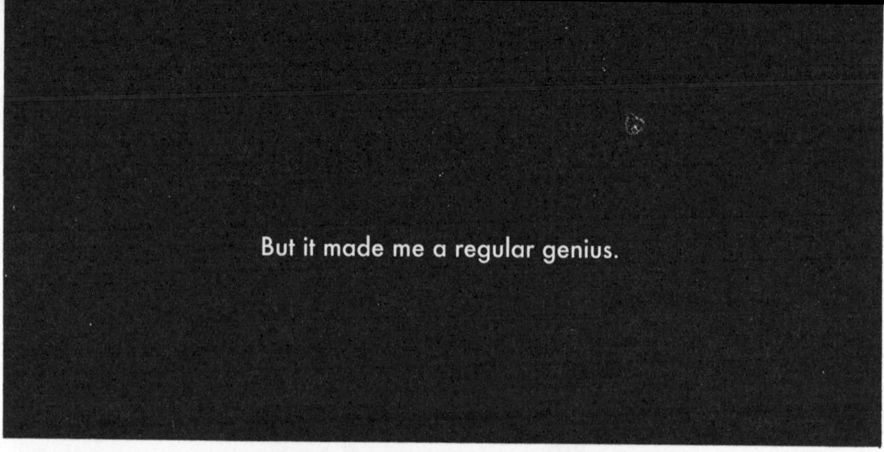
But it made me a regular genius.

## 10th track Bird Week

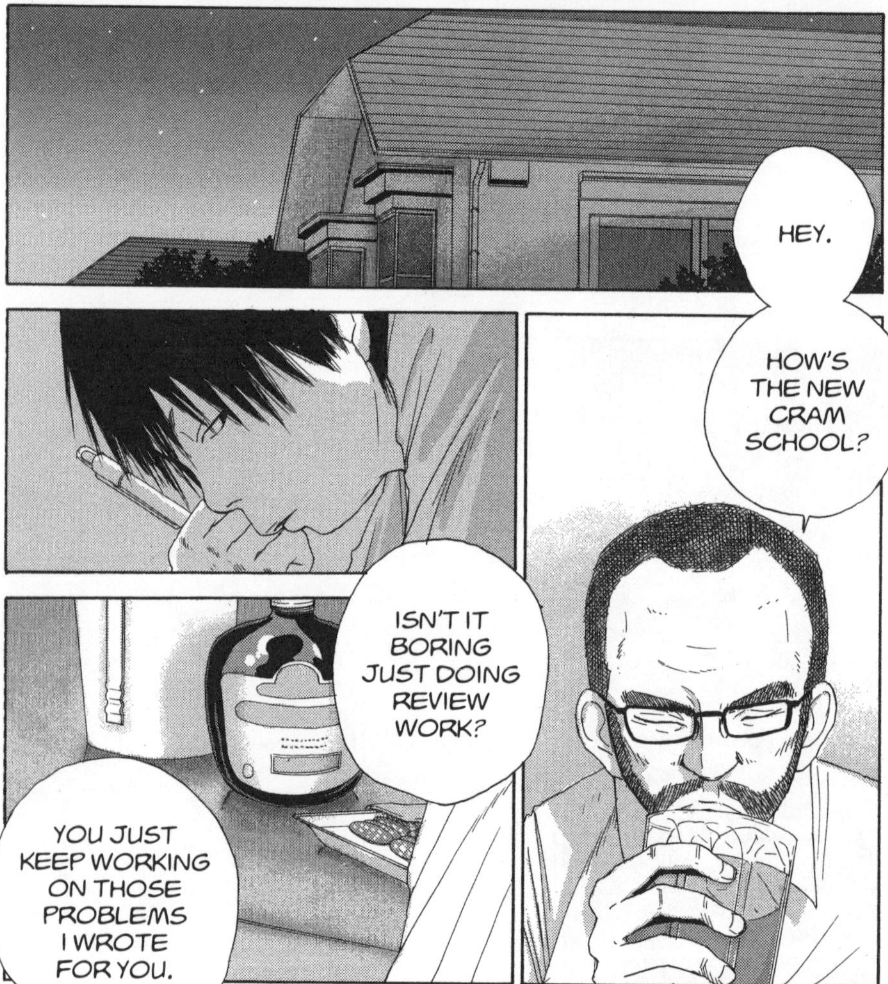
HEY.
HOW'S THE NEW CRAM SCHOOL?
ISN'T IT BORING JUST DOING REVIEW WORK?
YOU JUST KEEP WORKING ON THOSE PROBLEMS I WROTE FOR YOU.

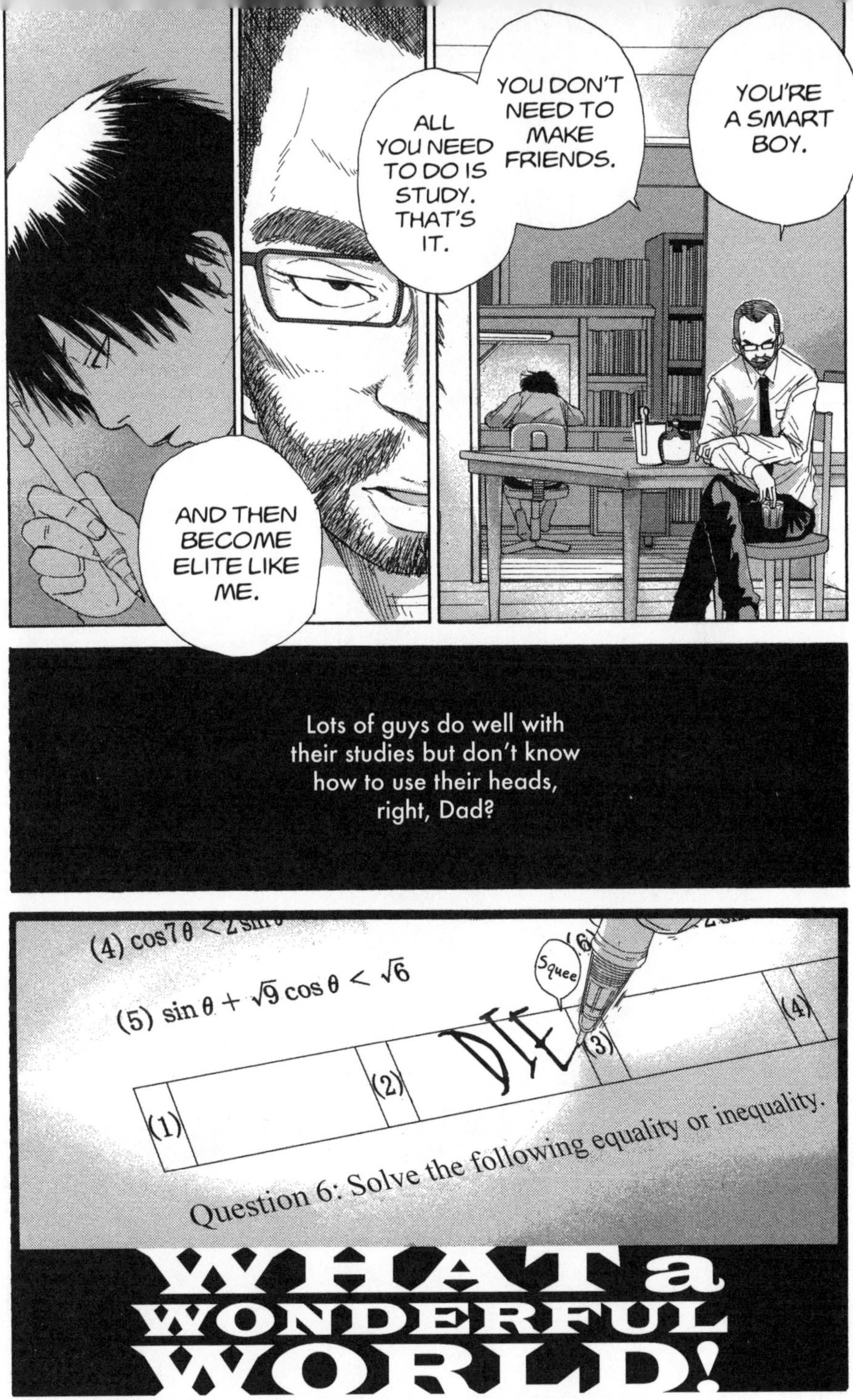
YOU'RE A SMART BOY.
YOU DON'T NEED TO MAKE FRIENDS.
ALL YOU NEED TO DO IS STUDY. THAT'S IT.
AND THEN BECOME ELITE LIKE ME.
Lots of guys do well with their studies but don't know how to use their heads, right, Dad?
(4) cos7θ
(5) sin θ + √9 cos θ < √6
Squee
DIE
(1)
(2)
(3)
(4)
Question 6: Solve the following equality or inequality.
WHAT a WONDERFUL WORLD!

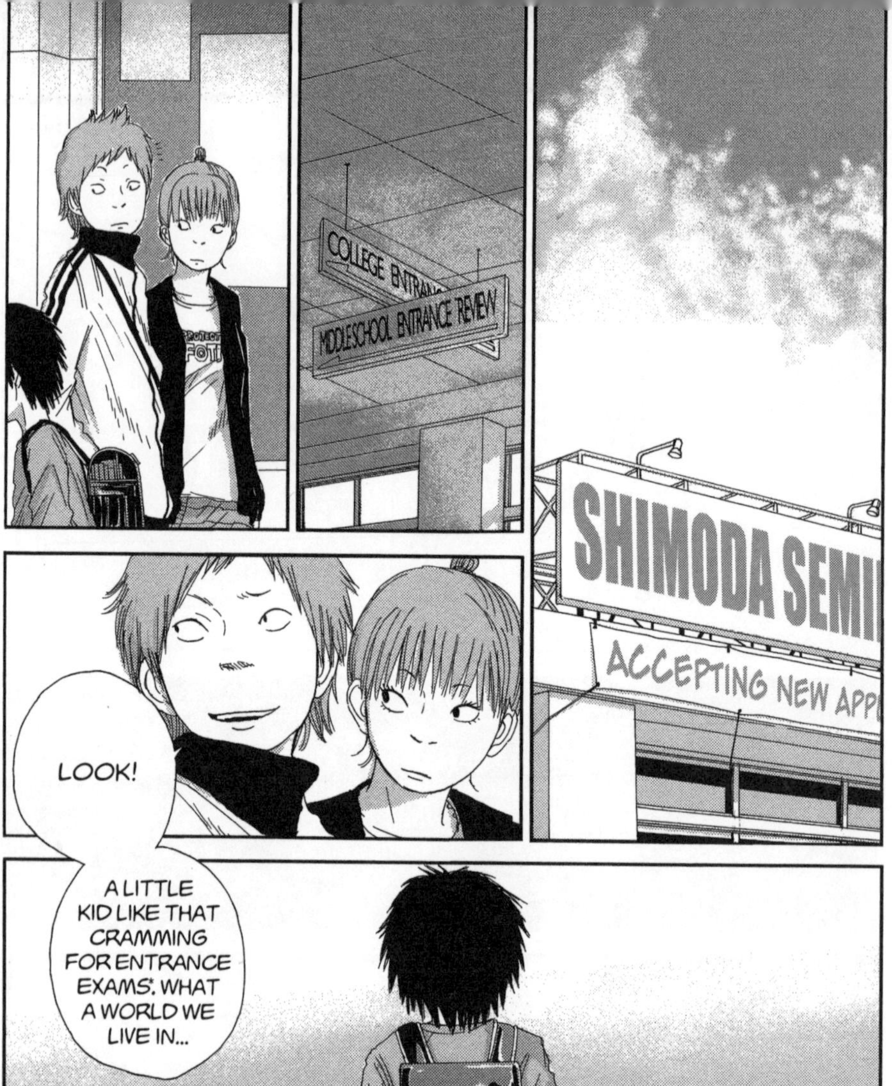
SHIMODA SEMI
ACCEPTING NEW APP
COLLEGE ENTRANC
MIDDLESCHOOL ENTRANCE REVIEW
LOOK!
A LITTLE KID LIKE THAT CRAMMING FOR ENTRANCE EXAMS*. WHAT A WORLD WE LIVE IN...

*IN JAPAN, HIGH SCHOOLS HAVE ENTRANCE EXAMS JUST LIKE COLLEGES DO.

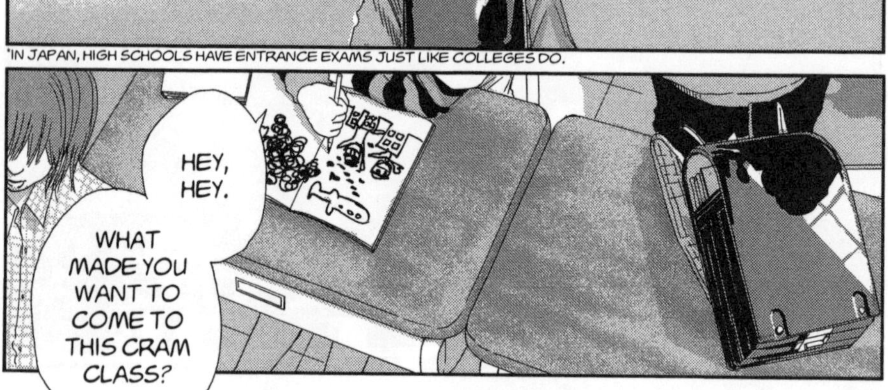
HEY, HEY.
WHAT MADE YOU WANT TO COME TO THIS CRAM CLASS?

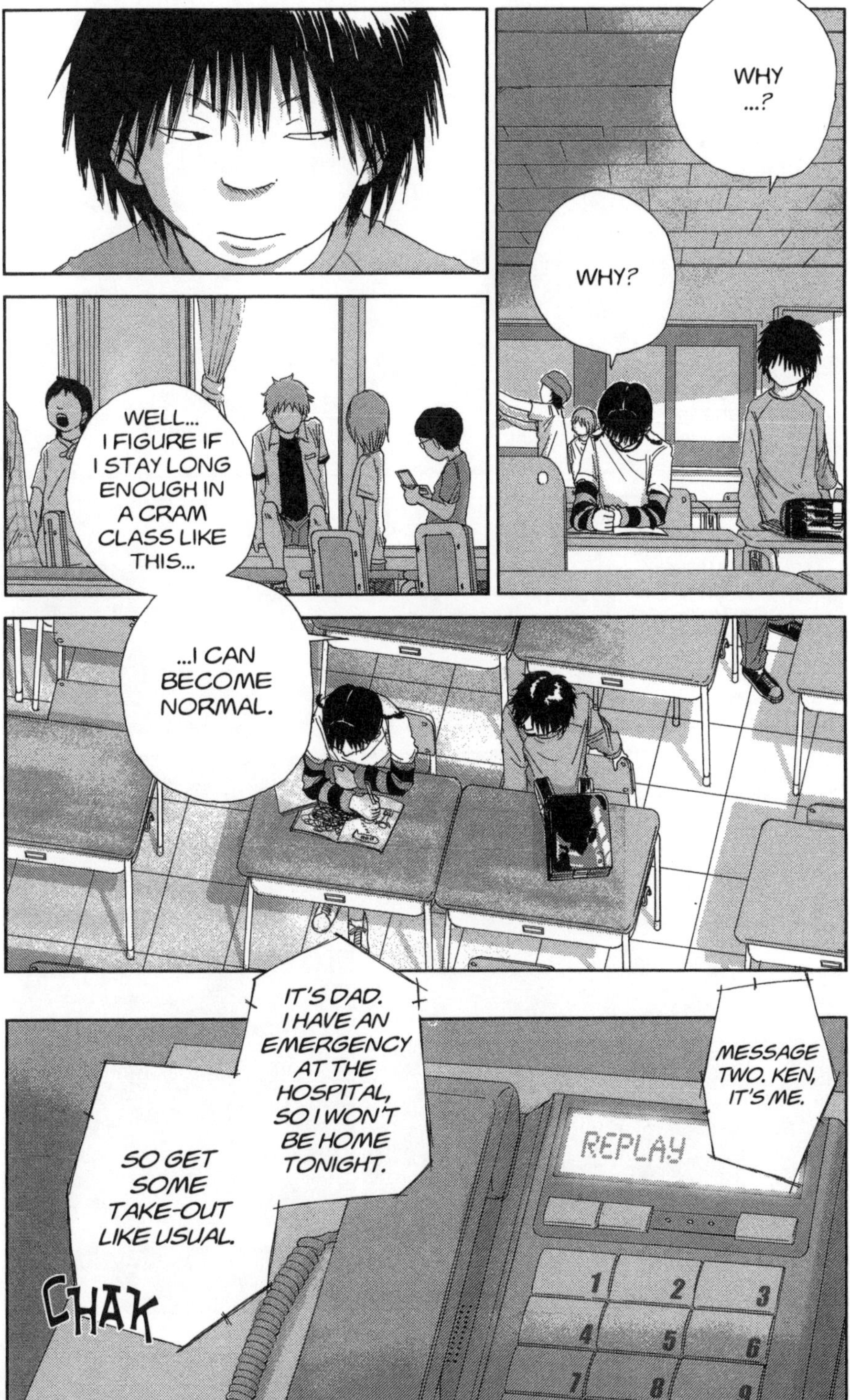
WHY ...?
WHY?
WELL... I FIGURE IF I STAY LONG ENOUGH IN A CRAM CLASS LIKE THIS...
...I CAN BECOME NORMAL.
MESSAGE TWO. KEN, IT'S ME.
REPLAY
IT'S DAD. I HAVE AN EMERGENCY AT THE HOSPITAL, SO I WON'T BE HOME TONIGHT.
SO GET SOME TAKE-OUT LIKE USUAL.
CHAK

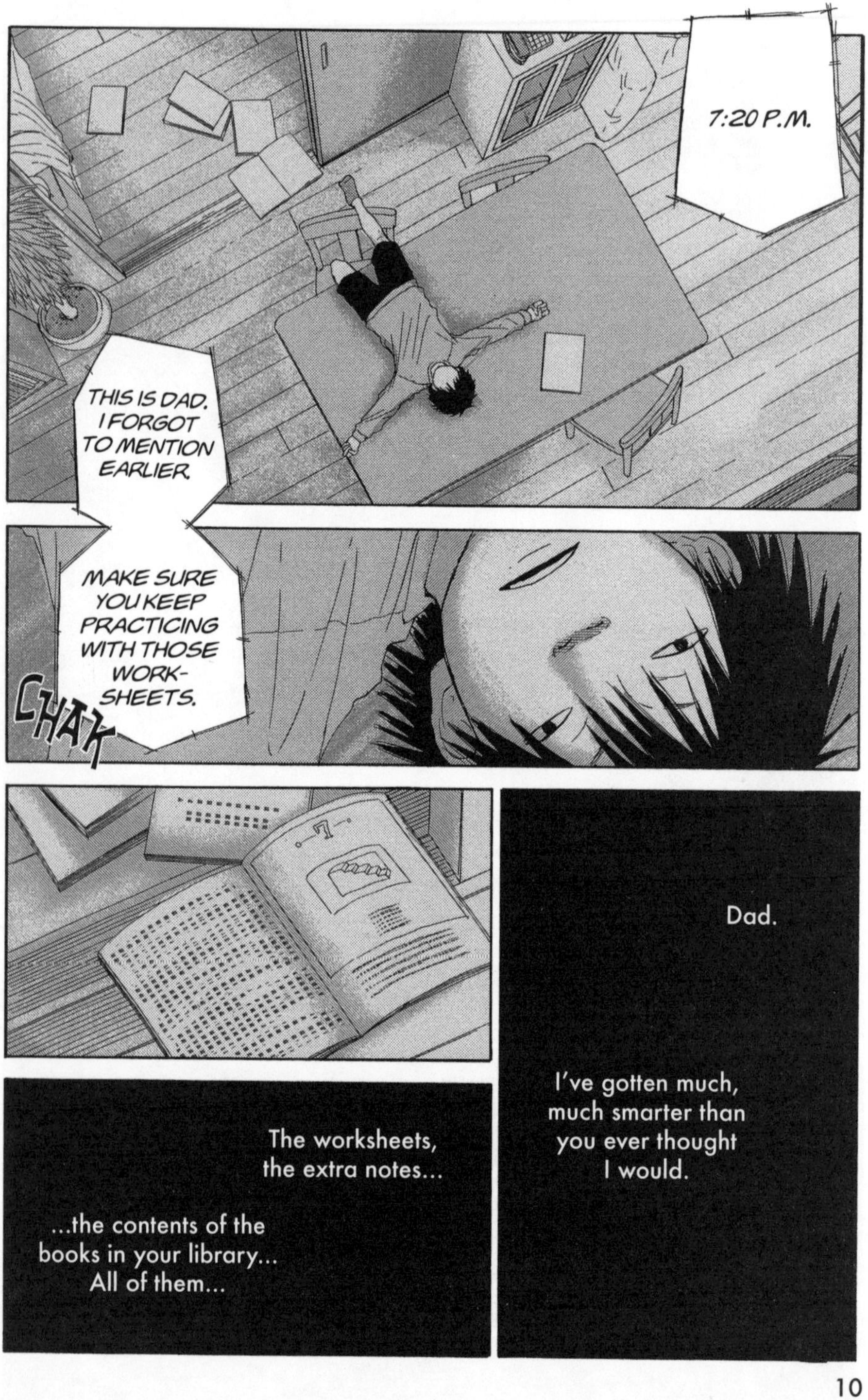
7:20 P.M.
THIS IS DAD. I FORGOT TO MENTION EARLIER.
MAKE SURE YOU KEEP PRACTICING WITH THOSE WORK-SHEETS.
CHAK
Dad.
I've gotten much, much smarter than you ever thought I would.
The worksheets, the extra notes...
...the contents of the books in your library... All of them...

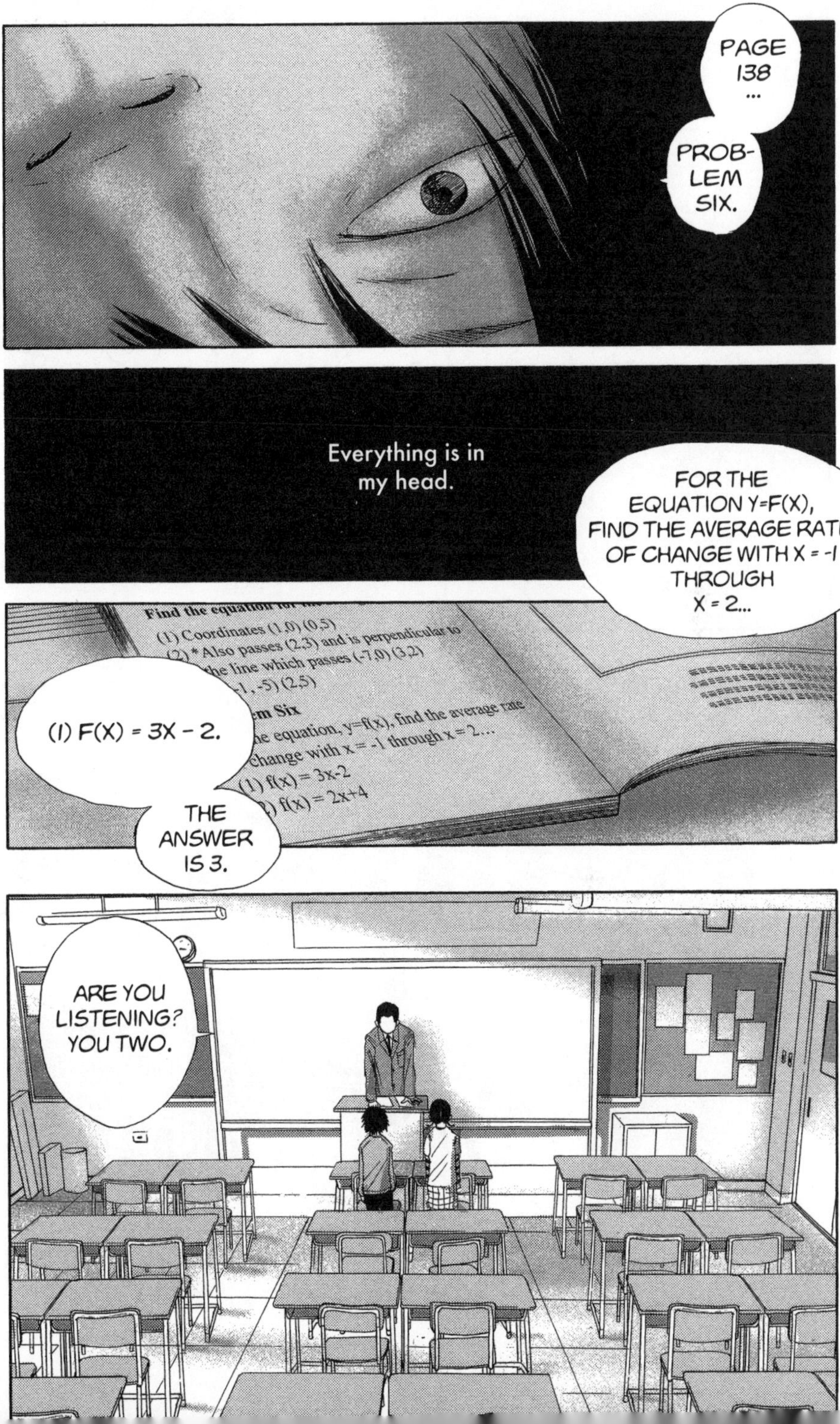
PAGE 138 ...
PROB-LEM SIX.
Everything is in my head.
FOR THE EQUATION Y=F(X), FIND THE AVERAGE RATE OF CHANGE WITH X = -1 THROUGH X = 2...
(1) Coordinates (1,0) (0,5)
the line which passes (-7,0) (3,2)
(1) f(x) = 3x-2
(1) F(X) = 3X – 2.
THE ANSWER IS 3.
ARE YOU LISTENING? YOU TWO.

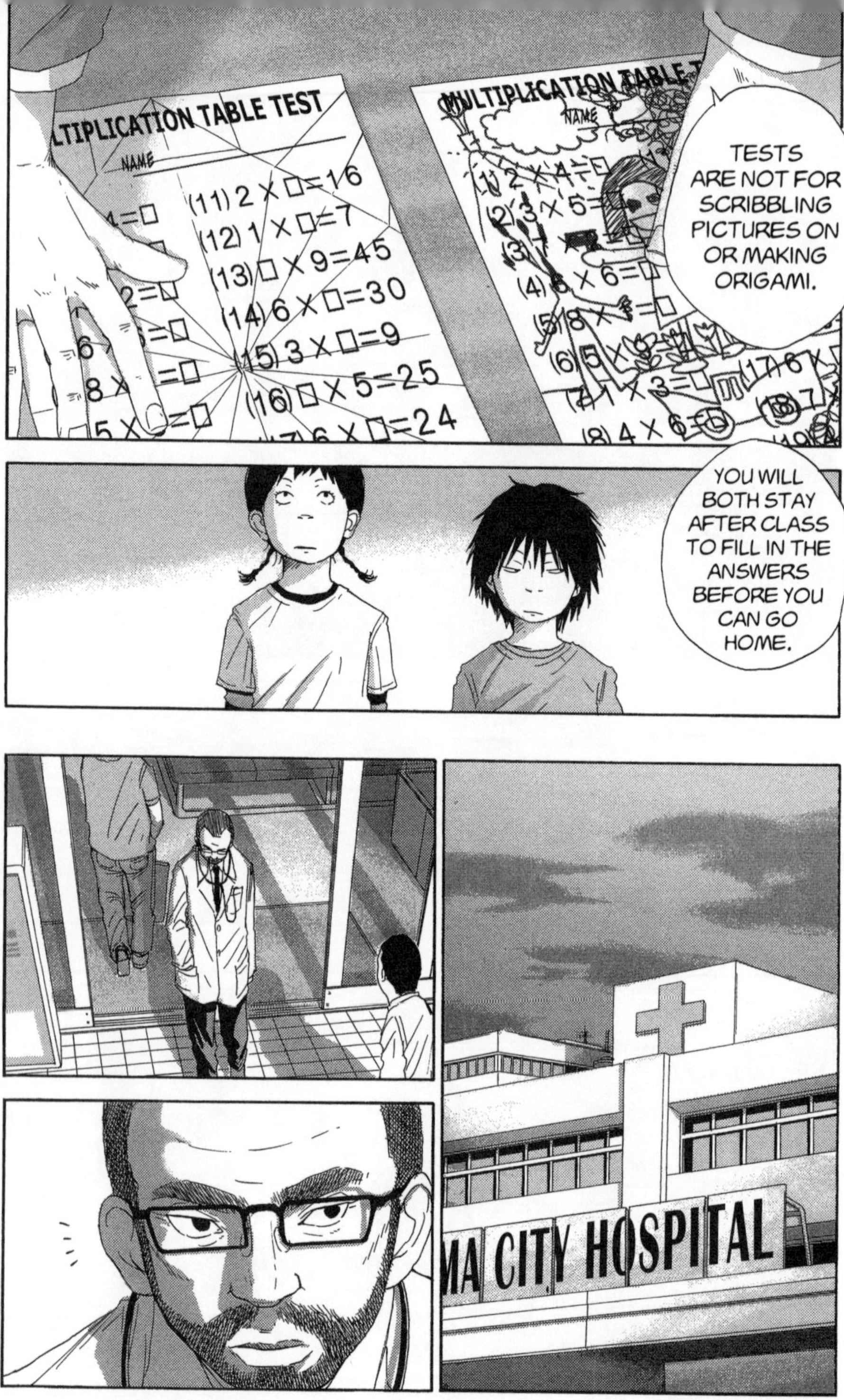
TESTS ARE NOT FOR SCRIBBLING PICTURES ON OR MAKING ORIGAMI.
MULTIPLICATION TABLE TEST
LTIPLICATION TABLE TEST
YOU WILL BOTH STAY AFTER CLASS TO FILL IN THE ANSWERS BEFORE YOU CAN GO HOME.
MA CITY HOSPITAL

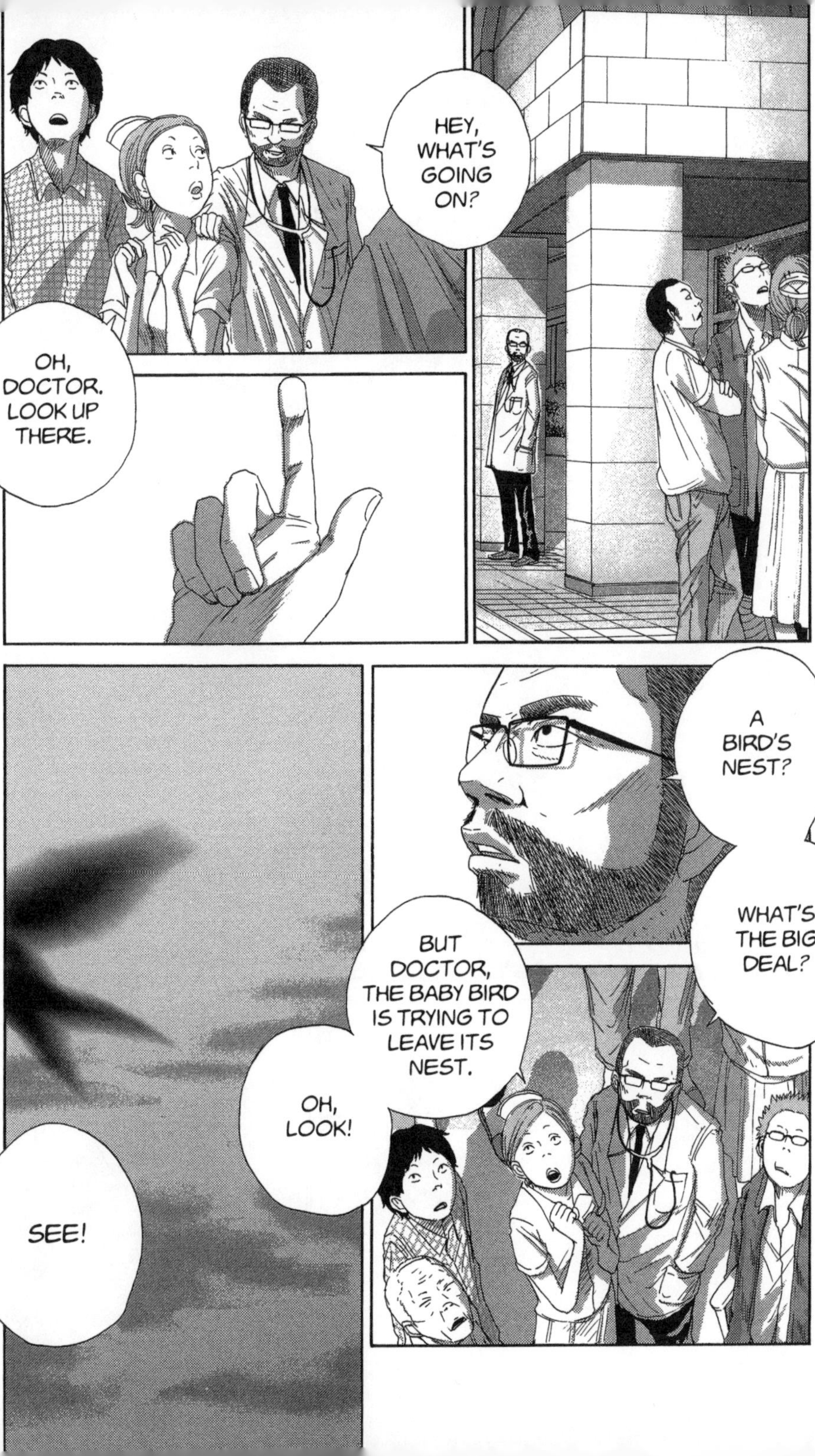
HEY, WHAT'S GOING ON?
OH, DOCTOR. LOOK UP THERE.
A BIRD'S NEST?
WHAT'S THE BIG DEAL?
BUT DOCTOR, THE BABY BIRD IS TRYING TO LEAVE ITS NEST.
OH, LOOK!
SEE!

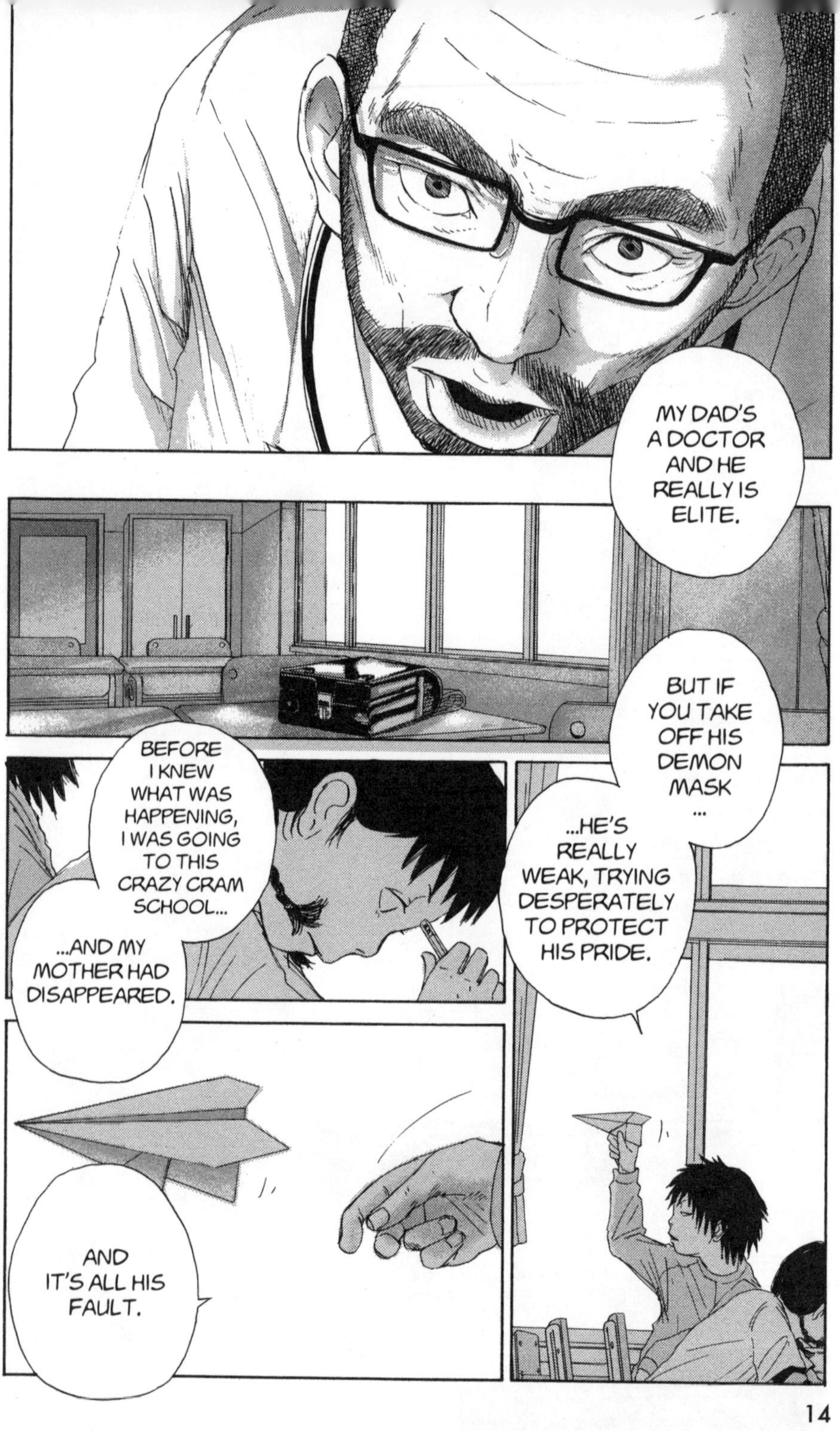
MY DAD'S A DOCTOR AND HE REALLY IS ELITE.
BUT IF YOU TAKE OFF HIS DEMON MASK ...
...HE'S REALLY WEAK, TRYING DESPERATELY TO PROTECT HIS PRIDE.
BEFORE I KNEW WHAT WAS HAPPENING, I WAS GOING TO THIS CRAZY CRAM SCHOOL...
...AND MY MOTHER HAD DISAPPEARED.
AND IT'S ALL HIS FAULT.

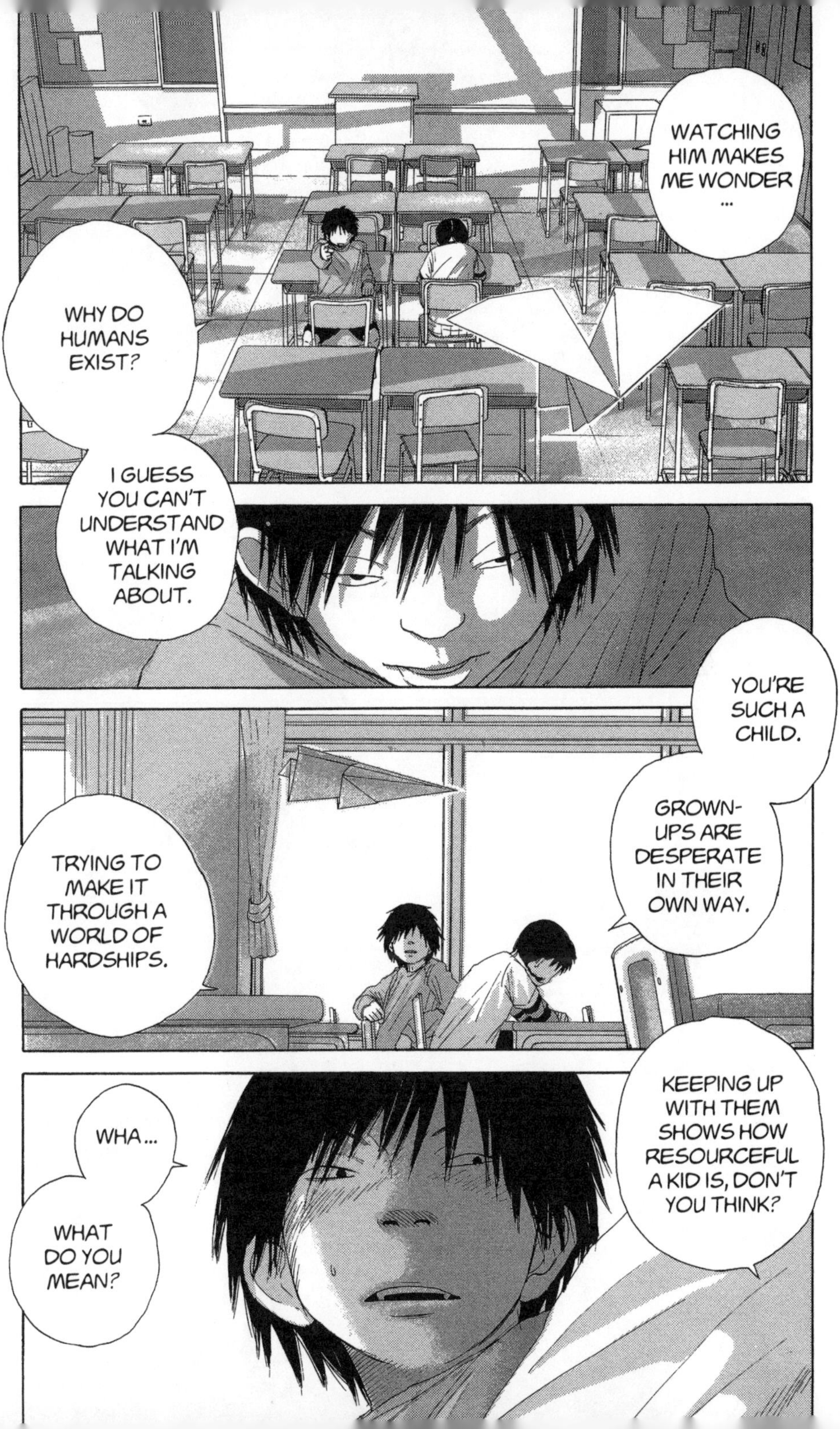
WATCHING HIM MAKES ME WONDER ...
WHY DO HUMANS EXIST?
I GUESS YOU CAN'T UNDERSTAND WHAT I'M TALKING ABOUT.
YOU'RE SUCH A CHILD.
GROWN-UPS ARE DESPERATE IN THEIR OWN WAY.
TRYING TO MAKE IT THROUGH A WORLD OF HARDSHIPS.
KEEPING UP WITH THEM SHOWS HOW RESOURCEFUL A KID IS, DON'T YOU THINK?
WHA...
WHAT DO YOU MEAN?

YOU'RE MUCH, MUCH DUMBER...

...THAN YOU THINK.

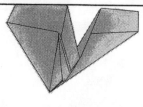

THEN I'D BE...

THEN...

CLATTER

DON'T RUN AWAY FROM REALITY!

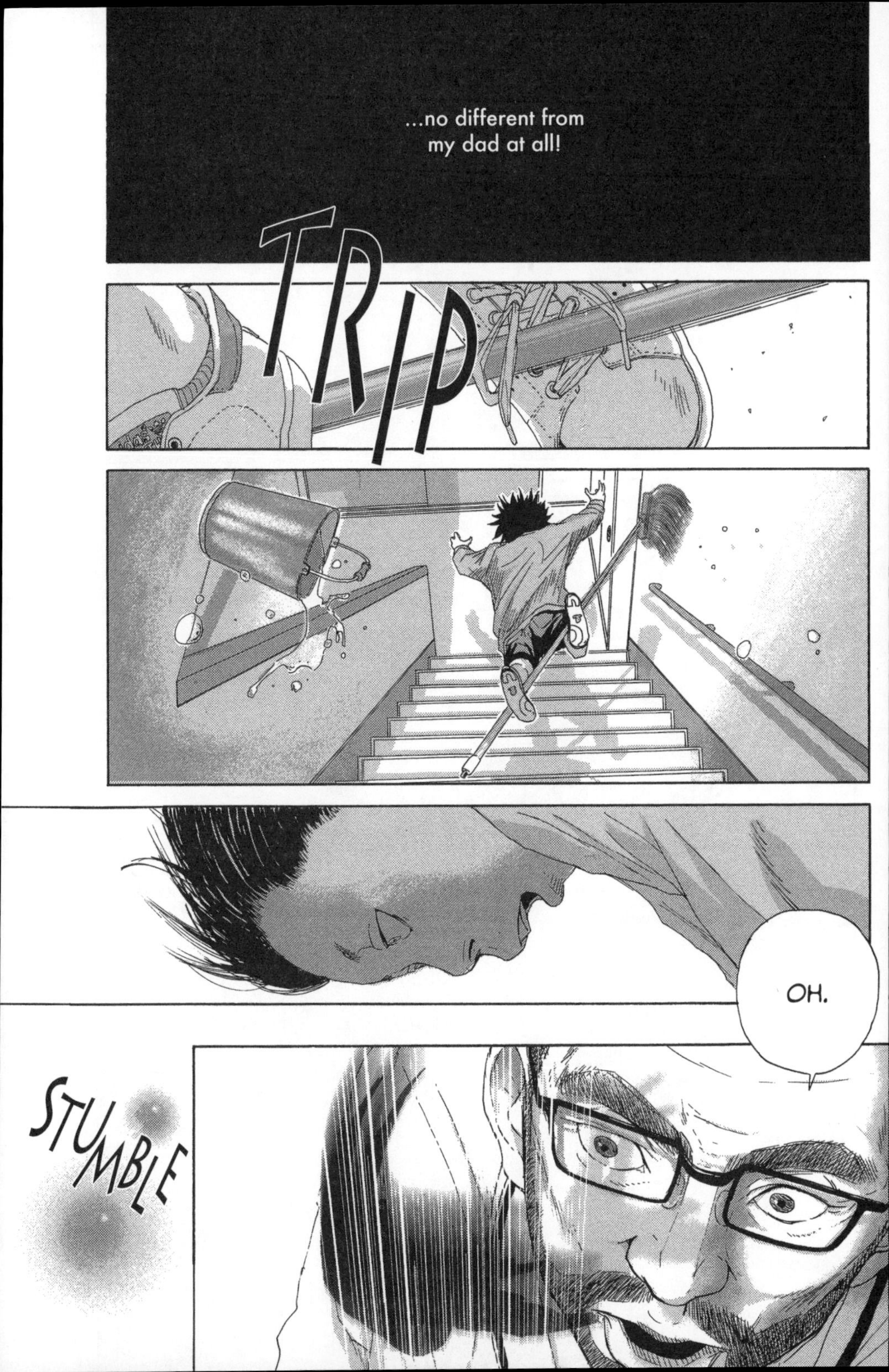
...no different from
my dad at all!
TRIP
OH.
STUMBLE

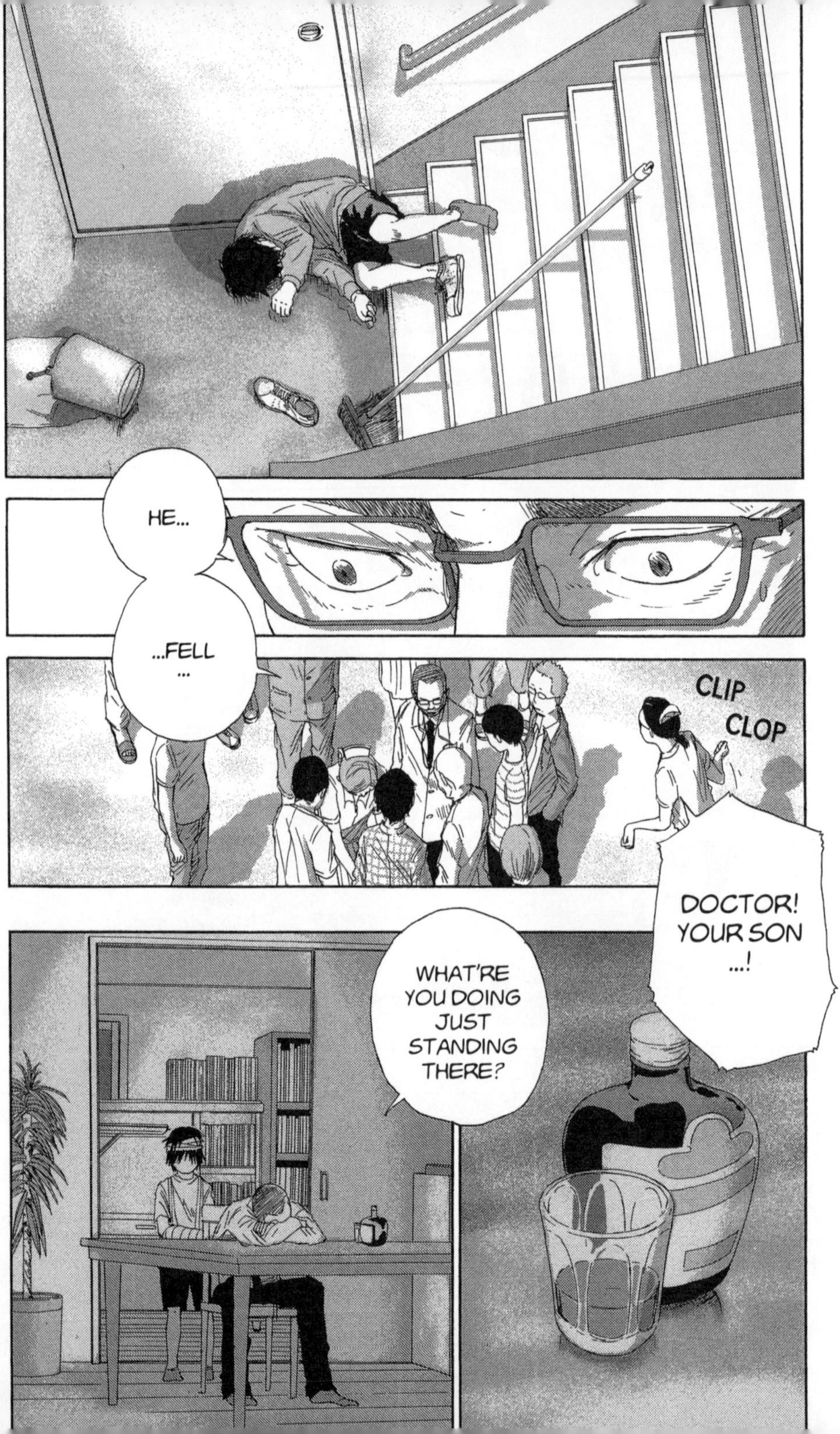
HE...
...FELL ...
CLIP CLOP
DOCTOR! YOUR SON ...!
WHAT'RE YOU DOING JUST STANDING THERE?

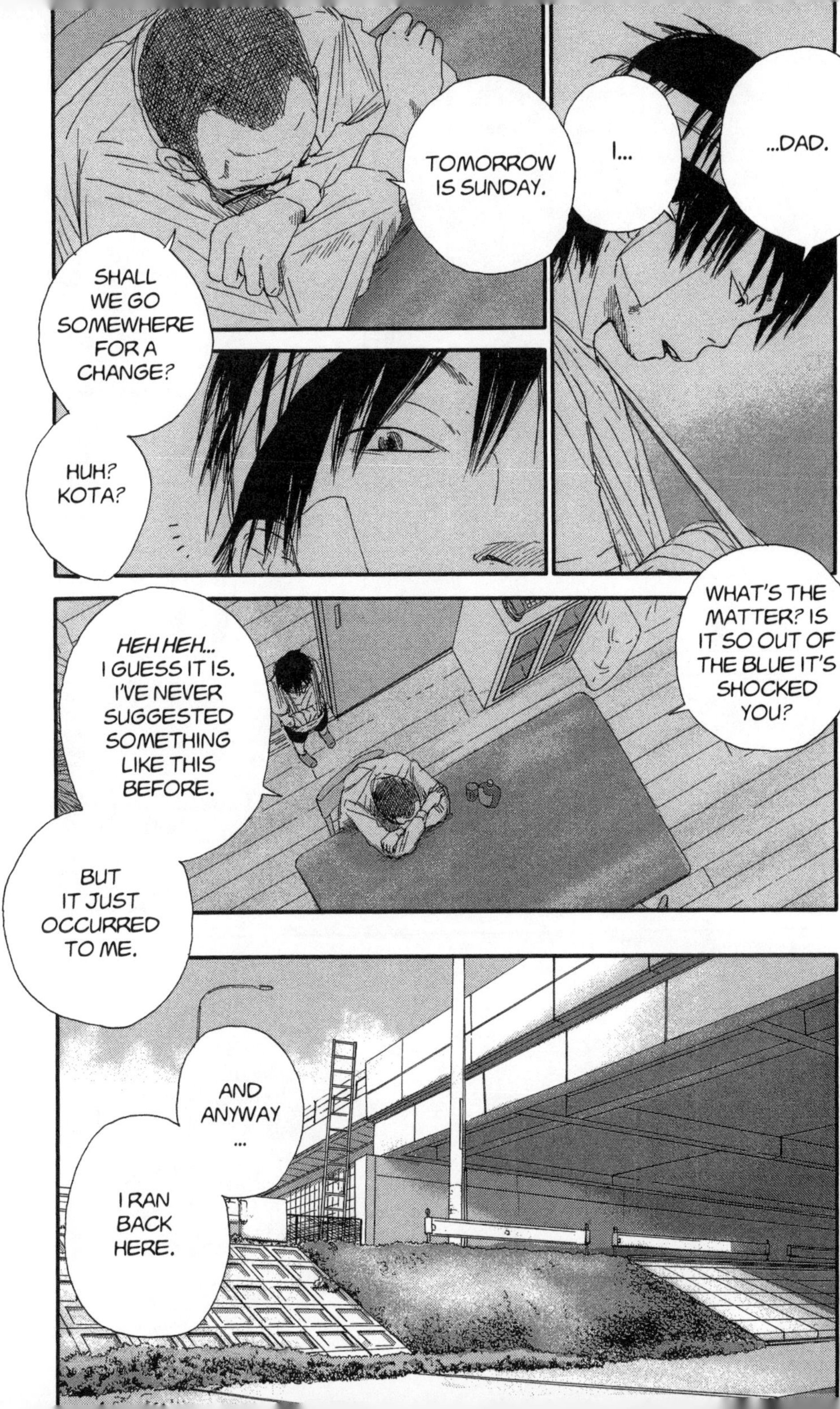
...DAD.
I...
TOMORROW IS SUNDAY.
SHALL WE GO SOMEWHERE FOR A CHANGE?
HUH? KOTA?
WHAT'S THE MATTER? IS IT SO OUT OF THE BLUE IT'S SHOCKED YOU?
*HEH HEH...* I GUESS IT IS. I'VE NEVER SUGGESTED SOMETHING LIKE THIS BEFORE.
BUT IT JUST OCCURRED TO ME.
AND ANYWAY ...
I RAN BACK HERE.

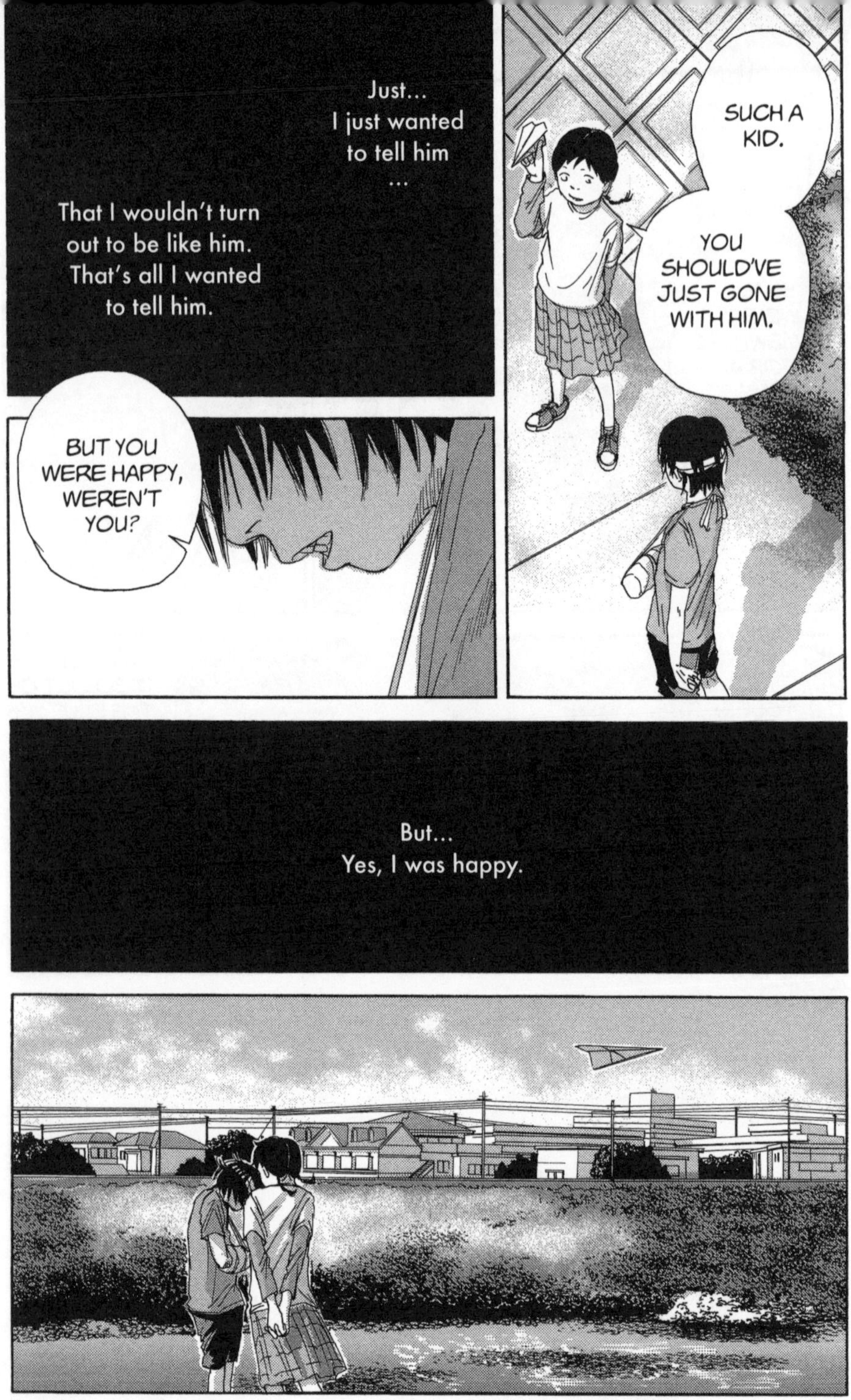
SUCH A KID.
YOU SHOULD'VE JUST GONE WITH HIM.
Just... I just wanted to tell him ...
That I wouldn't turn out to be like him. That's all I wanted to tell him.
BUT YOU WERE HAPPY, WEREN'T YOU?
But... Yes, I was happy.

# 11th track After the Rain

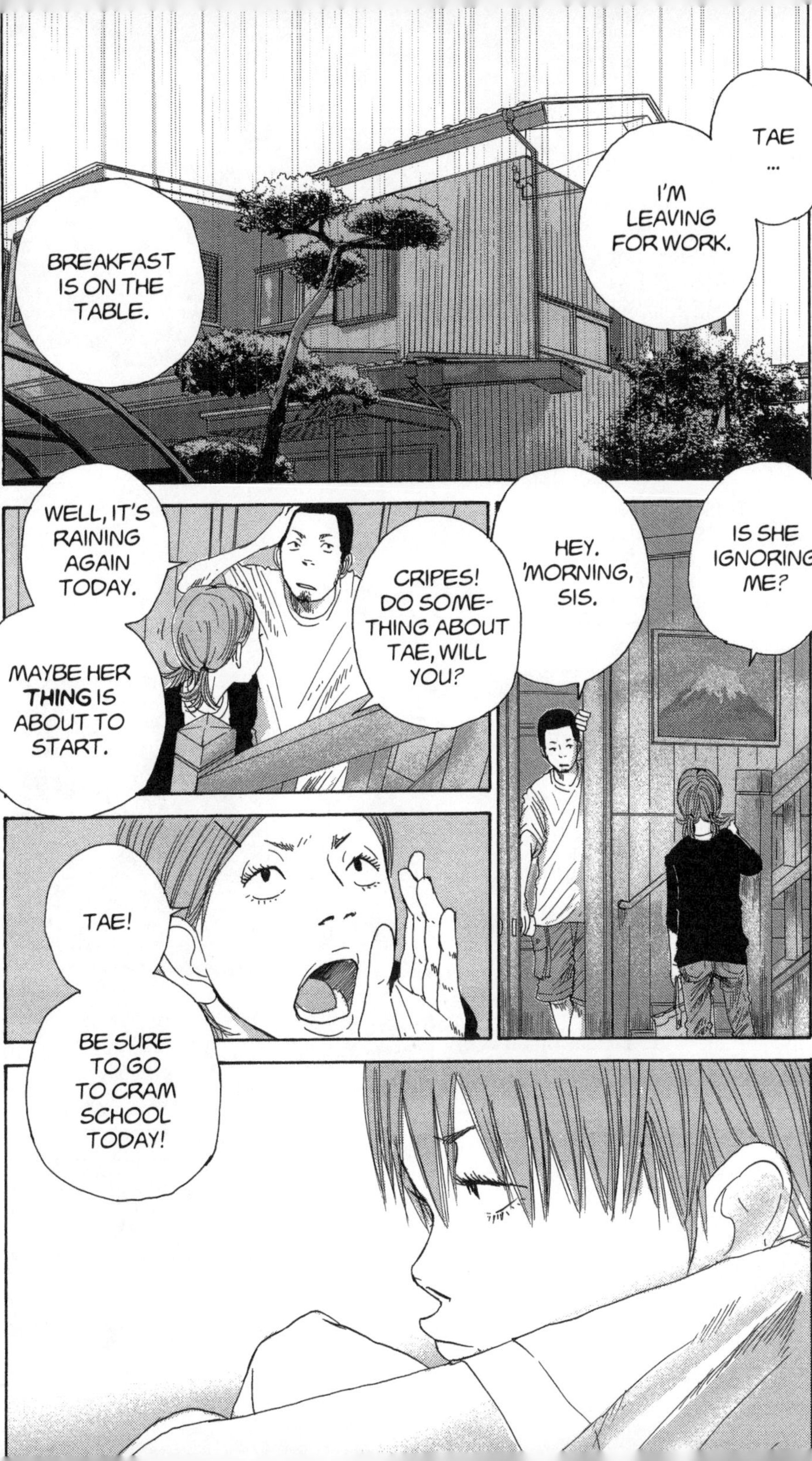

TAE ...
I'M LEAVING FOR WORK.
BREAKFAST IS ON THE TABLE.
IS SHE IGNORING ME?
HEY. 'MORNING, SIS.
CRIPES! DO SOME-THING ABOUT TAE, WILL YOU?
WELL, IT'S RAINING AGAIN TODAY.
MAYBE HER **THING** IS ABOUT TO START.
TAE!
BE SURE TO GO TO CRAM SCHOOL TODAY!

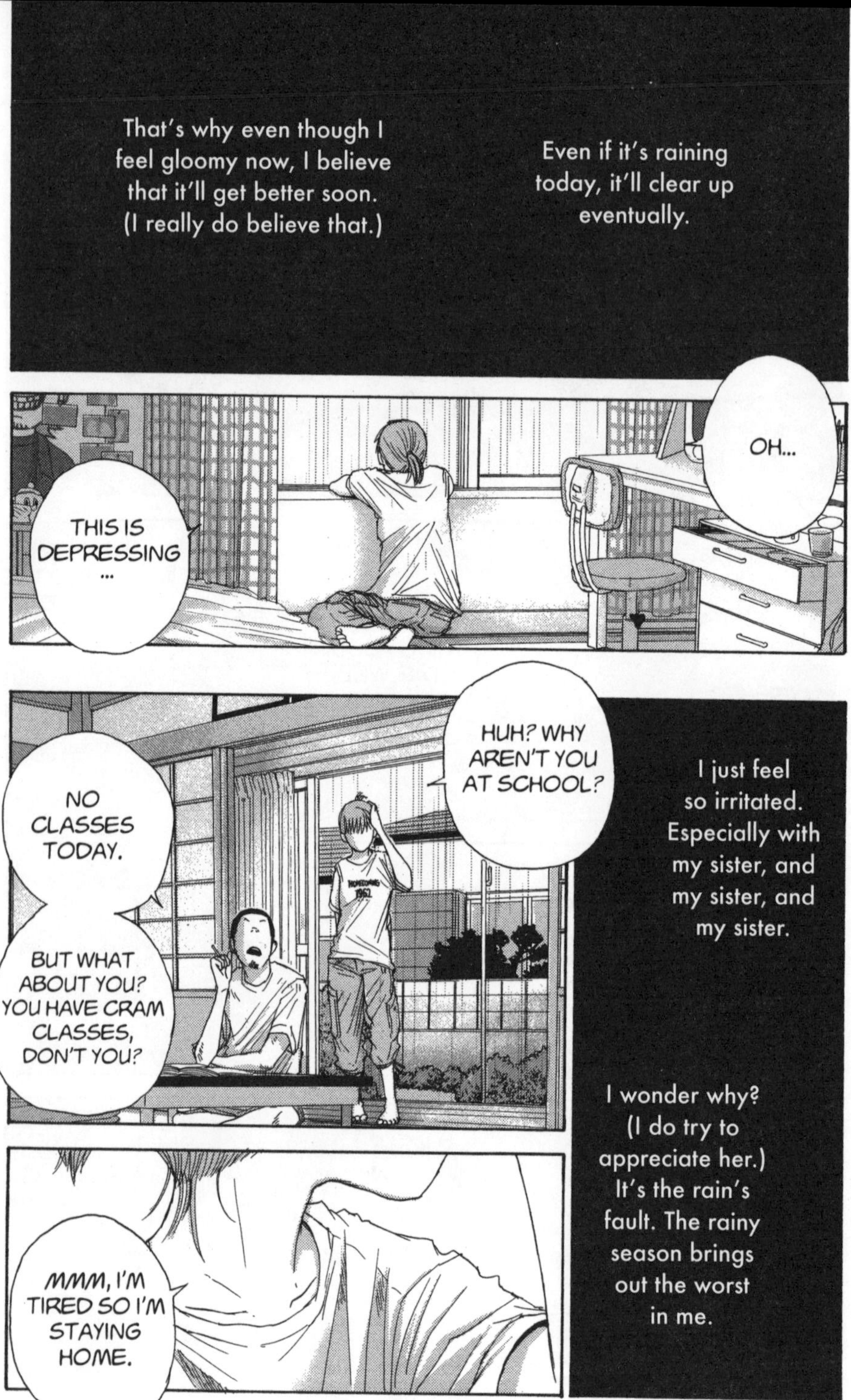
Even if it's raining today, it'll clear up eventually.
That's why even though I feel gloomy now, I believe that it'll get better soon. (I really do believe that.)
OH...
THIS IS DEPRESSING ...
I just feel so irritated. Especially with my sister, and my sister, and my sister.
I wonder why? (I do try to appreciate her.) It's the rain's fault. The rainy season brings out the worst in me.
HUH? WHY AREN'T YOU AT SCHOOL?
NO CLASSES TODAY.
BUT WHAT ABOUT YOU? YOU HAVE CRAM CLASSES, DON'T YOU?
MMM, I'M TIRED SO I'M STAYING HOME.

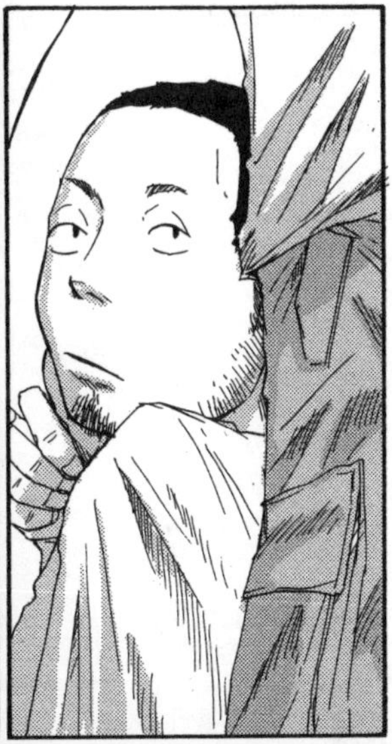

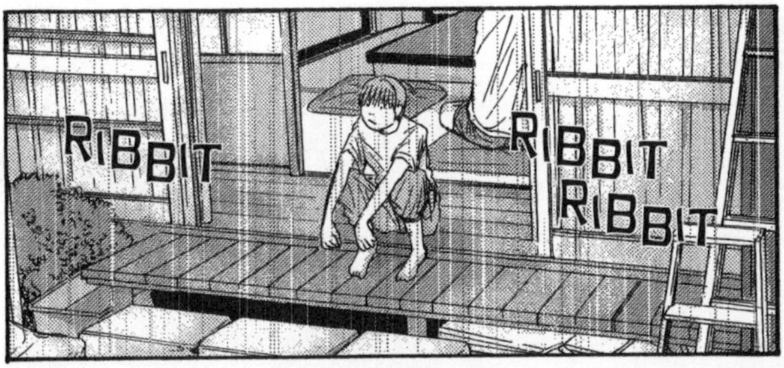
RIBBIT
RIBBIT RIBBIT
RIBBIT

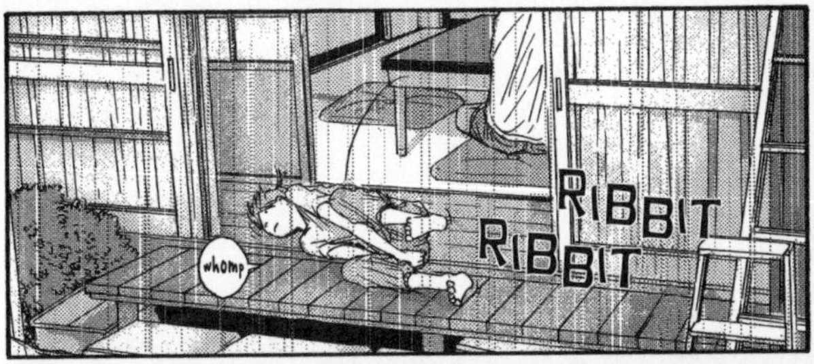
RIBBIT RIBBIT
whomp

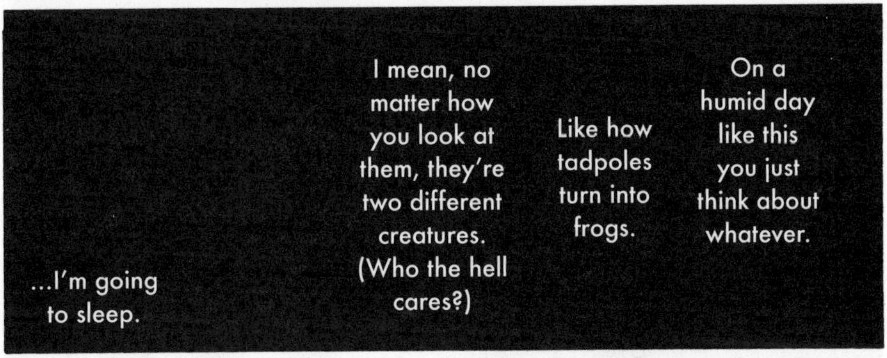
On a humid day like this you just think about whatever.
Like how tadpoles turn into frogs.
I mean, no matter how you look at them, they're two different creatures. (Who the hell cares?)
...I'm going to sleep.

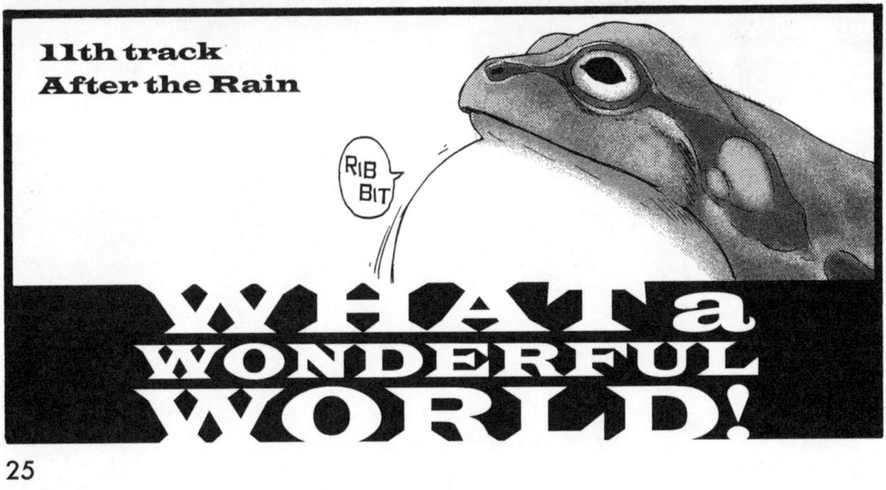
11th track
After the Rain
RIB BIT
WHAT a WONDERFUL WORLD!

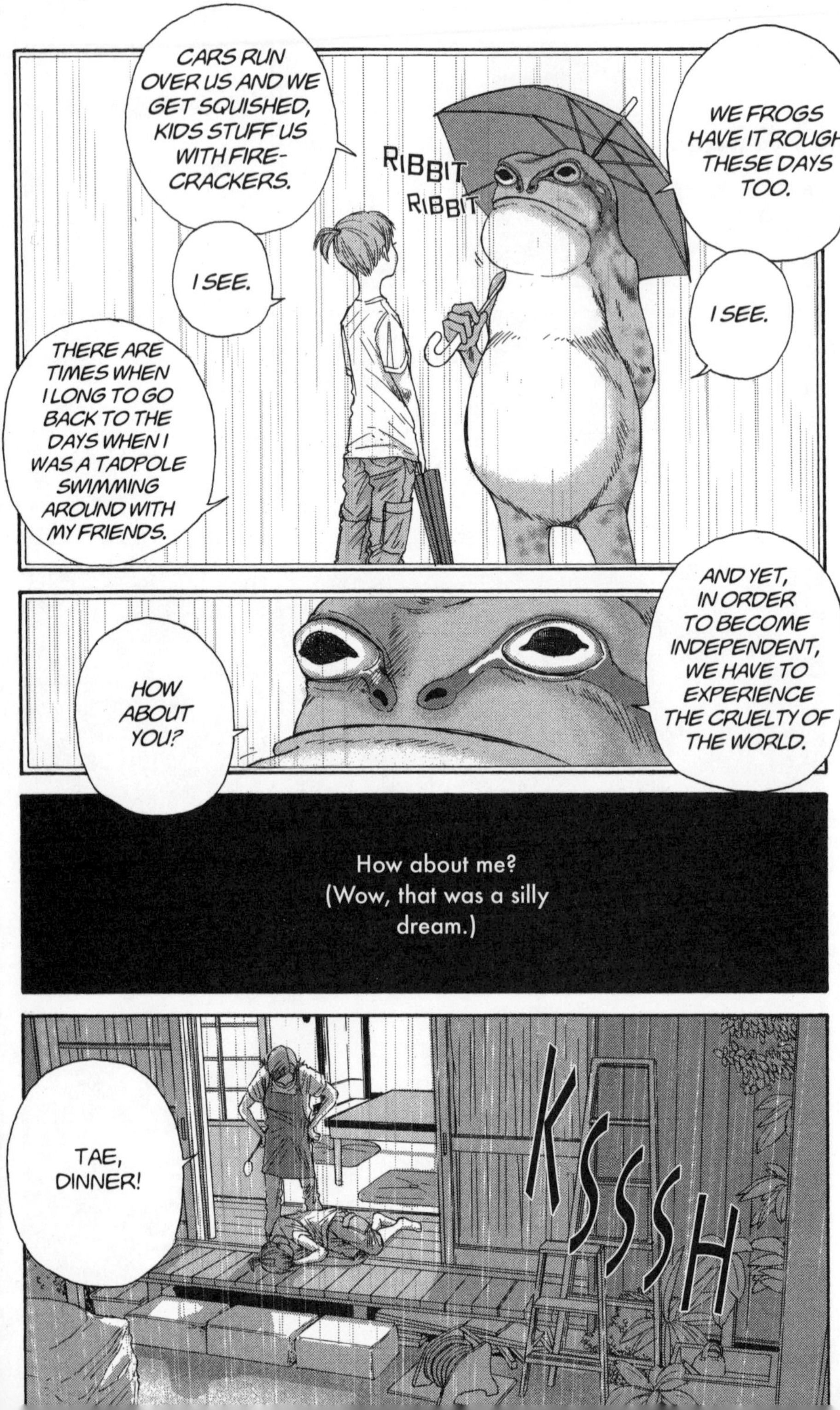
WE FROGS HAVE IT ROUGH THESE DAYS TOO.
CARS RUN OVER US AND WE GET SQUISHED, KIDS STUFF US WITH FIRE-CRACKERS.
RIBBIT RIBBIT
I SEE.
I SEE.
THERE ARE TIMES WHEN I LONG TO GO BACK TO THE DAYS WHEN I WAS A TADPOLE SWIMMING AROUND WITH MY FRIENDS.
AND YET, IN ORDER TO BECOME INDEPENDENT, WE HAVE TO EXPERIENCE THE CRUELTY OF THE WORLD.
HOW ABOUT YOU?
How about me? (Wow, that was a silly dream.)
KSSSH
TAE, DINNER!

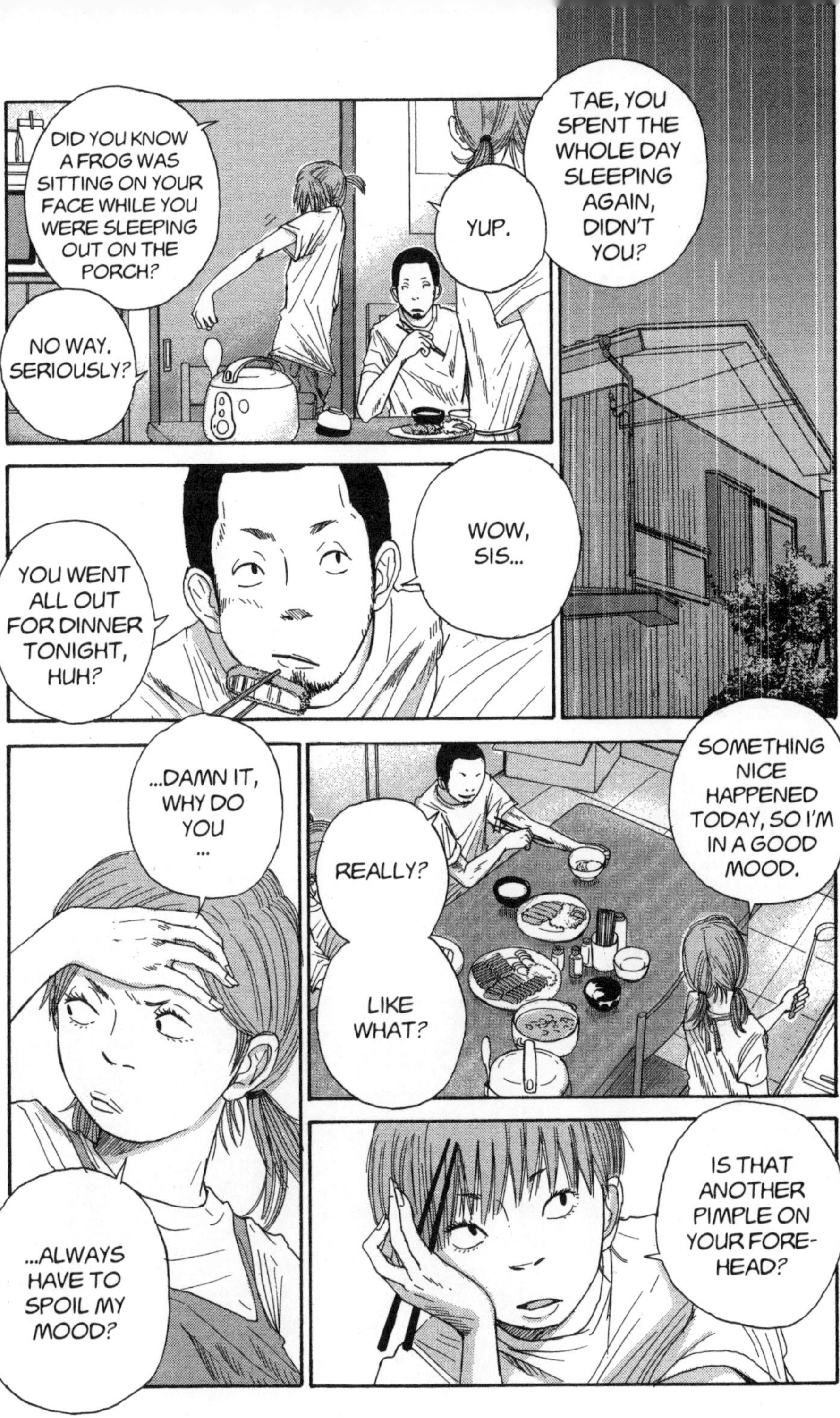

TAE, YOU SPENT THE WHOLE DAY SLEEPING AGAIN, DIDN'T YOU?
YUP.
DID YOU KNOW A FROG WAS SITTING ON YOUR FACE WHILE YOU WERE SLEEPING OUT ON THE PORCH?
NO WAY. SERIOUSLY?
WOW, SIS...
YOU WENT ALL OUT FOR DINNER TONIGHT, HUH?
SOMETHING NICE HAPPENED TODAY, SO I'M IN A GOOD MOOD.
REALLY?
LIKE WHAT?
IS THAT ANOTHER PIMPLE ON YOUR FORE-HEAD?
...DAMN IT, WHY DO YOU ...
...ALWAYS HAVE TO SPOIL MY MOOD?

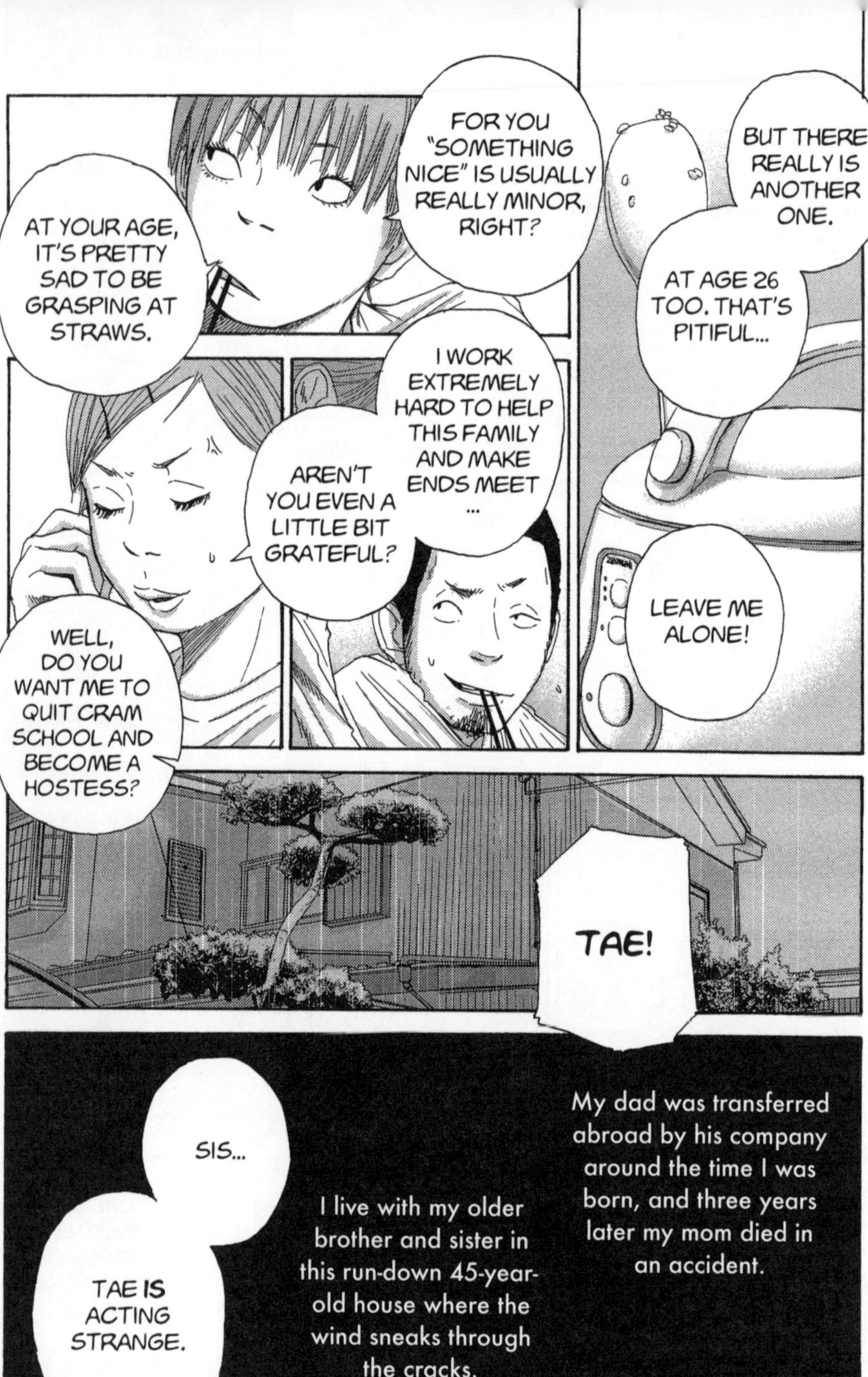
BUT THERE REALLY IS ANOTHER ONE.
AT AGE 26 TOO. THAT'S PITIFUL...
LEAVE ME ALONE!
FOR YOU "SOMETHING NICE" IS USUALLY REALLY MINOR, RIGHT?
AT YOUR AGE, IT'S PRETTY SAD TO BE GRASPING AT STRAWS.
I WORK EXTREMELY HARD TO HELP THIS FAMILY AND MAKE ENDS MEET ...
AREN'T YOU EVEN A LITTLE BIT GRATEFUL?
WELL, DO YOU WANT ME TO QUIT CRAM SCHOOL AND BECOME A HOSTESS?
TAE!
My dad was transferred abroad by his company around the time I was born, and three years later my mom died in an accident.
I live with my older brother and sister in this run-down 45-year-old house where the wind sneaks through the cracks.
SIS...
TAE IS ACTING STRANGE.

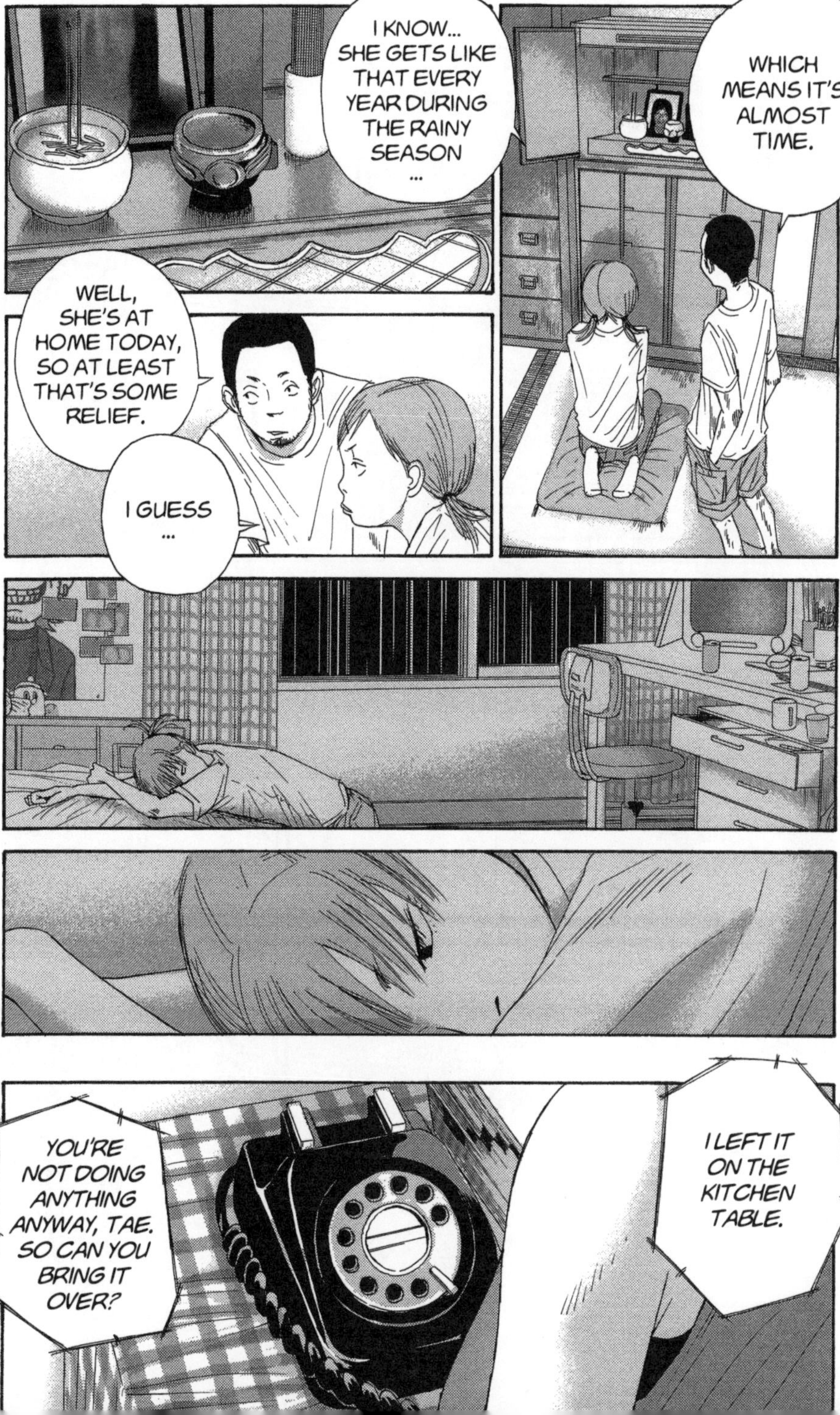
WHICH MEANS IT'S ALMOST TIME.
I KNOW... SHE GETS LIKE THAT EVERY YEAR DURING THE RAINY SEASON ...
WELL, SHE'S AT HOME TODAY, SO AT LEAST THAT'S SOME RELIEF.
I GUESS ...
I LEFT IT ON THE KITCHEN TABLE.
YOU'RE NOT DOING ANYTHING ANYWAY, TAE. SO CAN YOU BRING IT OVER?

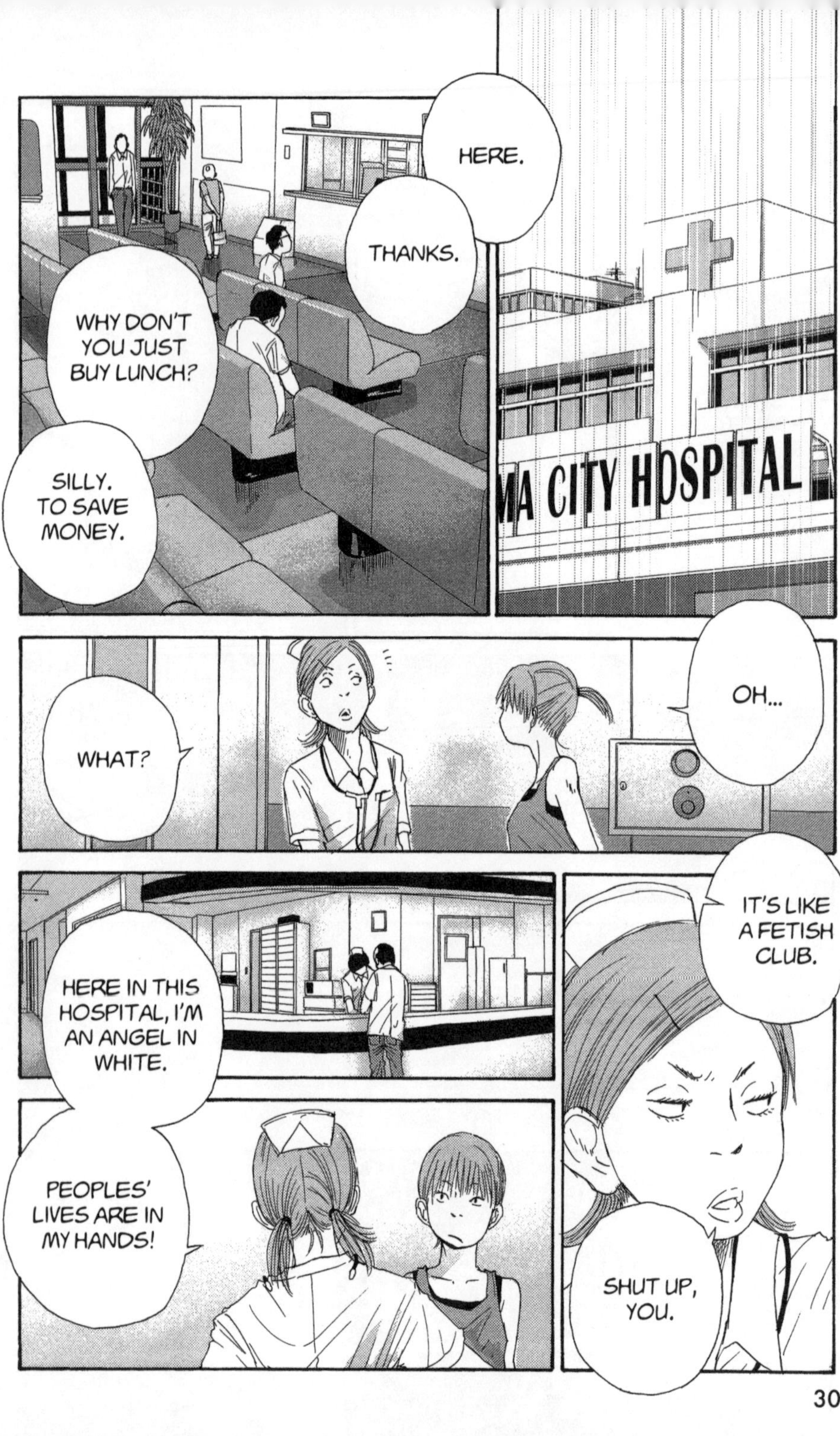
MA CITY HOSPITAL
HERE.
THANKS.
WHY DON'T YOU JUST BUY LUNCH?
SILLY. TO SAVE MONEY.
OH...
WHAT?
IT'S LIKE A FETISH CLUB.
SHUT UP, YOU.
HERE IN THIS HOSPITAL, I'M AN ANGEL IN WHITE.
PEOPLES' LIVES ARE IN MY HANDS!

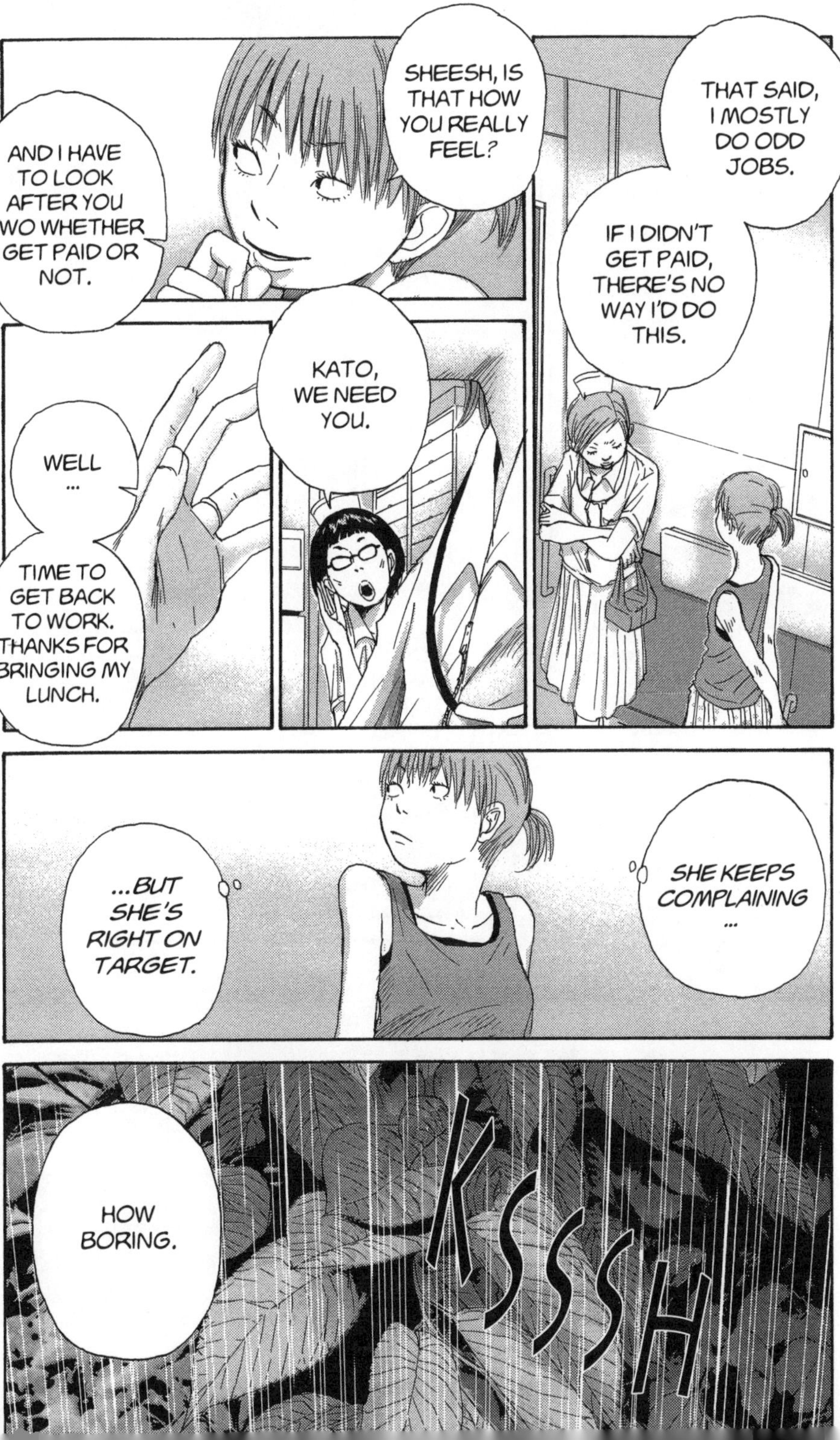
THAT SAID, I MOSTLY DO ODD JOBS.
IF I DIDN'T GET PAID, THERE'S NO WAY I'D DO THIS.
SHEESH, IS THAT HOW YOU REALLY FEEL?
AND I HAVE TO LOOK AFTER YOU TWO WHETHER I GET PAID OR NOT.
KATO, WE NEED YOU.
WELL ...
TIME TO GET BACK TO WORK. THANKS FOR BRINGING MY LUNCH.
SHE KEEPS COMPLAINING ...
...BUT SHE'S RIGHT ON TARGET.
KSSSH
HOW BORING.

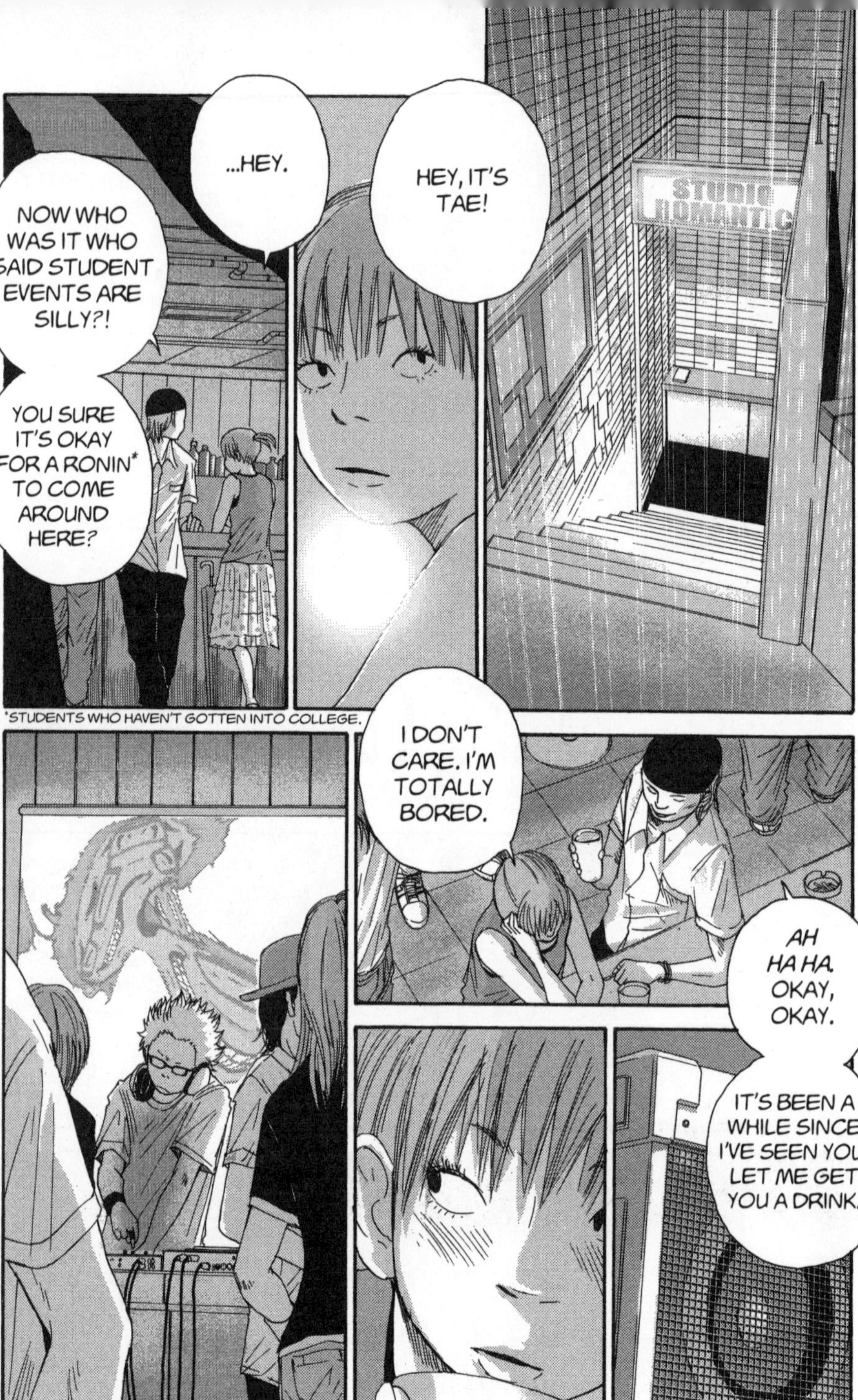
STUDIO ROMANTIC
HEY, IT'S TAE!
...HEY.
NOW WHO WAS IT WHO SAID STUDENT EVENTS ARE SILLY?!
YOU SURE IT'S OKAY FOR A RONIN* TO COME AROUND HERE?
I DON'T CARE. I'M TOTALLY BORED.
AH HA HA. OKAY, OKAY.
IT'S BEEN A WHILE SINCE I'VE SEEN YOU. LET ME GET YOU A DRINK.

*STUDENTS WHO HAVEN'T GOTTEN INTO COLLEGE.

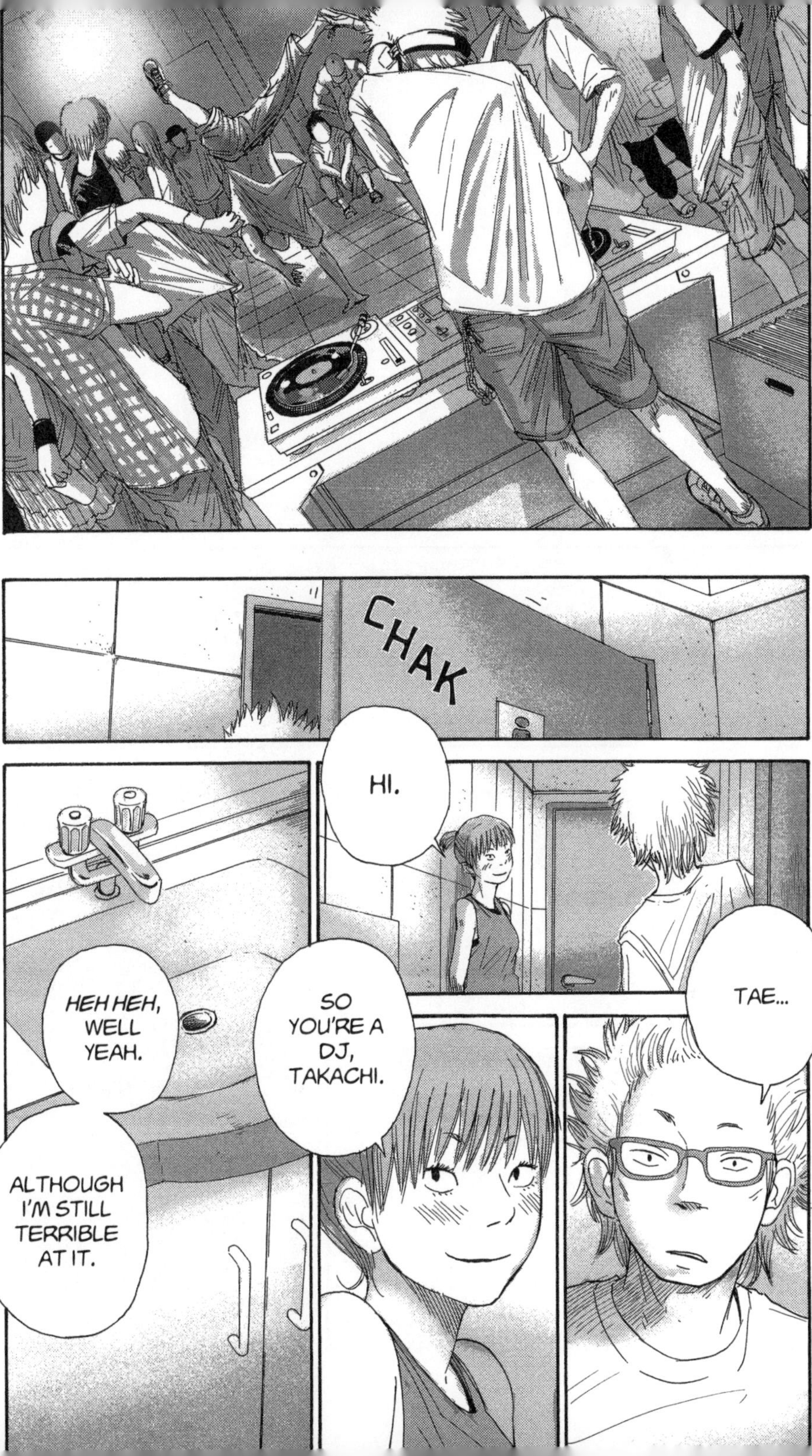
CHAK
HI.
TAE...
SO YOU'RE A DJ, TAKACHI.
HEH HEH, WELL YEAH.
ALTHOUGH I'M STILL TERRIBLE AT IT.

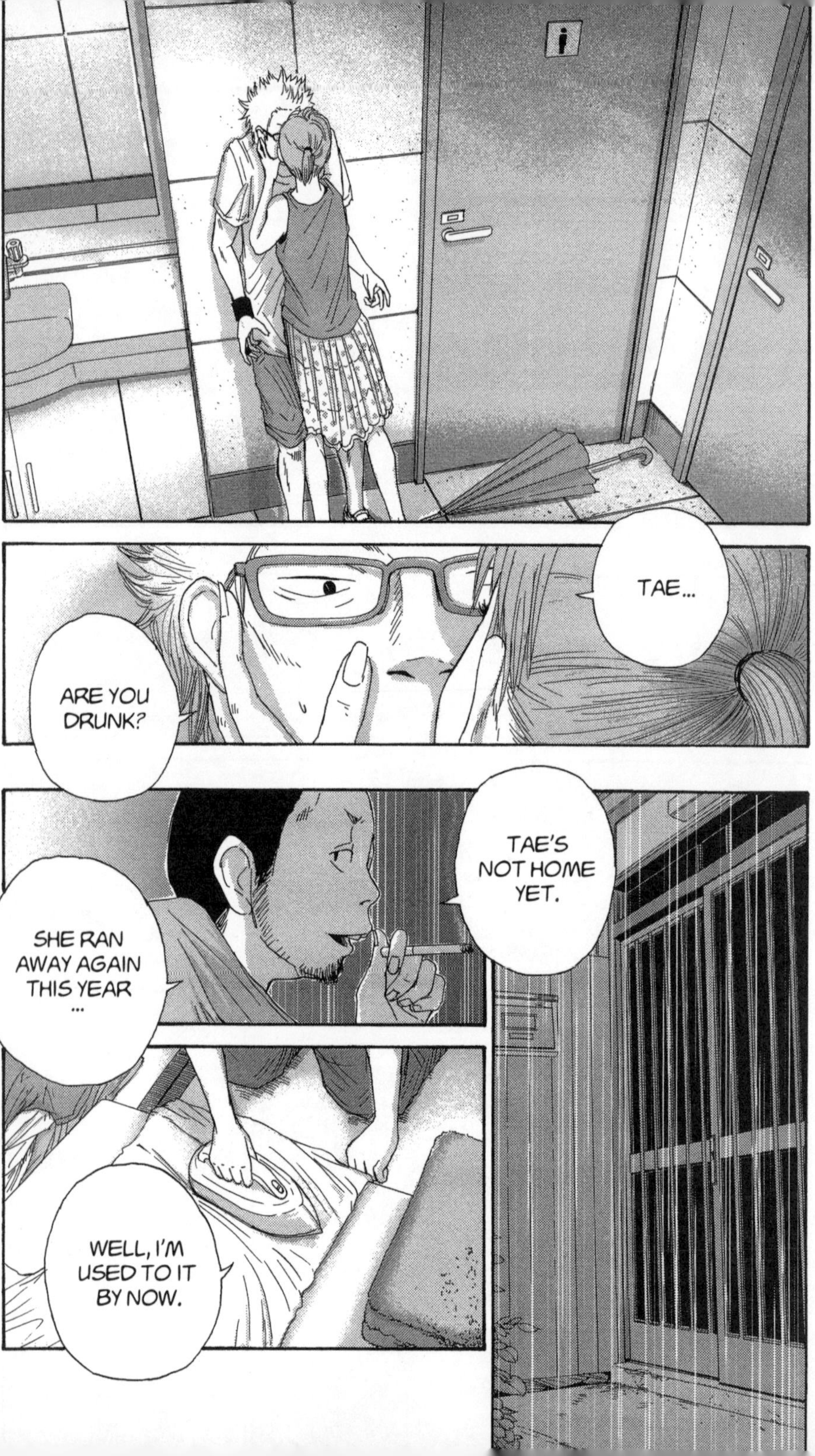
TAE...
ARE YOU DRUNK?
TAE'S NOT HOME YET.
SHE RAN AWAY AGAIN THIS YEAR...
WELL, I'M USED TO IT BY NOW.

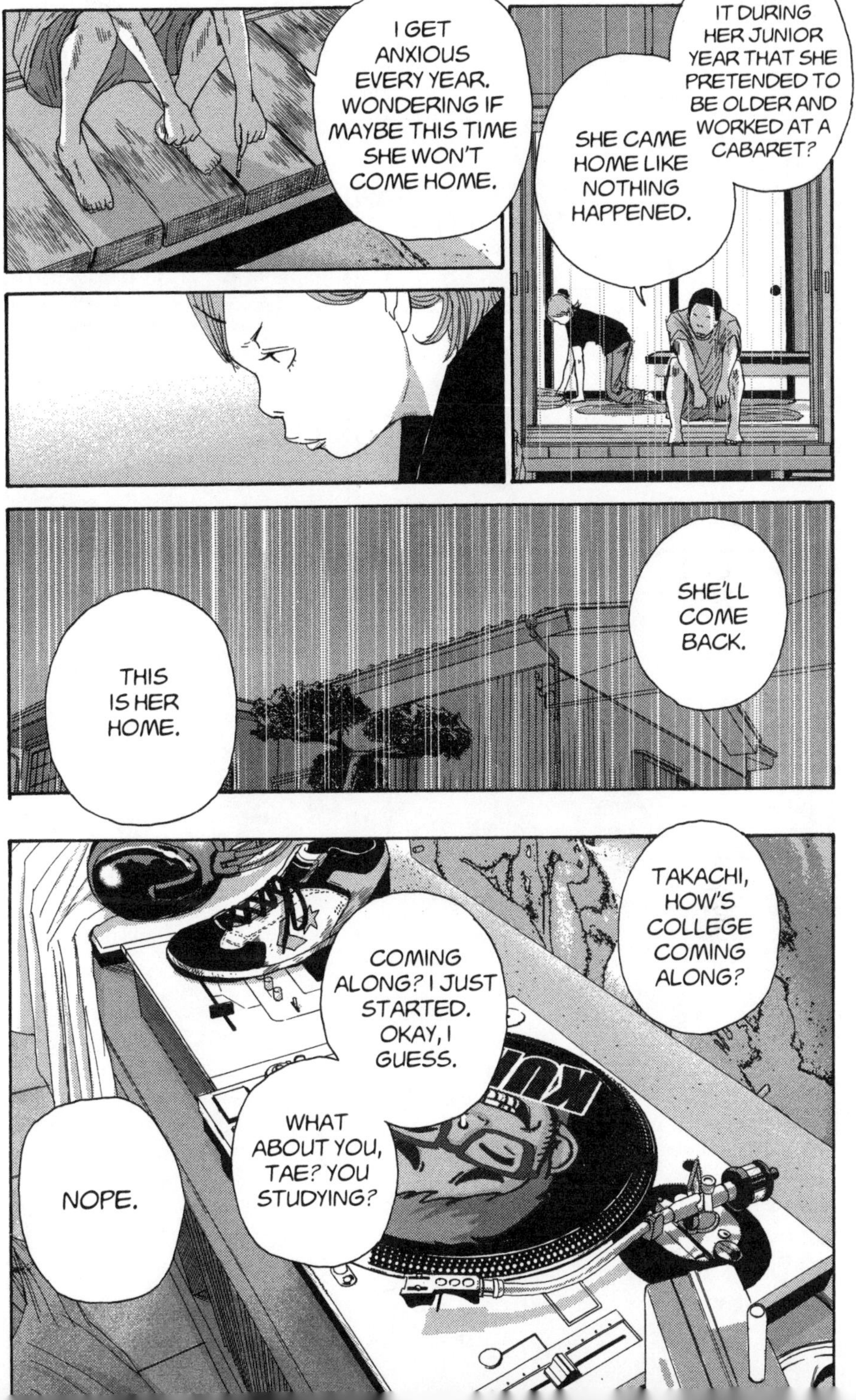
WAS IT DURING HER JUNIOR YEAR THAT SHE PRETENDED TO BE OLDER AND WORKED AT A CABARET?
SHE CAME HOME LIKE NOTHING HAPPENED.
I GET ANXIOUS EVERY YEAR. WONDERING IF MAYBE THIS TIME SHE WON'T COME HOME.
SHE'LL COME BACK.
THIS IS HER HOME.
TAKACHI, HOW'S COLLEGE COMING ALONG?
COMING ALONG? I JUST STARTED. OKAY, I GUESS.
WHAT ABOUT YOU, TAE? YOU STUDYING?
NOPE.

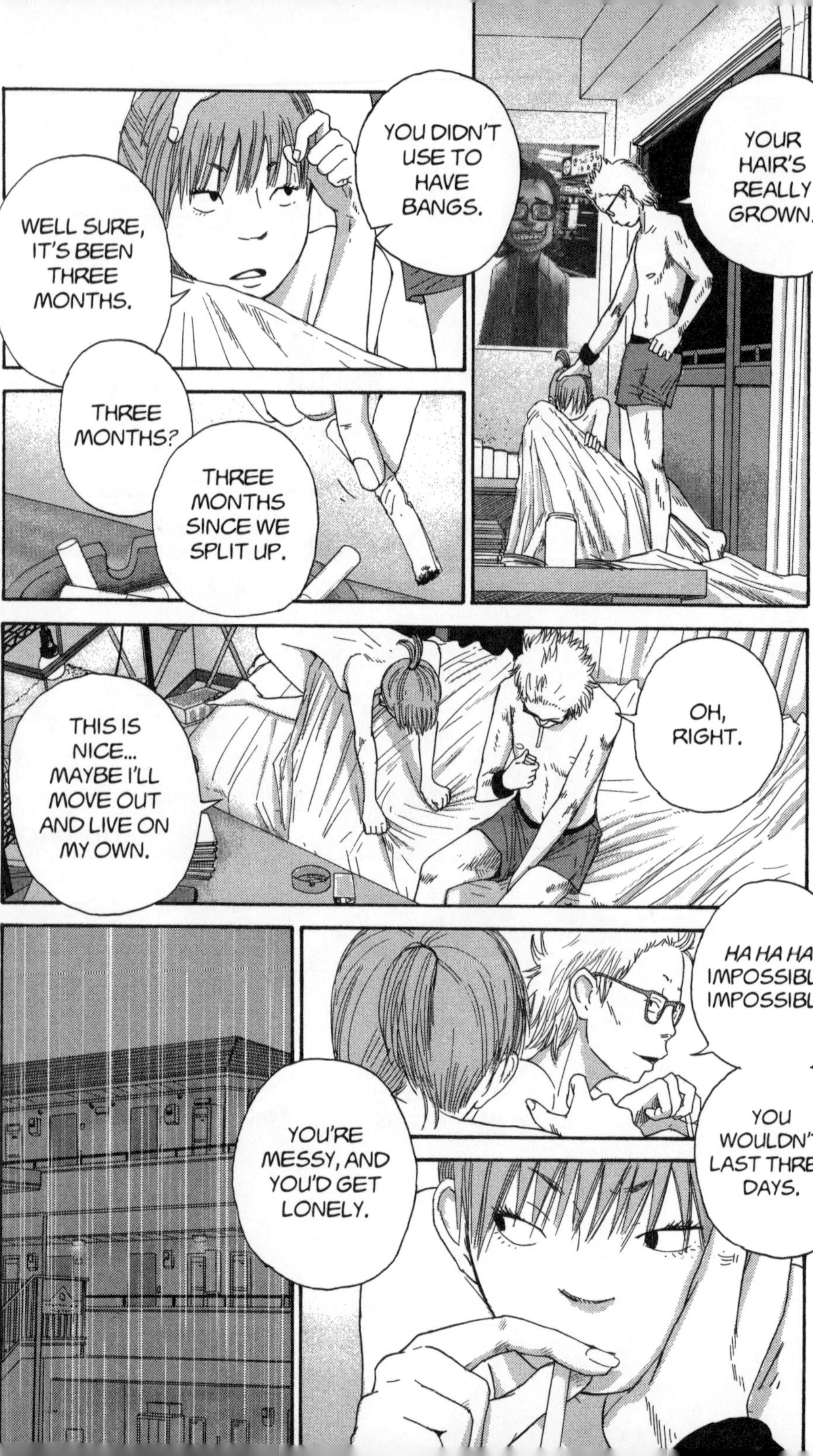
YOUR HAIR'S REALLY GROWN.
YOU DIDN'T USE TO HAVE BANGS.
WELL SURE, IT'S BEEN THREE MONTHS.
THREE MONTHS?
THREE MONTHS SINCE WE SPLIT UP.
OH, RIGHT.
THIS IS NICE... MAYBE I'LL MOVE OUT AND LIVE ON MY OWN.
*HA HA HA.* IMPOSSIBLE. IMPOSSIBLE.
YOU WOULDN'T LAST THREE DAYS.
YOU'RE MESSY, AND YOU'D GET LONELY.

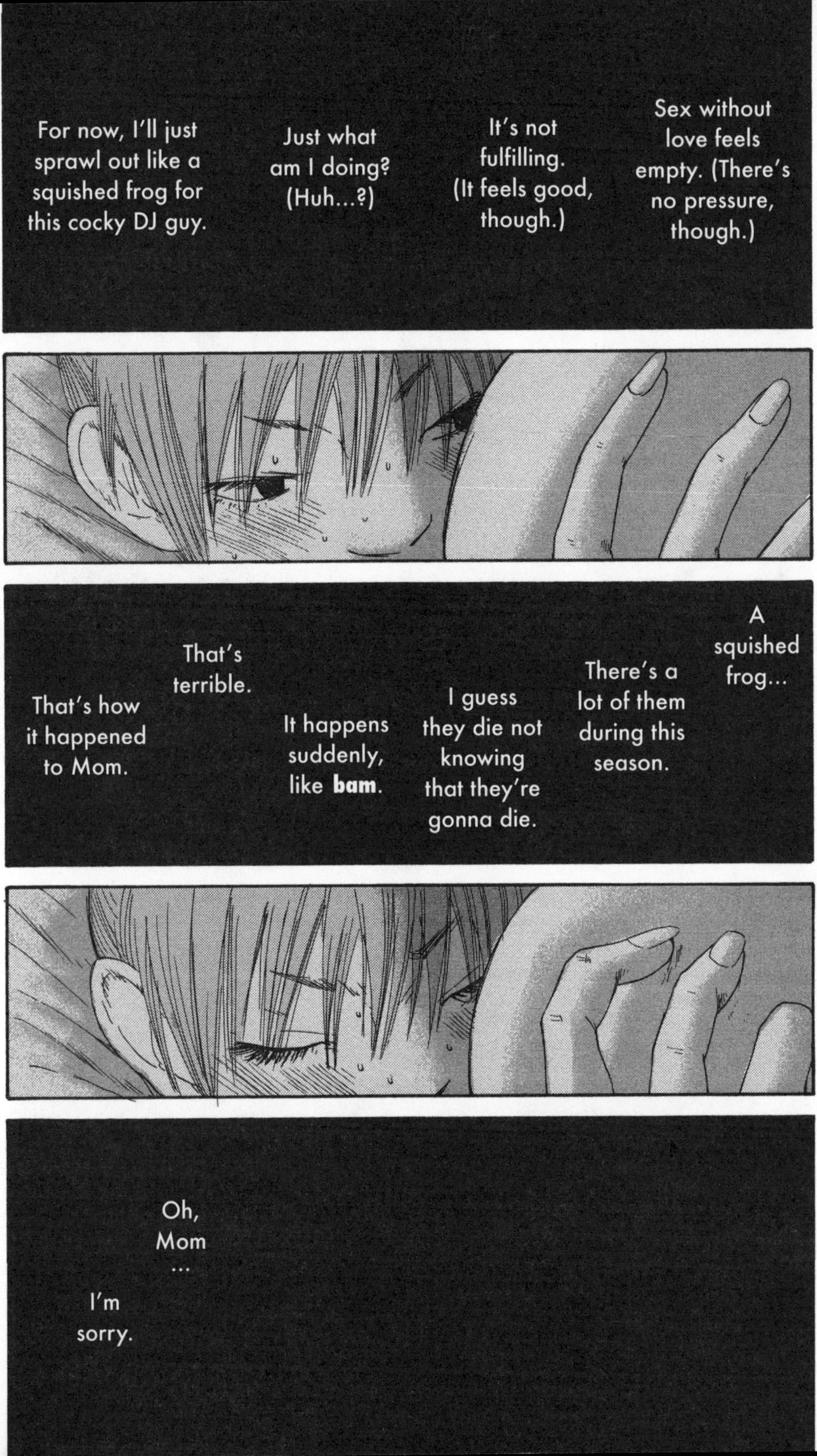
Sex without love feels empty. (There's no pressure, though.)
It's not fulfilling. (It feels good, though.)
Just what am I doing? (Huh...?)
For now, I'll just sprawl out like a squished frog for this cocky DJ guy.
A squished frog...
There's a lot of them during this season.
I guess they die not knowing that they're gonna die.
It happens suddenly, like **bam**.
That's terrible.
That's how it happened to Mom.
Oh, Mom ...
I'm sorry.

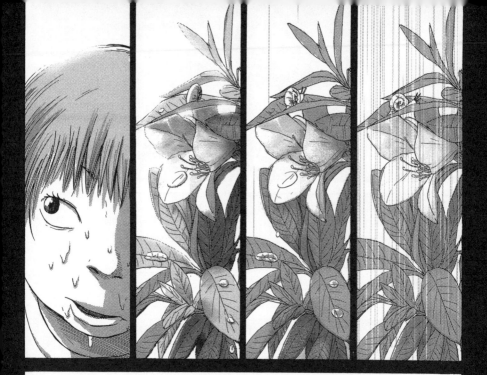

MOM.

That's right.
It's almost the
anniversary of
her death.

I can only
remember her
face through
photographs.

I was
three when
the accident
happened and
I'm pretty sure
Mom was 29
years old.

Twenty-nine...
that's so
young.

...Twenty-nine?
Sis is 26
years old
...

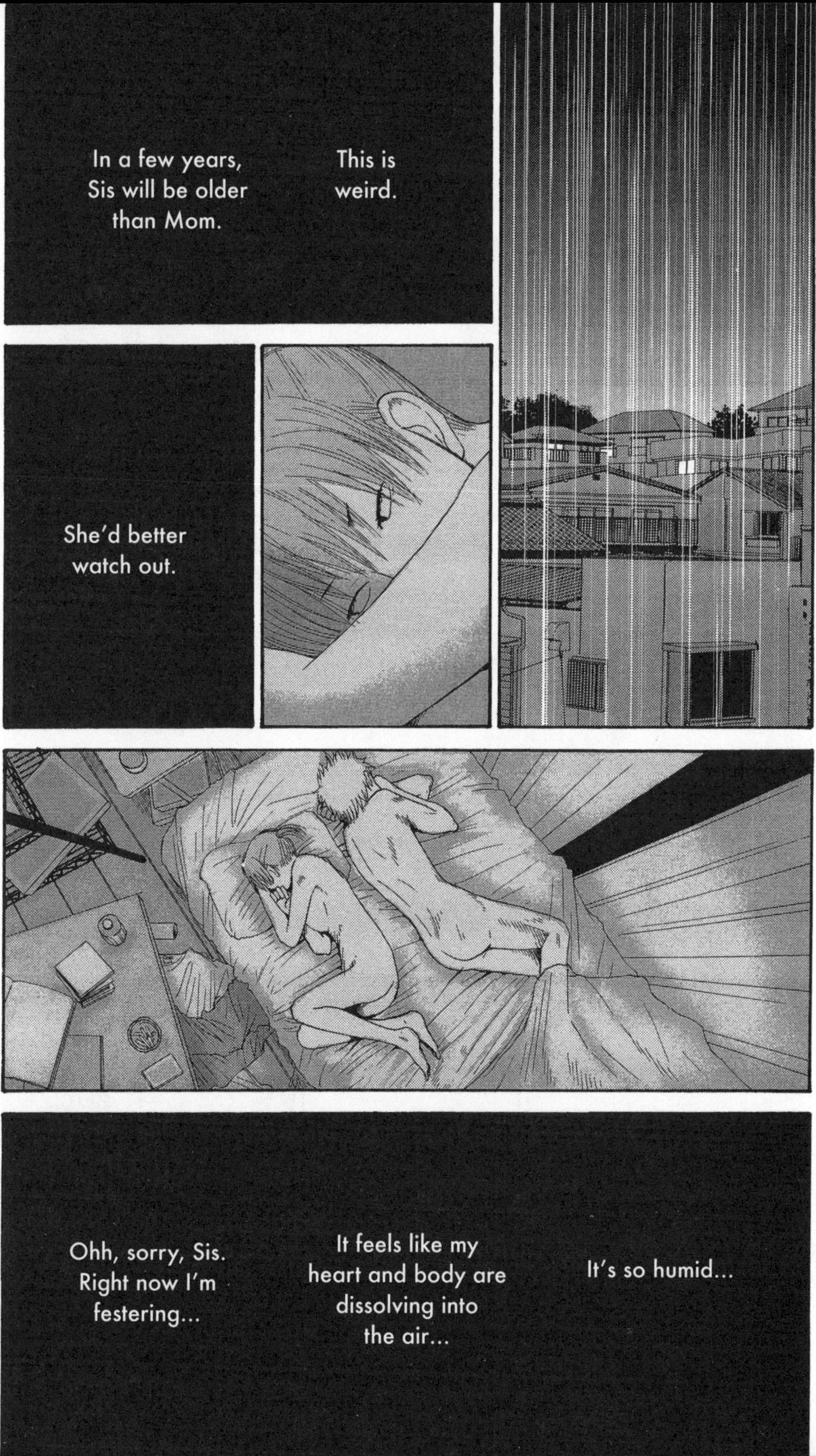
This is weird.
In a few years, Sis will be older than Mom.
She'd better watch out.
It's so humid...
It feels like my heart and body are dissolving into the air...
Ohh, sorry, Sis. Right now I'm festering...

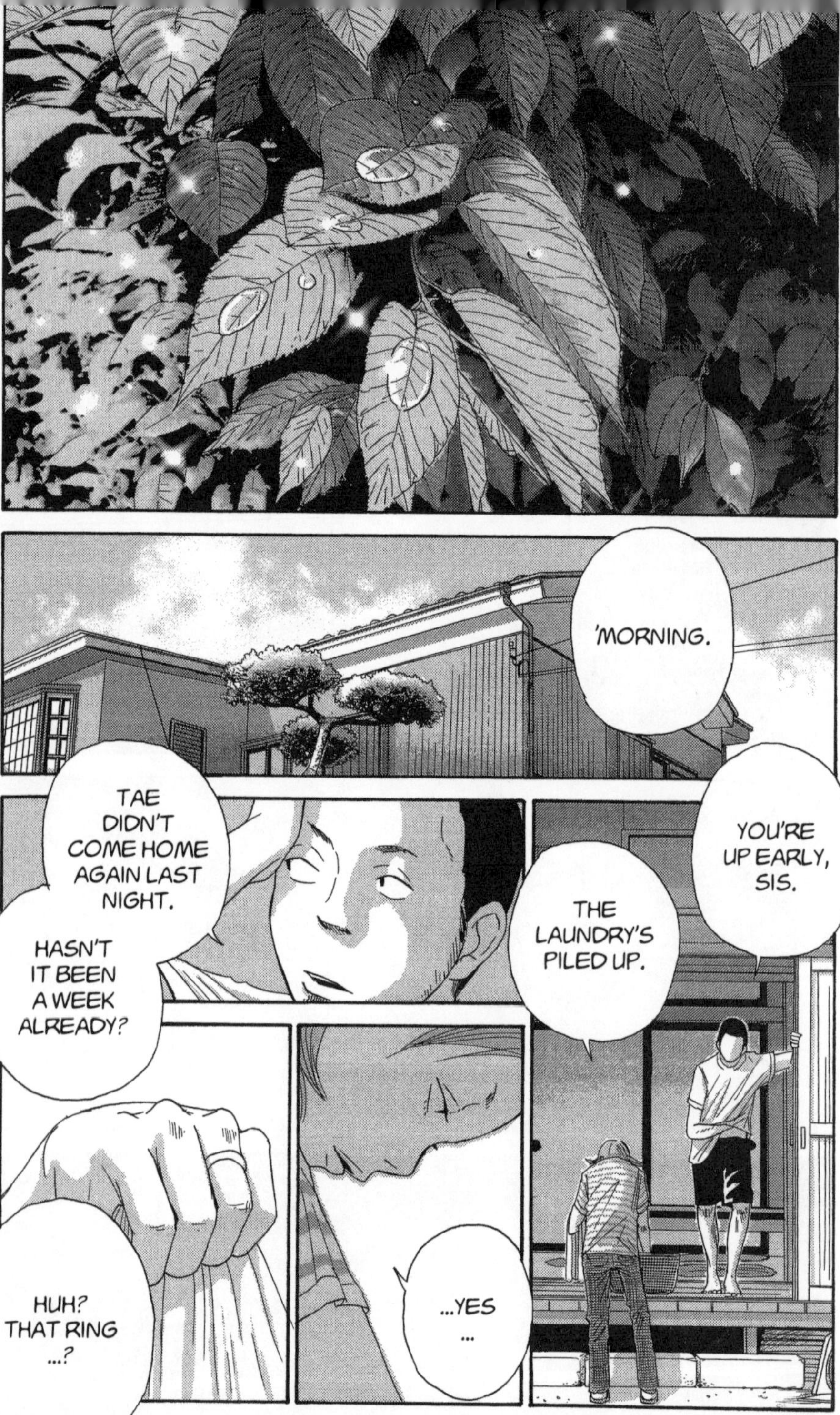
'MORNING.
YOU'RE UP EARLY, SIS.
THE LAUNDRY'S PILED UP.
TAE DIDN'T COME HOME AGAIN LAST NIGHT.
HASN'T IT BEEN A WEEK ALREADY?
...YES ...
HUH? THAT RING ...?

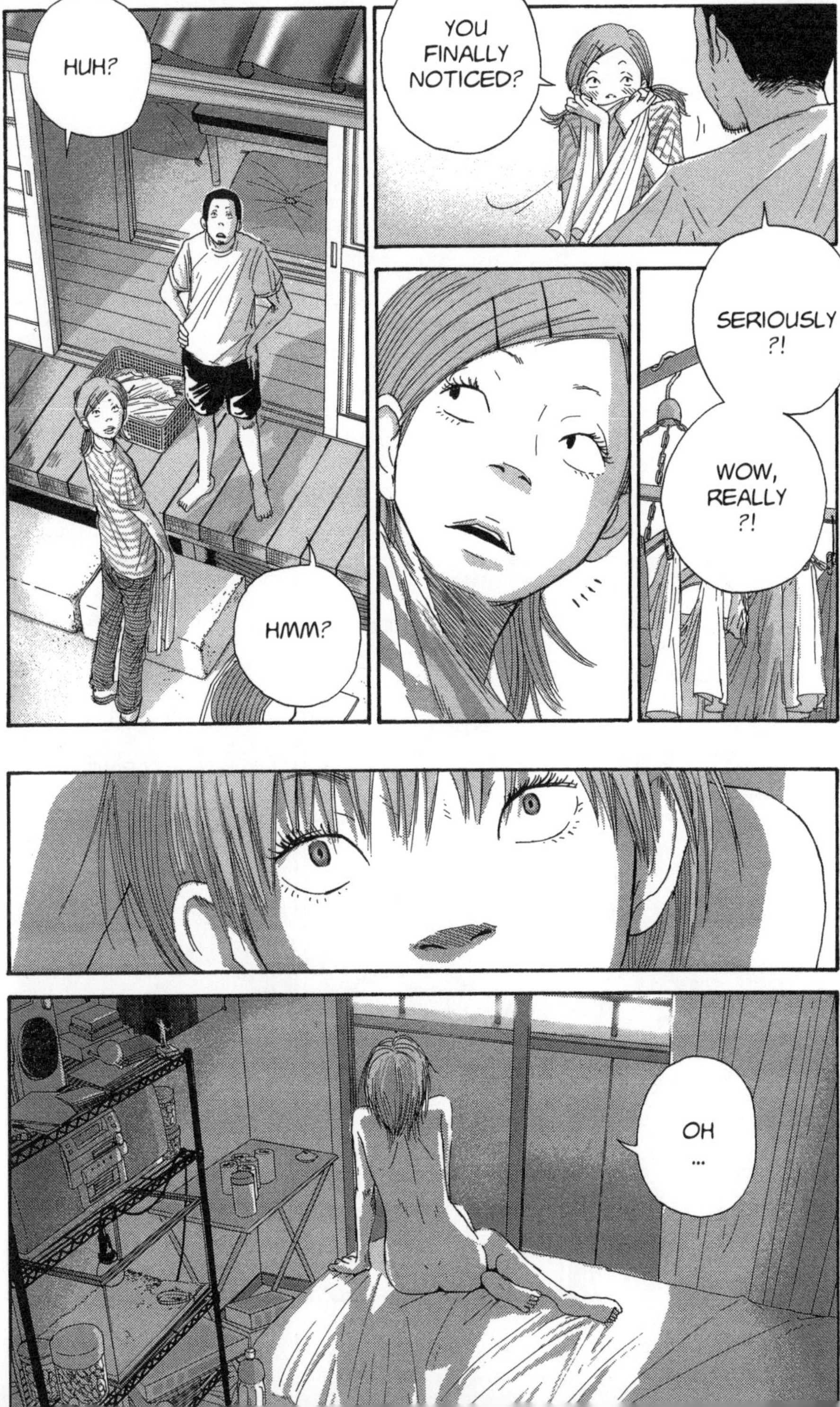
YOU FINALLY NOTICED?
SERIOUSLY ?!
WOW, REALLY ?!
HUH?
HMM?
OH ...

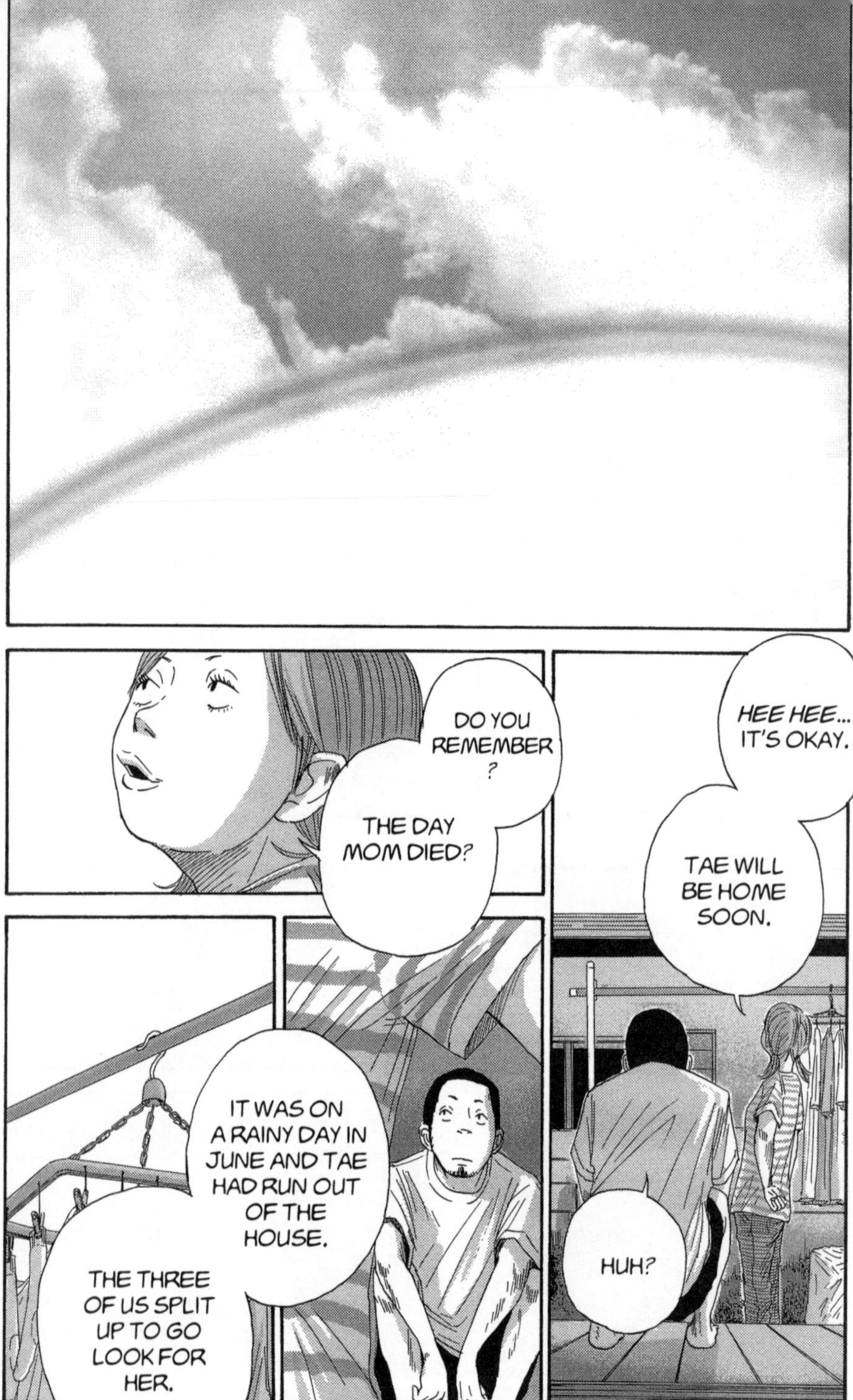
HEE HEE... IT'S OKAY.
TAE WILL BE HOME SOON.
DO YOU REMEMBER?
THE DAY MOM DIED?
HUH?
IT WAS ON A RAINY DAY IN JUNE AND TAE HAD RUN OUT OF THE HOUSE.
THE THREE OF US SPLIT UP TO GO LOOK FOR HER.

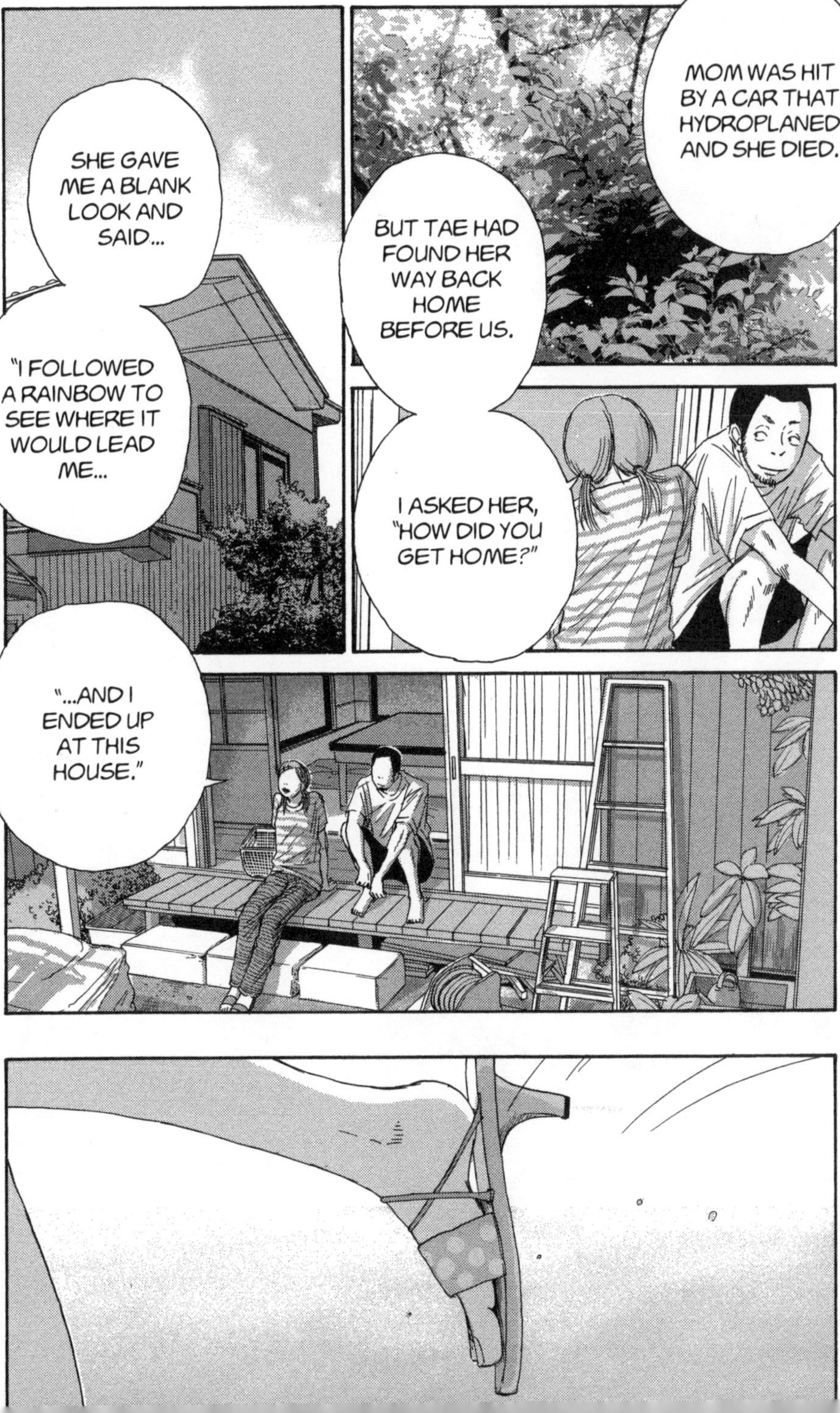
MOM WAS HIT BY A CAR THAT HYDROPLANED, AND SHE DIED.
BUT TAE HAD FOUND HER WAY BACK HOME BEFORE US.
I ASKED HER, "HOW DID YOU GET HOME?"
SHE GAVE ME A BLANK LOOK AND SAID...
"I FOLLOWED A RAINBOW TO SEE WHERE IT WOULD LEAD ME...
"...AND I ENDED UP AT THIS HOUSE."

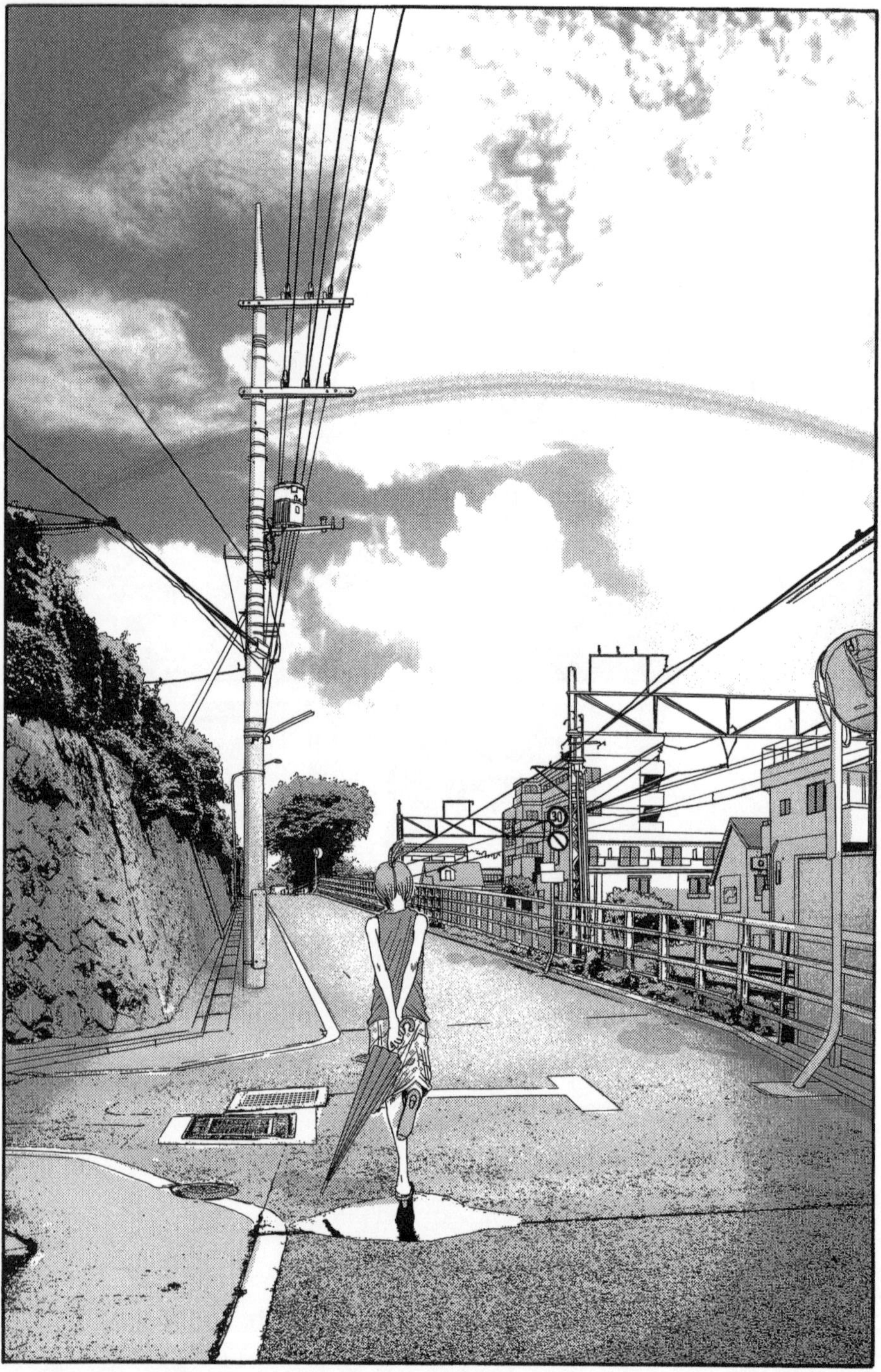
30

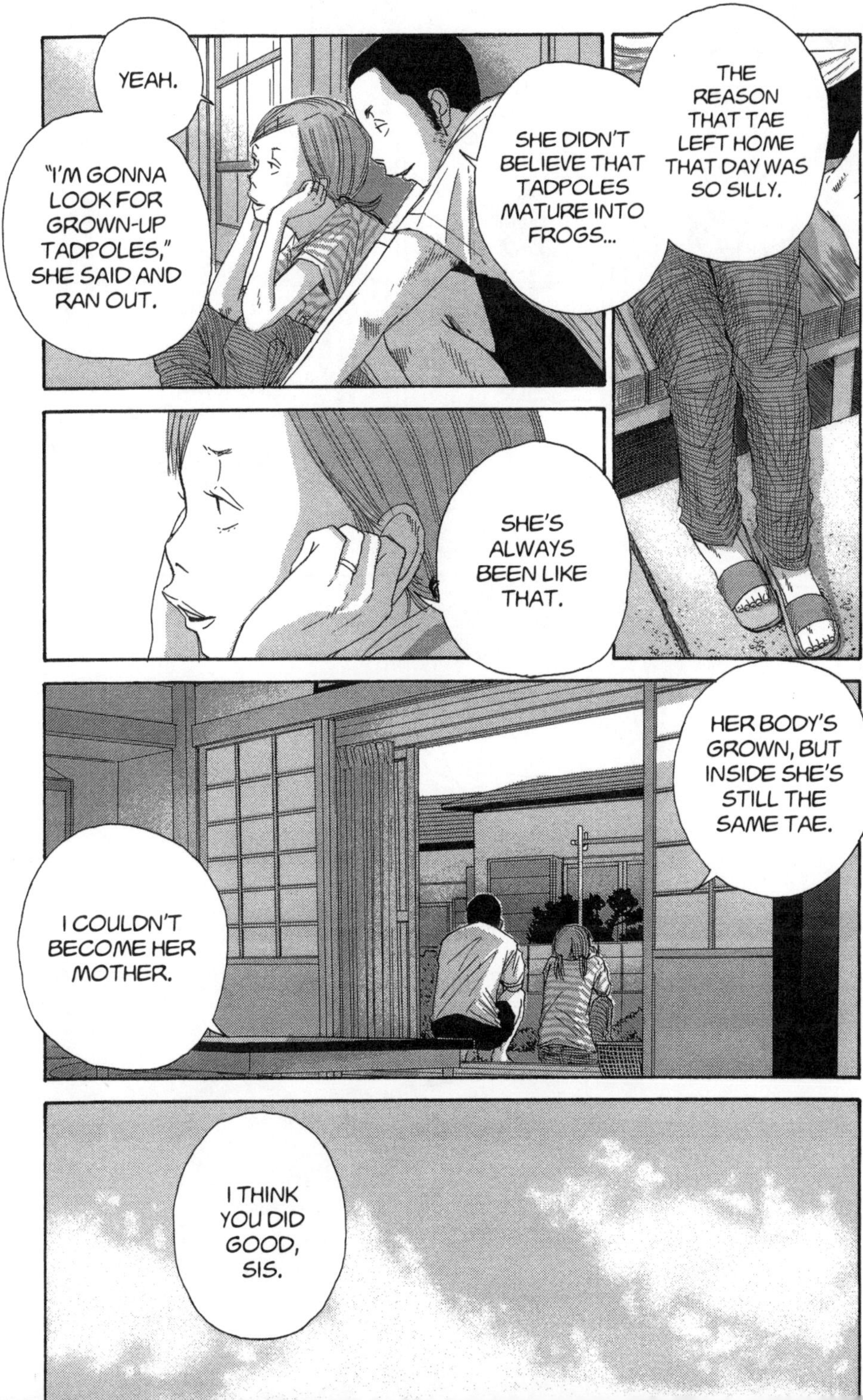
THE REASON THAT TAE LEFT HOME THAT DAY WAS SO SILLY.
SHE DIDN'T BELIEVE THAT TADPOLES MATURE INTO FROGS...
YEAH.
"I'M GONNA LOOK FOR GROWN-UP TADPOLES," SHE SAID AND RAN OUT.
SHE'S ALWAYS BEEN LIKE THAT.
HER BODY'S GROWN, BUT INSIDE SHE'S STILL THE SAME TAE.
I COULDN'T BECOME HER MOTHER.
I THINK YOU DID GOOD, SIS.

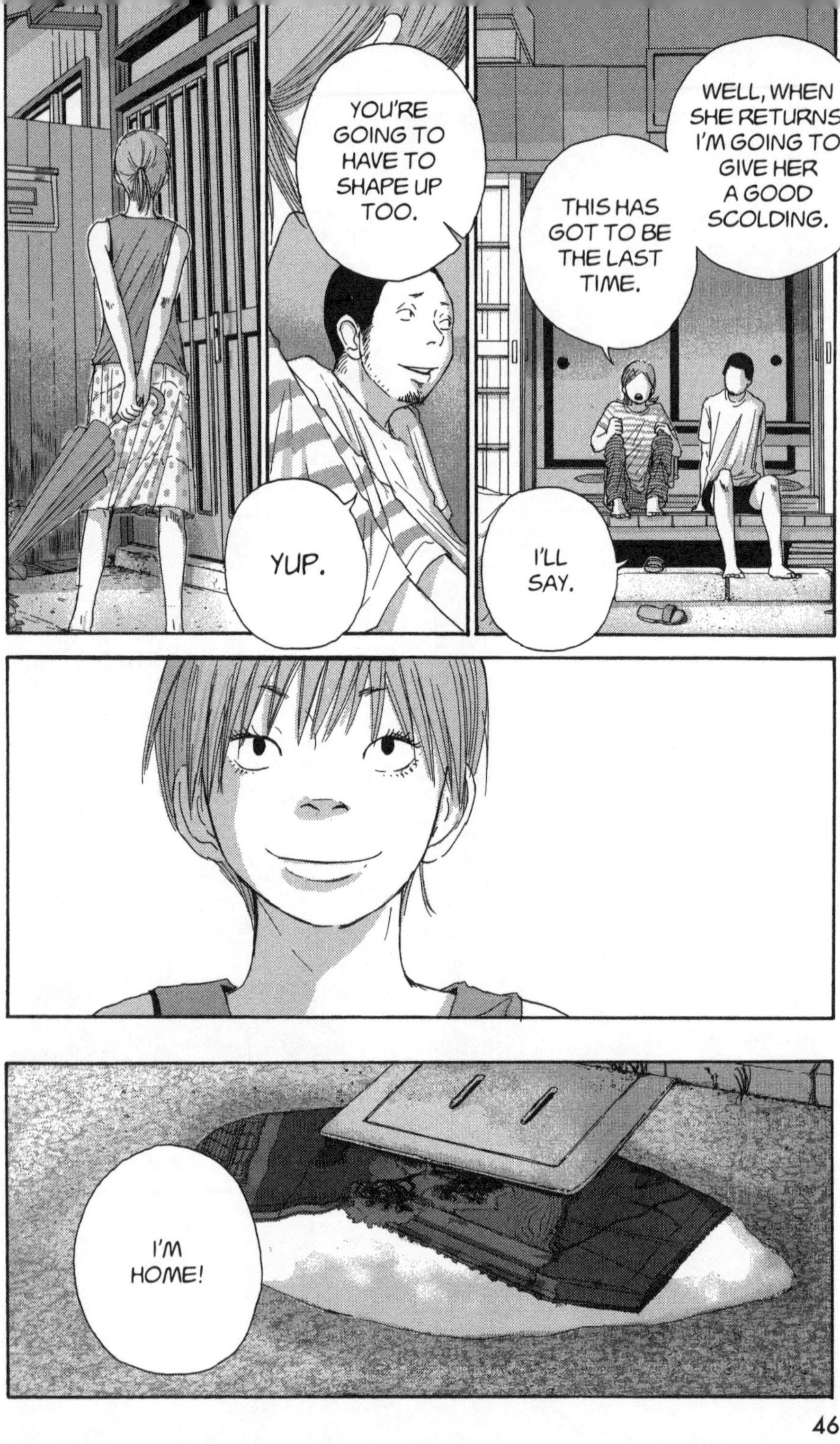
WELL, WHEN SHE RETURNS I'M GOING TO GIVE HER A GOOD SCOLDING.
THIS HAS GOT TO BE THE LAST TIME.
I'LL SAY.
YOU'RE GOING TO HAVE TO SHAPE UP TOO.
YUP.
I'M HOME!

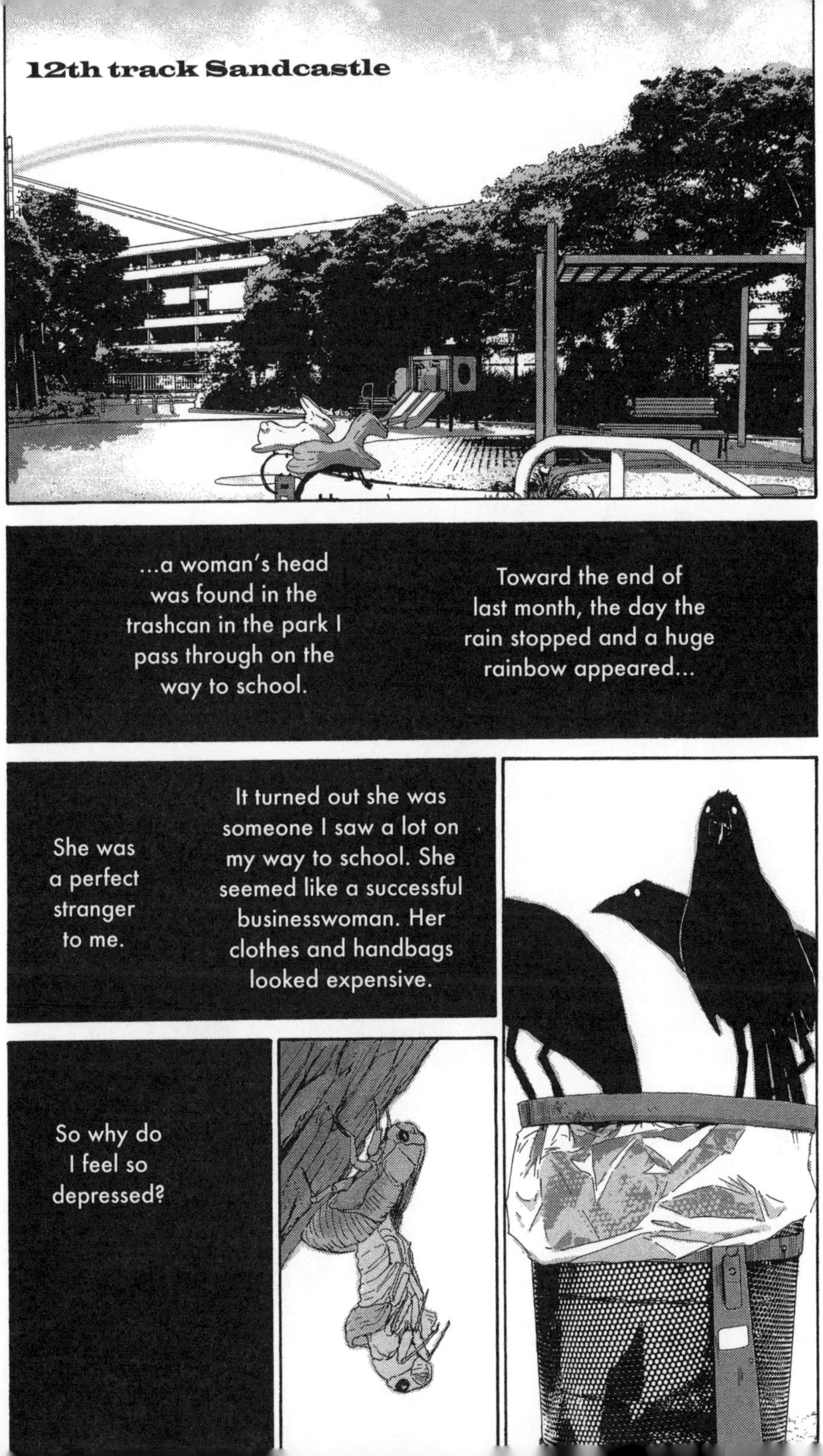
12th track Sandcastle
Toward the end of last month, the day the rain stopped and a huge rainbow appeared...
...a woman's head was found in the trashcan in the park I pass through on the way to school.
It turned out she was someone I saw a lot on my way to school. She seemed like a successful businesswoman. Her clothes and handbags looked expensive.
She was a perfect stranger to me.
So why do I feel so depressed?

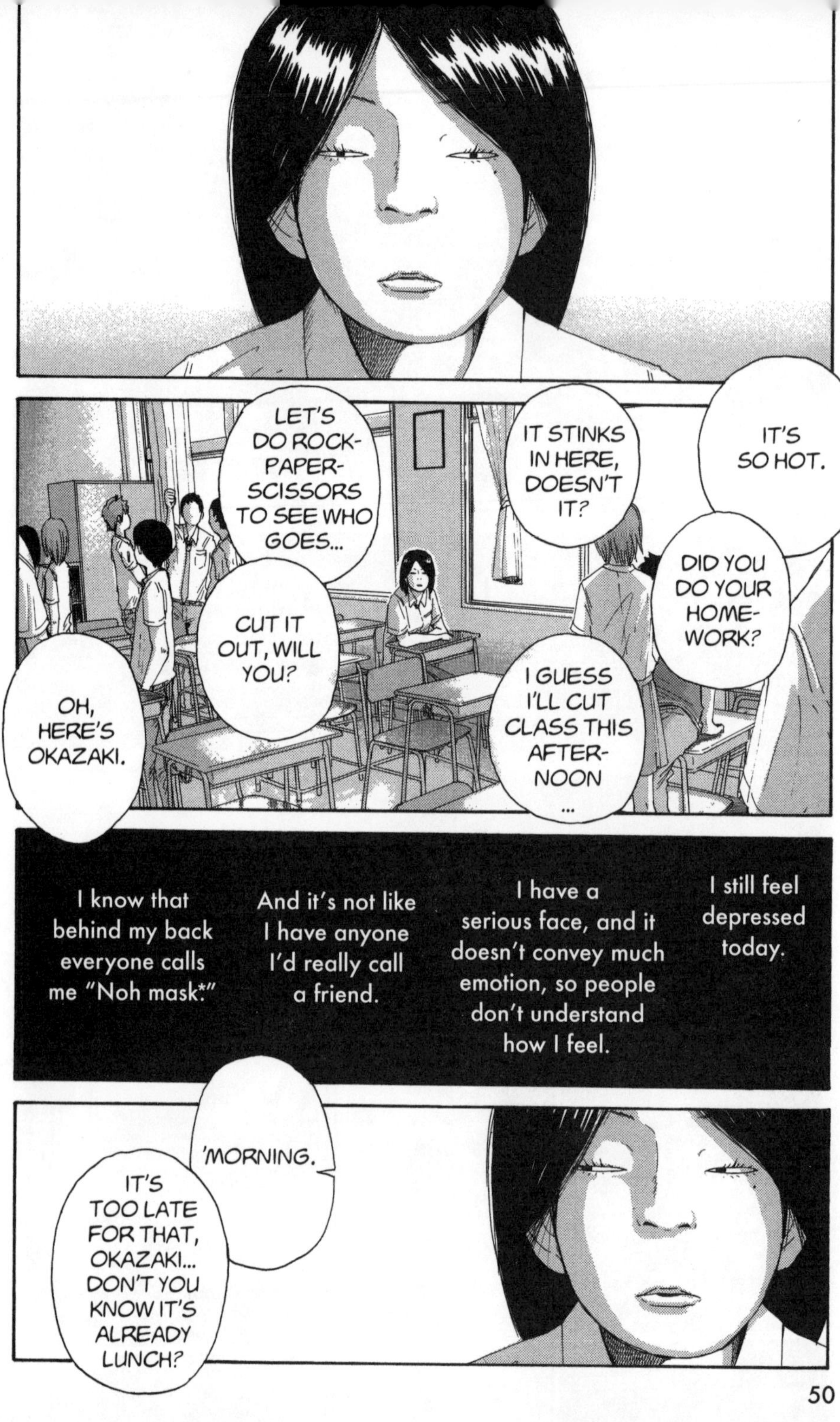
IT'S SO HOT.
IT STINKS IN HERE, DOESN'T IT?
LET'S DO ROCK-PAPER-SCISSORS TO SEE WHO GOES...
DID YOU DO YOUR HOMEWORK?
I GUESS I'LL CUT CLASS THIS AFTERNOON ...
CUT IT OUT, WILL YOU?
OH, HERE'S OKAZAKI.
I still feel depressed today.
I have a serious face, and it doesn't convey much emotion, so people don't understand how I feel.
And it's not like I have anyone I'd really call a friend.
I know that behind my back everyone calls me "Noh mask*"
'MORNING.
IT'S TOO LATE FOR THAT, OKAZAKI... DON'T YOU KNOW IT'S ALREADY LUNCH?

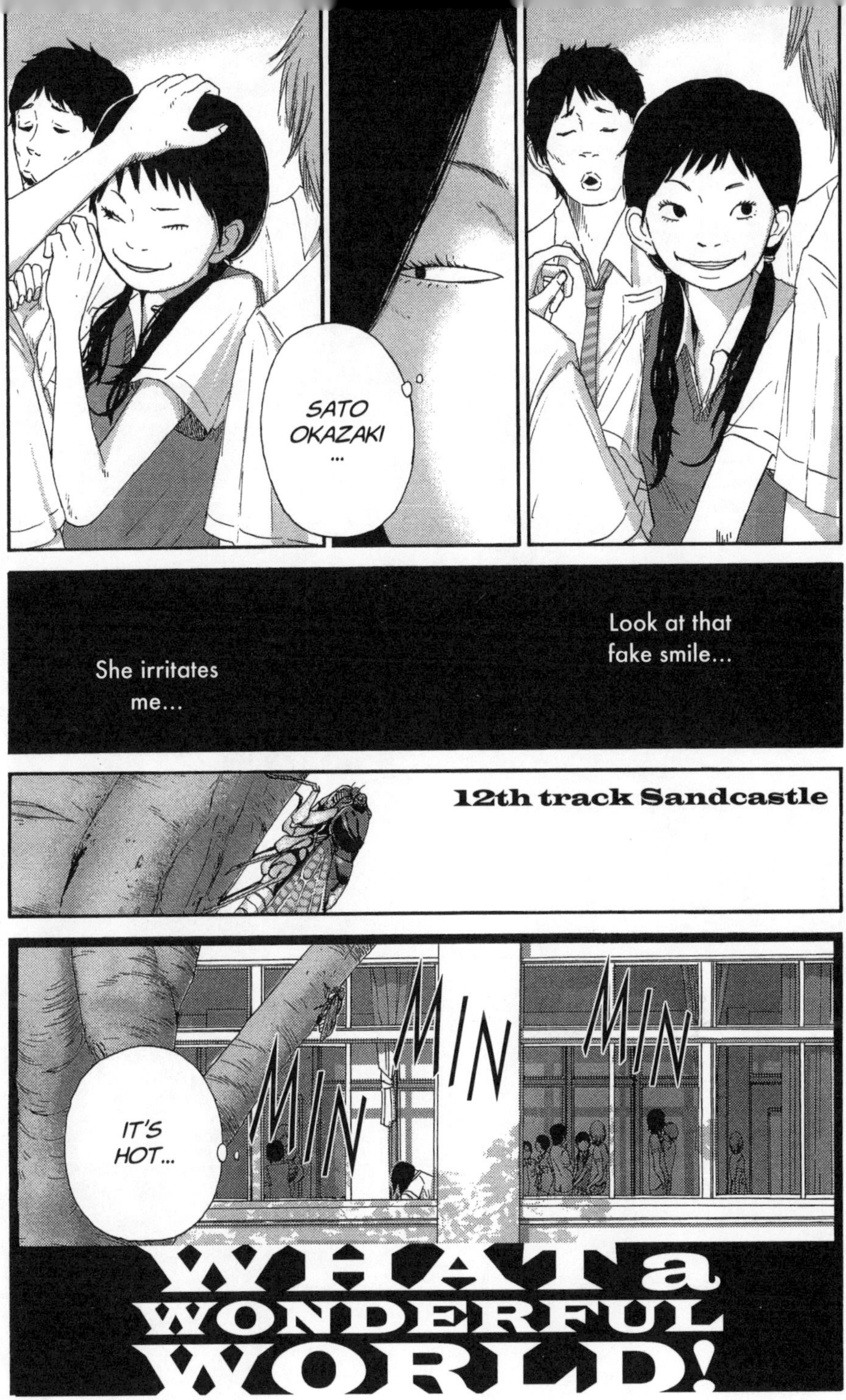
SATO OKAZAKI ...
Look at that fake smile...
She irritates me...
12th track Sandcastle
MIN MIN
MIN MIN
IT'S HOT...
WHAT a WONDERFUL WORLD!

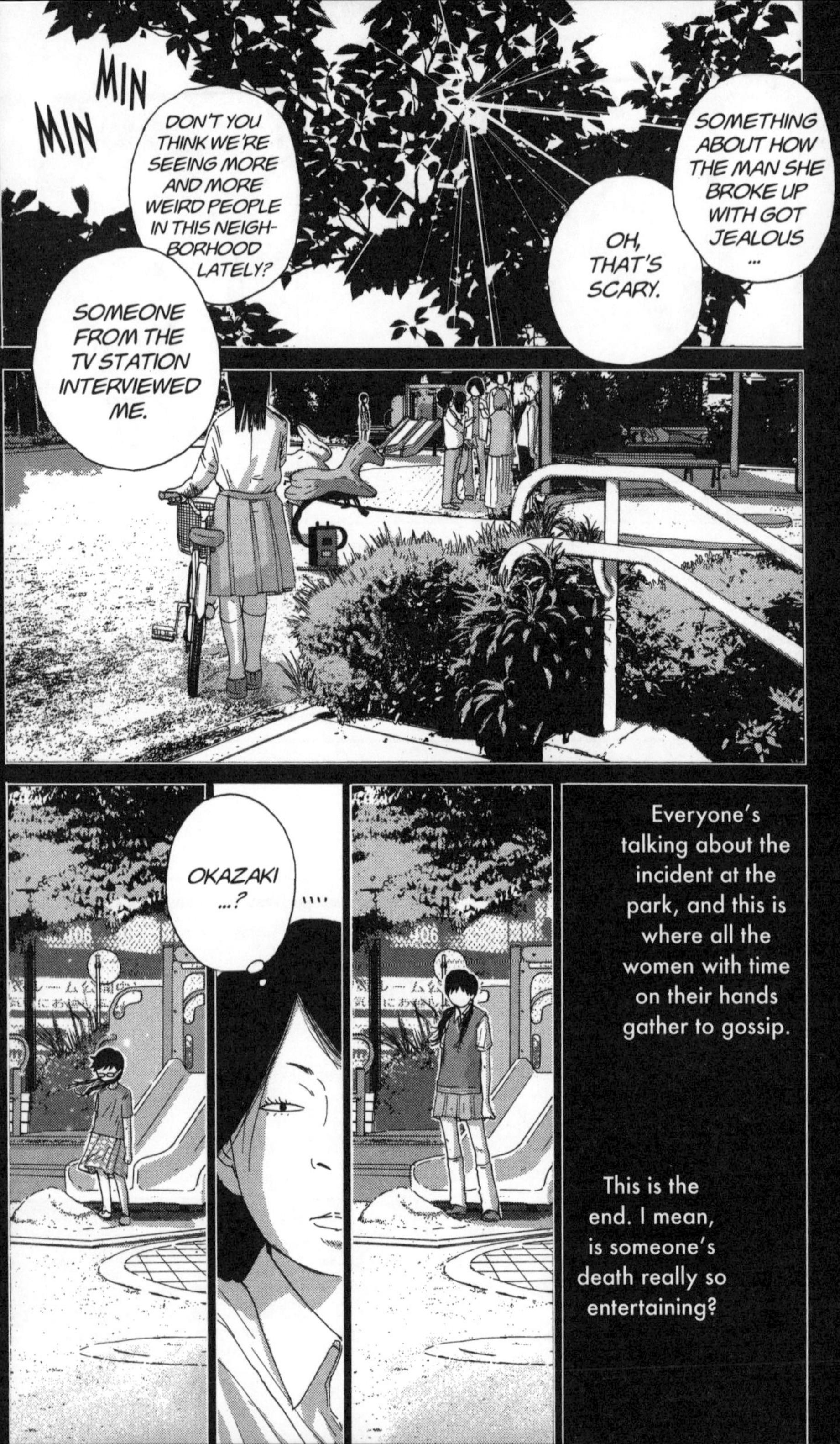
SOMETHING ABOUT HOW THE MAN SHE BROKE UP WITH GOT JEALOUS ...
OH, THAT'S SCARY.
MIN MIN
DON'T YOU THINK WE'RE SEEING MORE AND MORE WEIRD PEOPLE IN THIS NEIGHBORHOOD LATELY?
SOMEONE FROM THE TV STATION INTERVIEWED ME.
Everyone's talking about the incident at the park, and this is where all the women with time on their hands gather to gossip.
This is the end. I mean, is someone's death really so entertaining?
OKAZAKI ...?
''''

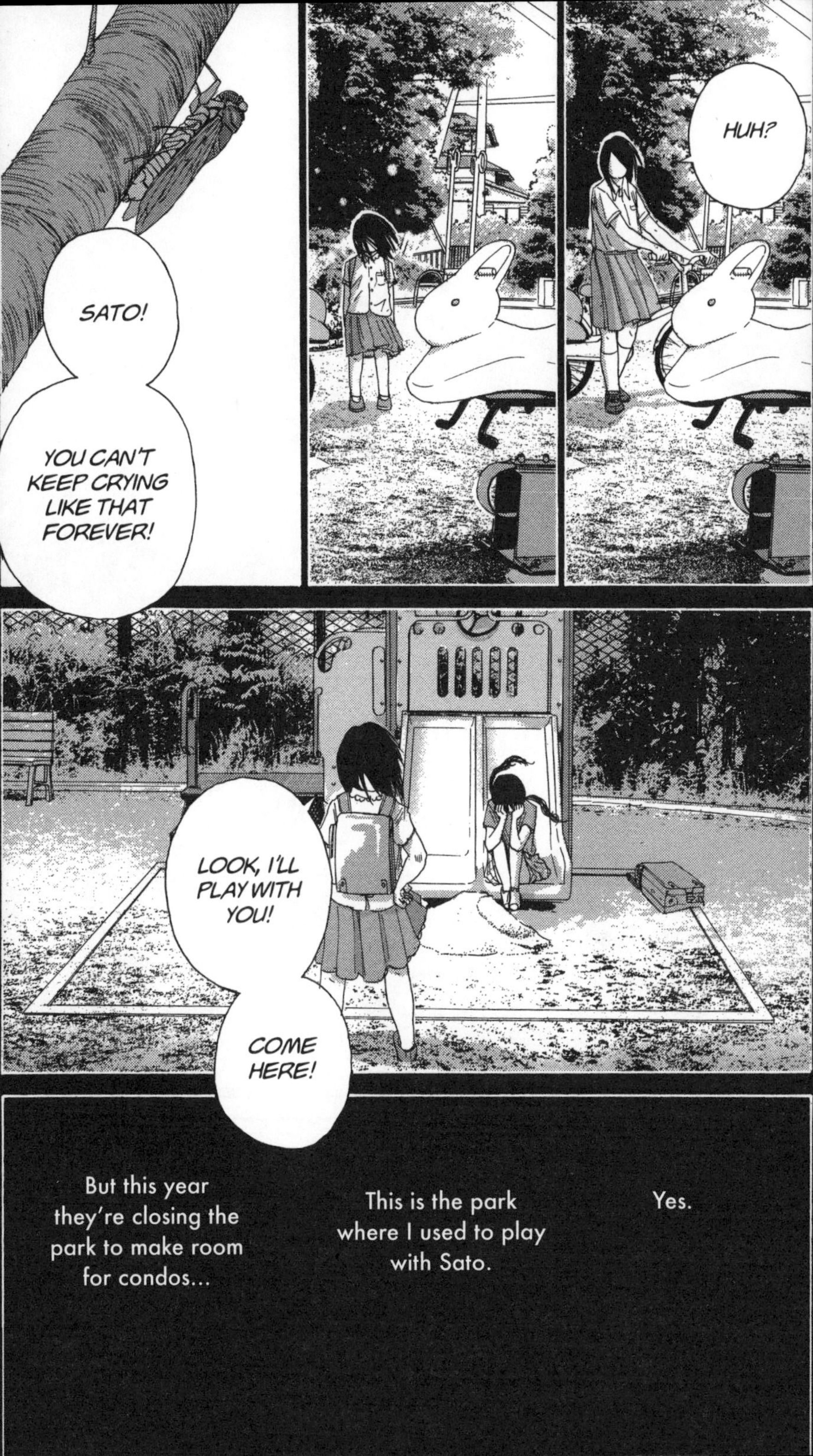
HUH?
SATO!
YOU CAN'T KEEP CRYING LIKE THAT FOREVER!
LOOK, I'LL PLAY WITH YOU!
COME HERE!
Yes.
This is the park where I used to play with Sato.
But this year they're closing the park to make room for condos...

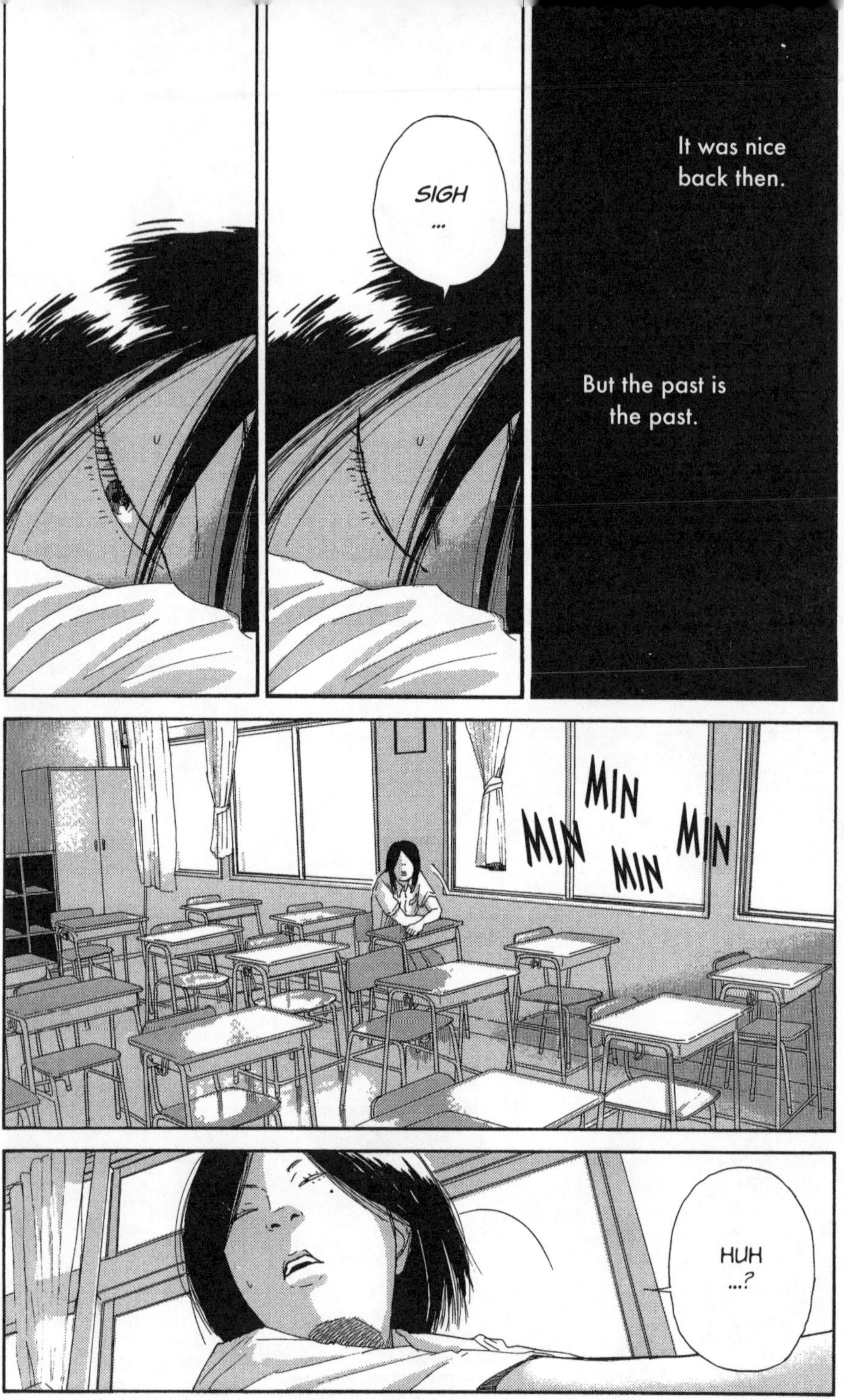
It was nice back then.
But the past is the past.
SIGH ...
MIN MIN MIN MIN
HUH ...?

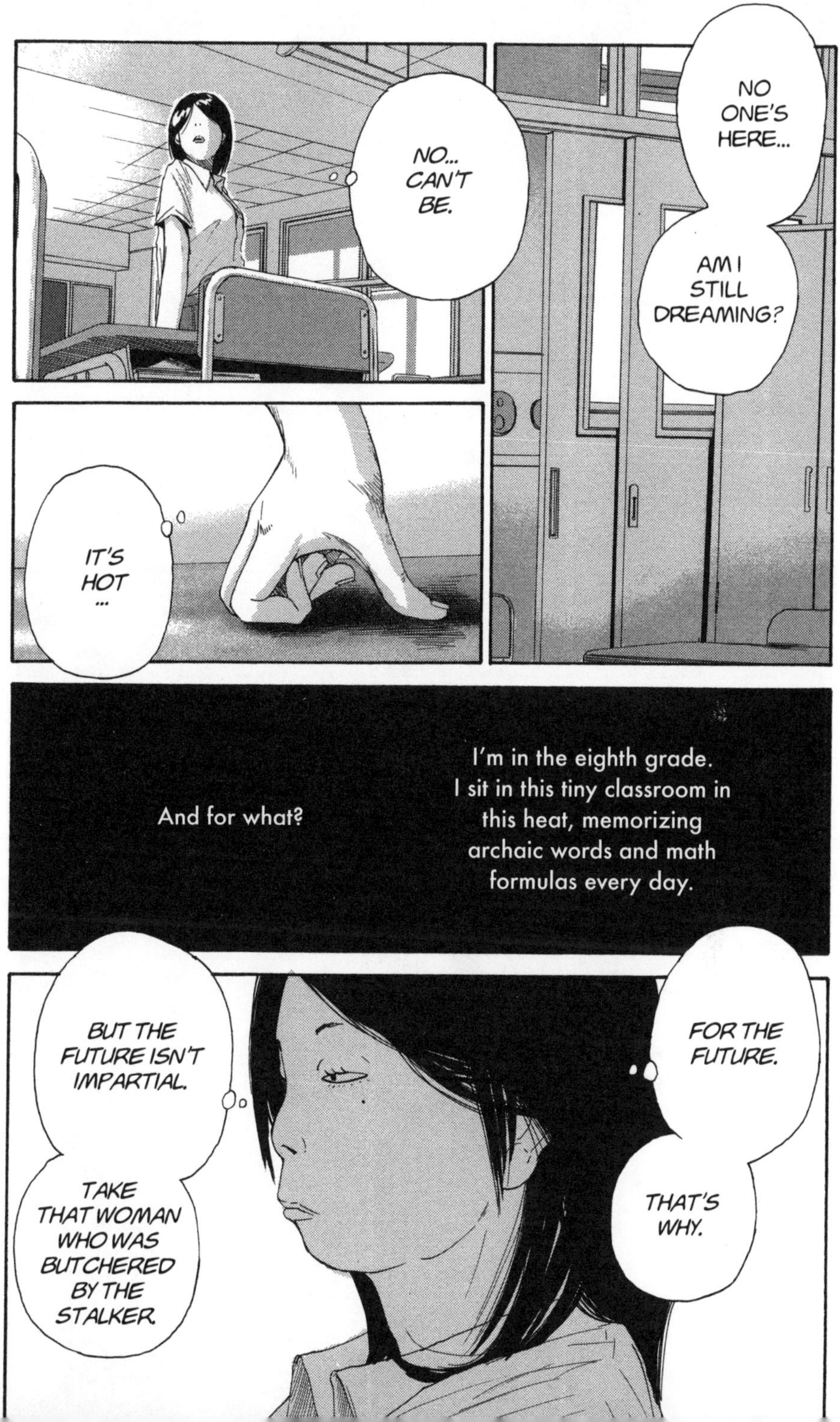
NO ONE'S HERE...
AM I STILL DREAMING?
NO... CAN'T BE.
IT'S HOT ...
I'm in the eighth grade. I sit in this tiny classroom in this heat, memorizing archaic words and math formulas every day.
And for what?
FOR THE FUTURE.
THAT'S WHY.
BUT THE FUTURE ISN'T IMPARTIAL.
TAKE THAT WOMAN WHO WAS BUTCHERED BY THE STALKER.

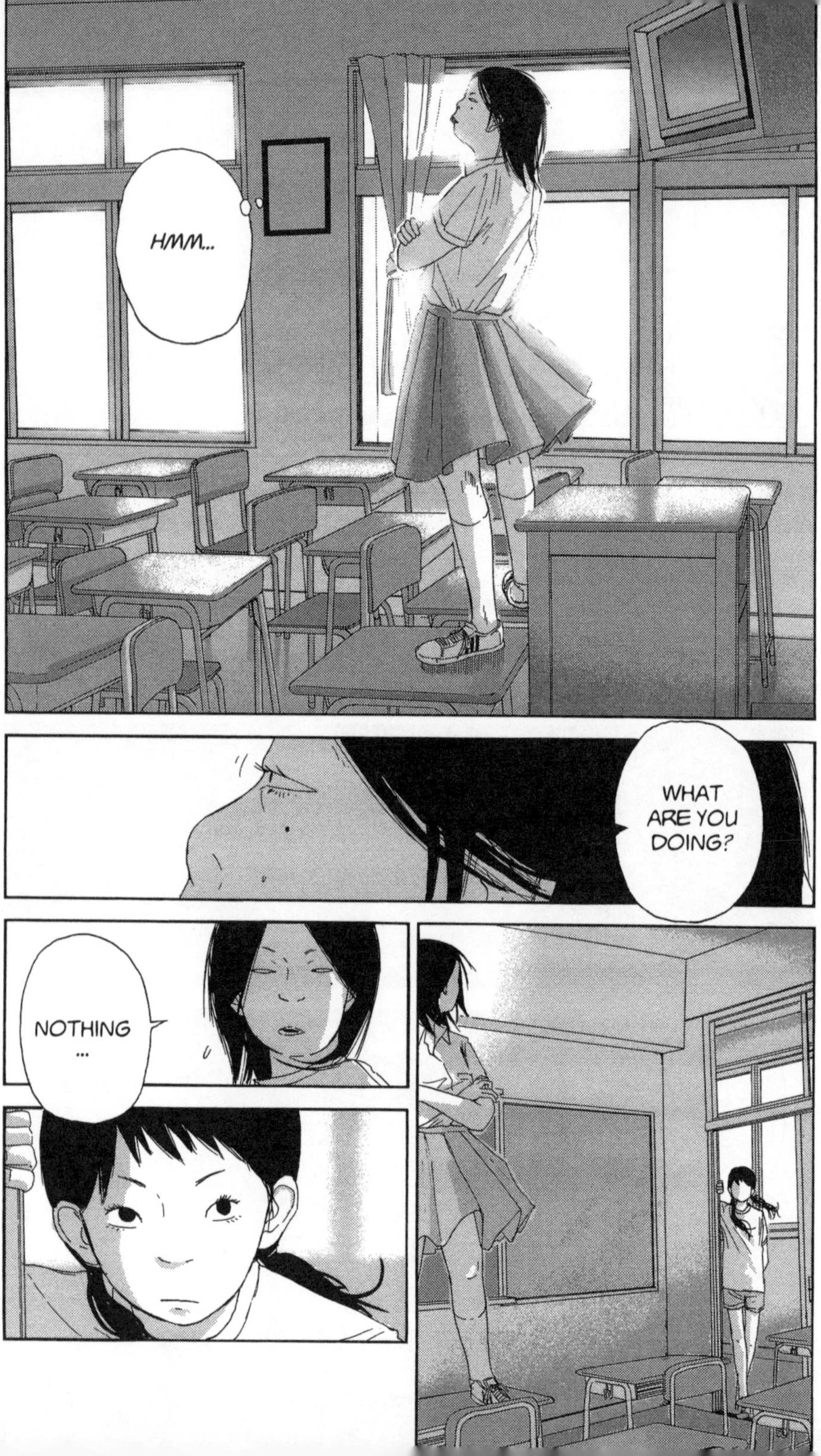
HMM...
WHAT ARE YOU DOING?
NOTHING ...

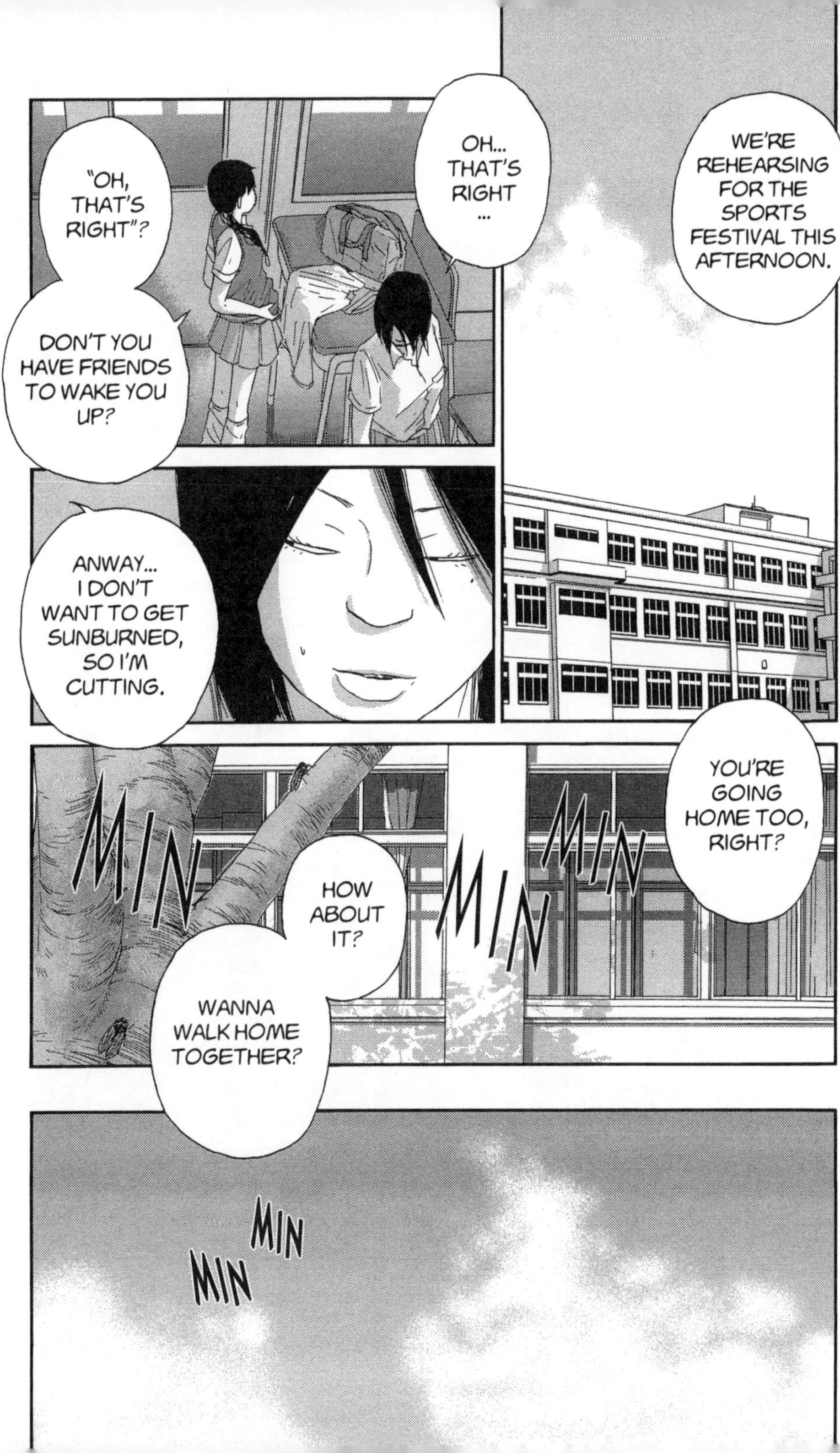
WE'RE REHEARSING FOR THE SPORTS FESTIVAL THIS AFTERNOON.
OH... THAT'S RIGHT ...
"OH, THAT'S RIGHT"?
DON'T YOU HAVE FRIENDS TO WAKE YOU UP?
ANWAY... I DON'T WANT TO GET SUNBURNED, SO I'M CUTTING.
YOU'RE GOING HOME TOO, RIGHT?
MIN MIN
MIN MIN
HOW ABOUT IT?
WANNA WALK HOME TOGETHER?
MIN
MIN

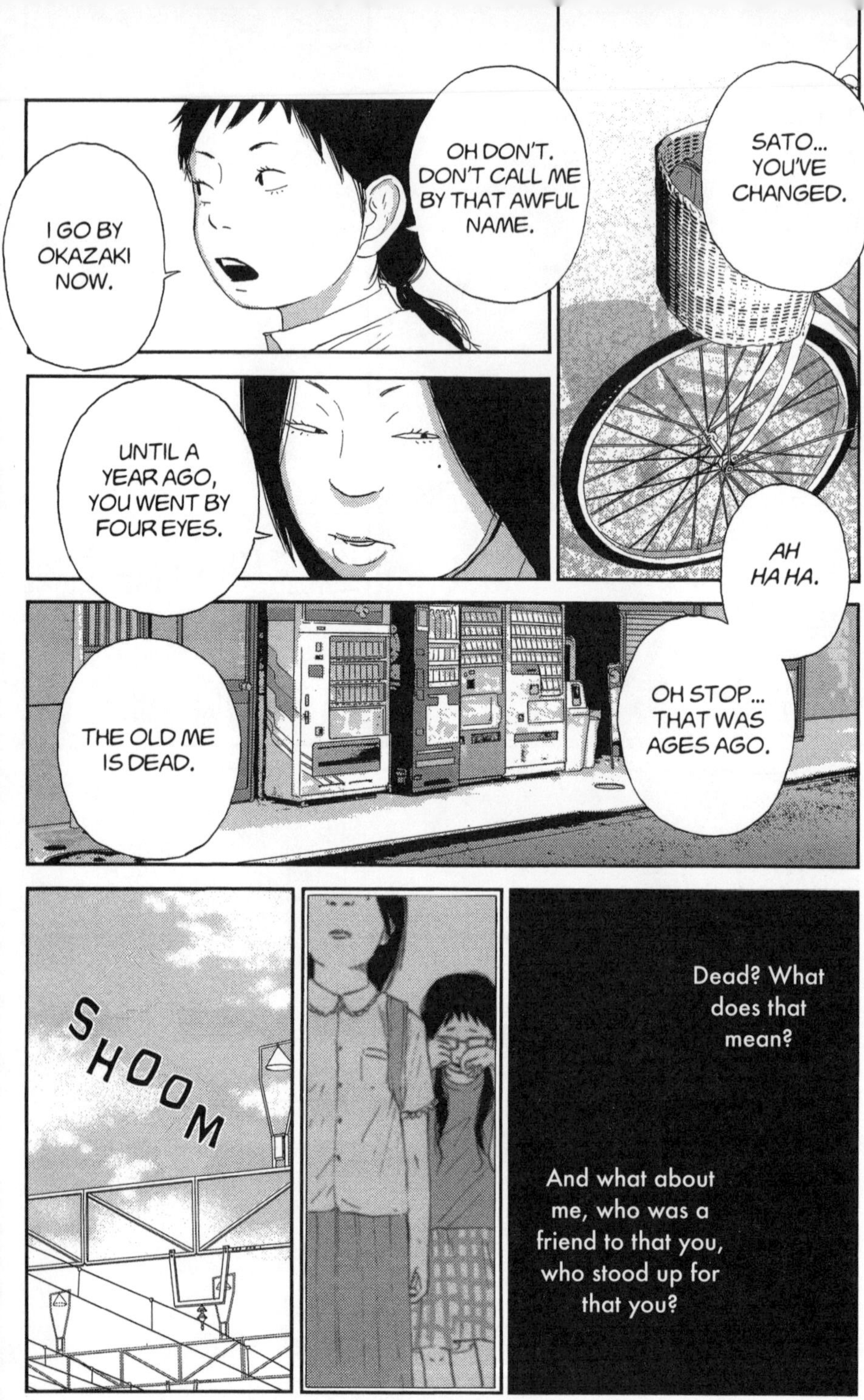
SATO... YOU'VE CHANGED.
AH HA HA.
OH DON'T. DON'T CALL ME BY THAT AWFUL NAME.
I GO BY OKAZAKI NOW.
UNTIL A YEAR AGO, YOU WENT BY FOUR EYES.
OH STOP... THAT WAS AGES AGO.
THE OLD ME IS DEAD.
Dead? What does that mean?
And what about me, who was a friend to that you, who stood up for that you?
SHOOM

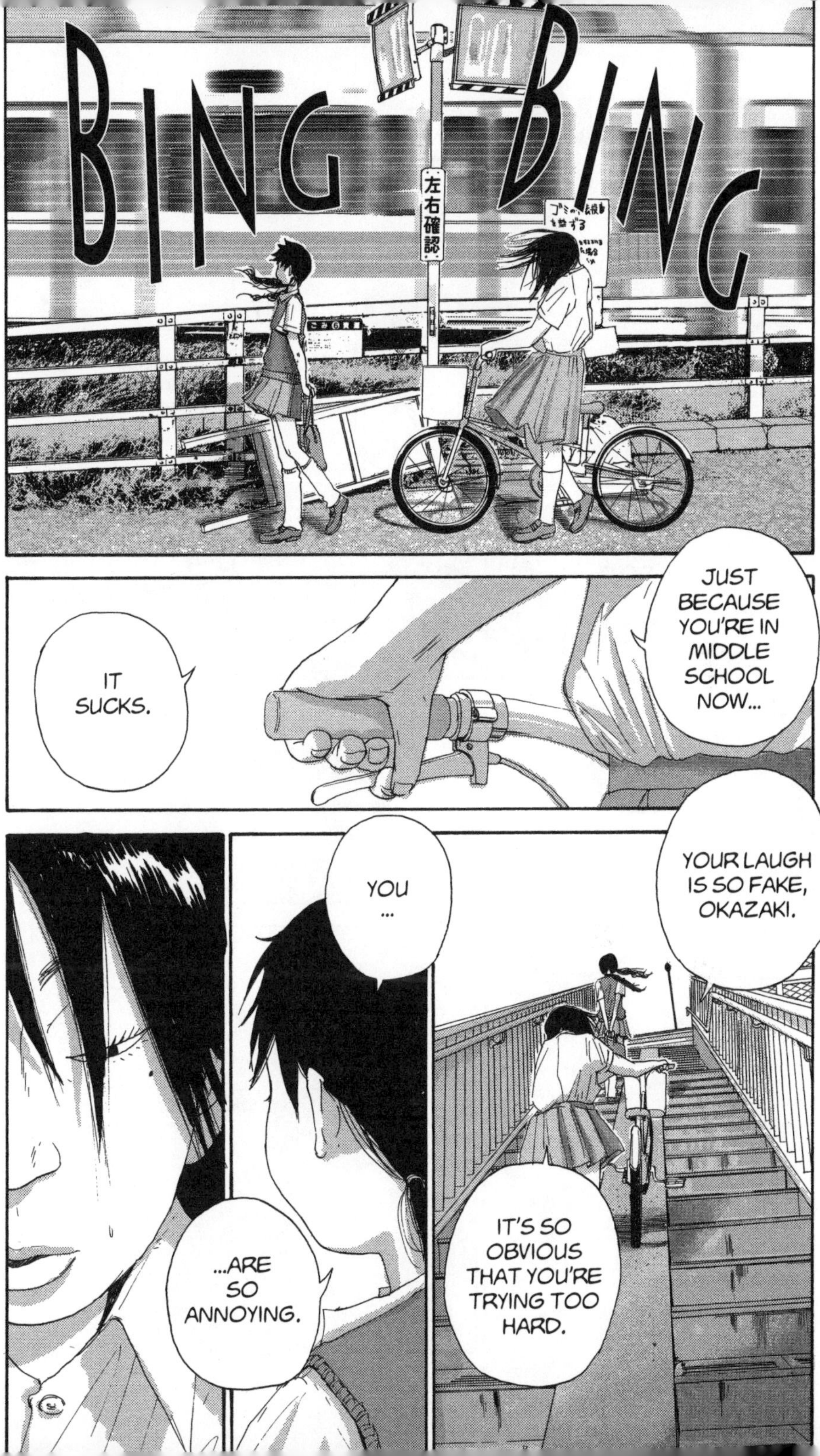
BING
BING
左右確認
JUST BECAUSE YOU'RE IN MIDDLE SCHOOL NOW...
IT SUCKS.
YOUR LAUGH IS SO FAKE, OKAZAKI.
IT'S SO OBVIOUS THAT YOU'RE TRYING TOO HARD.
YOU ...
...ARE SO ANNOYING.

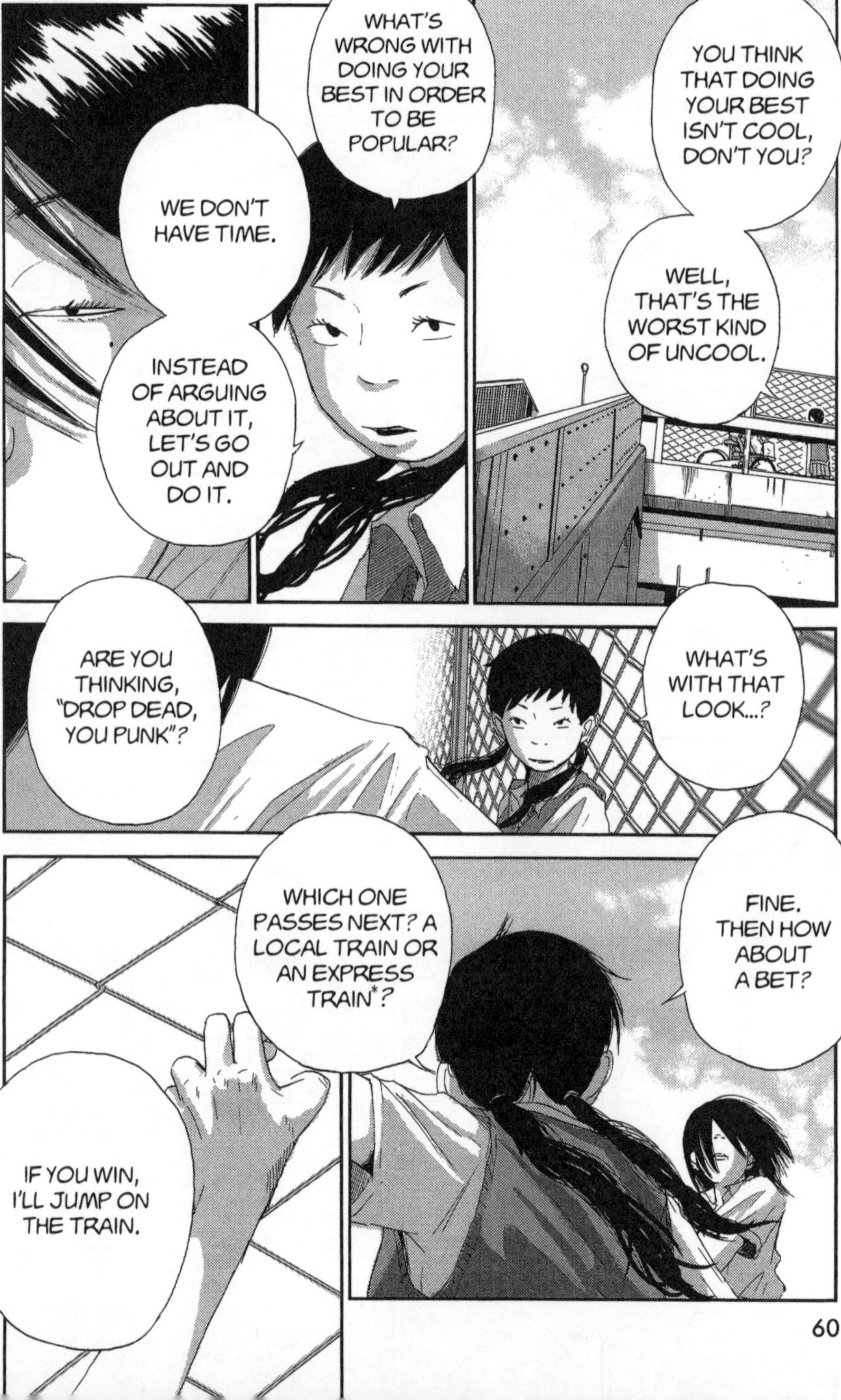
YOU THINK THAT DOING YOUR BEST ISN'T COOL, DON'T YOU?
WELL, THAT'S THE WORST KIND OF UNCOOL.
WHAT'S WRONG WITH DOING YOUR BEST IN ORDER TO BE POPULAR?
WE DON'T HAVE TIME.
INSTEAD OF ARGUING ABOUT IT, LET'S GO OUT AND DO IT.
WHAT'S WITH THAT LOOK...?
ARE YOU THINKING, "DROP DEAD, YOU PUNK"?
FINE. THEN HOW ABOUT A BET?
WHICH ONE PASSES NEXT? A LOCAL TRAIN OR AN EXPRESS TRAIN*?
IF YOU WIN, I'LL JUMP ON THE TRAIN.

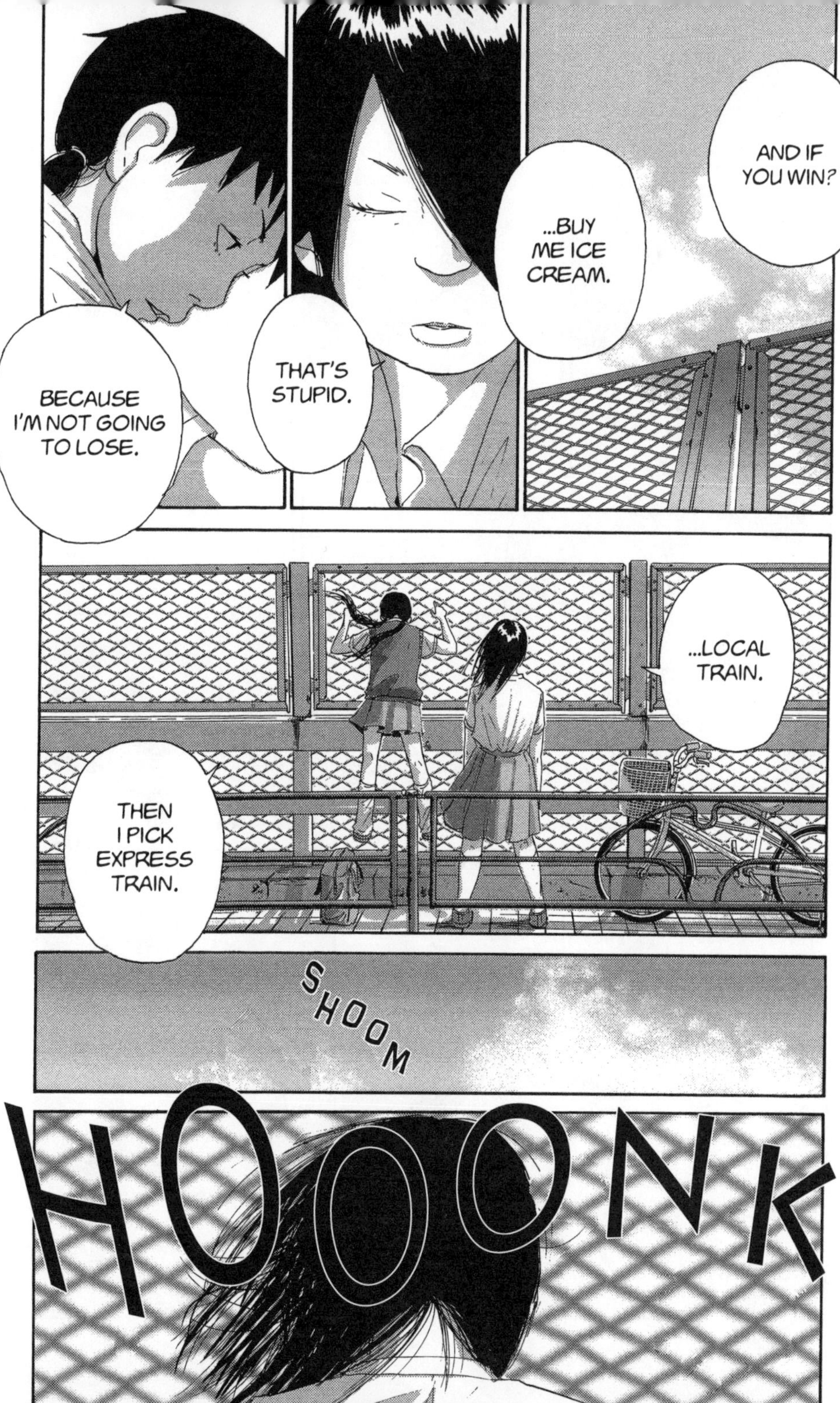
AND IF YOU WIN?
...BUY ME ICE CREAM.
THAT'S STUPID.
BECAUSE I'M NOT GOING TO LOSE.
...LOCAL TRAIN.
THEN I PICK EXPRESS TRAIN.
SHOOM
HOOONK

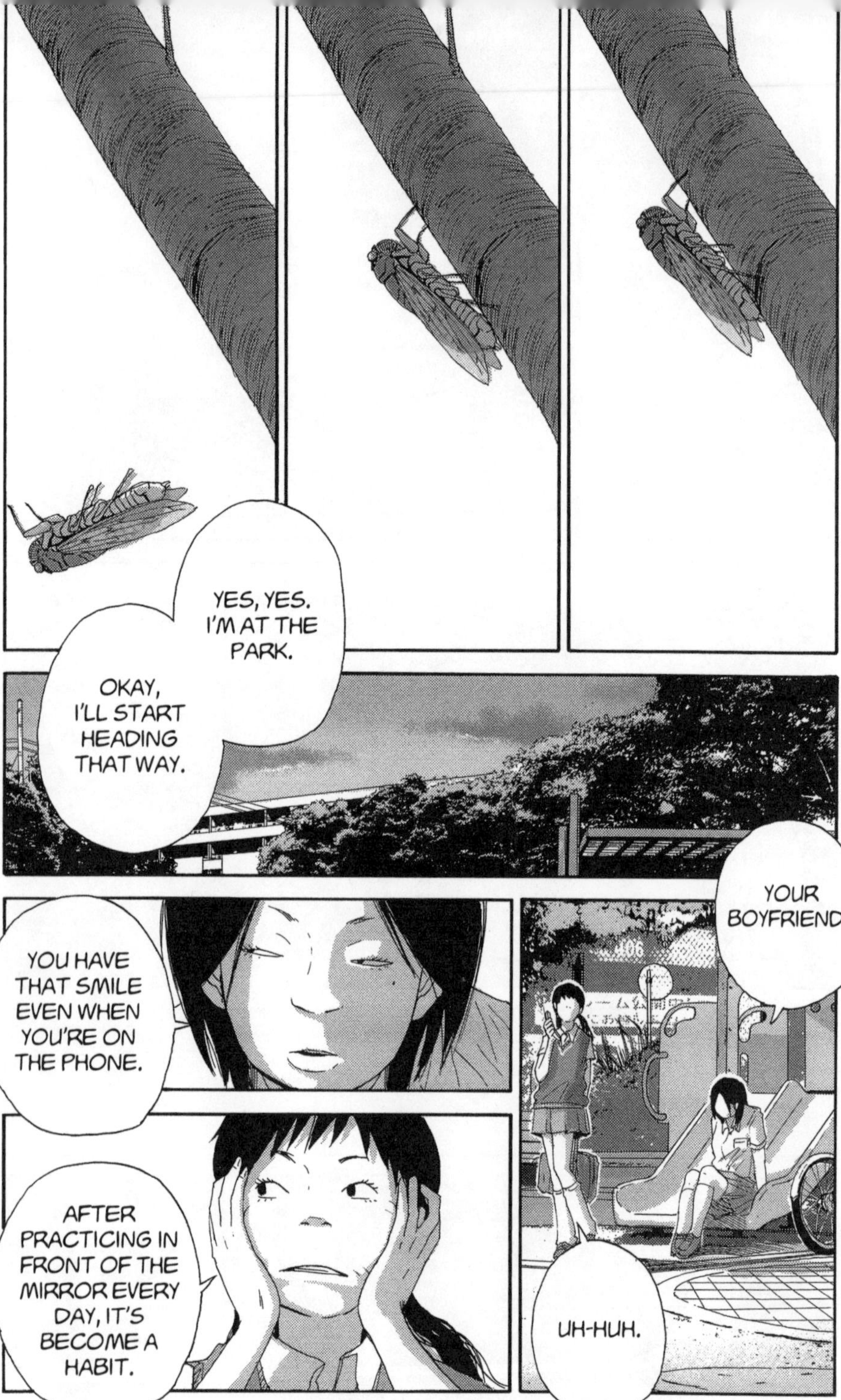
YES, YES. I'M AT THE PARK.
OKAY, I'LL START HEADING THAT WAY.
YOUR BOYFRIEND?
UH-HUH.
YOU HAVE THAT SMILE EVEN WHEN YOU'RE ON THE PHONE.
AFTER PRACTICING IN FRONT OF THE MIRROR EVERY DAY, IT'S BECOME A HABIT.

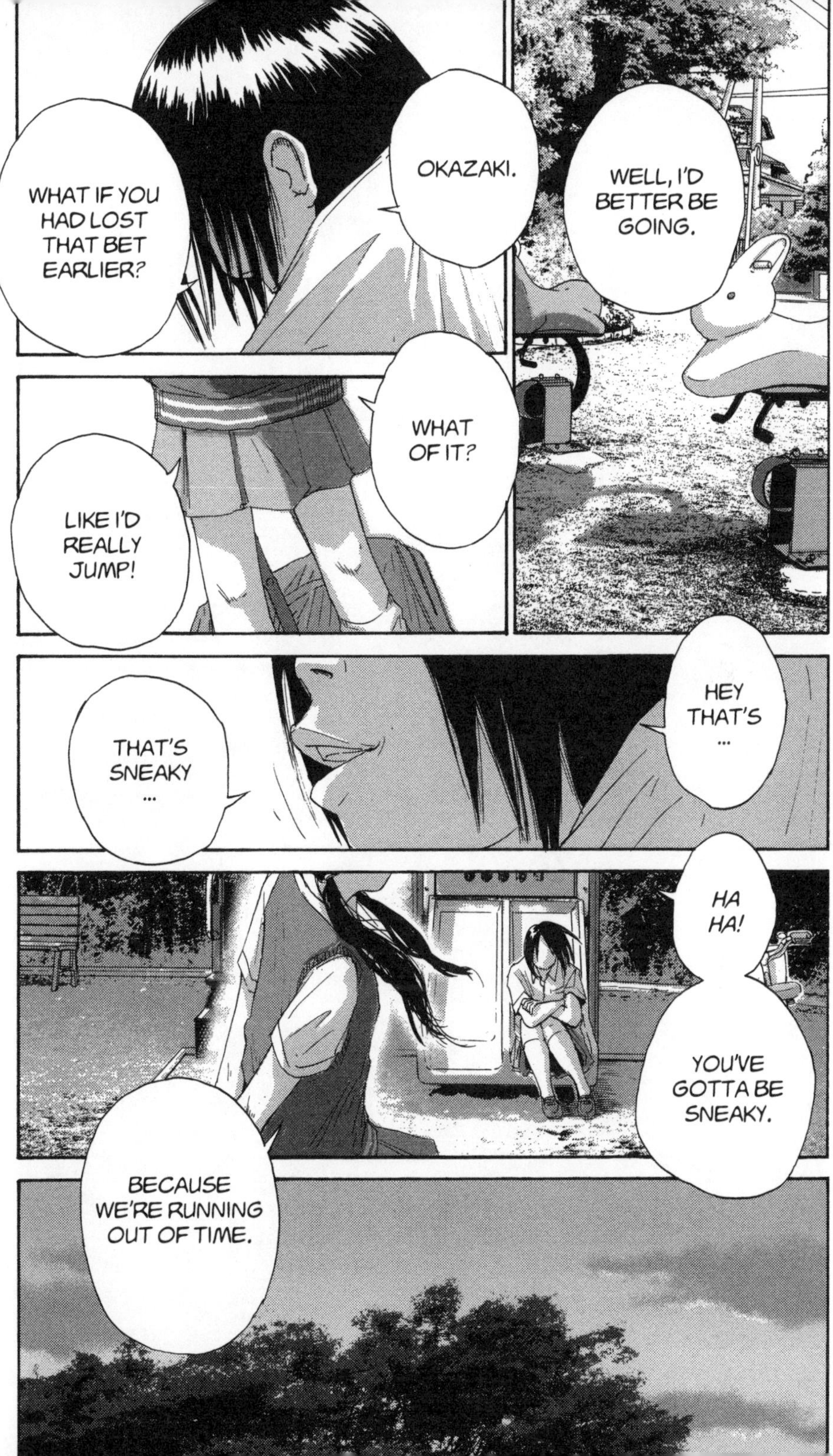
WELL, I'D BETTER BE GOING.
OKAZAKI.
WHAT IF YOU HAD LOST THAT BET EARLIER?
WHAT OF IT?
LIKE I'D REALLY JUMP!
HEY THAT'S ...
THAT'S SNEAKY ...
HA HA!
YOU'VE GOTTA BE SNEAKY.
BECAUSE WE'RE RUNNING OUT OF TIME.

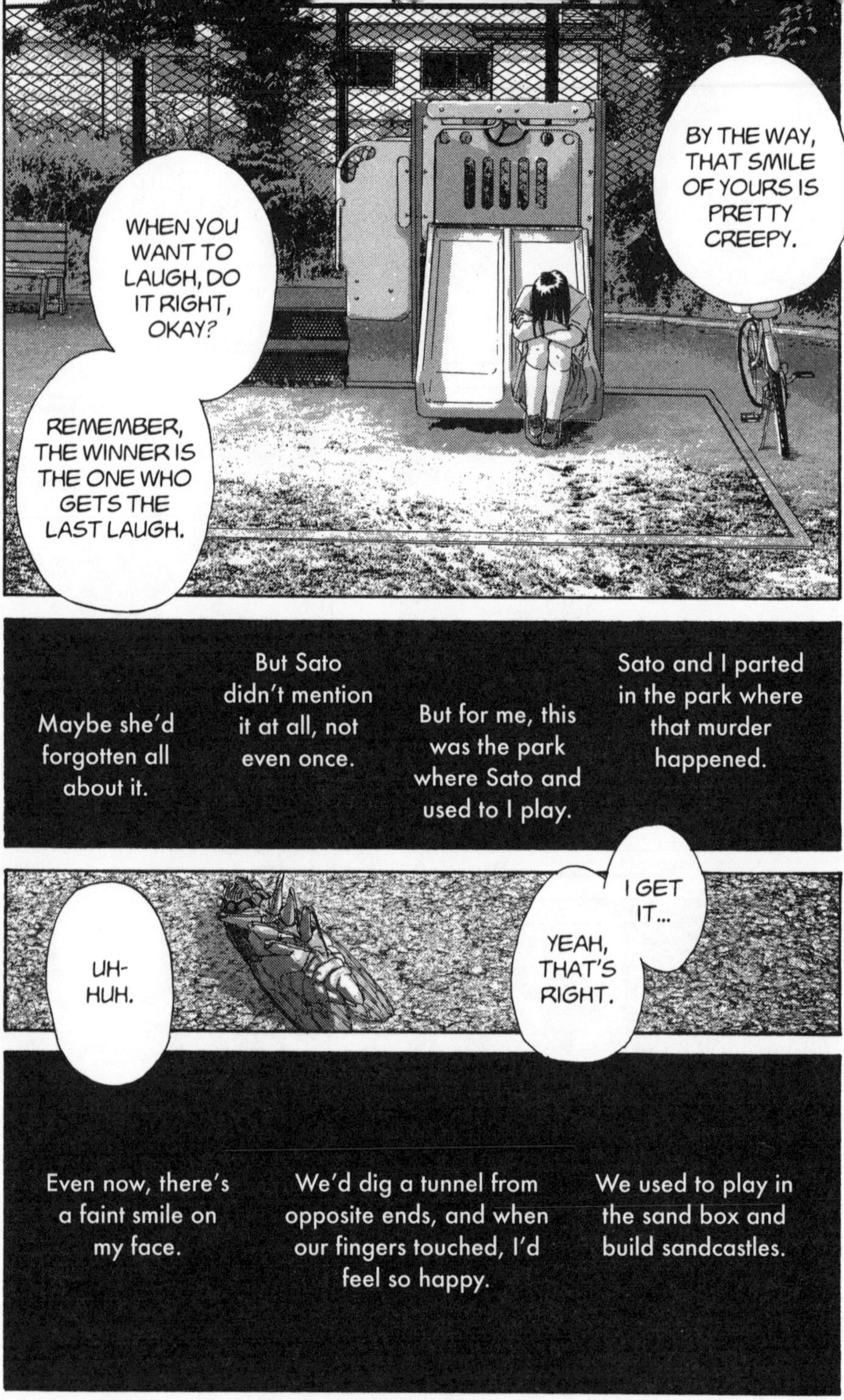
BY THE WAY, THAT SMILE OF YOURS IS PRETTY CREEPY.
WHEN YOU WANT TO LAUGH, DO IT RIGHT, OKAY?
REMEMBER, THE WINNER IS THE ONE WHO GETS THE LAST LAUGH.
Sato and I parted in the park where that murder happened.
But for me, this was the park where Sato and used to I play.
But Sato didn't mention it at all, not even once.
Maybe she'd forgotten all about it.
I GET IT...
YEAH, THAT'S RIGHT.
UH-HUH.
We used to play in the sand box and build sandcastles.
We'd dig a tunnel from opposite ends, and when our fingers touched, I'd feel so happy.
Even now, there's a faint smile on my face.

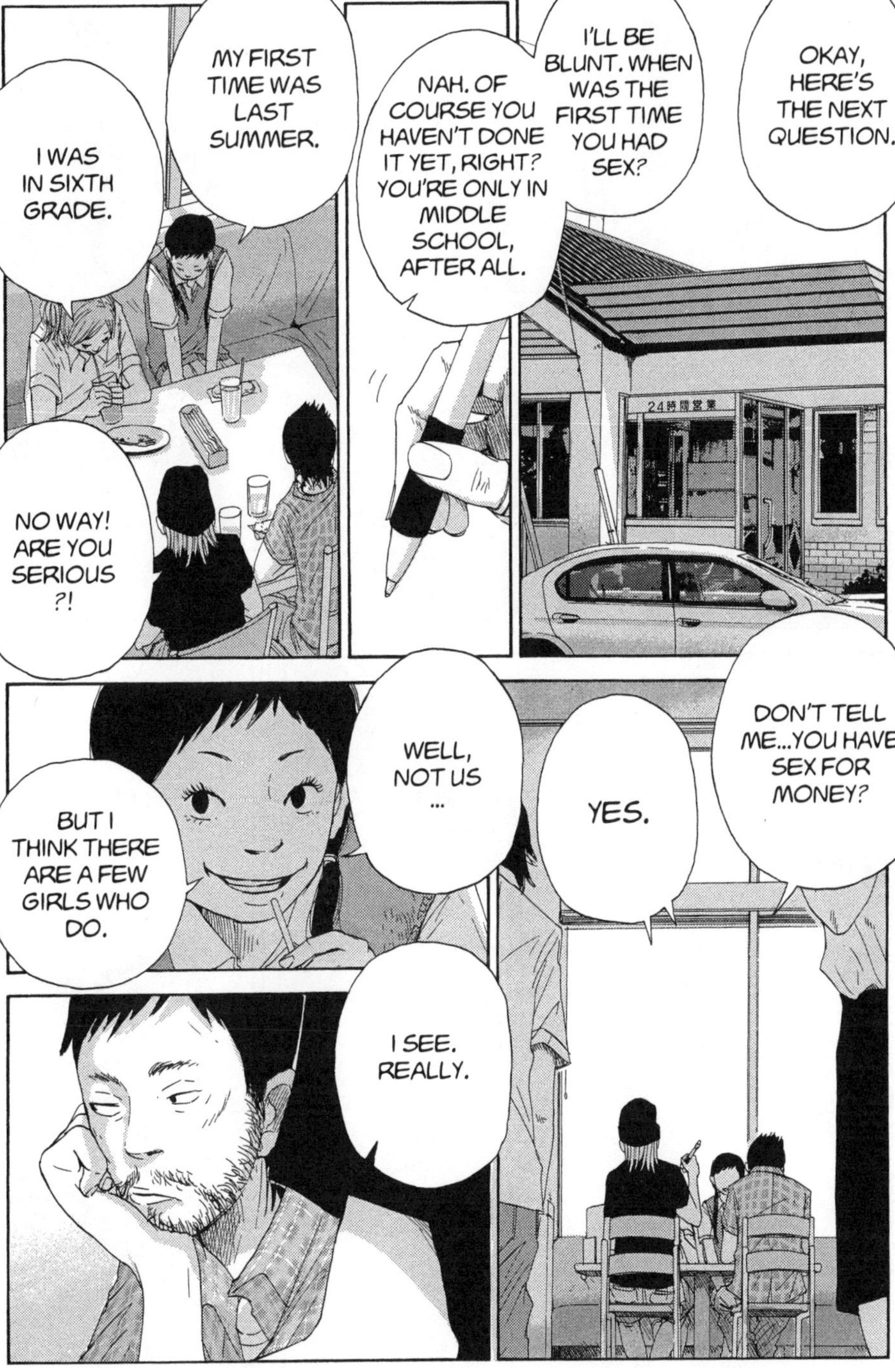
24時間営業
OKAY, HERE'S THE NEXT QUESTION.
I'LL BE BLUNT. WHEN WAS THE FIRST TIME YOU HAD SEX?
NAH. OF COURSE YOU HAVEN'T DONE IT YET, RIGHT? YOU'RE ONLY IN MIDDLE SCHOOL, AFTER ALL.
MY FIRST TIME WAS LAST SUMMER.
I WAS IN SIXTH GRADE.
NO WAY! ARE YOU SERIOUS?!
DON'T TELL ME...YOU HAVE SEX FOR MONEY?
YES.
WELL, NOT US...
BUT I THINK THERE ARE A FEW GIRLS WHO DO.
I SEE. REALLY.

**13th track Good Night**

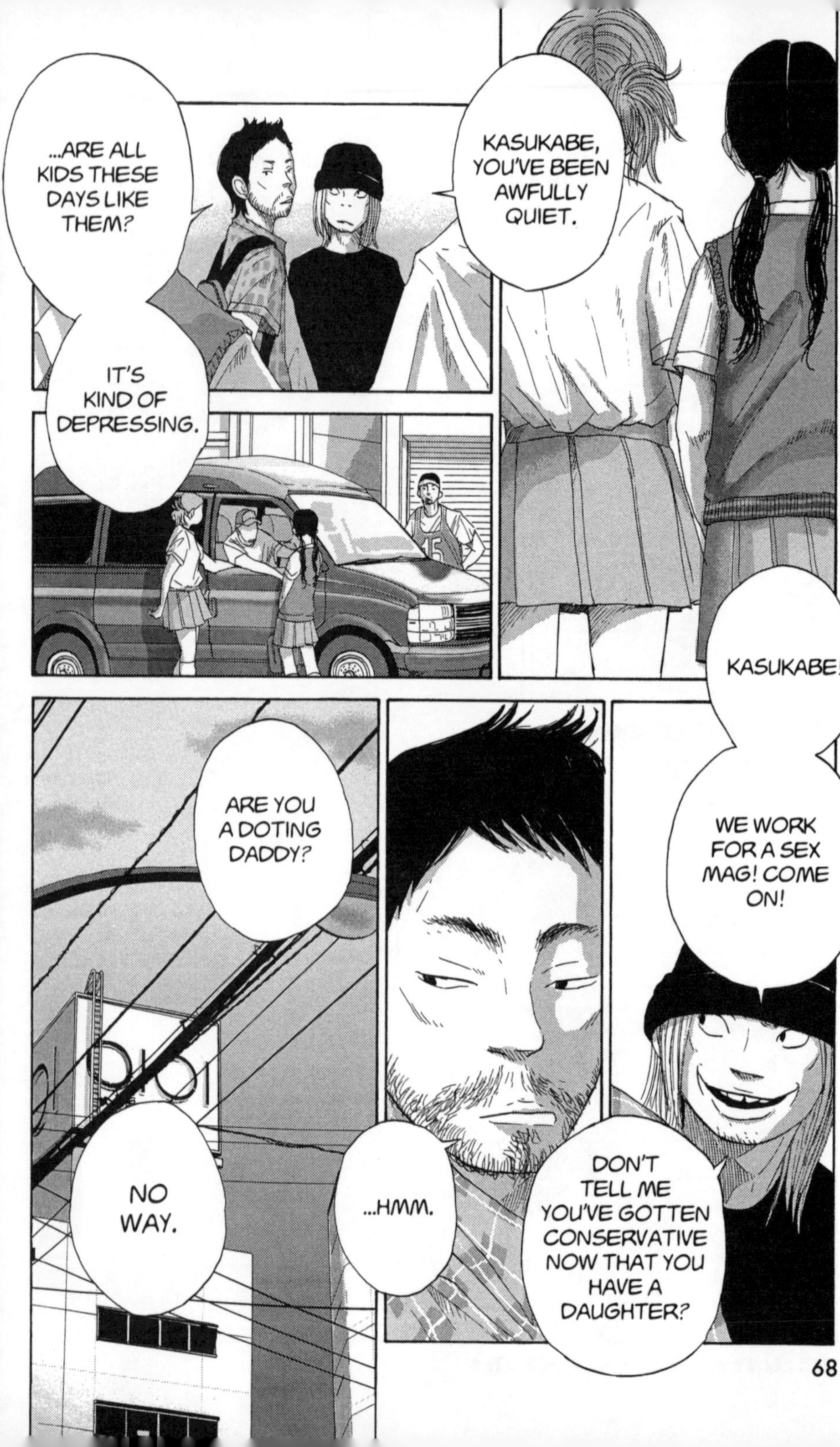
...ARE ALL KIDS THESE DAYS LIKE THEM?
IT'S KIND OF DEPRESSING.
KASUKABE, YOU'VE BEEN AWFULLY QUIET.
KASUKABE!
WE WORK FOR A SEX MAG! COME ON!
DON'T TELL ME YOU'VE GOTTEN CONSERVATIVE NOW THAT YOU HAVE A DAUGHTER?
...HMM.
ARE YOU A DOTING DADDY?
NO WAY.

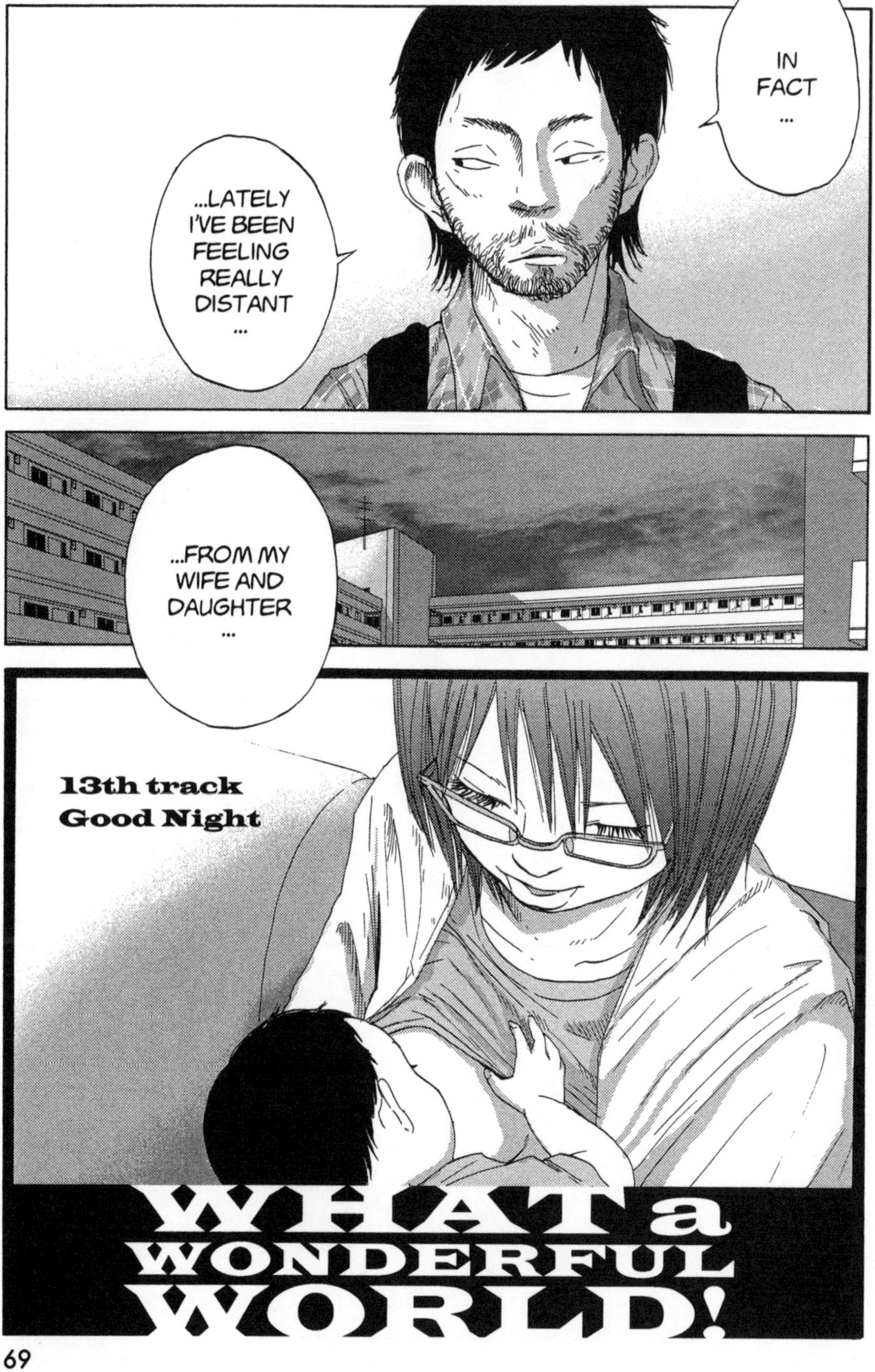
IN FACT ...
...LATELY I'VE BEEN FEELING REALLY DISTANT ...
...FROM MY WIFE AND DAUGHTER ...
13th track
Good Night
WHAT a WONDERFUL WORLD!

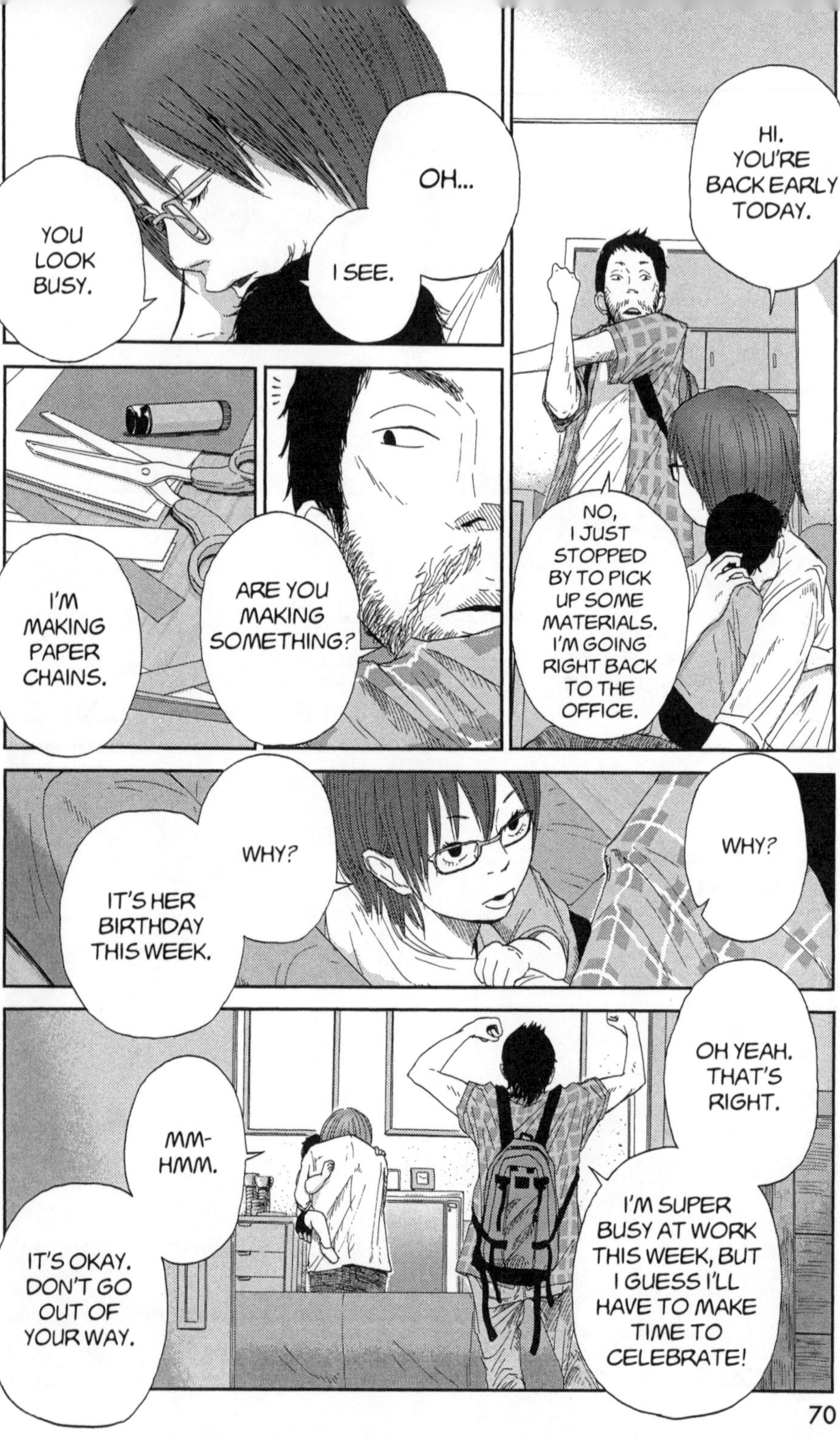
HI. YOU'RE BACK EARLY TODAY.
NO, I JUST STOPPED BY TO PICK UP SOME MATERIALS. I'M GOING RIGHT BACK TO THE OFFICE.
OH...
I SEE.
YOU LOOK BUSY.
ARE YOU MAKING SOMETHING?
I'M MAKING PAPER CHAINS.
WHY?
WHY?
IT'S HER BIRTHDAY THIS WEEK.
OH YEAH. THAT'S RIGHT.
I'M SUPER BUSY AT WORK THIS WEEK, BUT I GUESS I'LL HAVE TO MAKE TIME TO CELEBRATE!
MM-HMM.
IT'S OKAY. DON'T GO OUT OF YOUR WAY.

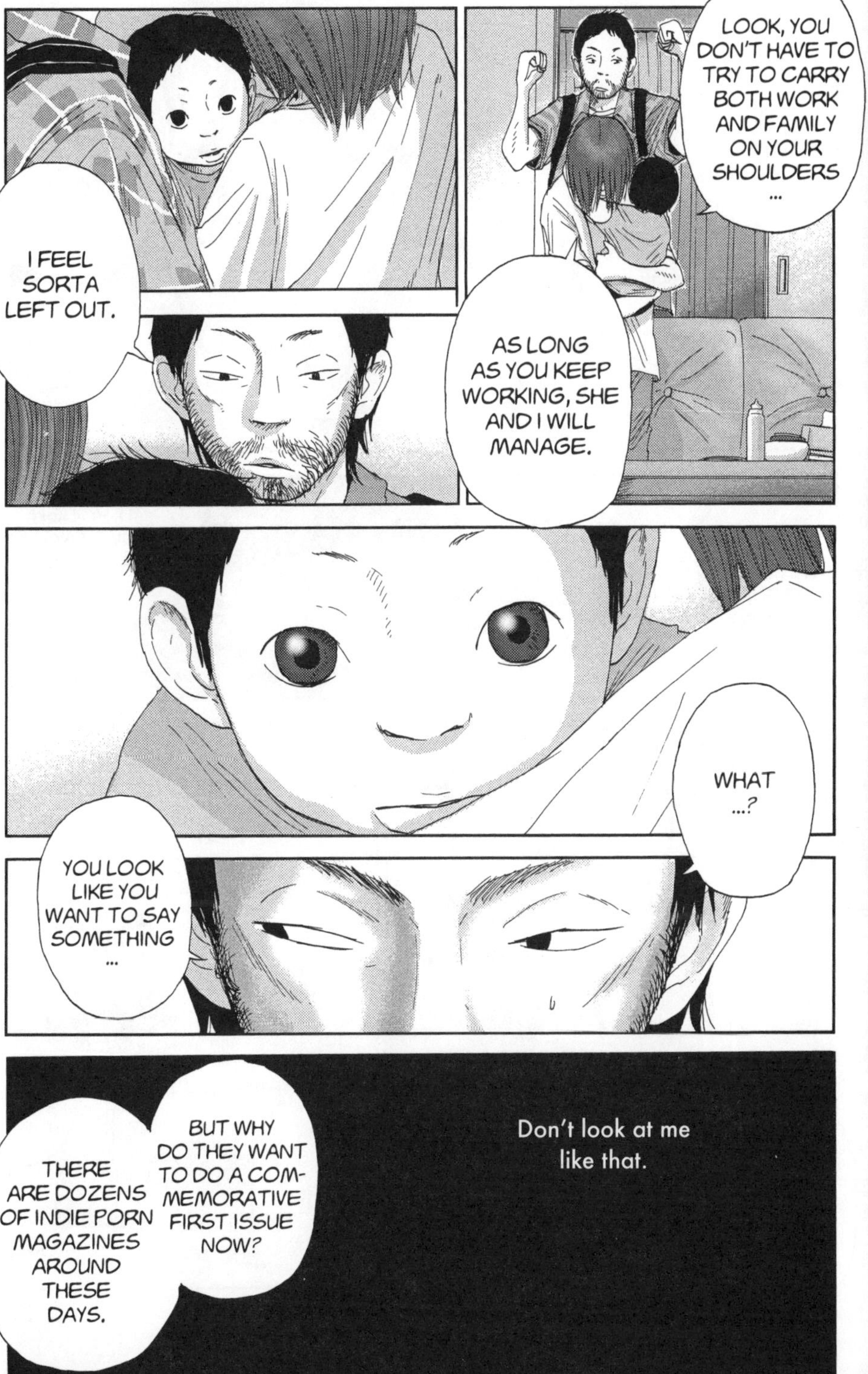
LOOK, YOU DON'T HAVE TO TRY TO CARRY BOTH WORK AND FAMILY ON YOUR SHOULDERS ...
AS LONG AS YOU KEEP WORKING, SHE AND I WILL MANAGE.
I FEEL SORTA LEFT OUT.
WHAT ...?
YOU LOOK LIKE YOU WANT TO SAY SOMETHING ...
Don't look at me like that.
BUT WHY DO THEY WANT TO DO A COM-MEMORATIVE FIRST ISSUE NOW?
THERE ARE DOZENS OF INDIE PORN MAGAZINES AROUND THESE DAYS.

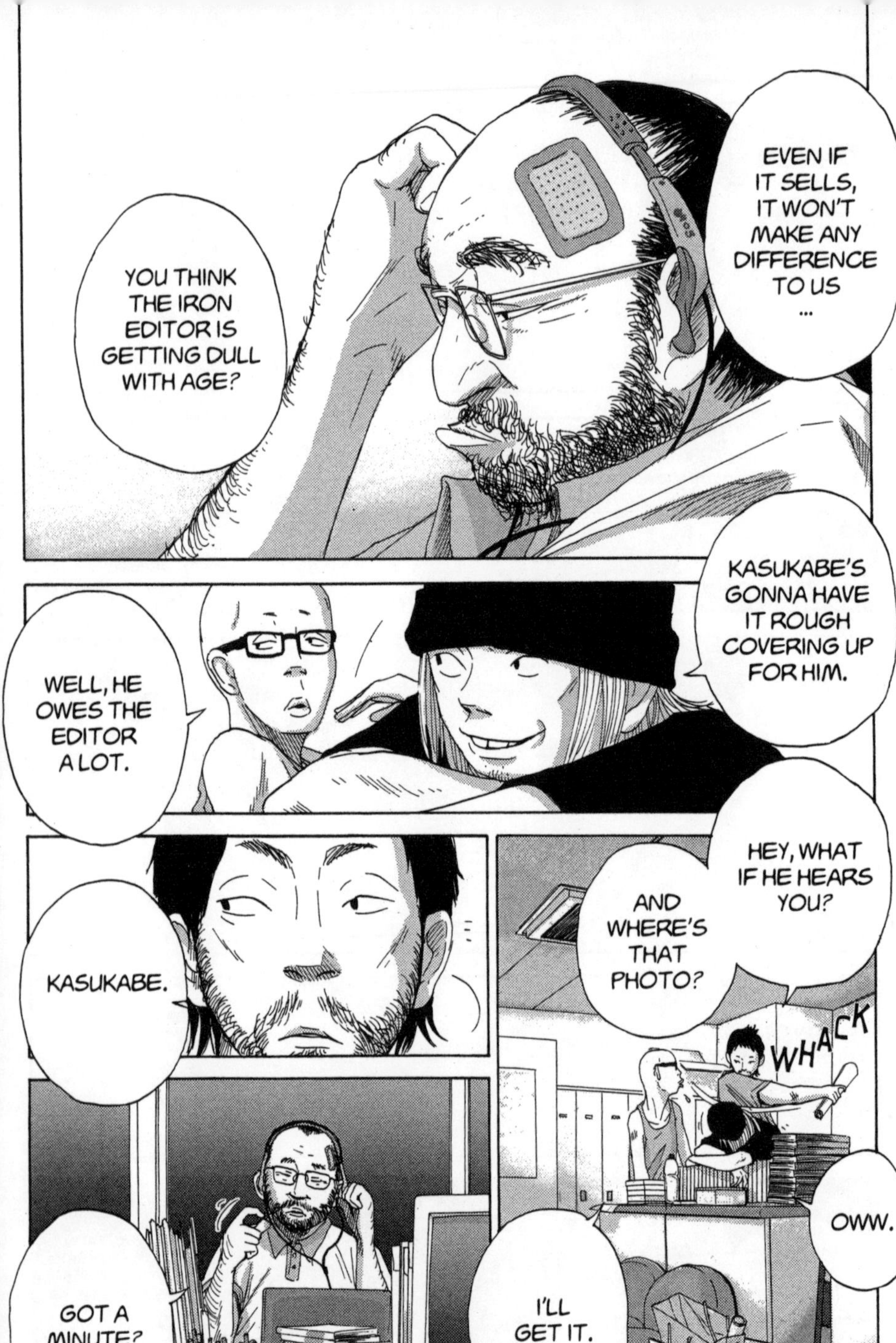
EVEN IF IT SELLS, IT WON'T MAKE ANY DIFFERENCE TO US ...
YOU THINK THE IRON EDITOR IS GETTING DULL WITH AGE?
KASUKABE'S GONNA HAVE IT ROUGH COVERING UP FOR HIM.
WELL, HE OWES THE EDITOR A LOT.
HEY, WHAT IF HE HEARS YOU?
AND WHERE'S THAT PHOTO?
WHACK
OWW.
I'LL GET IT.
KASUKABE.
GOT A MINUTE?

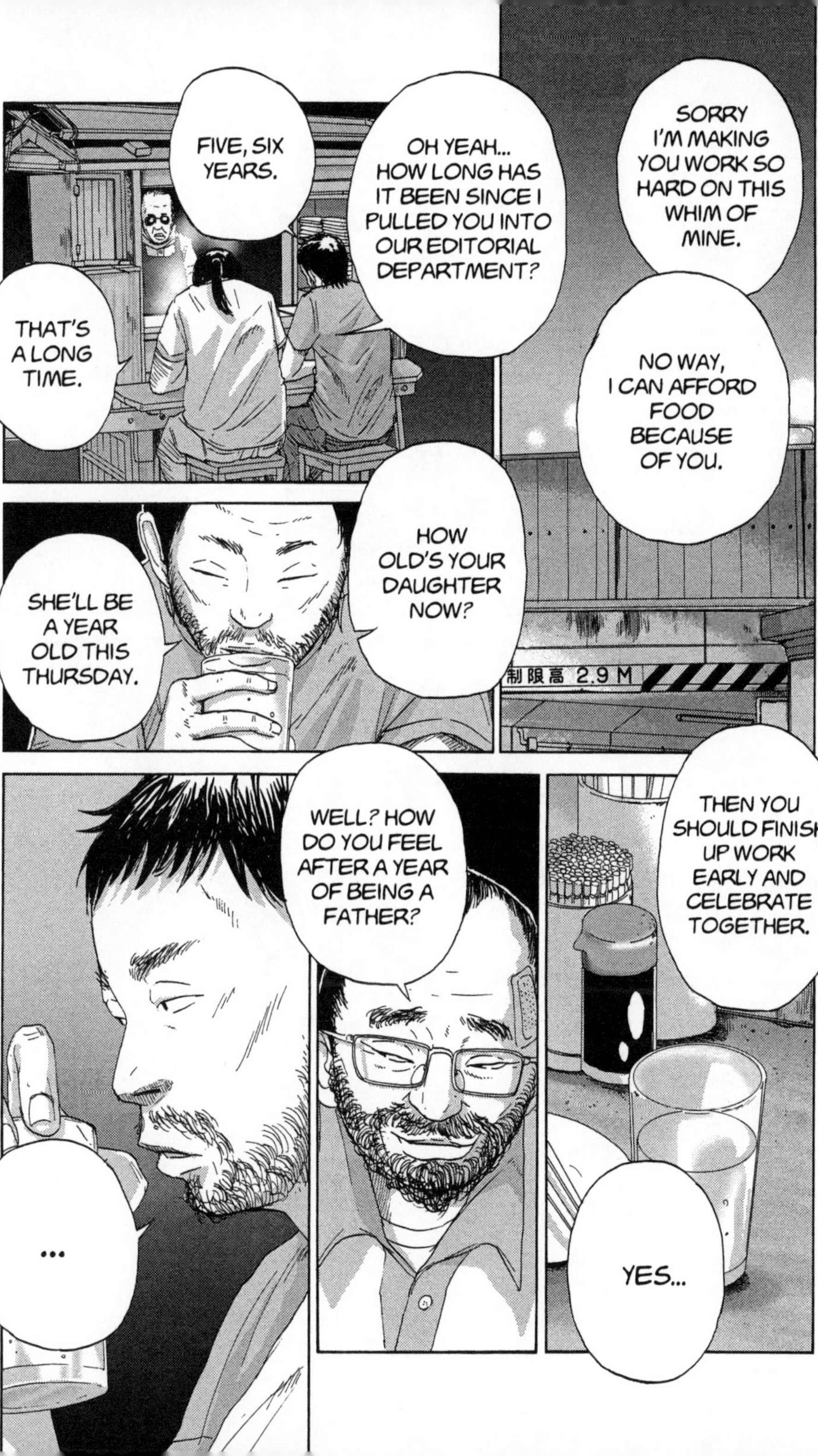
SORRY I'M MAKING YOU WORK SO HARD ON THIS WHIM OF MINE.
NO WAY, I CAN AFFORD FOOD BECAUSE OF YOU.
制限高 2.9 M
OH YEAH... HOW LONG HAS IT BEEN SINCE I PULLED YOU INTO OUR EDITORIAL DEPARTMENT?
FIVE, SIX YEARS.
THAT'S A LONG TIME.
HOW OLD'S YOUR DAUGHTER NOW?
SHE'LL BE A YEAR OLD THIS THURSDAY.
THEN YOU SHOULD FINISH UP WORK EARLY AND CELEBRATE TOGETHER.
YES...
WELL? HOW DO YOU FEEL AFTER A YEAR OF BEING A FATHER?
...

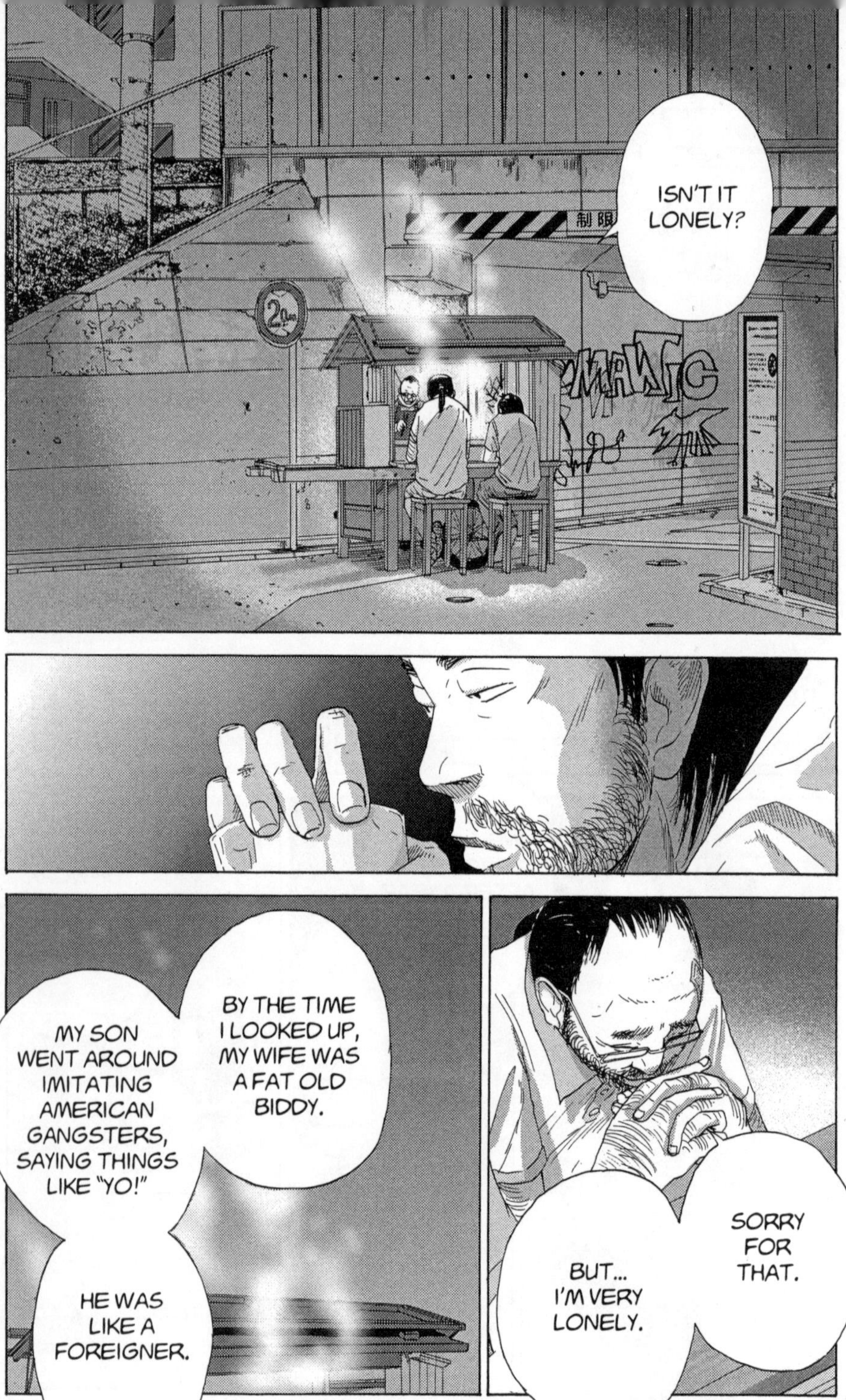
ISN'T IT LONELY?
制限
SORRY FOR THAT.
BUT... I'M VERY LONELY.
BY THE TIME I LOOKED UP, MY WIFE WAS A FAT OLD BIDDY.
MY SON WENT AROUND IMITATING AMERICAN GANGSTERS, SAYING THINGS LIKE "YO!"
HE WAS LIKE A FOREIGNER.

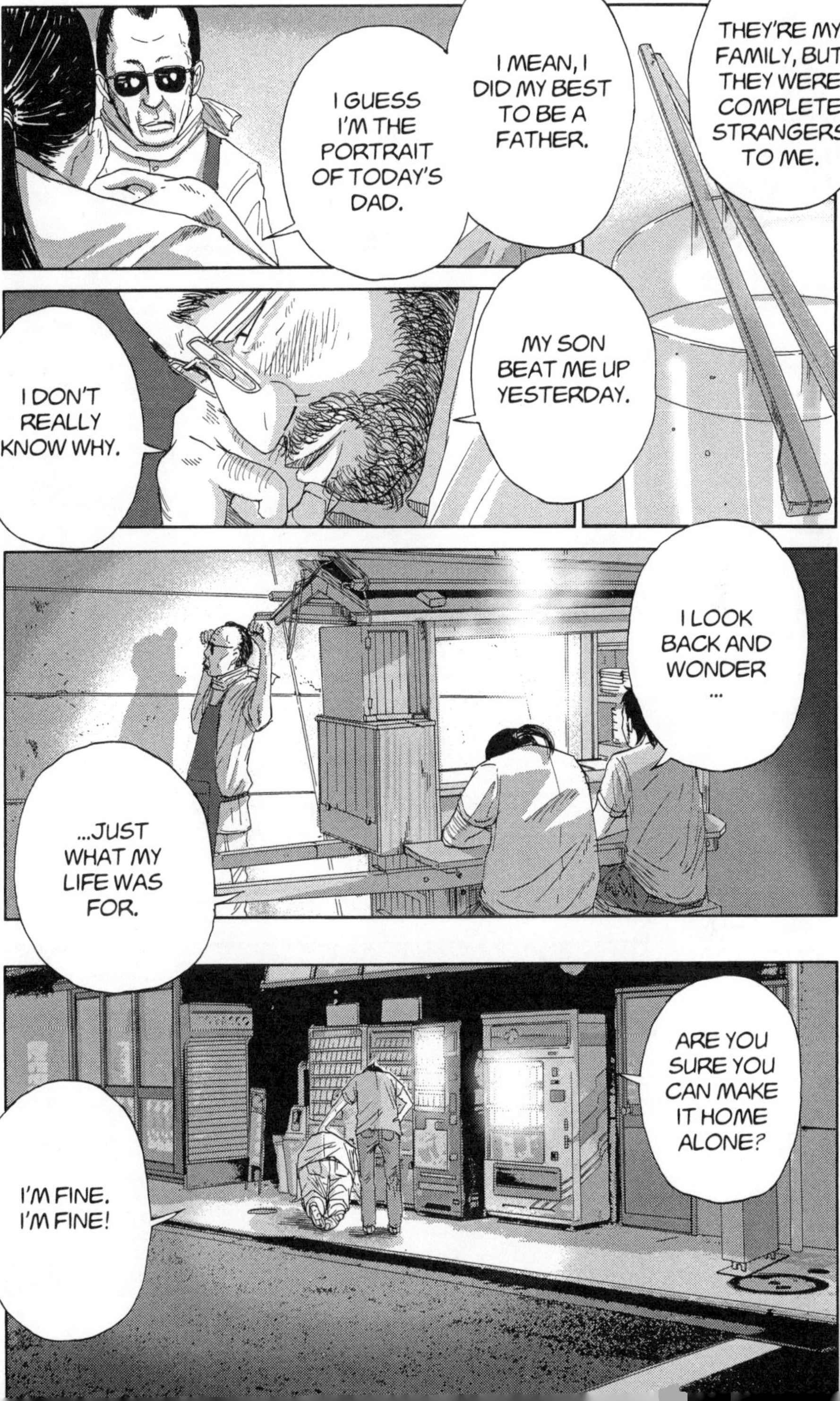
THEY'RE MY FAMILY, BUT THEY WERE COMPLETE STRANGERS TO ME.
I MEAN, I DID MY BEST TO BE A FATHER.
I GUESS I'M THE PORTRAIT OF TODAY'S DAD.
MY SON BEAT ME UP YESTERDAY.
I DON'T REALLY KNOW WHY.
I LOOK BACK AND WONDER ...
...JUST WHAT MY LIFE WAS FOR.
ARE YOU SURE YOU CAN MAKE IT HOME ALONE?
I'M FINE. I'M FINE!

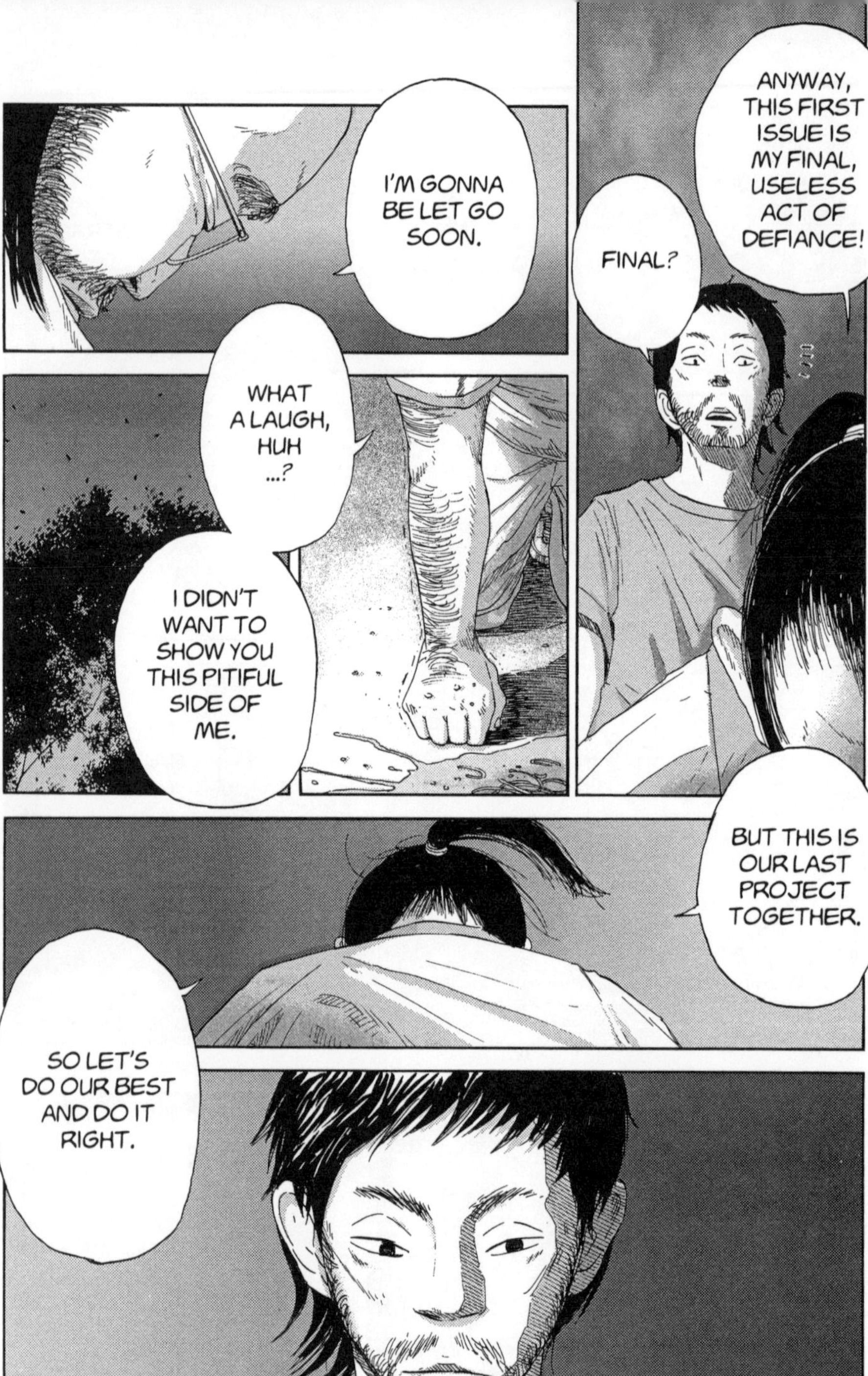
ANYWAY, THIS FIRST ISSUE IS MY FINAL, USELESS ACT OF DEFIANCE!
FINAL?
I'M GONNA BE LET GO SOON.
WHAT A LAUGH, HUH ...?
I DIDN'T WANT TO SHOW YOU THIS PITIFUL SIDE OF ME.
BUT THIS IS OUR LAST PROJECT TOGETHER.
SO LET'S DO OUR BEST AND DO IT RIGHT.

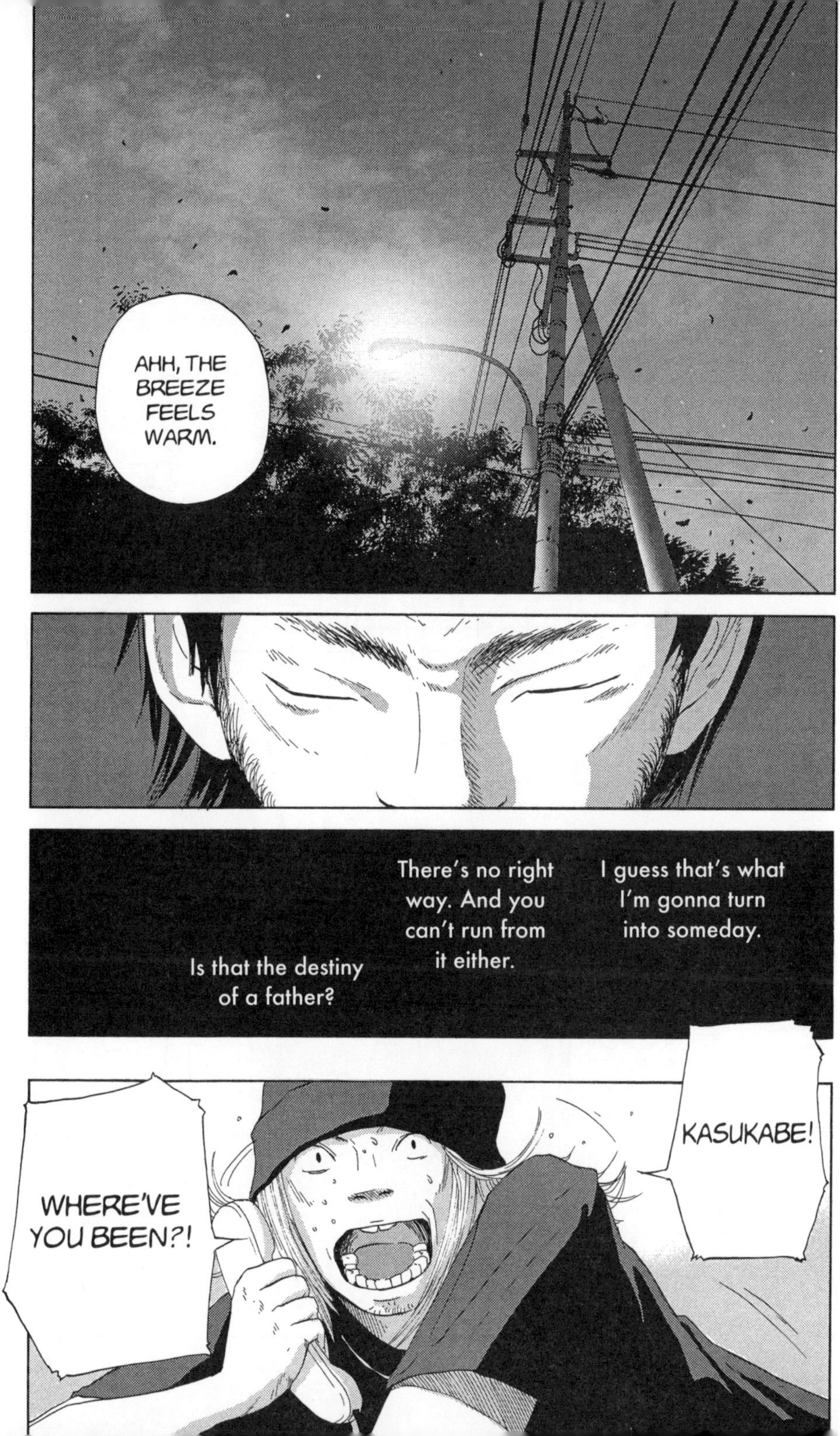
AHH, THE BREEZE FEELS WARM.
I guess that's what I'm gonna turn into someday.
There's no right way. And you can't run from it either.
Is that the destiny of a father?
KASUKABE!
WHERE'VE YOU BEEN?!

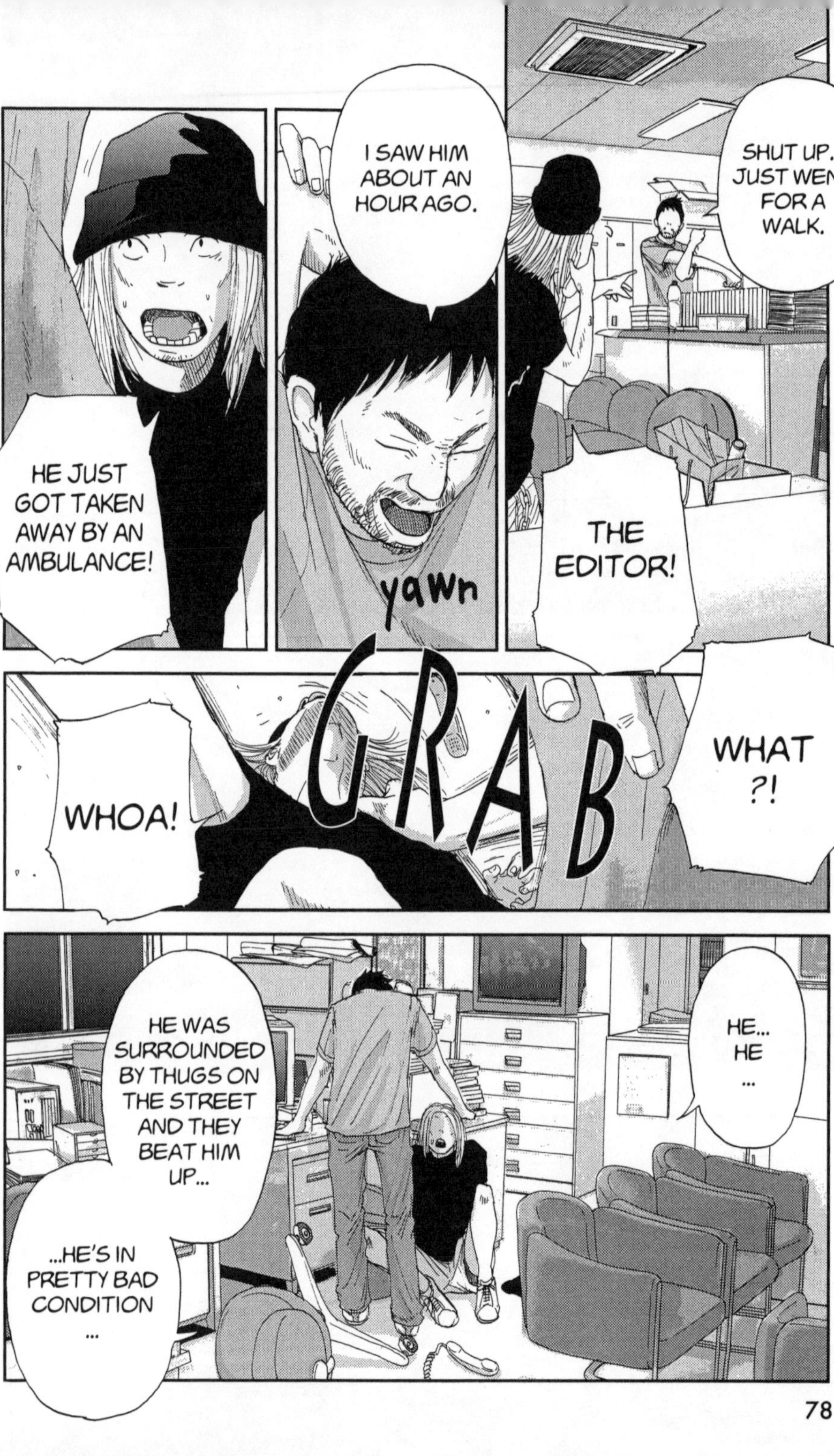
SHUT UP. I JUST WENT FOR A WALK.
THE EDITOR!
I SAW HIM ABOUT AN HOUR AGO.
yawn
HE JUST GOT TAKEN AWAY BY AN AMBULANCE!
WHAT ?!
GRAB
WHOA!
HE... HE ...
HE WAS SURROUNDED BY THUGS ON THE STREET AND THEY BEAT HIM UP...
...HE'S IN PRETTY BAD CONDITION ...

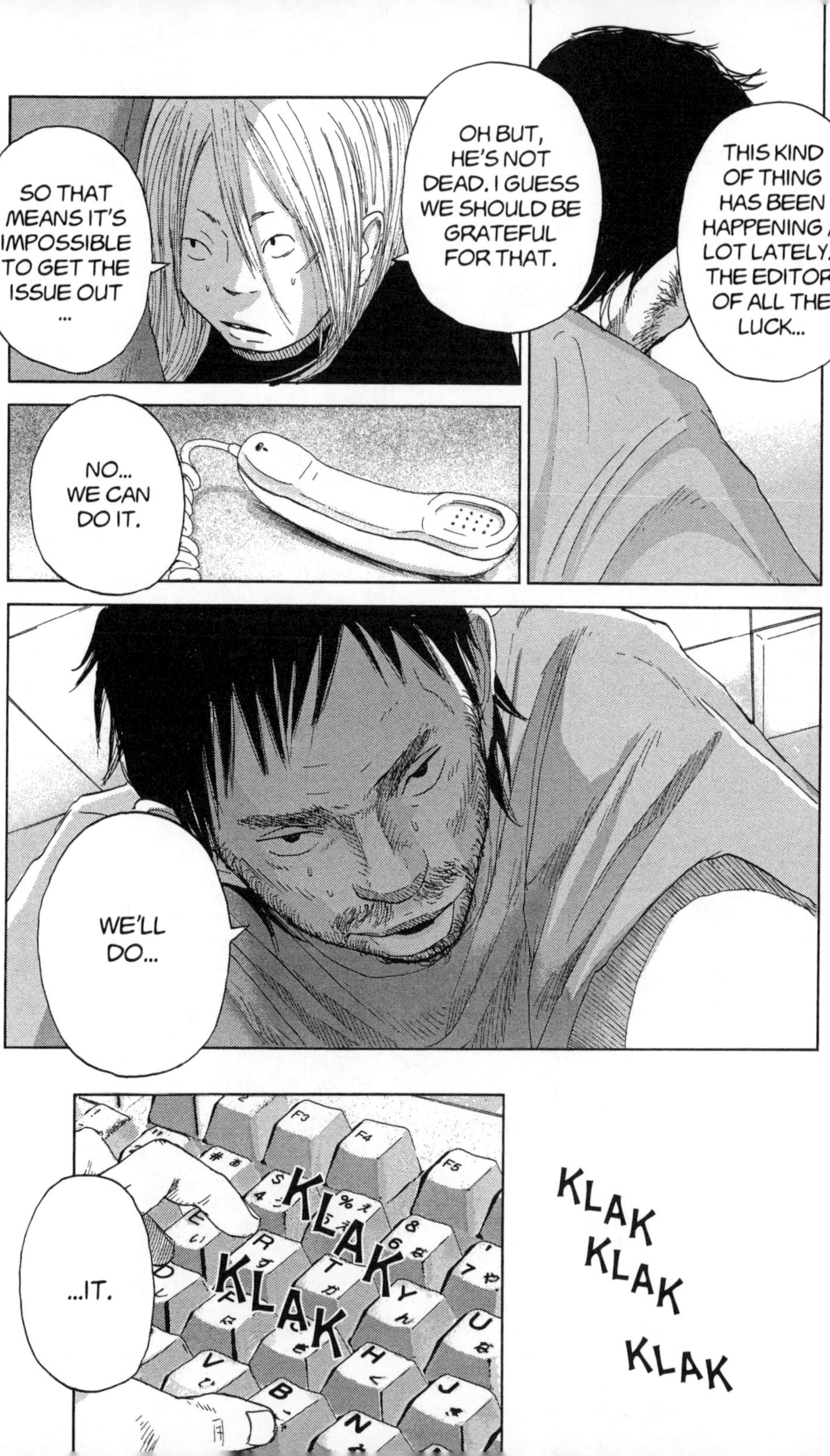
THIS KIND OF THING HAS BEEN HAPPENING A LOT LATELY... THE EDITOR, OF ALL THE LUCK...
OH BUT, HE'S NOT DEAD. I GUESS WE SHOULD BE GRATEFUL FOR THAT.
SO THAT MEANS IT'S IMPOSSIBLE TO GET THE ISSUE OUT ...
NO... WE CAN DO IT.
WE'LL DO...
KLAK KLAK KLAK
KLAK KLAK KLAK
...IT.

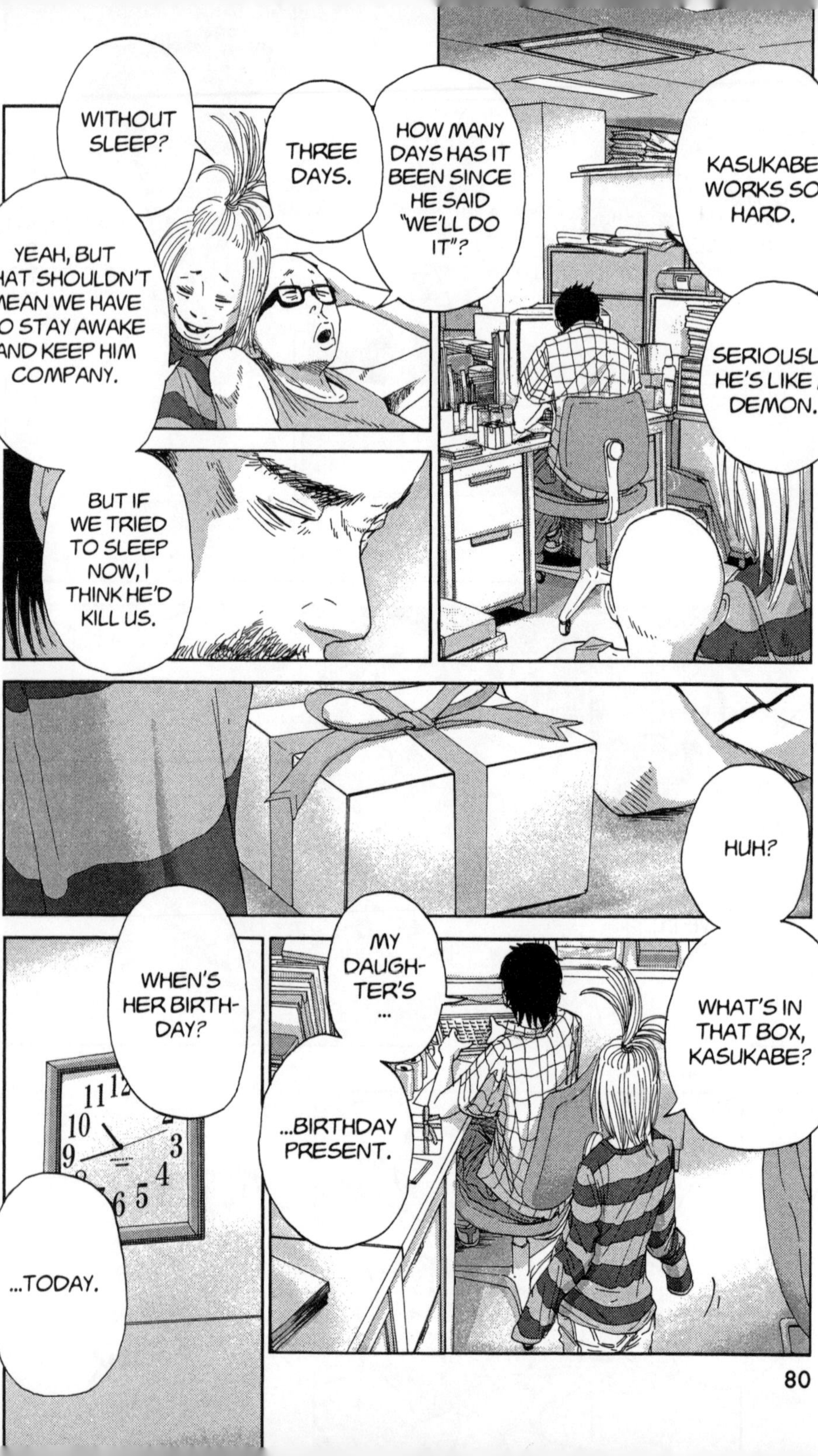
KASUKABE WORKS SO HARD.
SERIOUSLY, HE'S LIKE A DEMON.
HOW MANY DAYS HAS IT BEEN SINCE HE SAID "WE'LL DO IT"?
THREE DAYS.
WITHOUT SLEEP?
YEAH, BUT THAT SHOULDN'T MEAN WE HAVE TO STAY AWAKE AND KEEP HIM COMPANY.
BUT IF WE TRIED TO SLEEP NOW, I THINK HE'D KILL US.
HUH?
WHAT'S IN THAT BOX, KASUKABE?
MY DAUGH-TER'S ...
...BIRTHDAY PRESENT.
WHEN'S HER BIRTH-DAY?
...TODAY.

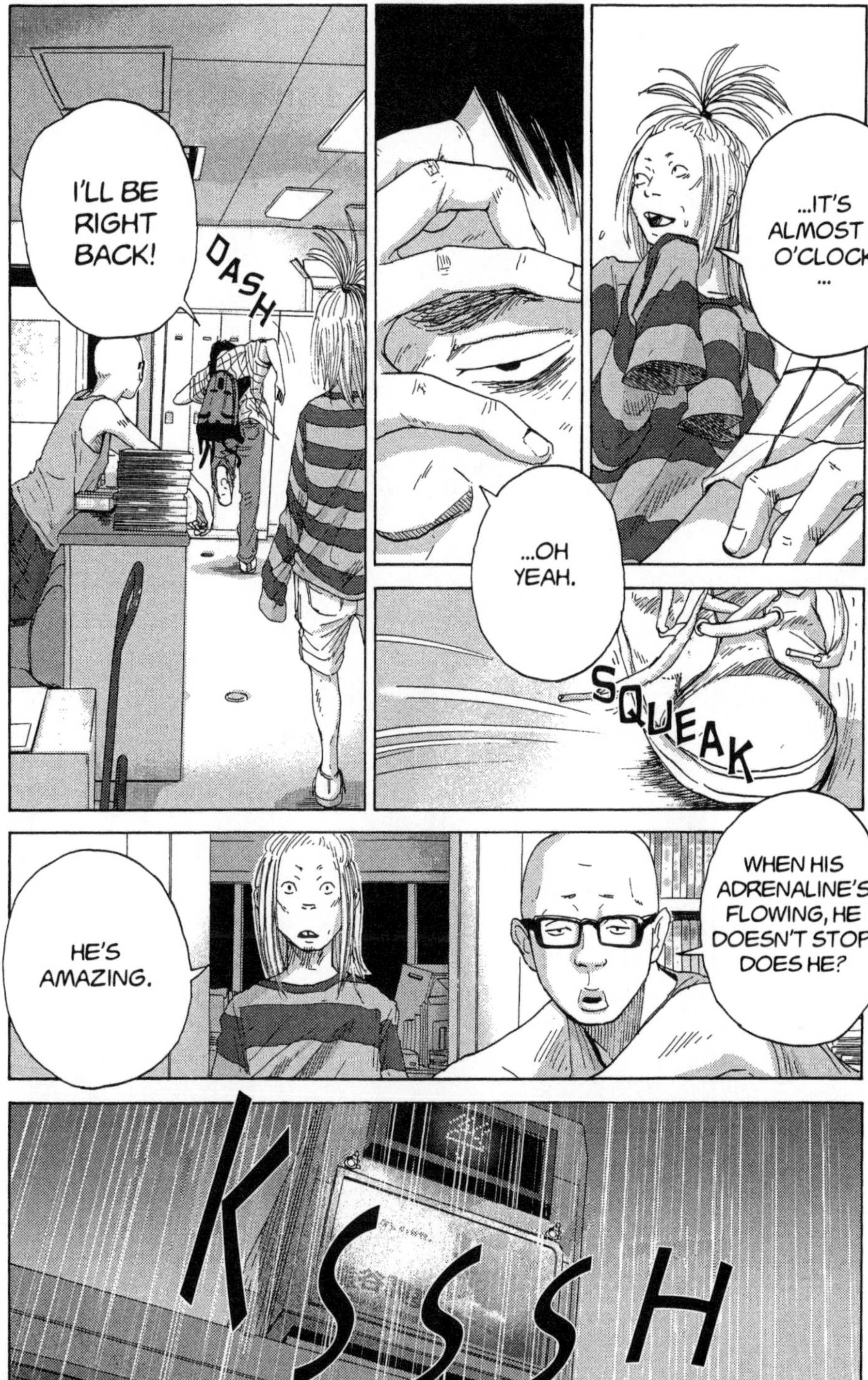
...IT'S ALMOST 11 O'CLOCK ...
...OH YEAH.
SQUEAK
I'LL BE RIGHT BACK!
DASH
WHEN HIS ADRENALINE'S FLOWING, HE DOESN'T STOP, DOES HE?
HE'S AMAZING.
KSSSH

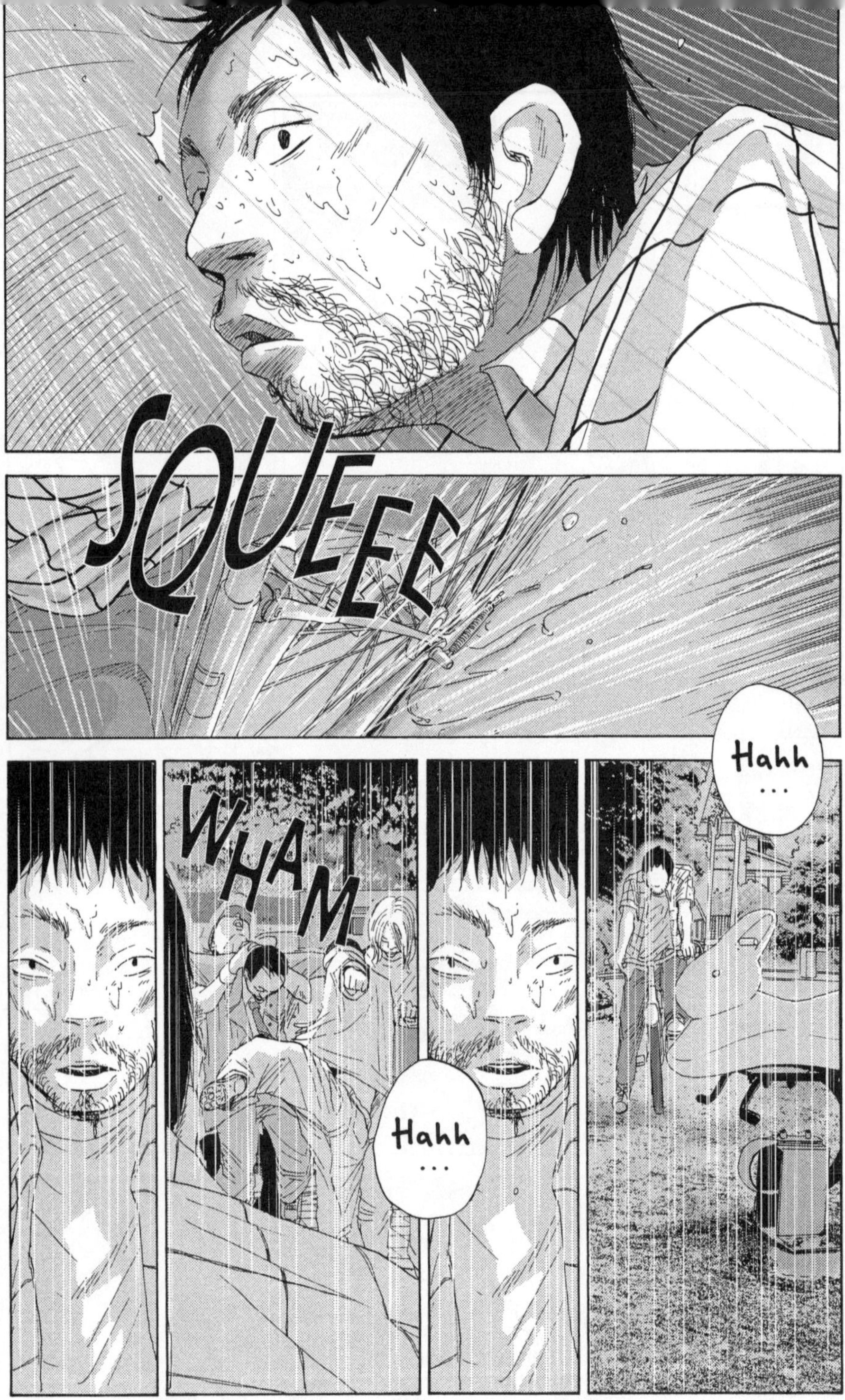
SQUEEE
Hahh ...
Hahh ...
WHAM

WHAT A LAUGH.

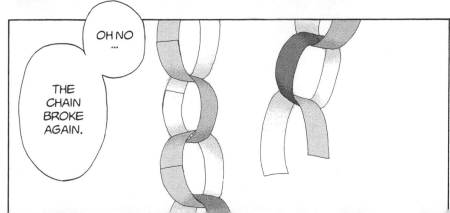

OH NO
...

THE
CHAIN
BROKE
AGAIN.

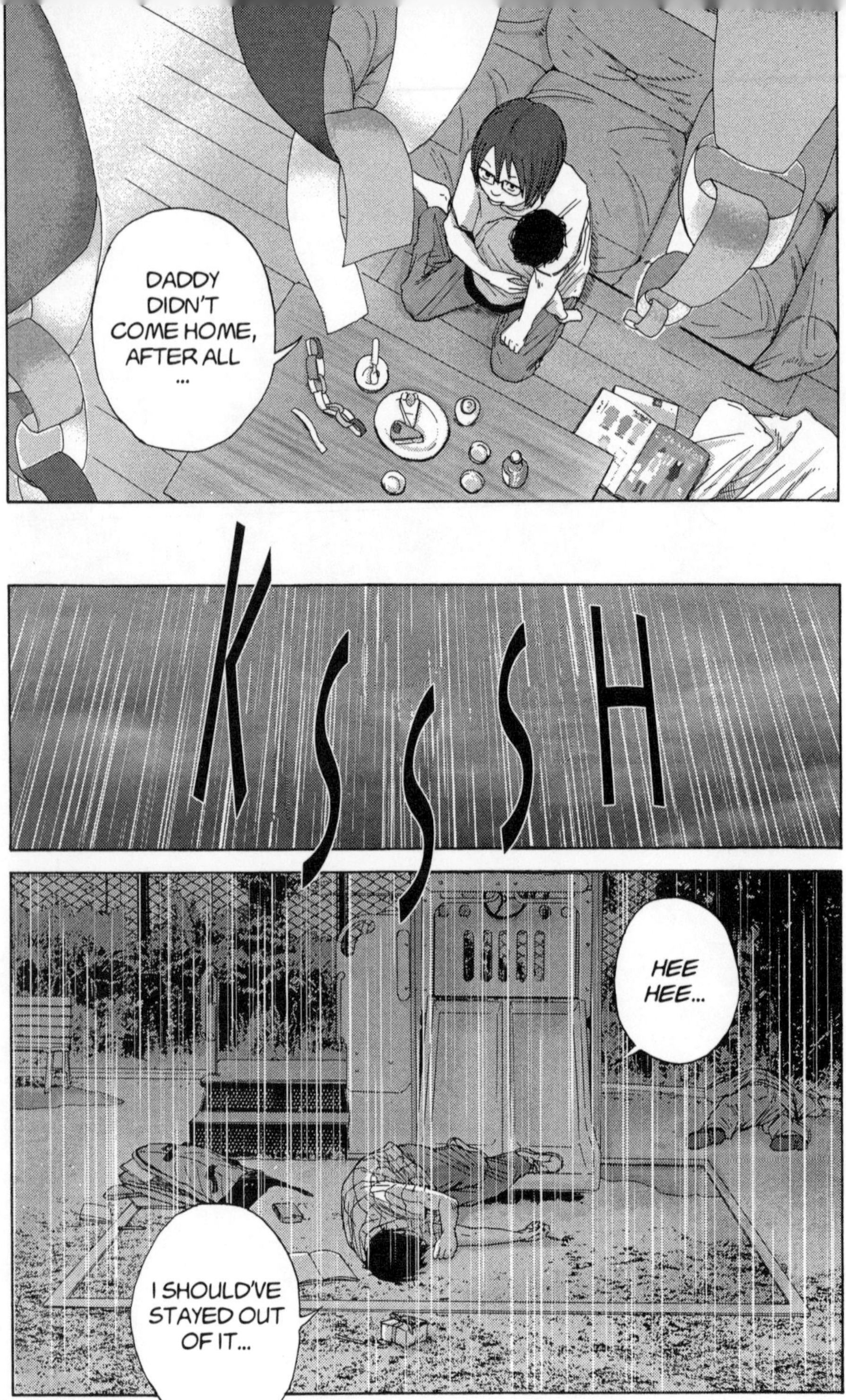
DADDY DIDN'T COME HOME, AFTER ALL ...
KSSSH
HEE HEE...
I SHOULD'VE STAYED OUT OF IT...

AM I LIKE THAT TOO?
AM I...
...GONNA LOSE TOO?
No, right?
It's not about winning or losing...
It's whether I'm satisfied with myself...
THEN ...
OWW...
DAMN, IT HURTS ...
JUST WHAT...
...AM I?
WHAT ARE YOU?

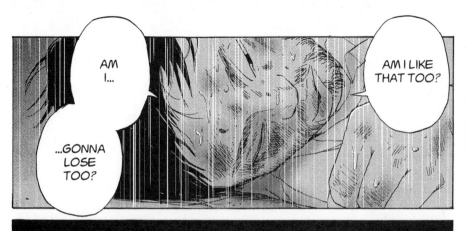

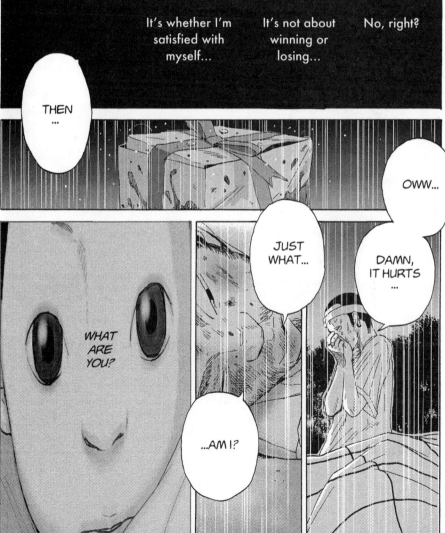

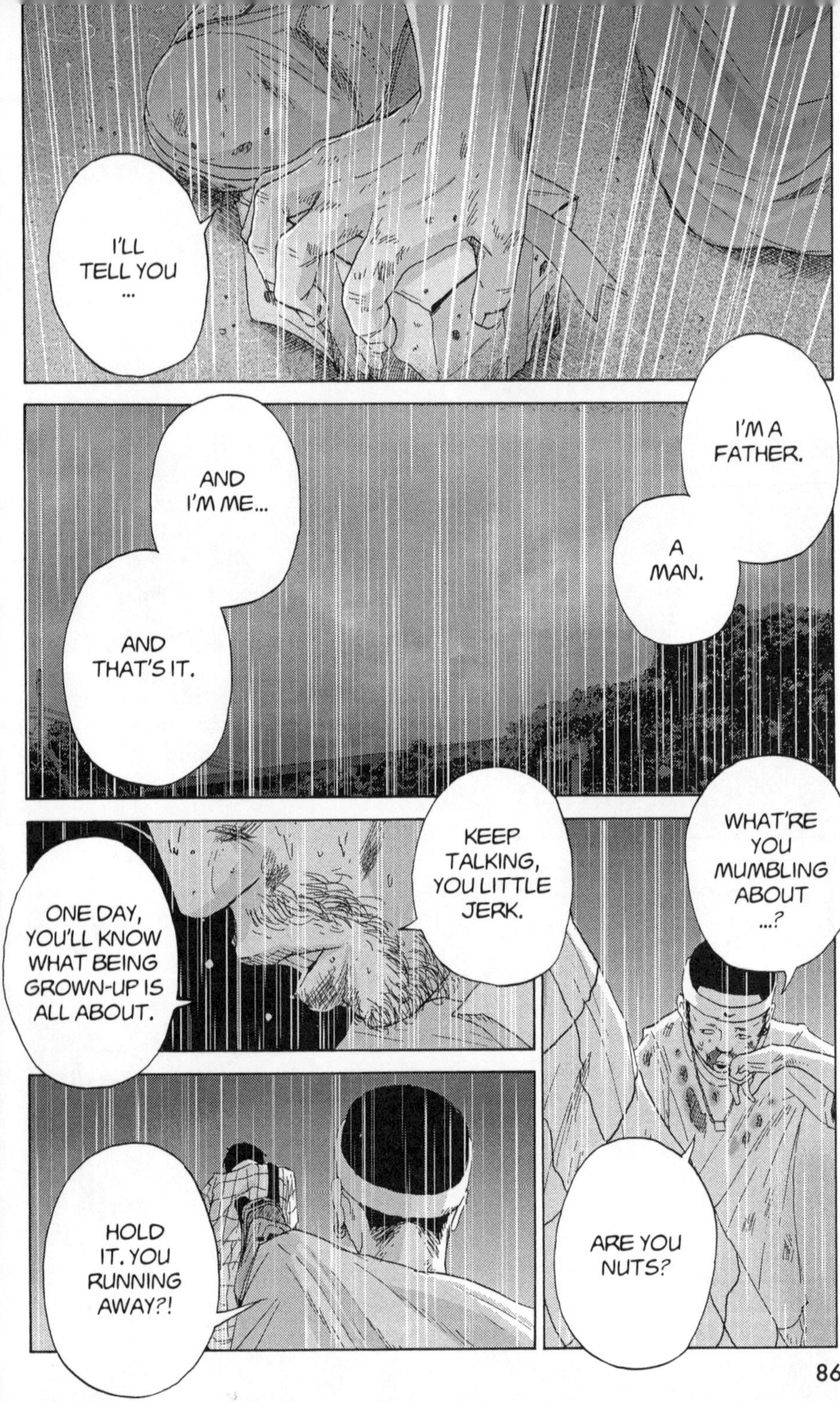
I'LL TELL YOU ...
I'M A FATHER.
A MAN.
AND I'M ME...
AND THAT'S IT.
WHAT'RE YOU MUMBLING ABOUT ...?
ARE YOU NUTS?
KEEP TALKING, YOU LITTLE JERK.
ONE DAY, YOU'LL KNOW WHAT BEING GROWN-UP IS ALL ABOUT.
HOLD IT. YOU RUNNING AWAY?!

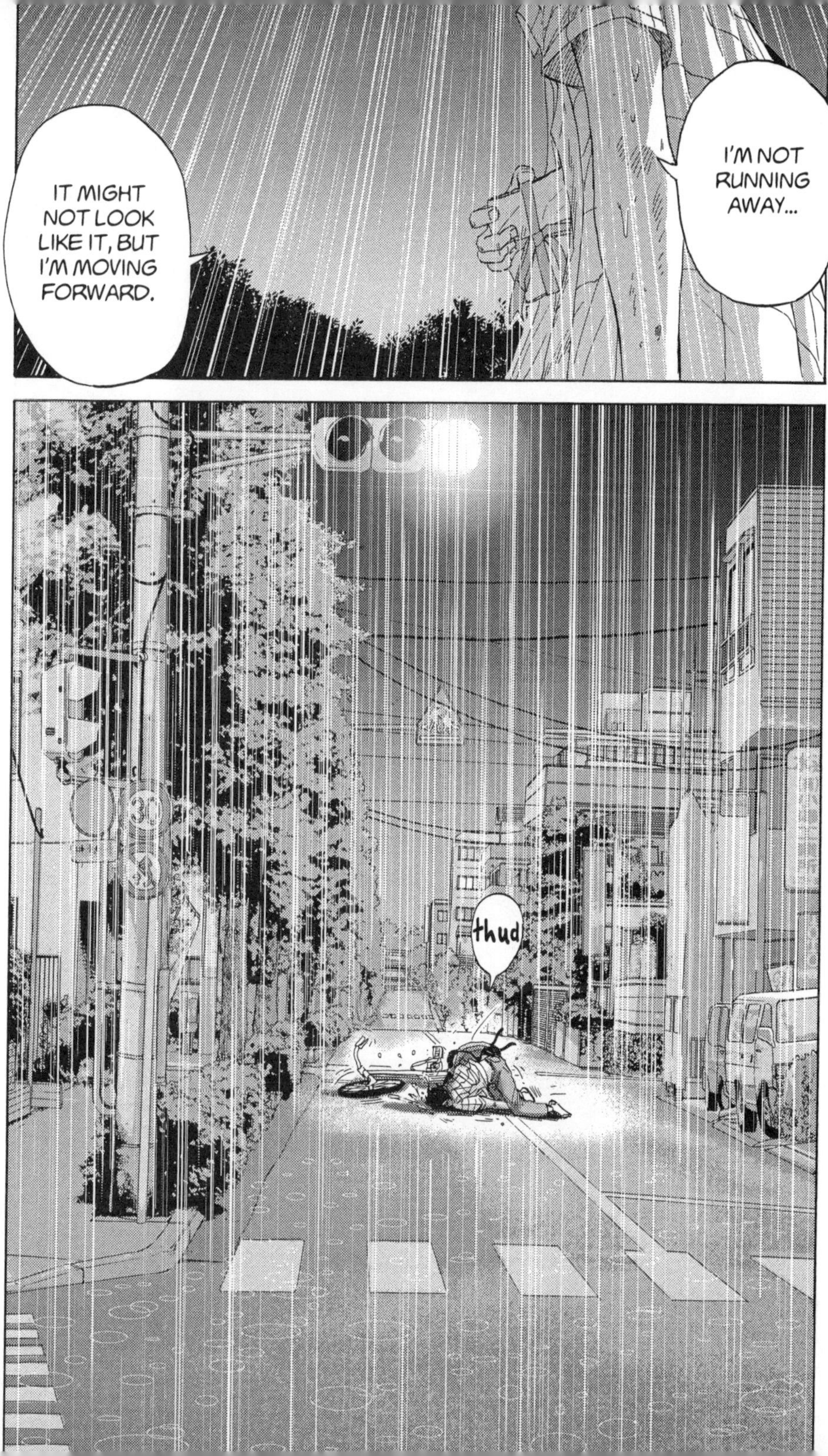
I'M NOT RUNNING AWAY...
IT MIGHT NOT LOOK LIKE IT, BUT I'M MOVING FORWARD.
thud

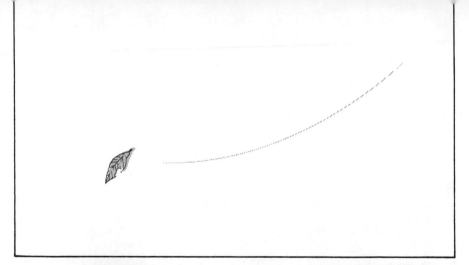

YOU
FINALLY
WOKE UP
...

YOU
HAD US
WORRIED.

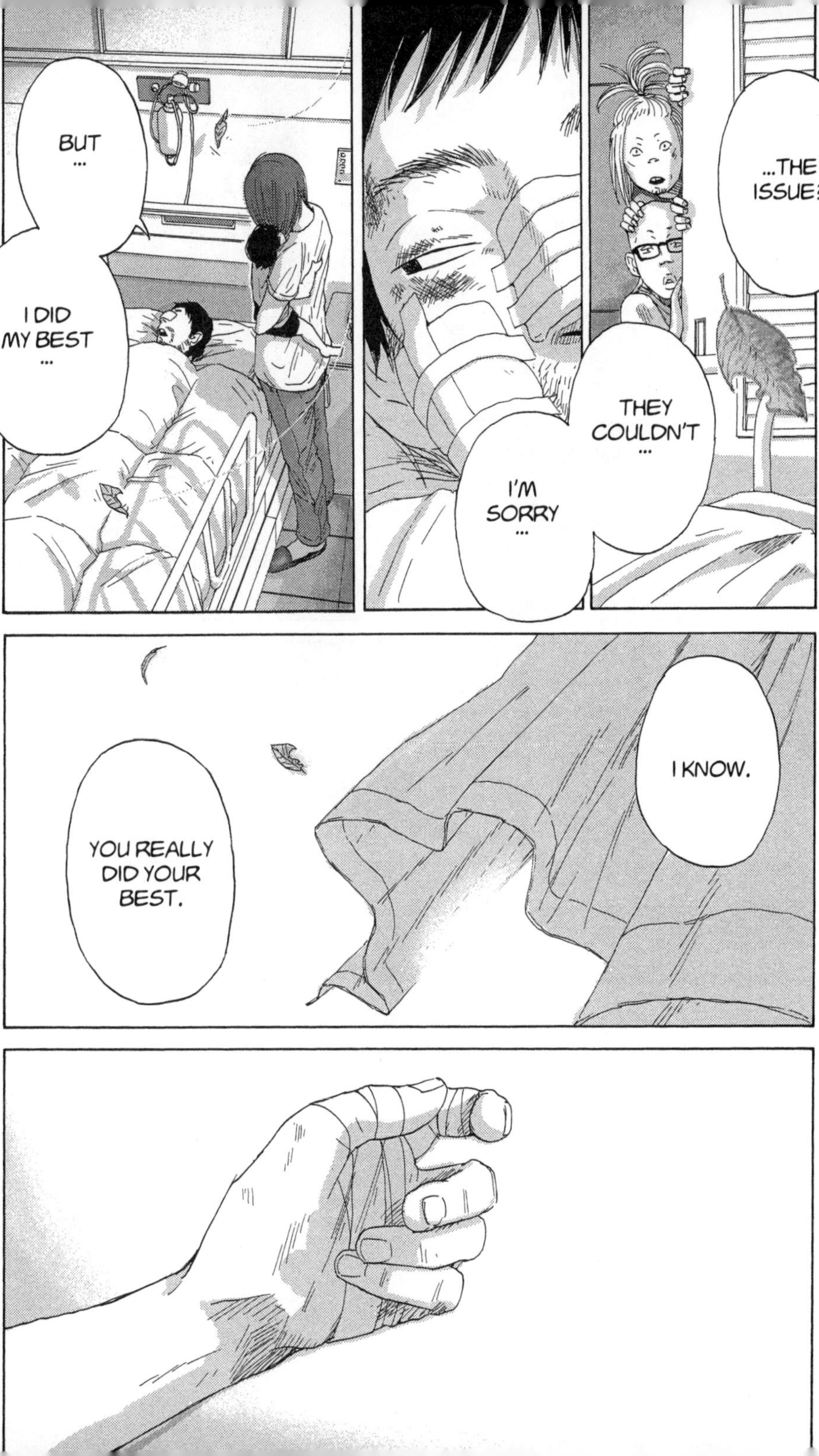
...THE ISSUE?
THEY COULDN'T ...
I'M SORRY ...
BUT ...
I DID MY BEST ...
I KNOW.
YOU REALLY DID YOUR BEST.

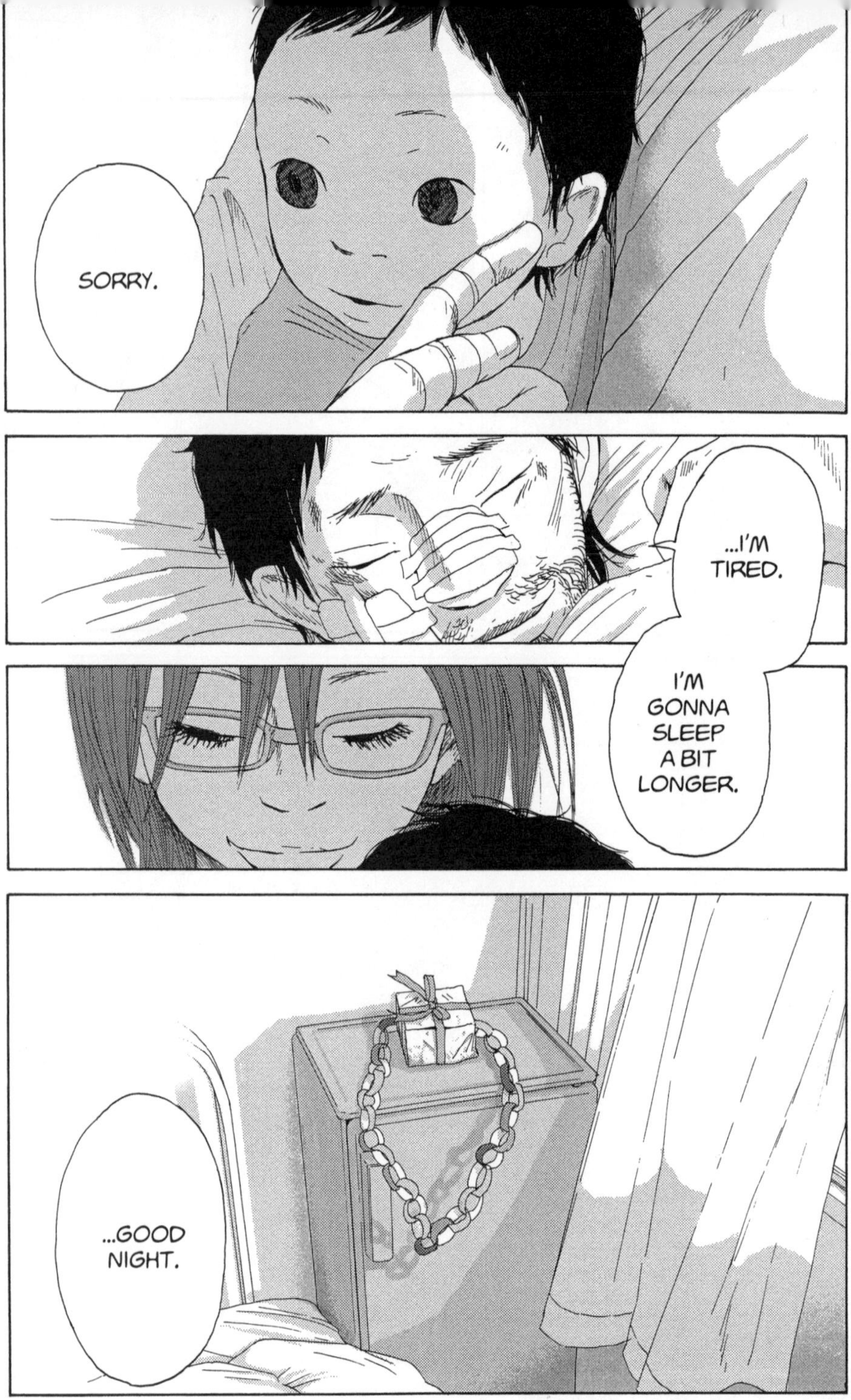
SORRY.
...I'M TIRED.
I'M GONNA SLEEP A BIT LONGER.
...GOOD NIGHT.

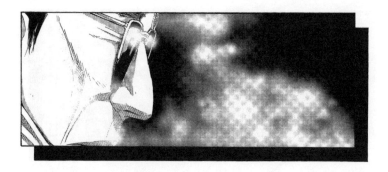

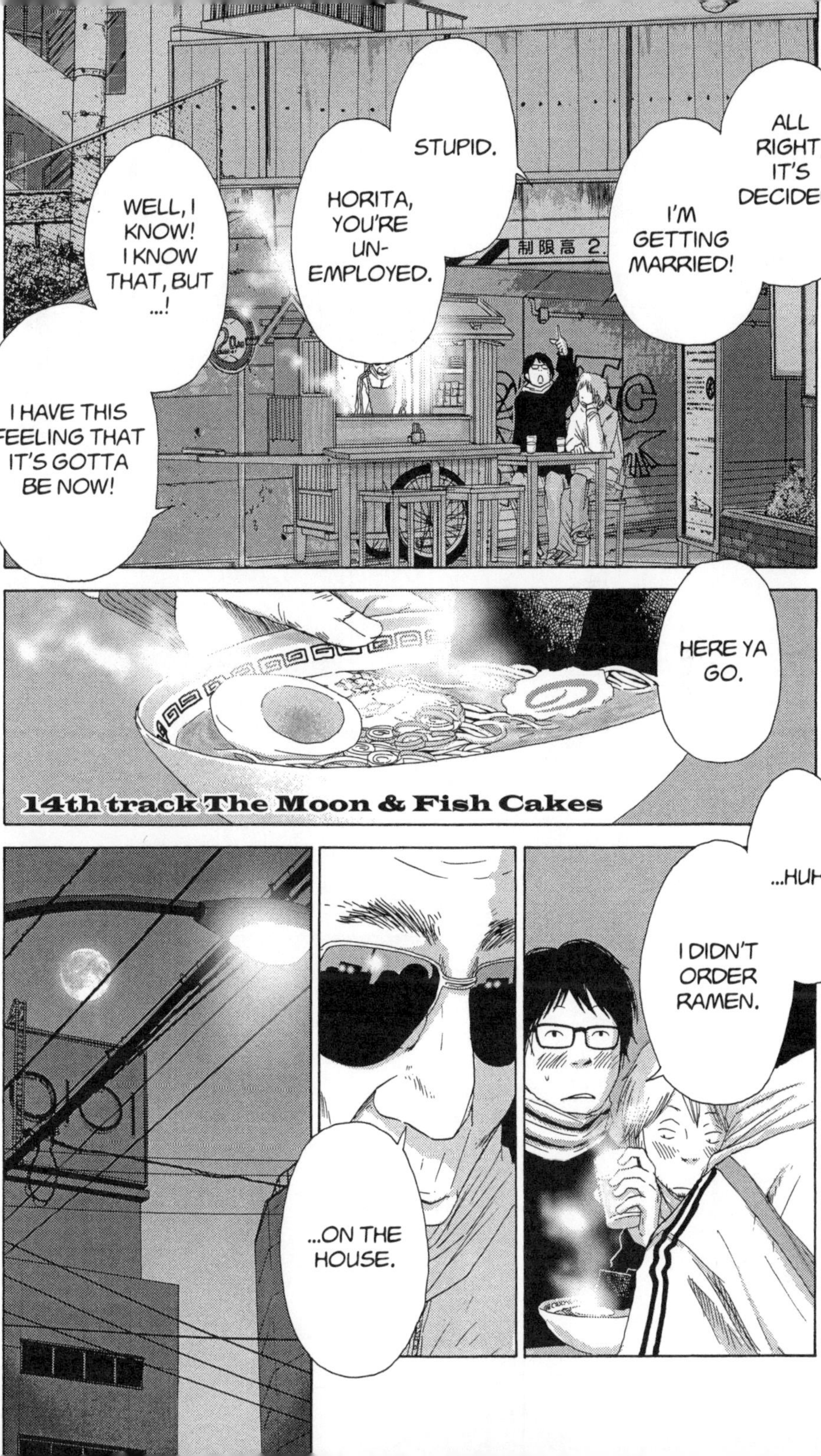
ALL RIGHT, IT'S DECIDED!
I'M GETTING MARRIED!
STUPID.
HORITA, YOU'RE UN-EMPLOYED.
WELL, I KNOW! I KNOW THAT, BUT ...!
I HAVE THIS FEELING THAT IT'S GOTTA BE NOW!
制限高 2.
HERE YA GO.
14th track The Moon & Fish Cakes
...HUH?
I DIDN'T ORDER RAMEN.
...ON THE HOUSE.

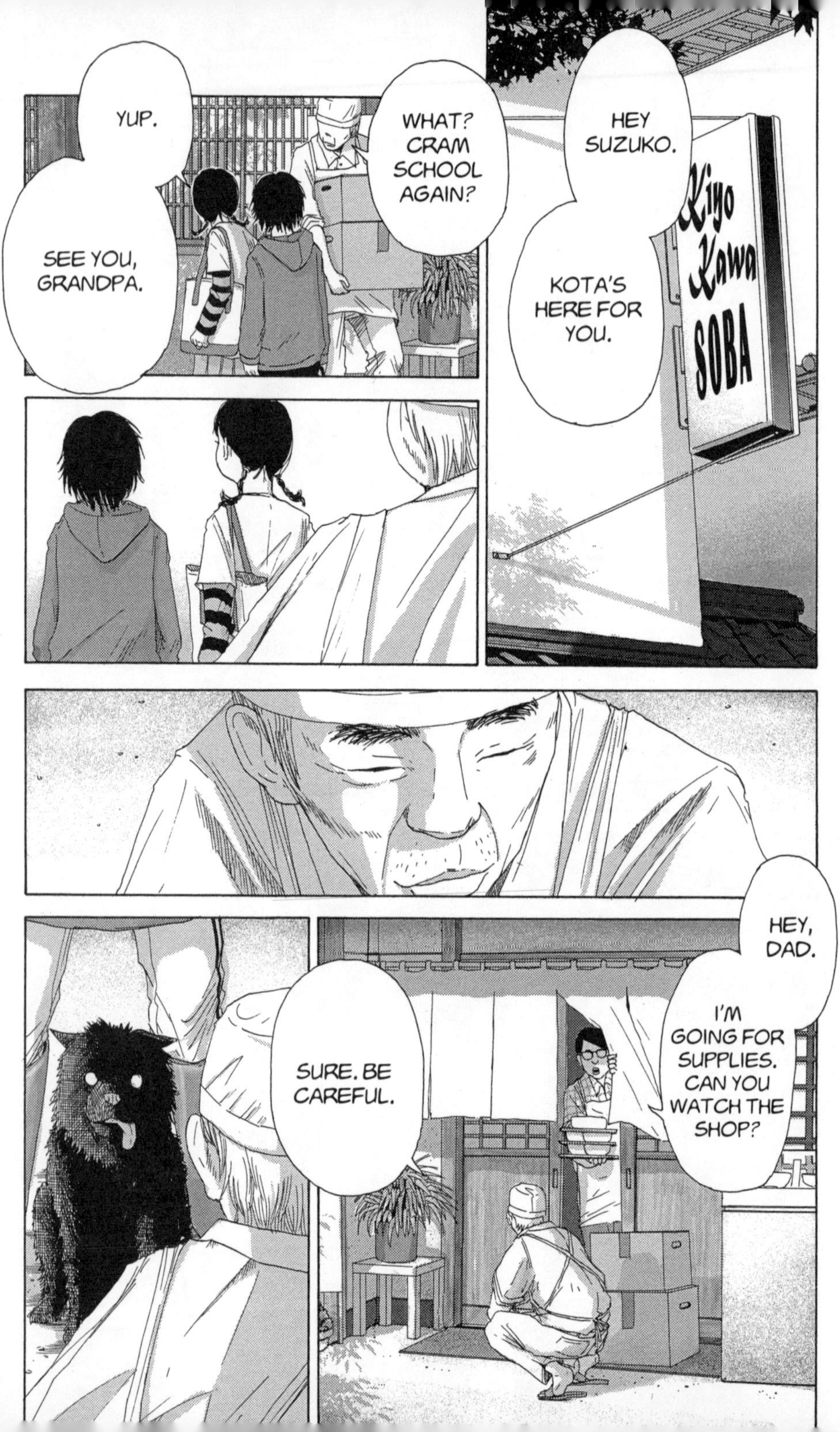
HEY SUZUKO.
KOTA'S HERE FOR YOU.
Kiyo Kawa SOBA
WHAT? CRAM SCHOOL AGAIN?
YUP.
SEE YOU, GRANDPA.
HEY, DAD.
I'M GOING FOR SUPPLIES. CAN YOU WATCH THE SHOP?
SURE. BE CAREFUL.

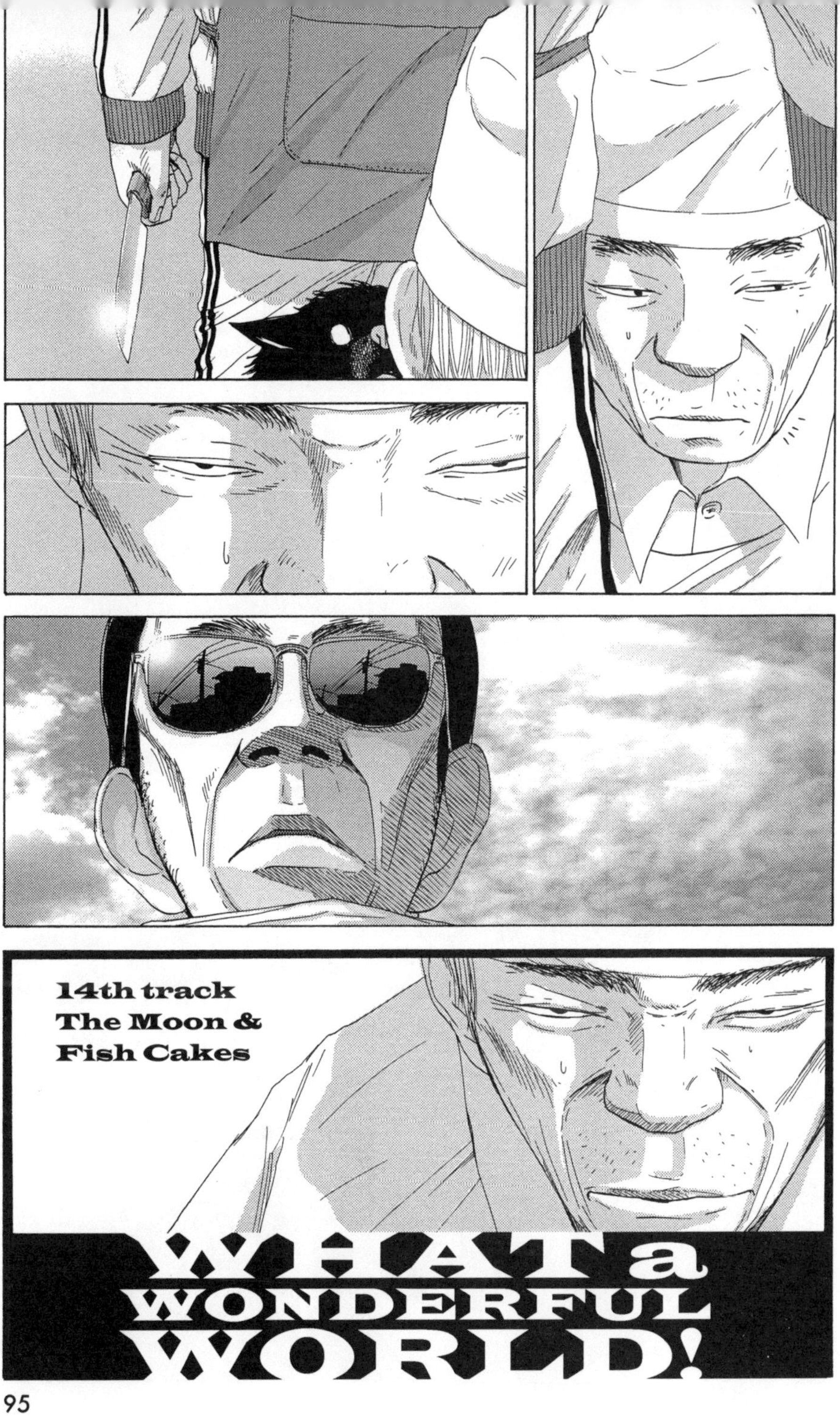
14th track
The Moon &
Fish Cakes
WHAT a
WONDERFUL
WORLD!

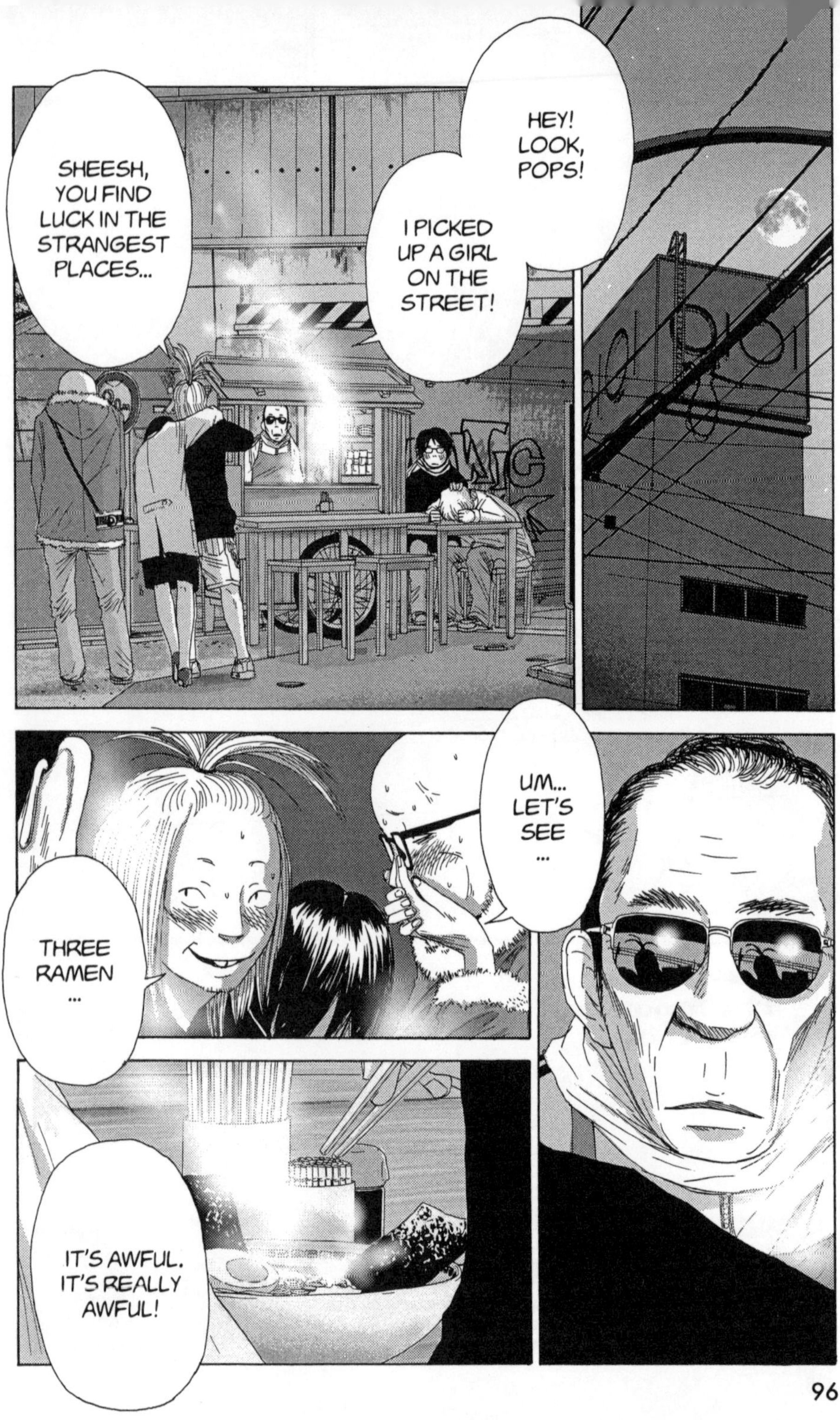
HEY! LOOK, POPS!
I PICKED UP A GIRL ON THE STREET!
SHEESH, YOU FIND LUCK IN THE STRANGEST PLACES...
UM... LET'S SEE ...
THREE RAMEN ...
IT'S AWFUL. IT'S REALLY AWFUL!

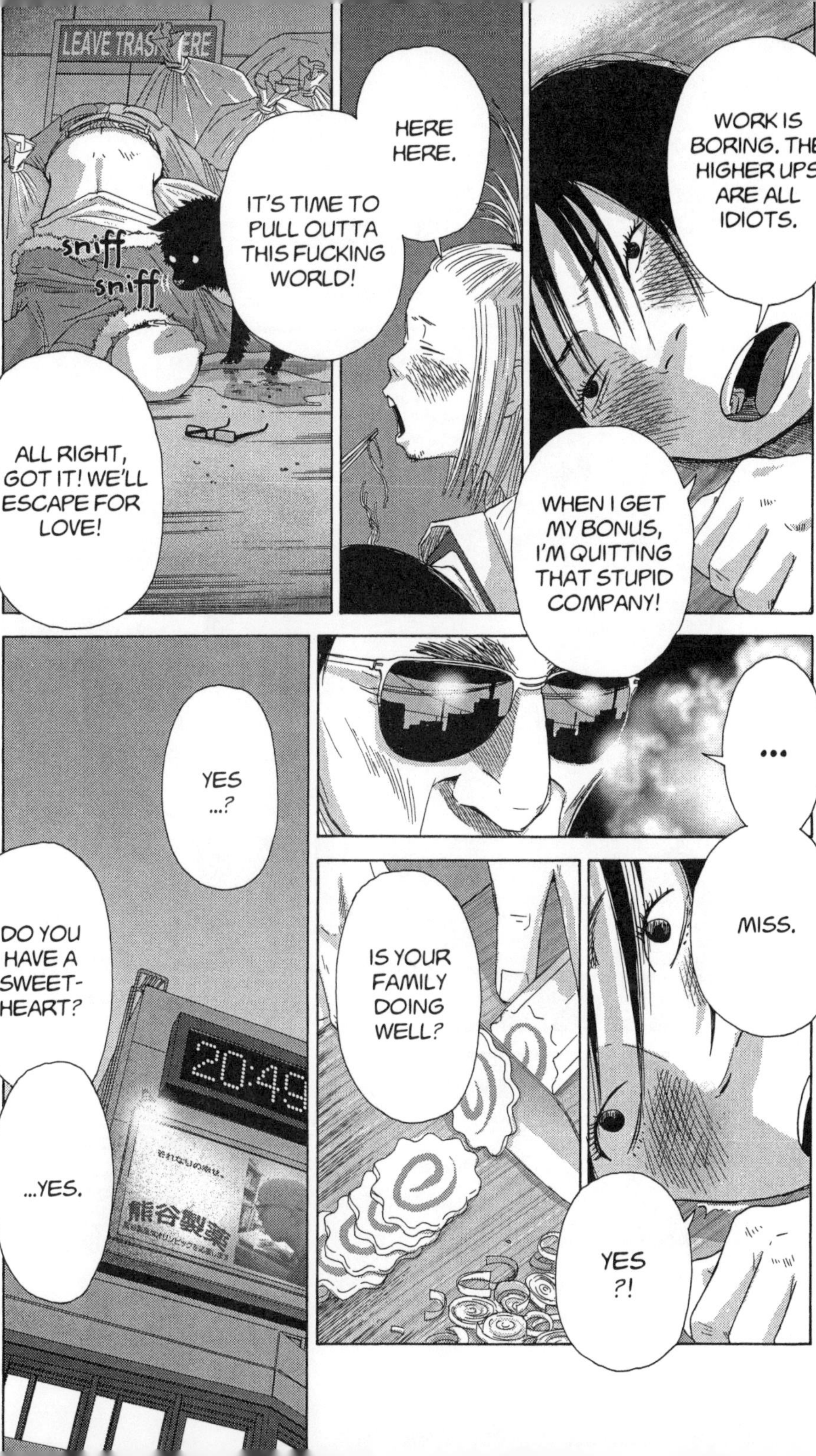
WORK IS BORING. THE HIGHER UPS ARE ALL IDIOTS.
WHEN I GET MY BONUS, I'M QUITTING THAT STUPID COMPANY!
HERE HERE.
IT'S TIME TO PULL OUTTA THIS FUCKING WORLD!
sniff
sniff
ALL RIGHT, I GOT IT! WE'LL ESCAPE FOR LOVE!
...
MISS.
YES ?!
IS YOUR FAMILY DOING WELL?
YES ...?
DO YOU HAVE A SWEET-HEART?
20:49
熊谷製薬
...YES.

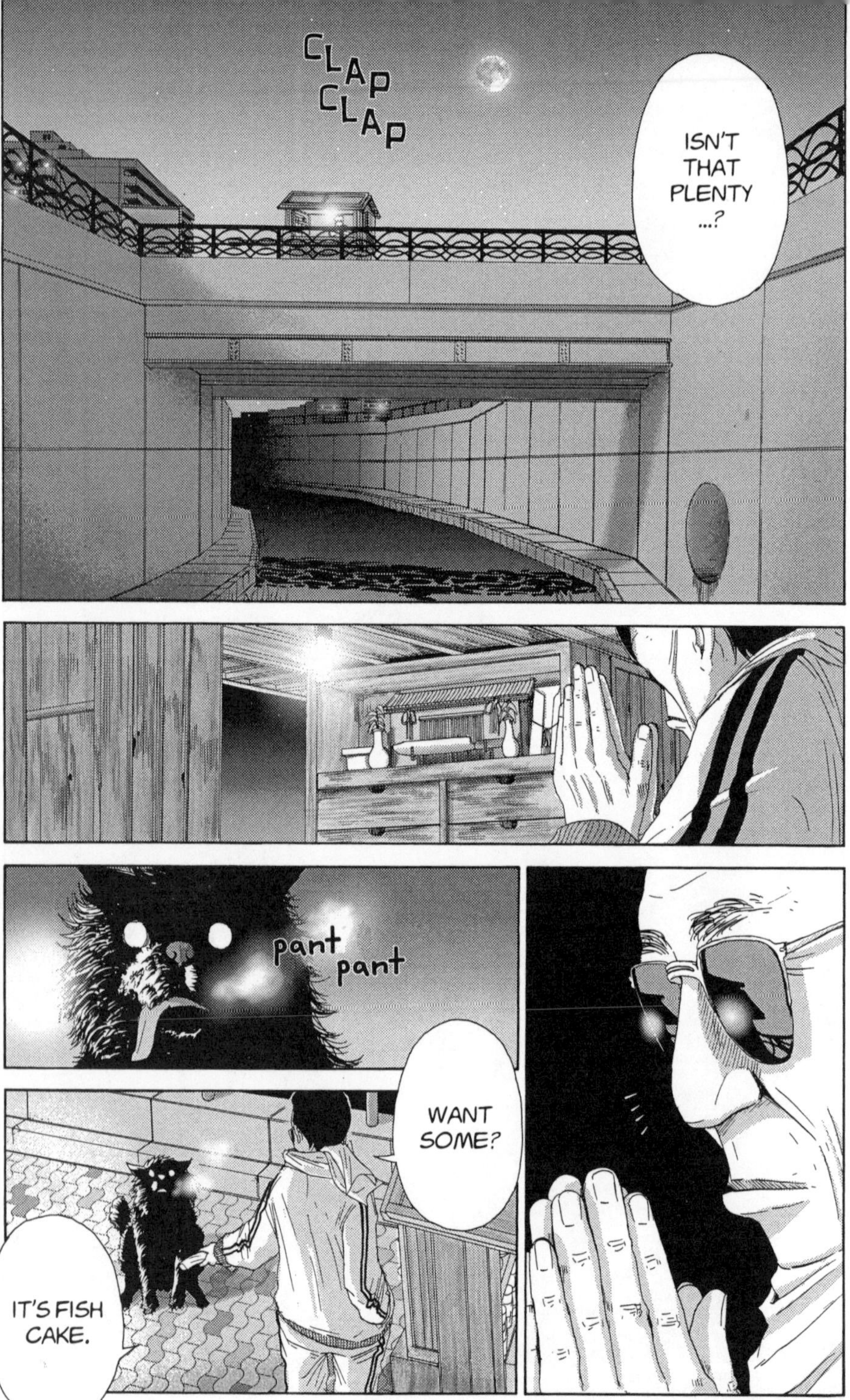
ISN'T THAT PLENTY ...?
CLAP CLAP
WANT SOME?
pant pant
IT'S FISH CAKE.

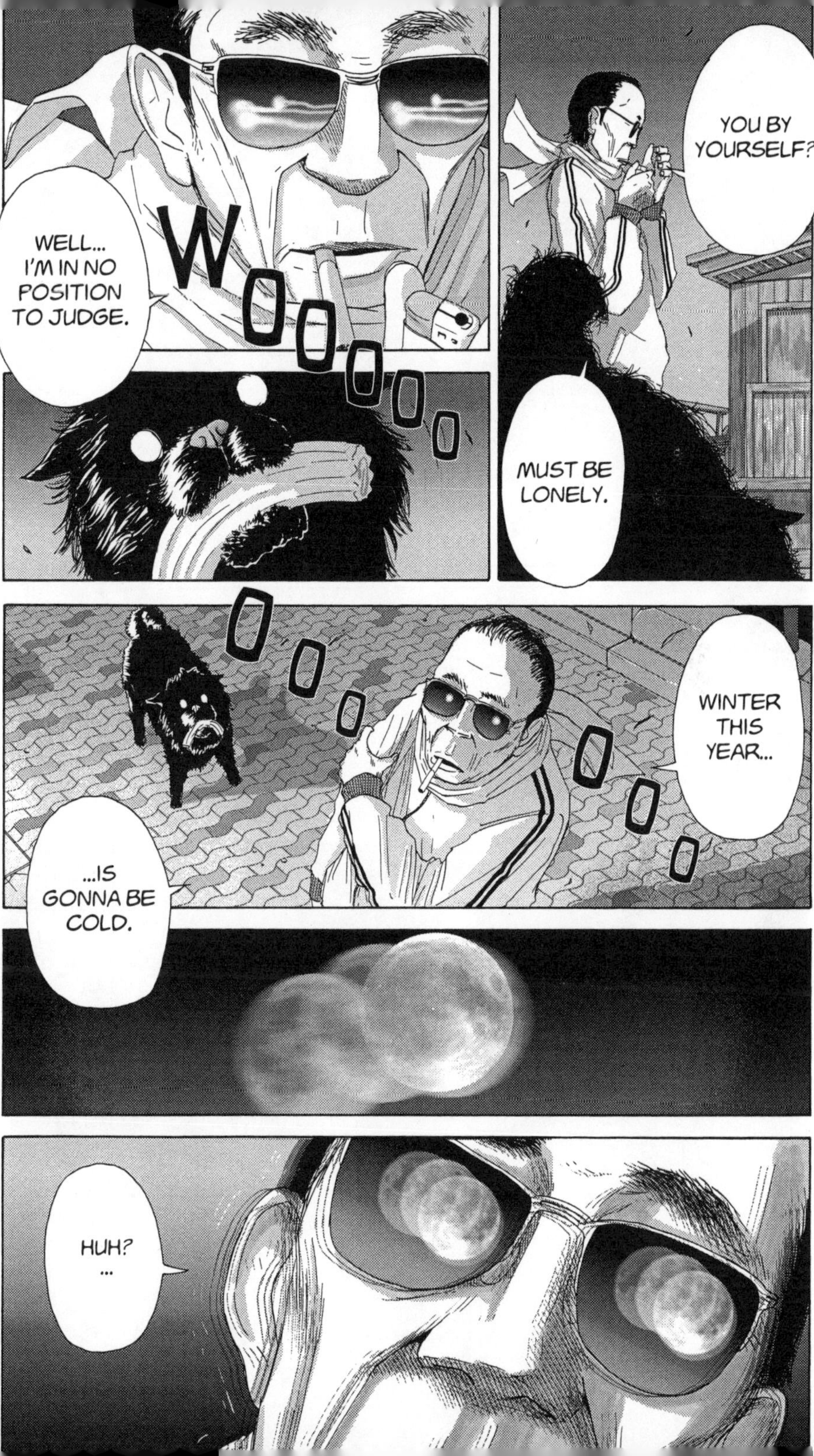
YOU BY YOURSELF?
MUST BE LONELY.
WELL... I'M IN NO POSITION TO JUDGE.
WOOOOOO
OOOOOOO
WINTER THIS YEAR...
...IS GONNA BE COLD.
HUH? ...

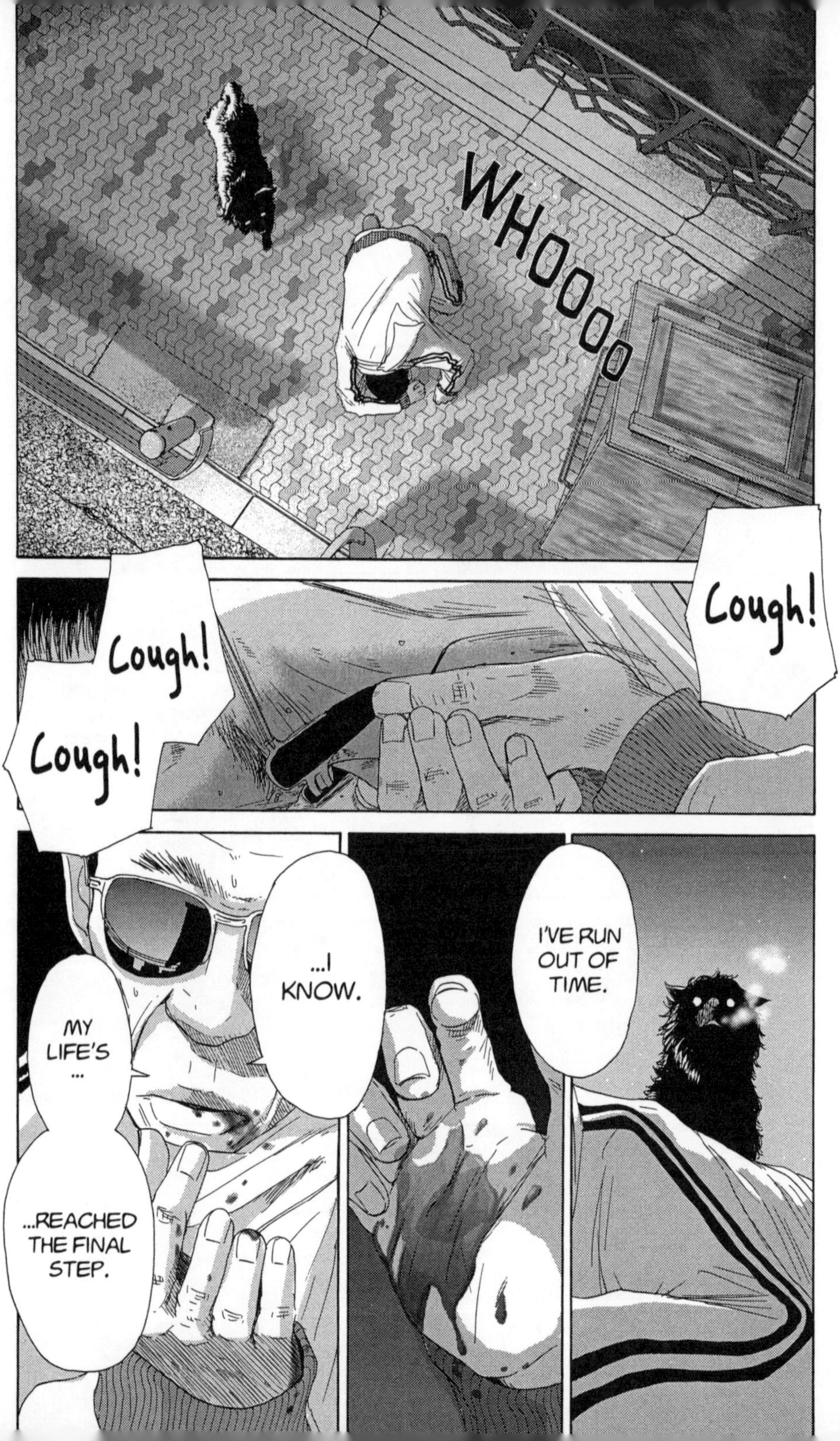
WHOOOOO
Cough!
Cough!
Cough!
I'VE RUN OUT OF TIME.
...I KNOW.
MY LIFE'S ...
...REACHED THE FINAL STEP.

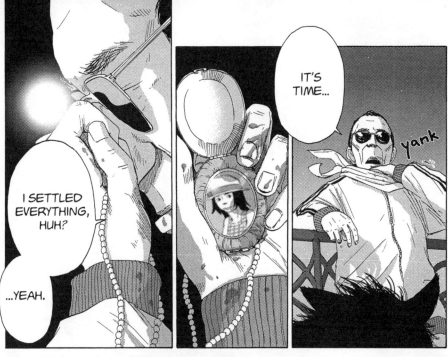

IT'S TIME...

I SETTLED EVERYTHING, HUH?

...YEAH.

*yank*

IT'S BEEN...

...THIRTY YEARS...

THAT KNIFE BELONGED TO OUR GRAND-FATHER!

WHAT'RE YOU DOING WITH IT?

KSSSH

HEY.

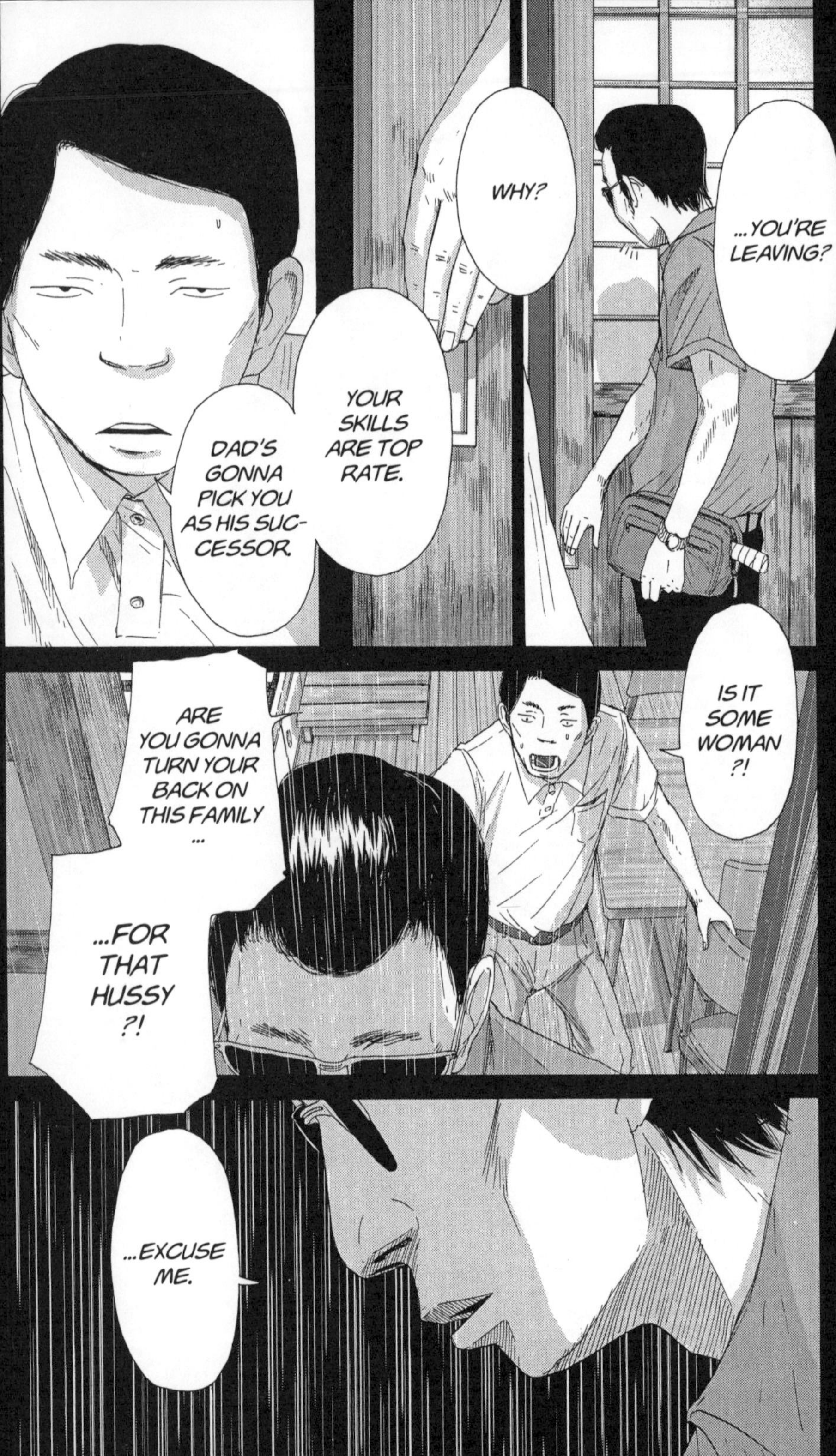
...YOU'RE LEAVING?
WHY?
YOUR SKILLS ARE TOP RATE.
DAD'S GONNA PICK YOU AS HIS SUC-CESSOR.
IS IT SOME WOMAN ?!
ARE YOU GONNA TURN YOUR BACK ON THIS FAMILY ...
...FOR THAT HUSSY ?!
...EXCUSE ME.

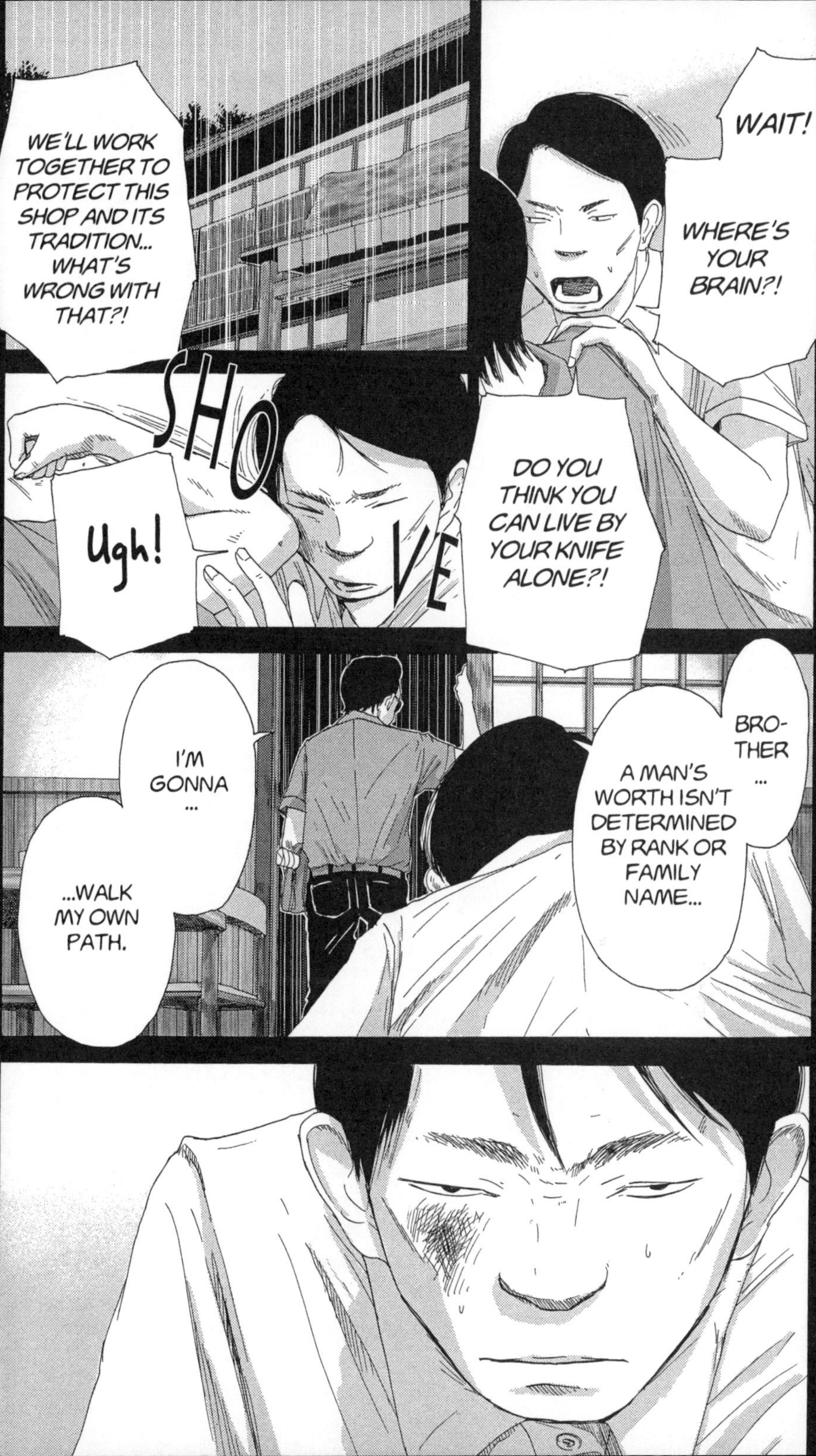
WAIT!
WHERE'S YOUR BRAIN?!
DO YOU THINK YOU CAN LIVE BY YOUR KNIFE ALONE?!
WE'LL WORK TOGETHER TO PROTECT THIS SHOP AND ITS TRADITION... WHAT'S WRONG WITH THAT?!
SHOVE
Ugh!
BROTHER...
A MAN'S WORTH ISN'T DETERMINED BY RANK OR FAMILY NAME...
I'M GONNA...
...WALK MY OWN PATH.

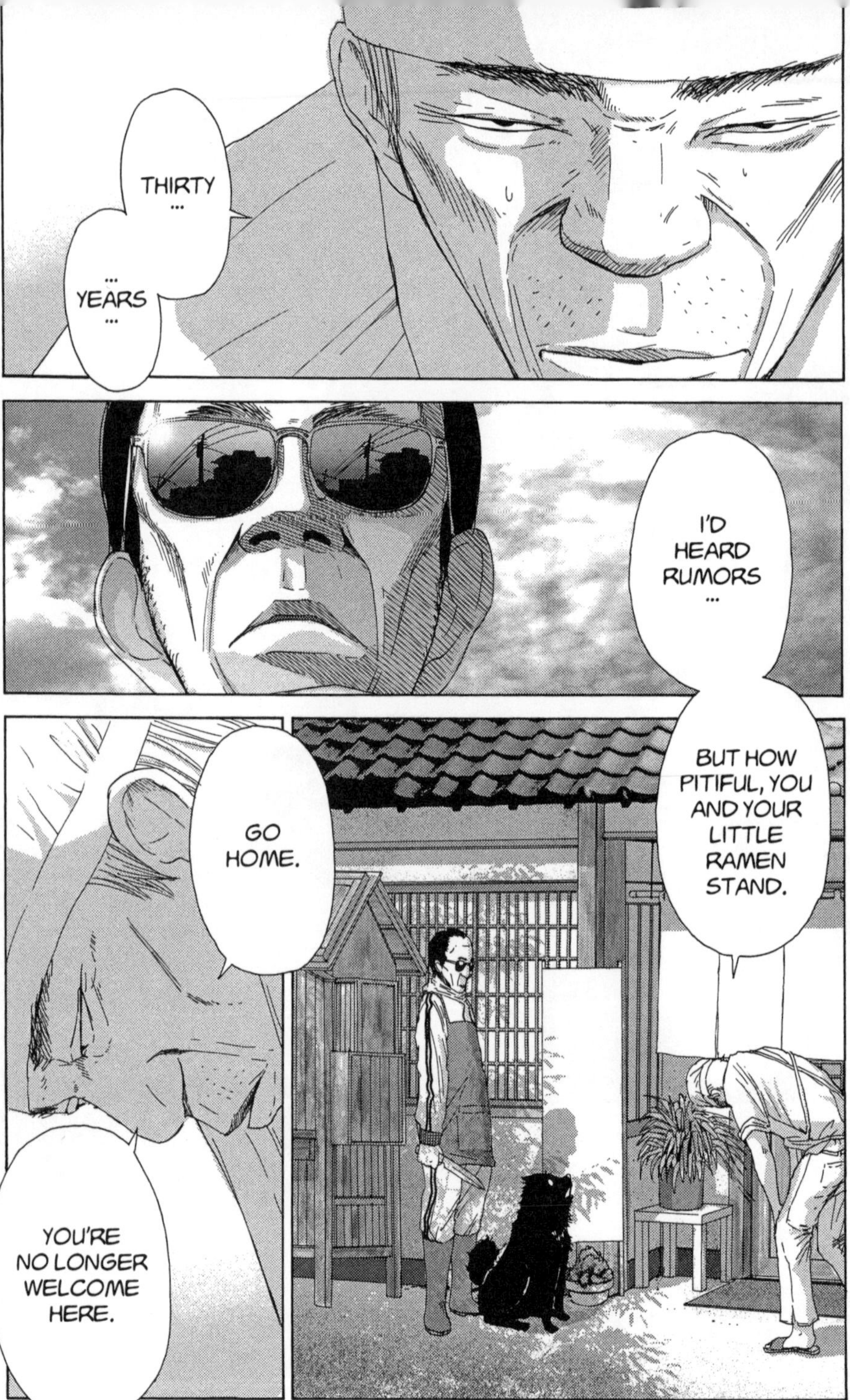
THIRTY ...
... YEARS ...
I'D HEARD RUMORS ...
BUT HOW PITIFUL, YOU AND YOUR LITTLE RAMEN STAND.
GO HOME.
YOU'RE NO LONGER WELCOME HERE.

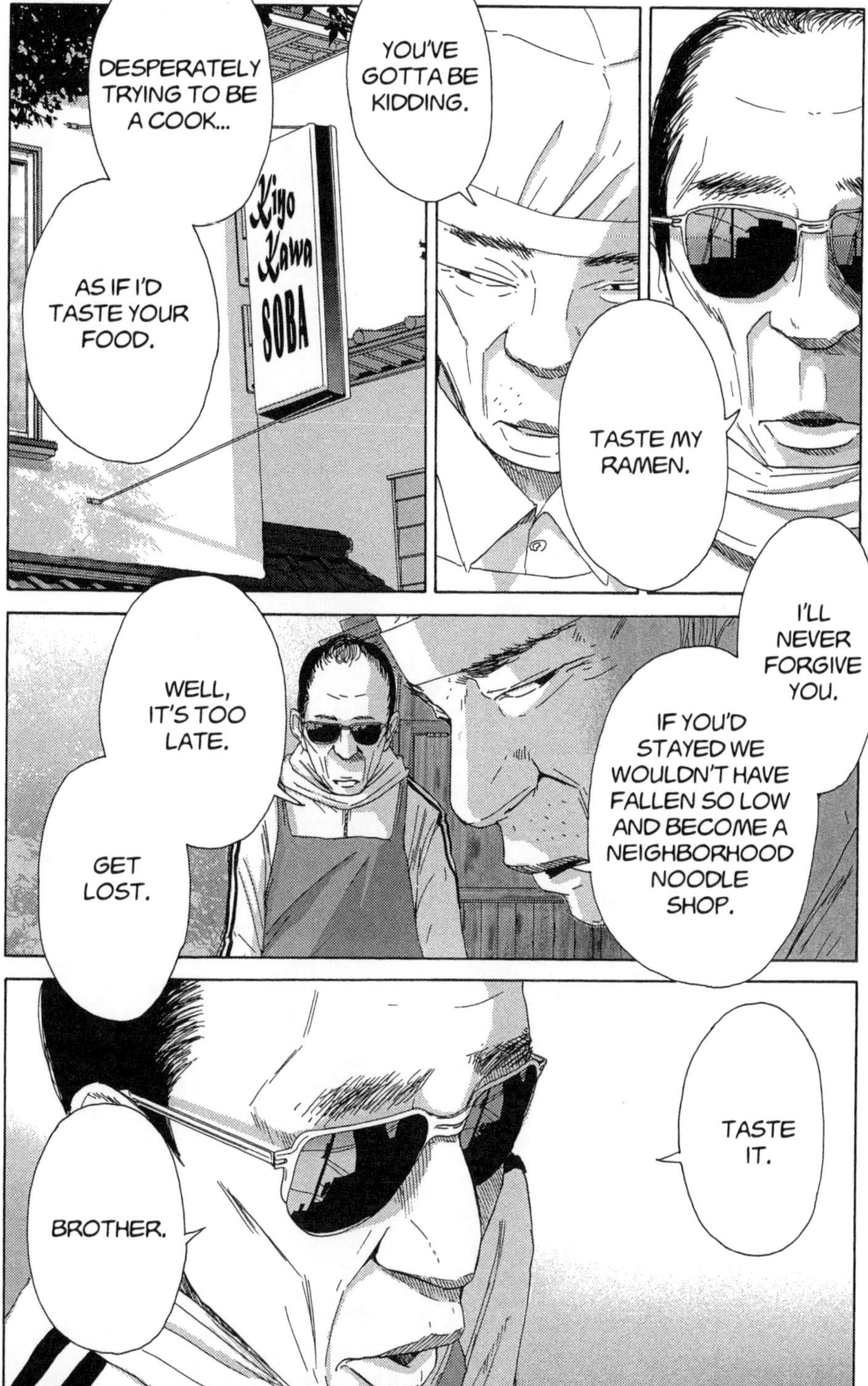
TASTE MY RAMEN.
YOU'VE GOTTA BE KIDDING.
DESPERATELY TRYING TO BE A COOK...
AS IF I'D TASTE YOUR FOOD.
Kiyo Kawa SOBA
I'LL NEVER FORGIVE YOU.
IF YOU'D STAYED WE WOULDN'T HAVE FALLEN SO LOW AND BECOME A NEIGHBORHOOD NOODLE SHOP.
WELL, IT'S TOO LATE.
GET LOST.
TASTE IT.
BROTHER.

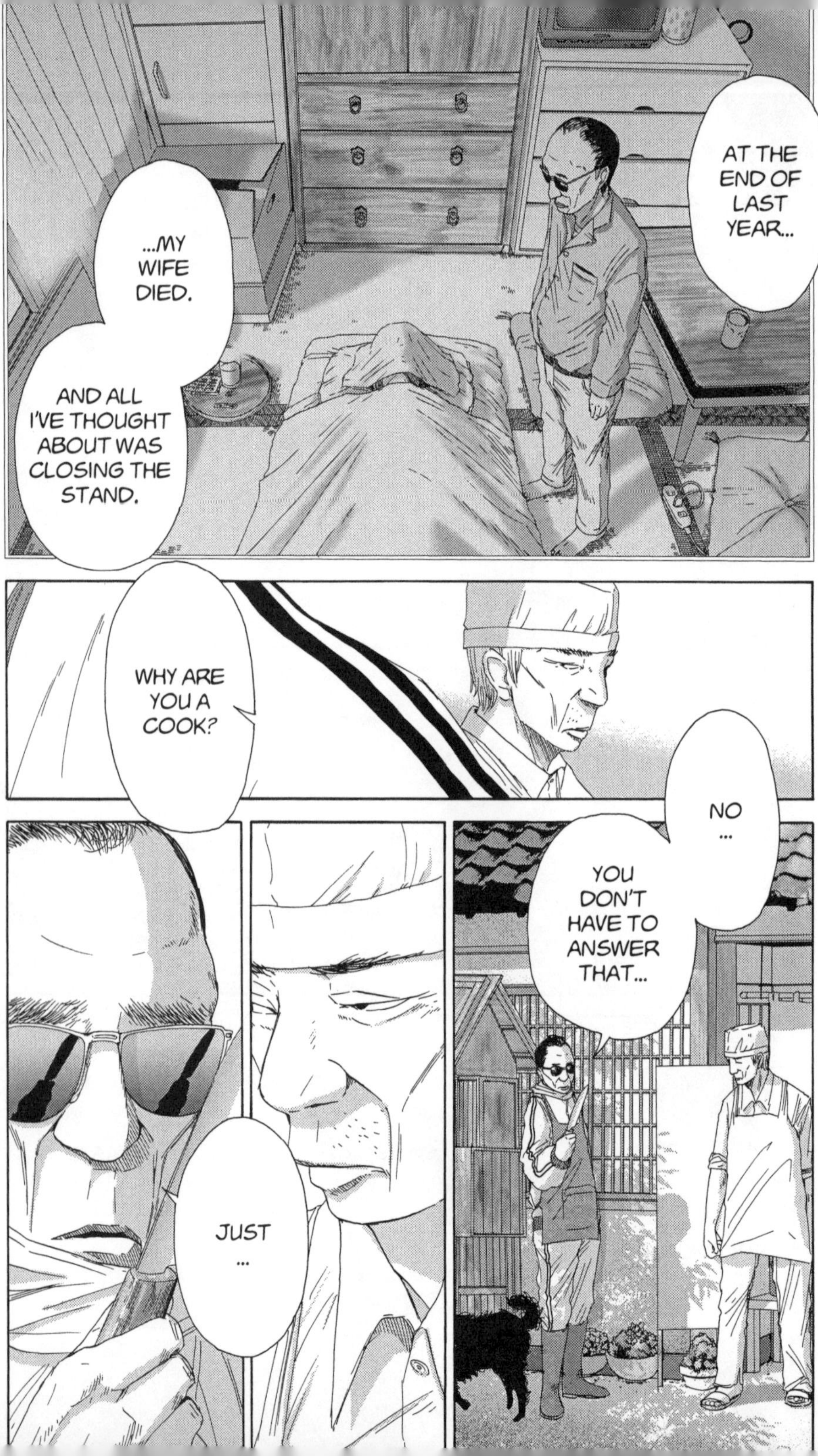
AT THE END OF LAST YEAR...
...MY WIFE DIED.
AND ALL I'VE THOUGHT ABOUT WAS CLOSING THE STAND.
WHY ARE YOU A COOK?
NO ...
YOU DON'T HAVE TO ANSWER THAT...
JUST ...

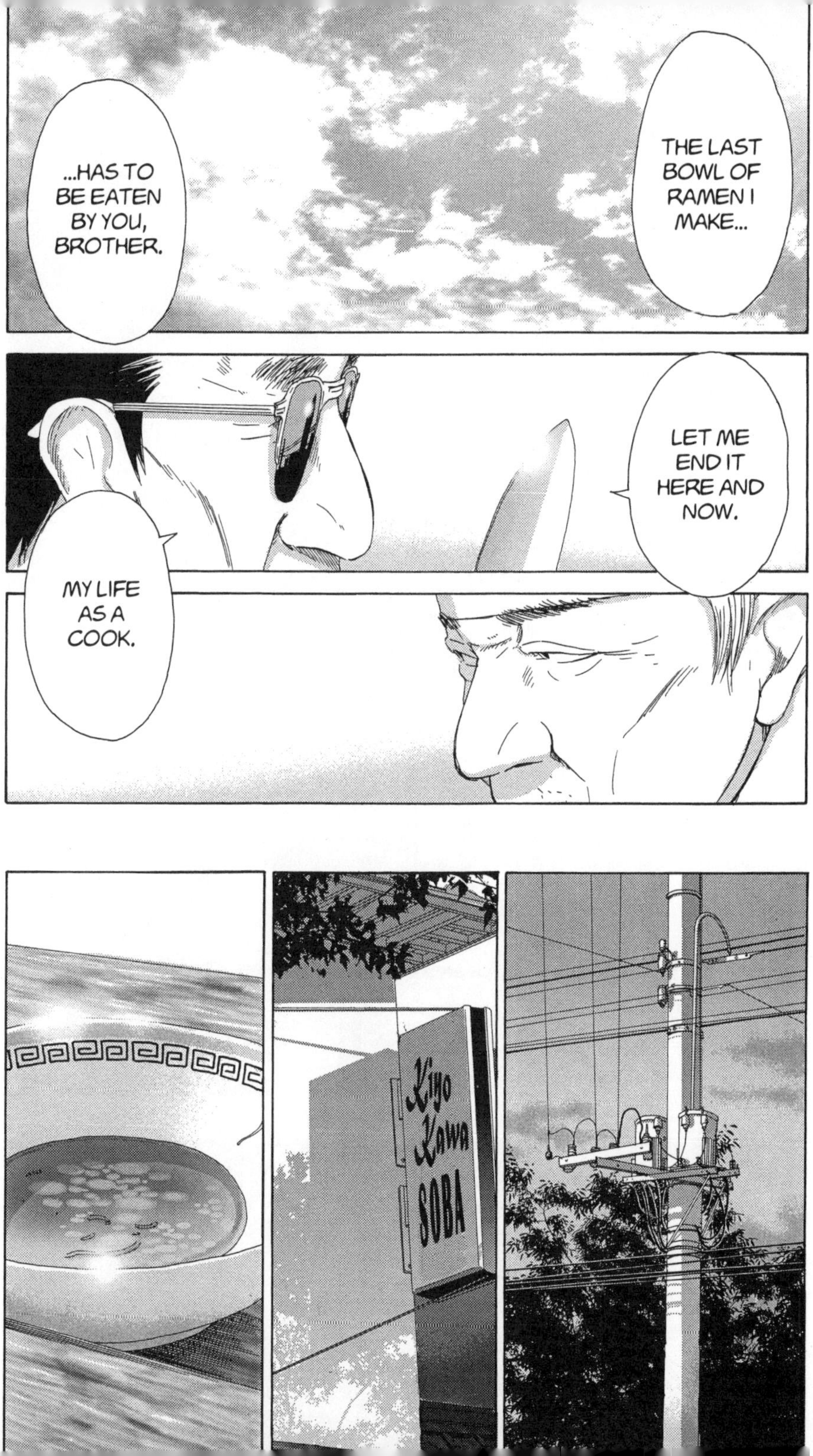
THE LAST BOWL OF RAMEN I MAKE...
...HAS TO BE EATEN BY YOU, BROTHER.
LET ME END IT HERE AND NOW.
MY LIFE AS A COOK.
Kiyo Kawa SOBA

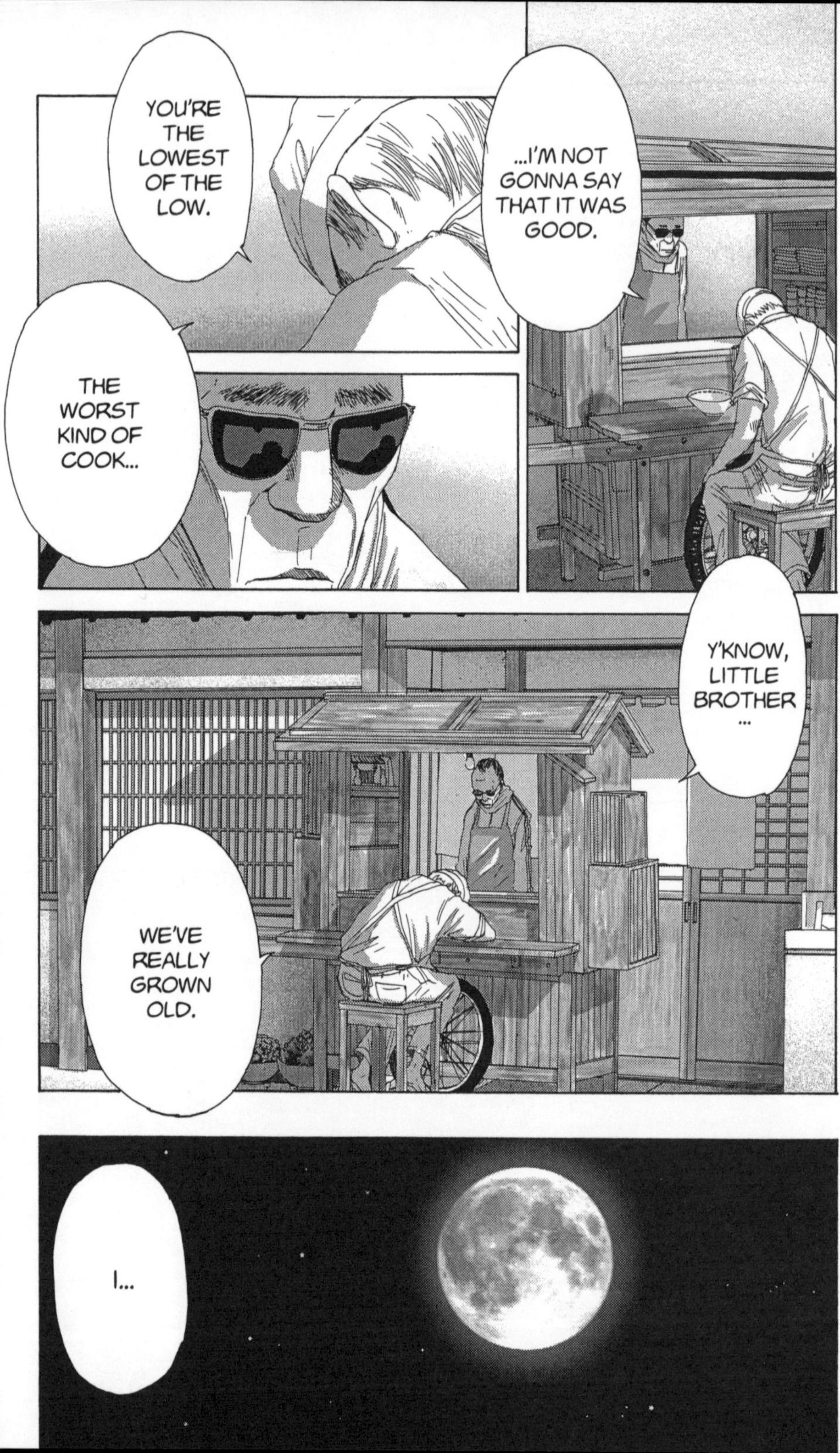
...I'M NOT GONNA SAY THAT IT WAS GOOD.
YOU'RE THE LOWEST OF THE LOW.
THE WORST KIND OF COOK...
Y'KNOW, LITTLE BROTHER ...
WE'VE REALLY GROWN OLD.
I...

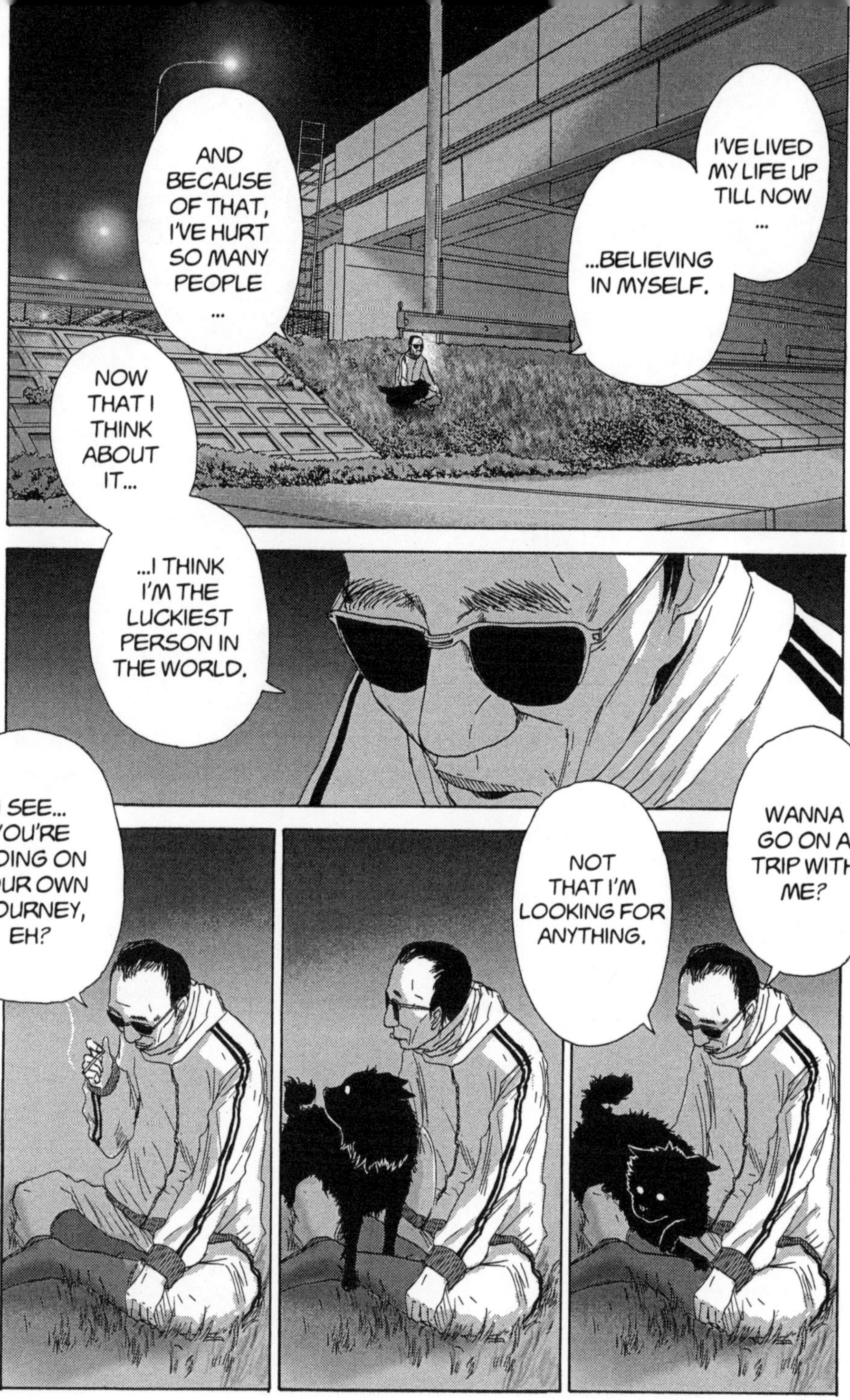
I'VE LIVED MY LIFE UP TILL NOW ...
...BELIEVING IN MYSELF.
AND BECAUSE OF THAT, I'VE HURT SO MANY PEOPLE ...
NOW THAT I THINK ABOUT IT...
...I THINK I'M THE LUCKIEST PERSON IN THE WORLD.
WANNA GO ON A TRIP WITH ME?
NOT THAT I'M LOOKING FOR ANYTHING.
I SEE... YOU'RE GOING ON YOUR OWN JOURNEY, EH?

THAT KNIFE...

YOU DON'T HAVE TO RETURN IT.

ISN'T THAT RIGHT?

THE TWO OF US...

...WON'T BE NEEDING THAT ANYMORE.

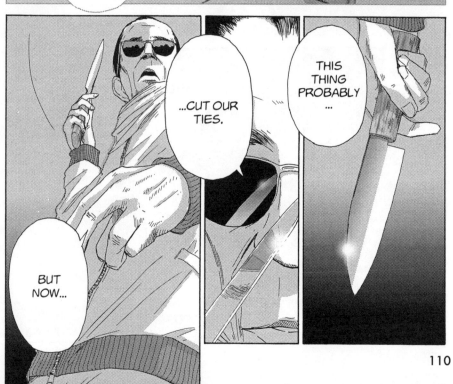

THIS THING PROBABLY...

...CUT OUR TIES.

BUT NOW...

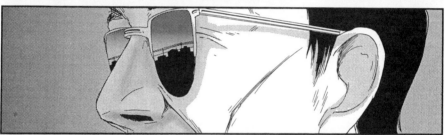

Okay...

SERIOUSLY, IT'S THAT GOOD.

JUST COME WITH ME AND TRY IT.

REALLY?

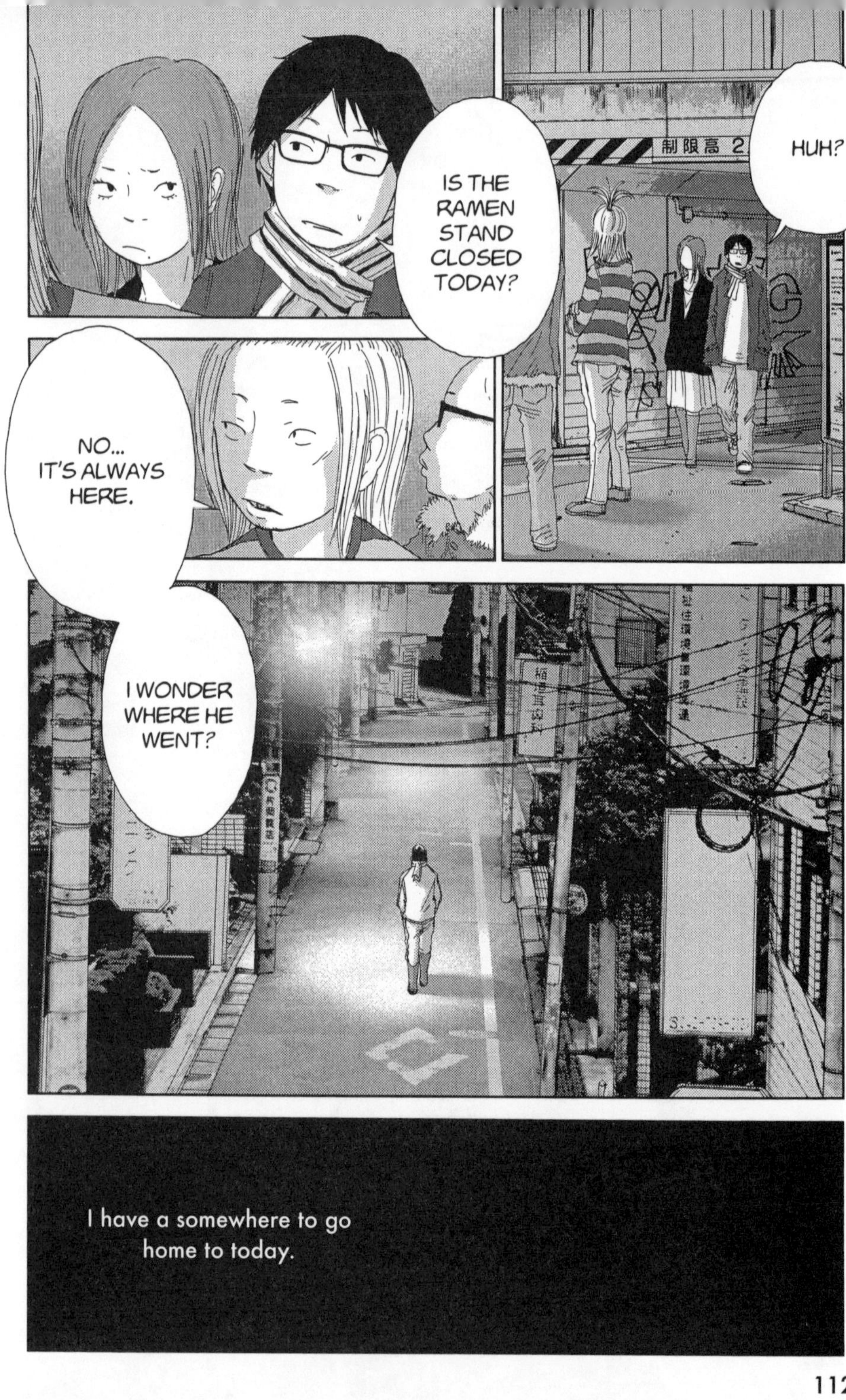
HUH?
IS THE RAMEN STAND CLOSED TODAY?
NO... IT'S ALWAYS HERE.
I WONDER WHERE HE WENT?
I have a somewhere to go home to today.

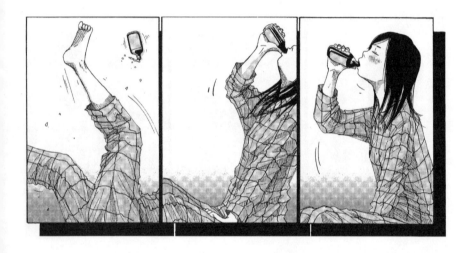

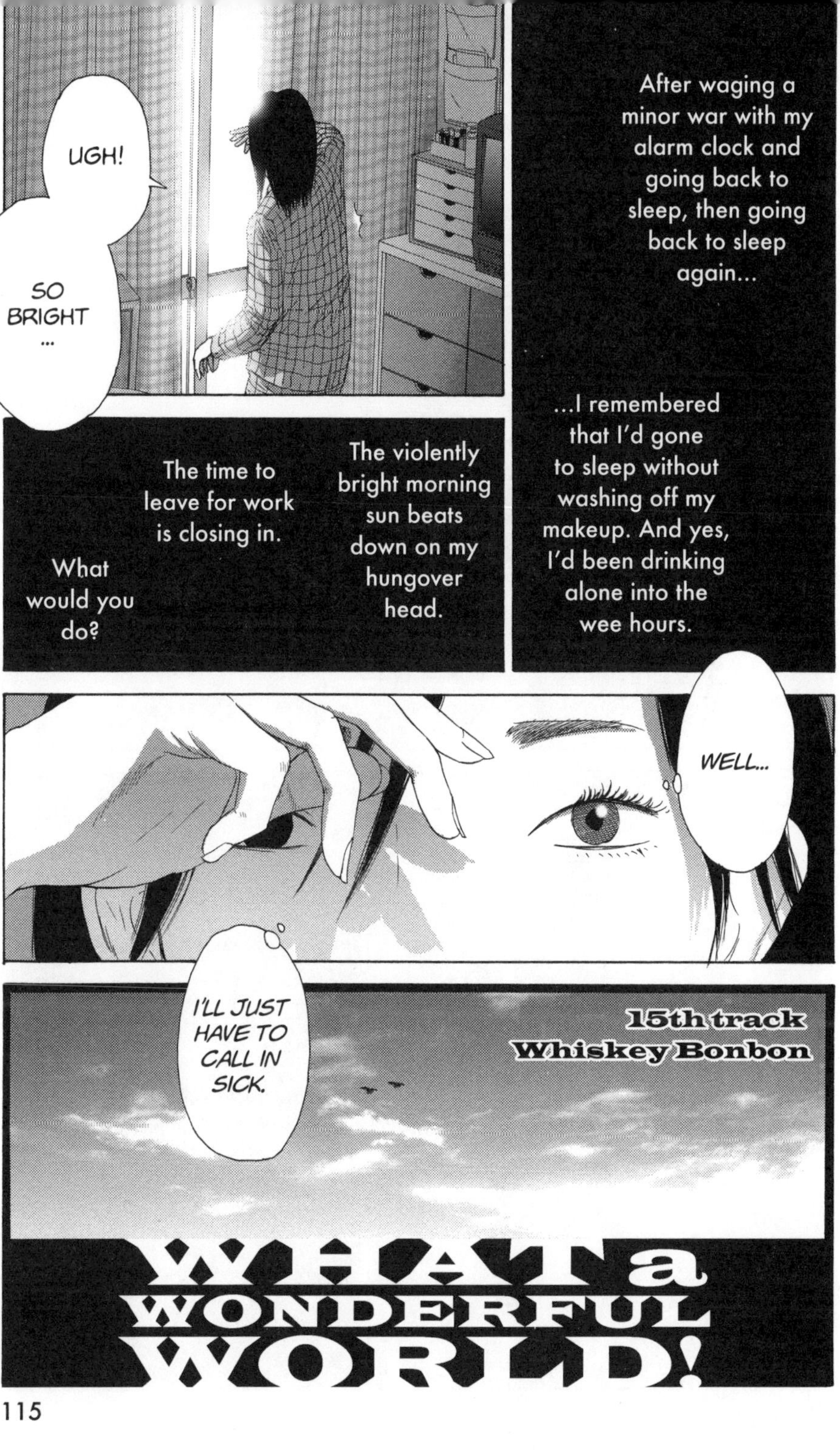
After waging a minor war with my alarm clock and going back to sleep, then going back to sleep again...
...I remembered that I'd gone to sleep without washing off my makeup. And yes, I'd been drinking alone into the wee hours.
UGH!
SO BRIGHT ...
The violently bright morning sun beats down on my hungover head.
The time to leave for work is closing in.
What would you do?
WELL...
I'LL JUST HAVE TO CALL IN SICK.
15th track
Whiskey Bonbon
WHAT a WONDERFUL WORLD!

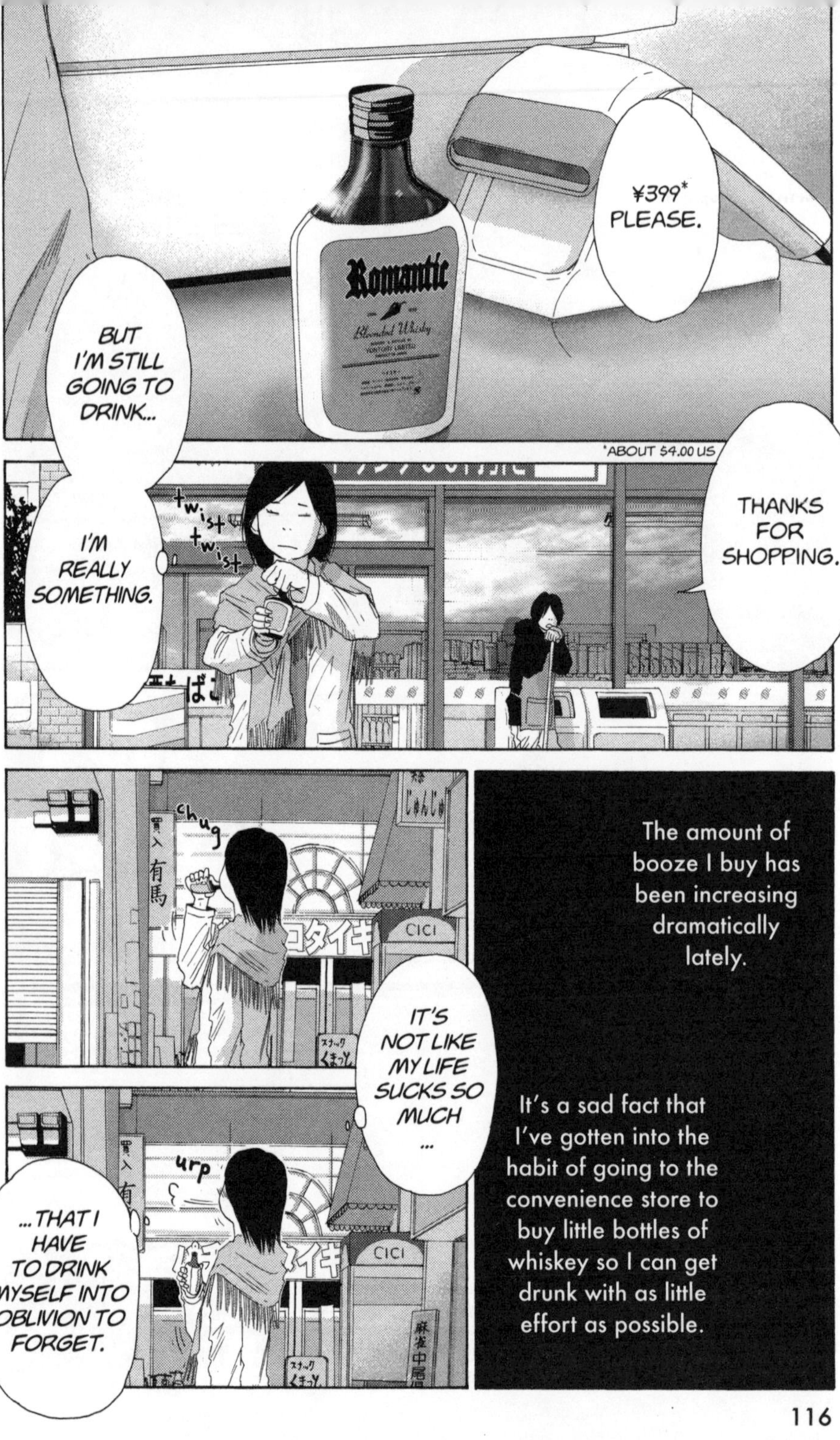
¥399* PLEASE.
BUT I'M STILL GOING TO DRINK...
*ABOUT $4.00 US
THANKS FOR SHOPPING.
twist twist
I'M REALLY SOMETHING.
The amount of booze I buy has been increasing dramatically lately.
It's a sad fact that I've gotten into the habit of going to the convenience store to buy little bottles of whiskey so I can get drunk with as little effort as possible.
chug
IT'S NOT LIKE MY LIFE SUCKS SO MUCH ...
urp
...THAT I HAVE TO DRINK MYSELF INTO OBLIVION TO FORGET.

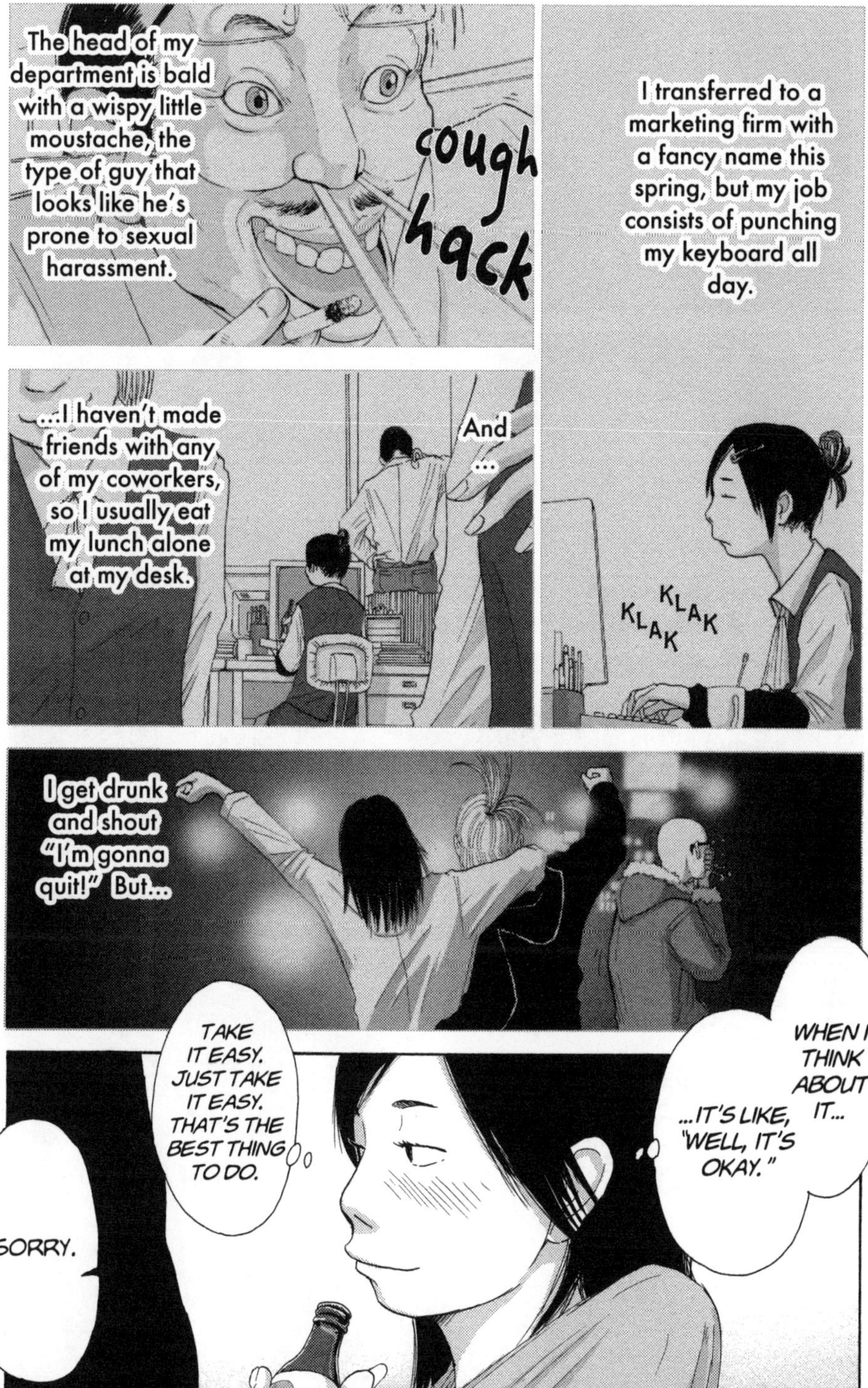
I transferred to a marketing firm with a fancy name this spring, but my job consists of punching my keyboard all day.
KLAK KLAK
The head of my department is bald with a wispy little moustache, the type of guy that looks like he's prone to sexual harassment.
cough hack
And ...
...I haven't made friends with any of my coworkers, so I usually eat my lunch alone at my desk.
I get drunk and shout "I'm gonna quit!" But...
WHEN I THINK ABOUT IT...
...IT'S LIKE, "WELL, IT'S OKAY."
TAKE IT EASY. JUST TAKE IT EASY. THAT'S THE BEST THING TO DO.
SORRY.

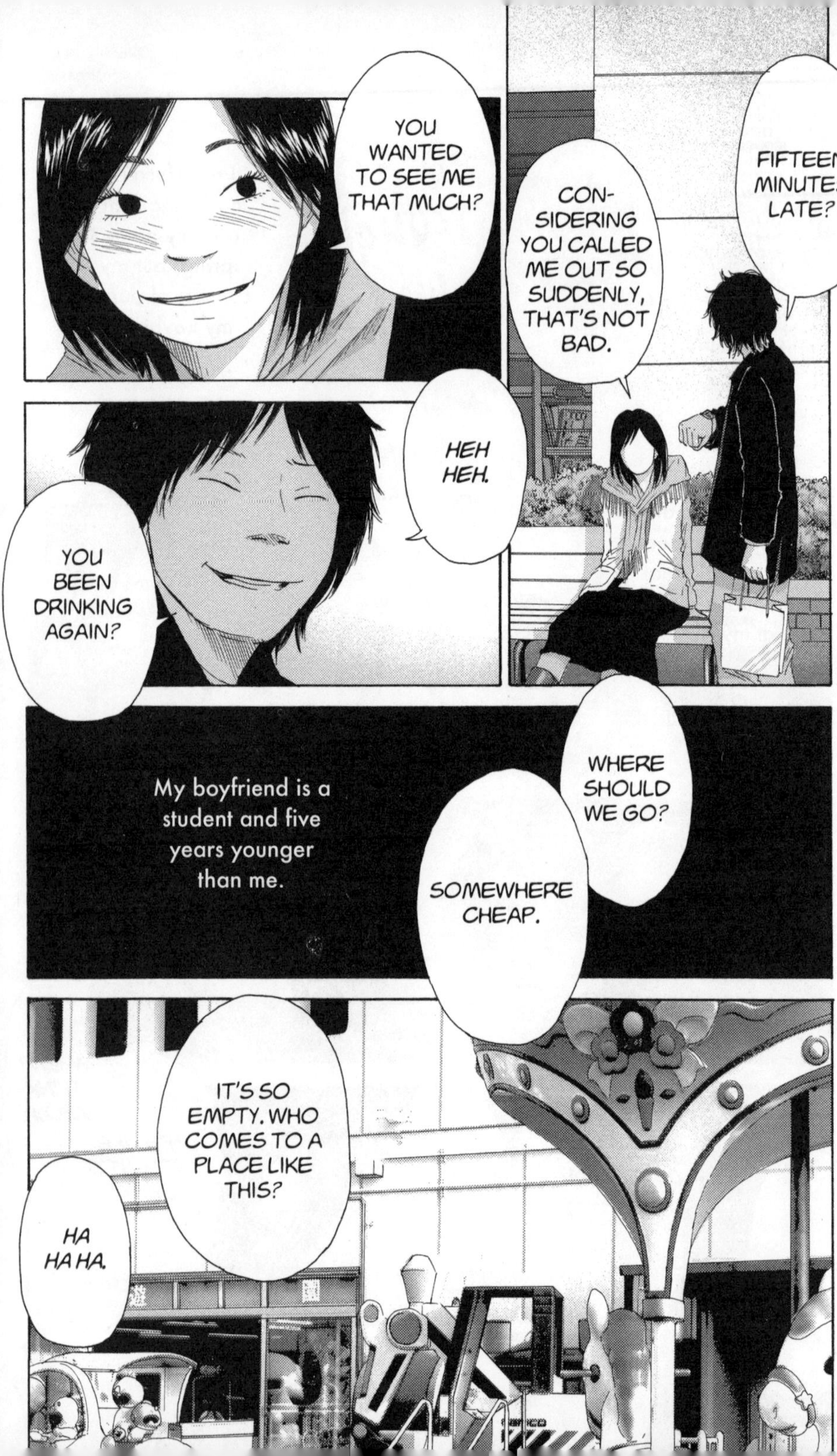
FIFTEEN MINUTES LATE?
CON-SIDERING YOU CALLED ME OUT SO SUDDENLY, THAT'S NOT BAD.
YOU WANTED TO SEE ME THAT MUCH?
HEH HEH.
YOU BEEN DRINKING AGAIN?
WHERE SHOULD WE GO?
SOMEWHERE CHEAP.
My boyfriend is a student and five years younger than me.
IT'S SO EMPTY. WHO COMES TO A PLACE LIKE THIS?
HA HA HA.

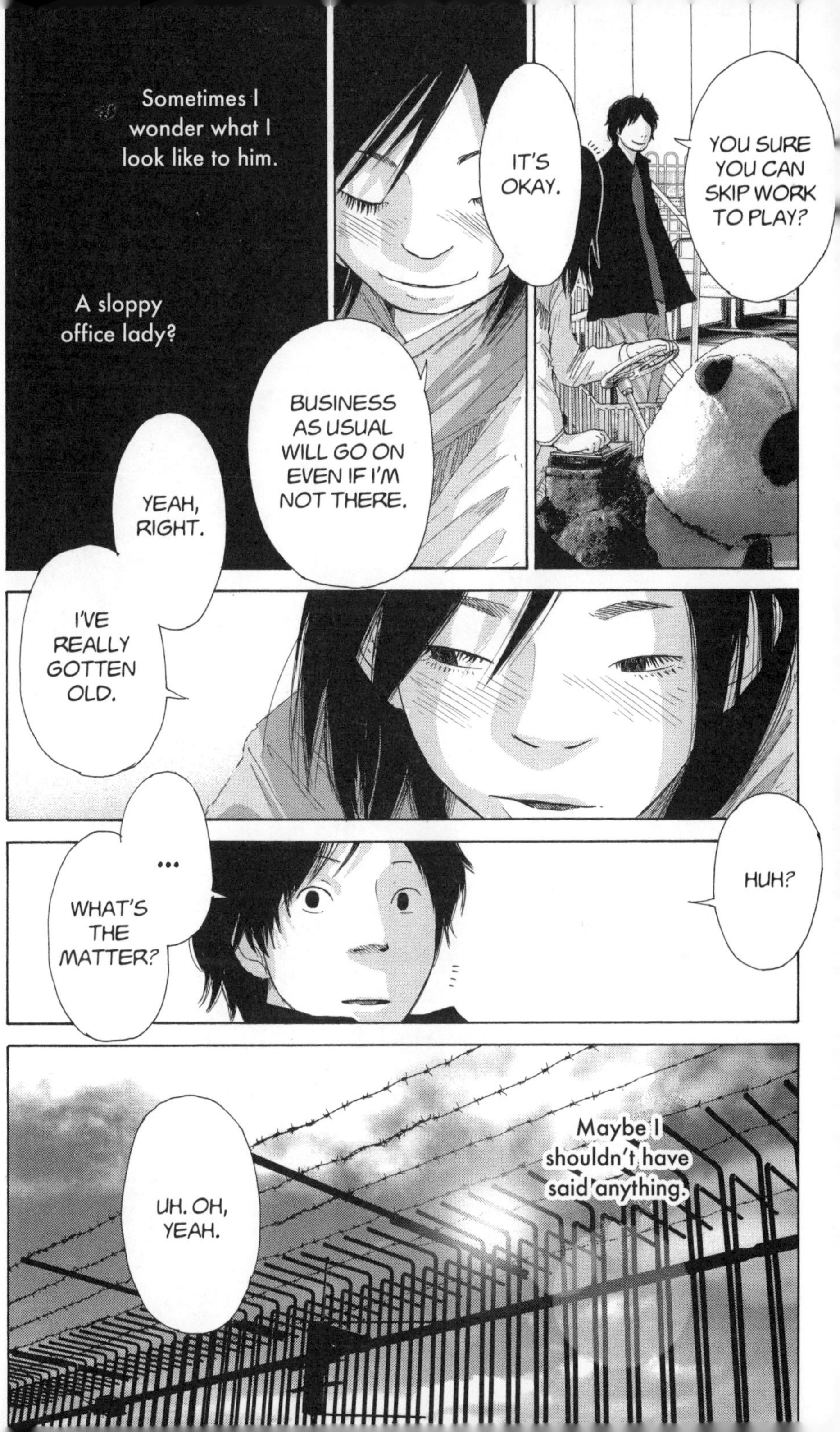

YOU SURE YOU CAN SKIP WORK TO PLAY?
IT'S OKAY.
BUSINESS AS USUAL WILL GO ON EVEN IF I'M NOT THERE.
Sometimes I wonder what I look like to him.
A sloppy office lady?
YEAH, RIGHT.
I'VE REALLY GOTTEN OLD.
HUH?
...
WHAT'S THE MATTER?
Maybe I shouldn't have said anything.
UH. OH, YEAH.

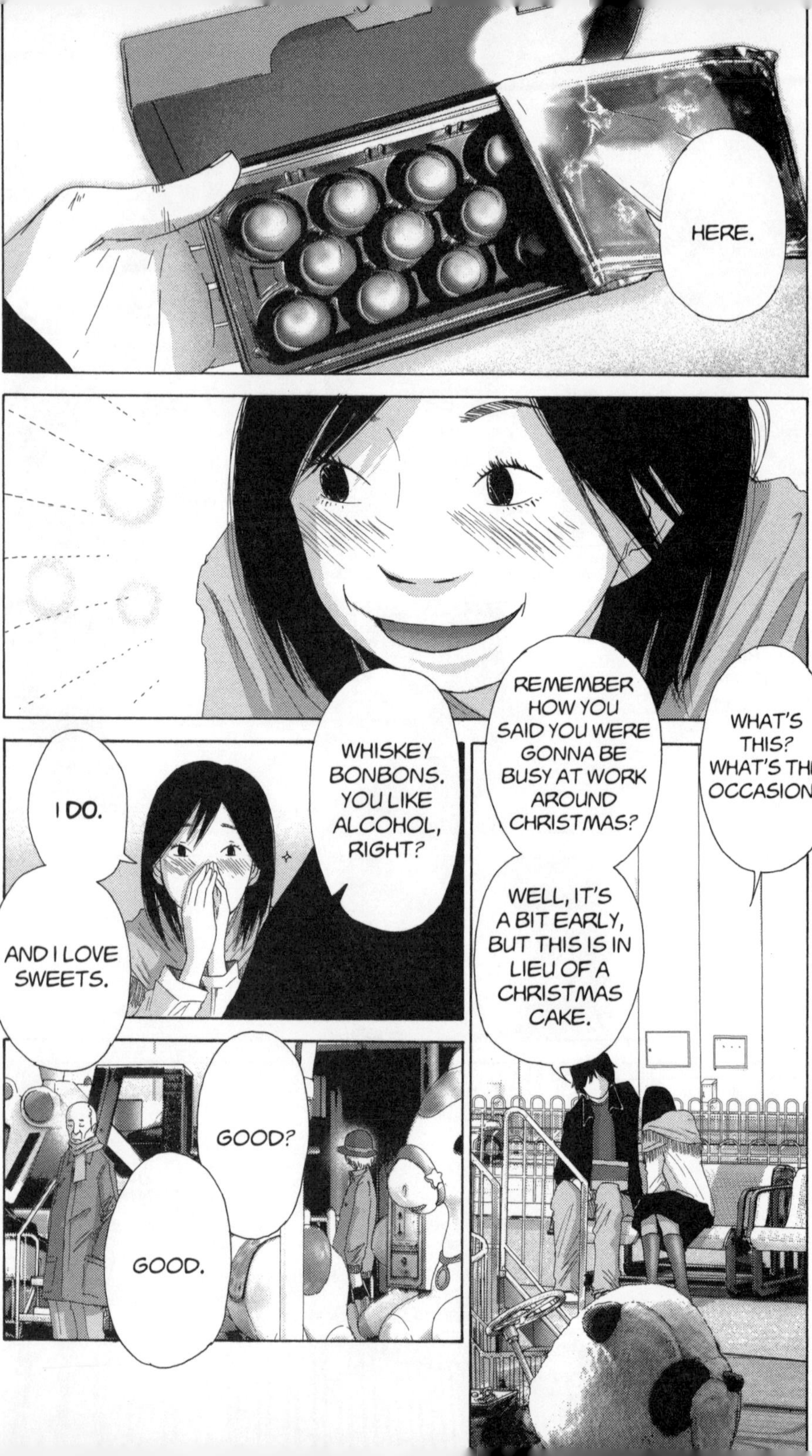
HERE.
WHAT'S THIS? WHAT'S THE OCCASION?
REMEMBER HOW YOU SAID YOU WERE GONNA BE BUSY AT WORK AROUND CHRISTMAS?
WELL, IT'S A BIT EARLY, BUT THIS IS IN LIEU OF A CHRISTMAS CAKE.
WHISKEY BONBONS. YOU LIKE ALCOHOL, RIGHT?
I DO.
AND I LOVE SWEETS.
GOOD?
GOOD.

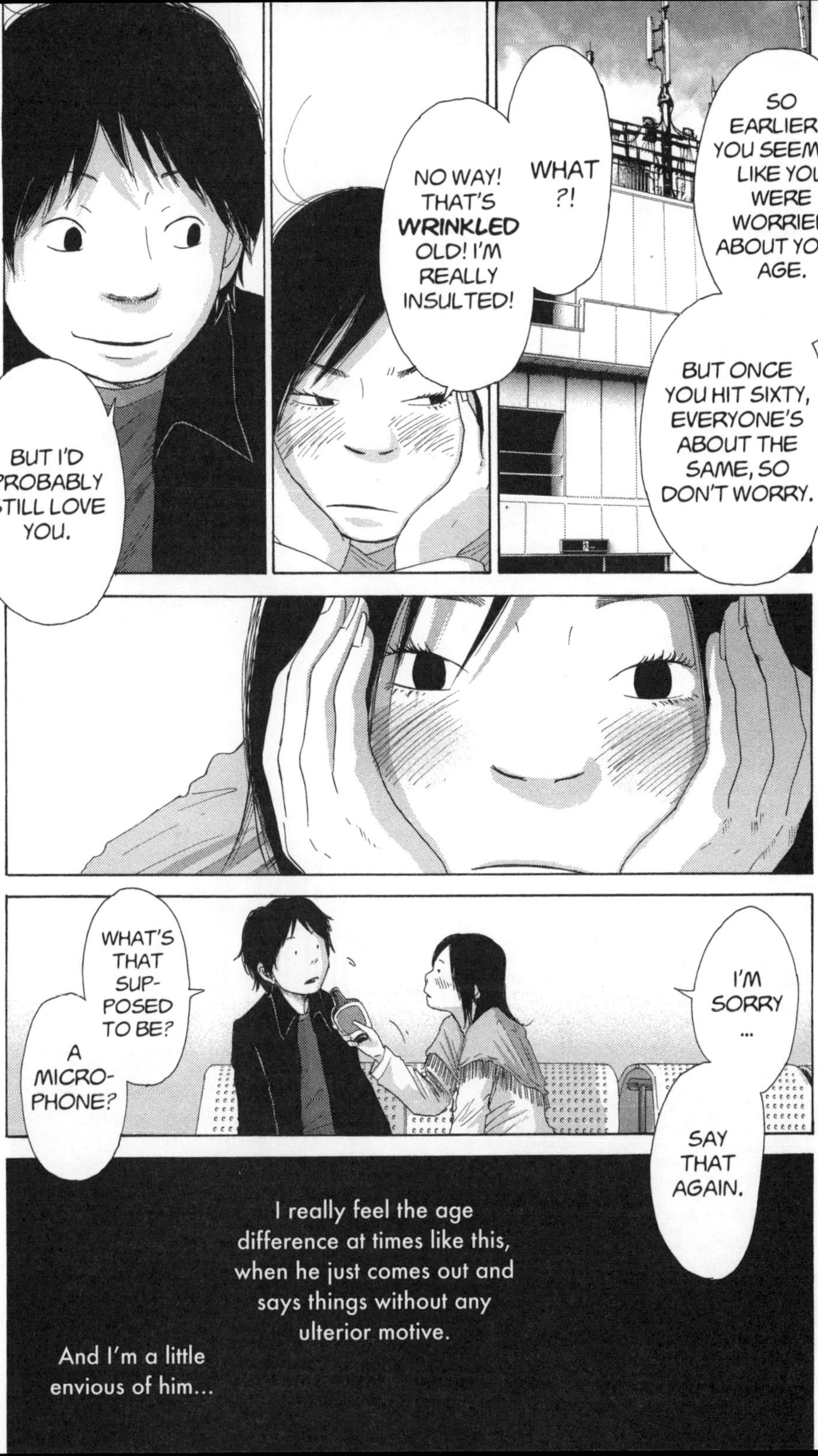
SO EARLIER... YOU SEEMED LIKE YOU WERE WORRIED ABOUT YOUR AGE.
BUT ONCE YOU HIT SIXTY, EVERYONE'S ABOUT THE SAME, SO DON'T WORRY.
WHAT ?!
NO WAY! THAT'S **WRINKLED** OLD! I'M REALLY INSULTED!
BUT I'D PROBABLY STILL LOVE YOU.
I'M SORRY ...
SAY THAT AGAIN.
WHAT'S THAT SUP-POSED TO BE?
A MICRO-PHONE?
I really feel the age difference at times like this, when he just comes out and says things without any ulterior motive.
And I'm a little envious of him...

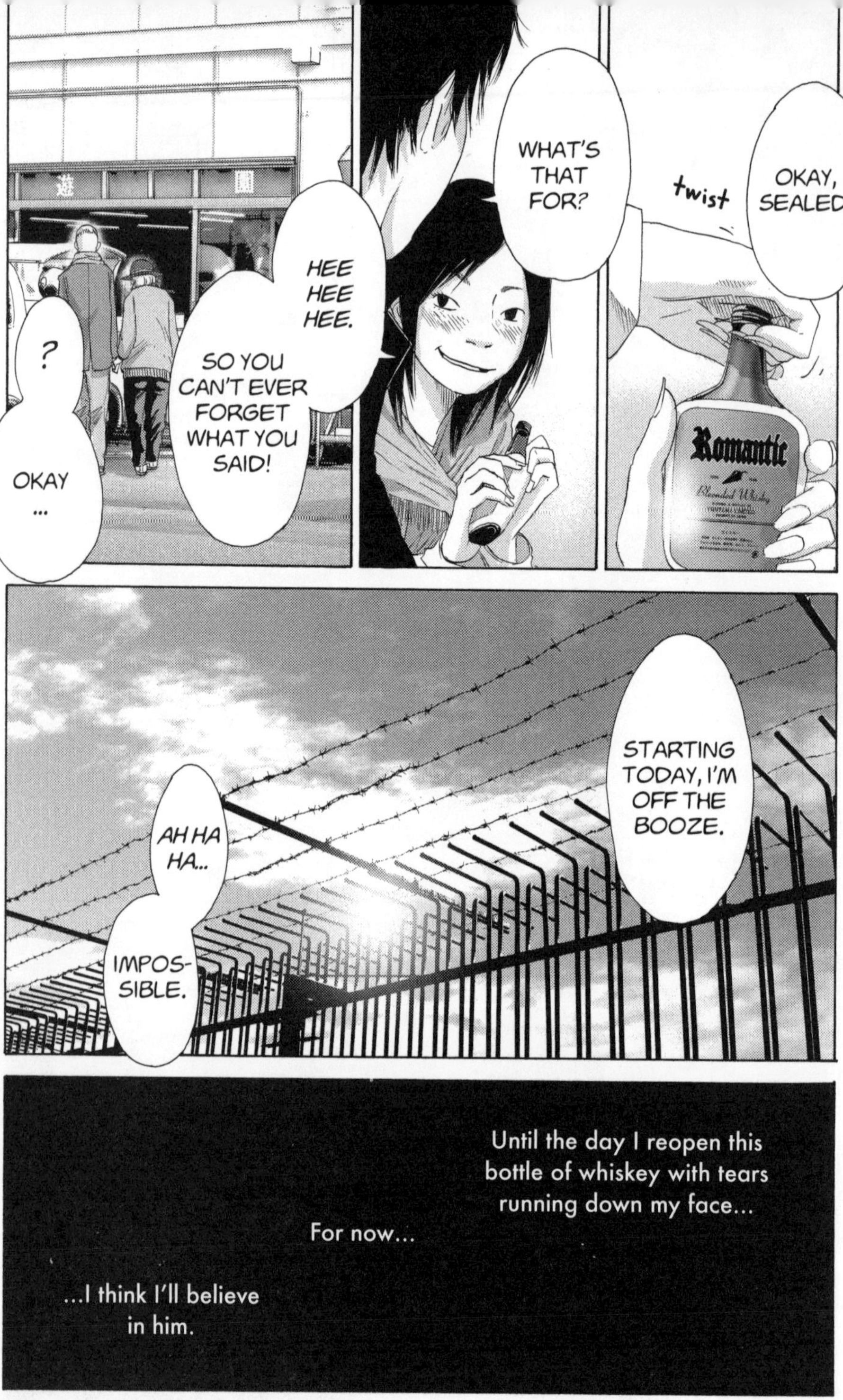
twist
OKAY, SEALED.
Romantic
Blended Whisky
WHAT'S THAT FOR?
HEE HEE HEE.
SO YOU CAN'T EVER FORGET WHAT YOU SAID!
?
OKAY ...
STARTING TODAY, I'M OFF THE BOOZE.
AH HA HA...
IMPOSSIBLE.
Until the day I reopen this bottle of whiskey with tears running down my face...
For now...
...I think I'll believe in him.

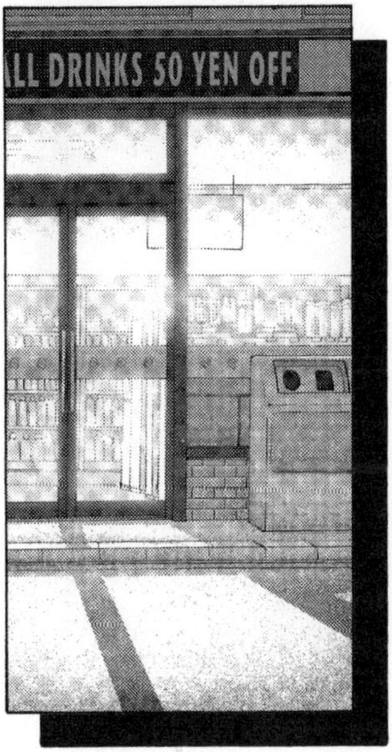
ALL DRINKS 50 YEN OFF

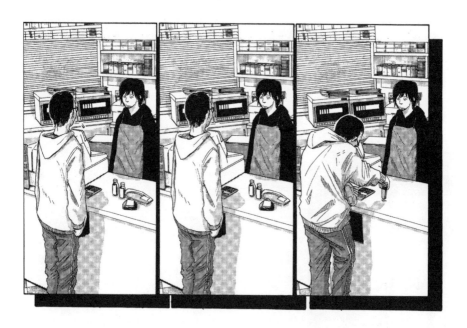

# 16th track What a Wonderful World

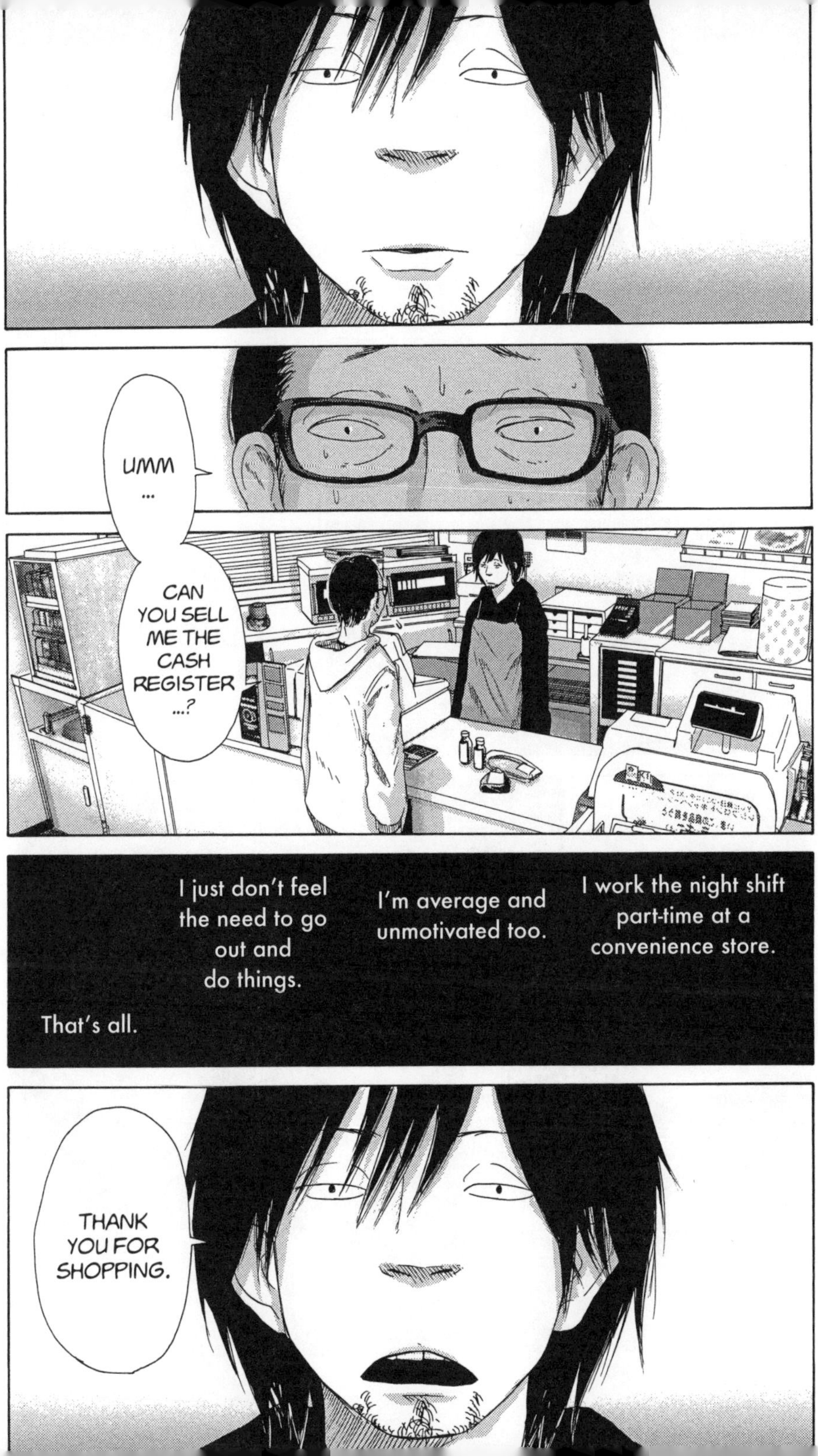
UMM ...
CAN YOU SELL ME THE CASH REGISTER ...?
I work the night shift part-time at a convenience store.
I'm average and unmotivated too.
I just don't feel the need to go out and do things.
That's all.
THANK YOU FOR SHOPPING.

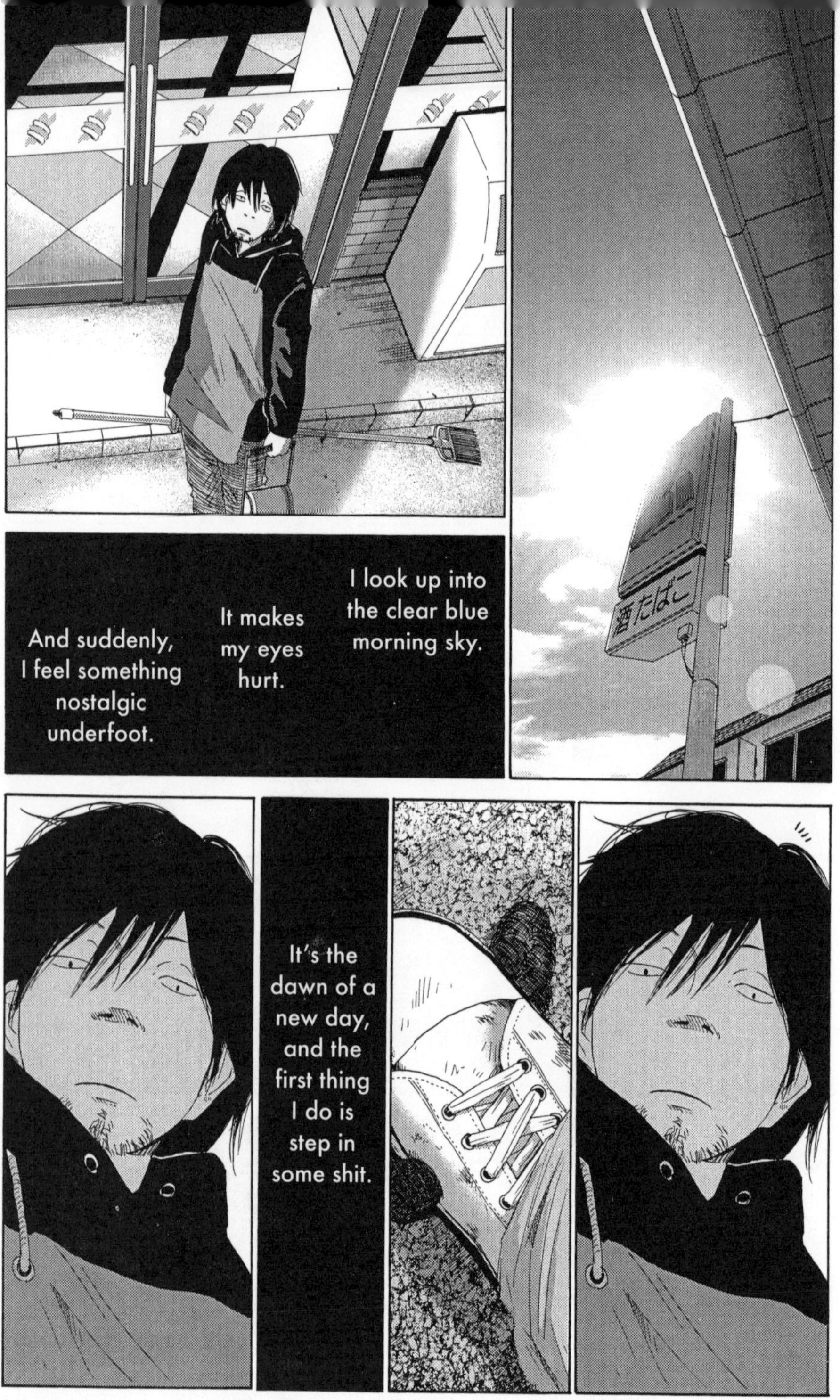
酒たばこ
I look up into the clear blue morning sky.
It makes my eyes hurt.
And suddenly, I feel something nostalgic underfoot.
It's the dawn of a new day, and the first thing I do is step in some shit.

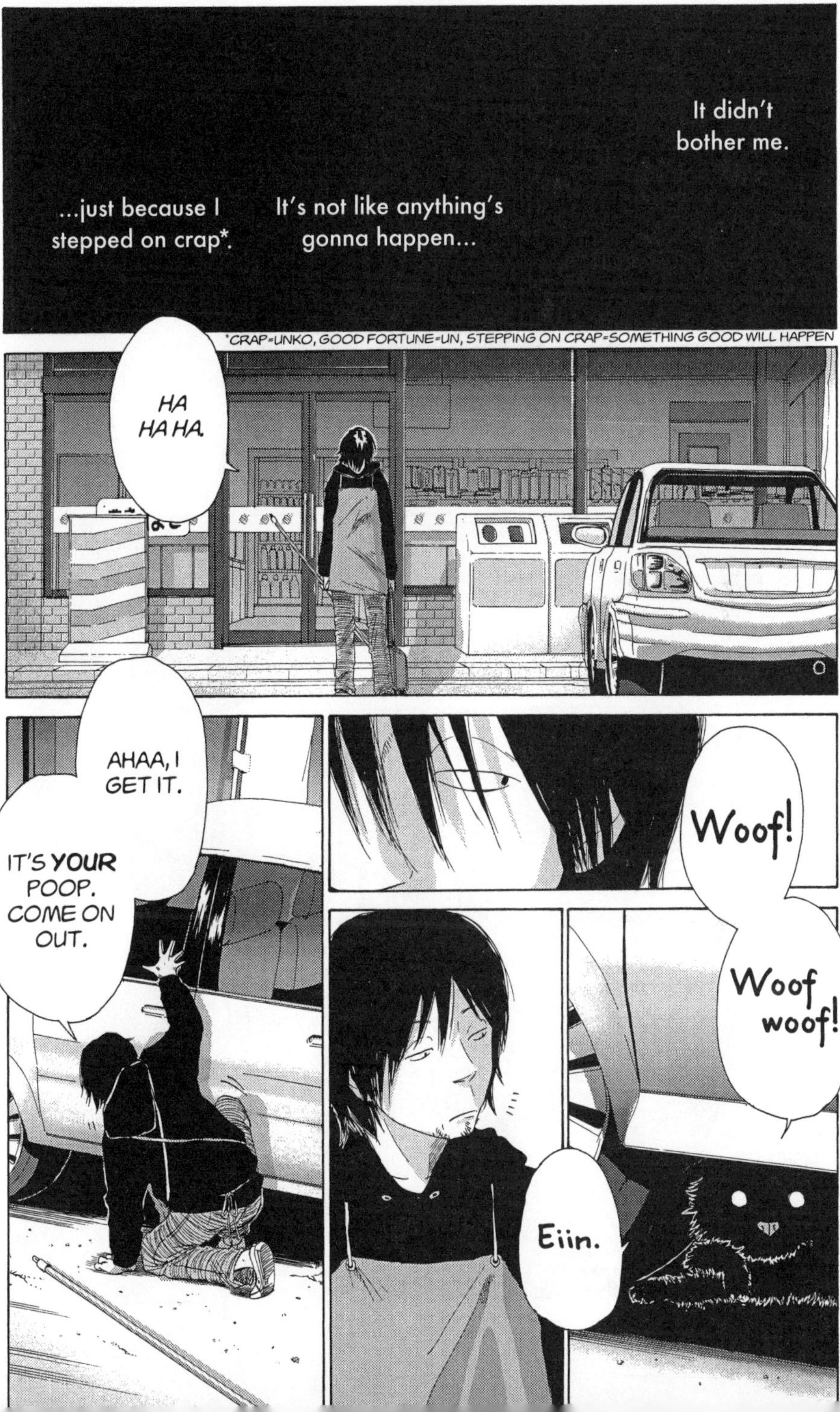
It didn't bother me.
It's not like anything's gonna happen...
...just because I stepped on crap*.
*CRAP=UNKO, GOOD FORTUNE=UN, STEPPING ON CRAP=SOMETHING GOOD WILL HAPPEN
HA HA HA.
Woof!
Woof woof!
Eiin.
AHAA, I GET IT.
IT'S **YOUR** POOP. COME ON OUT.

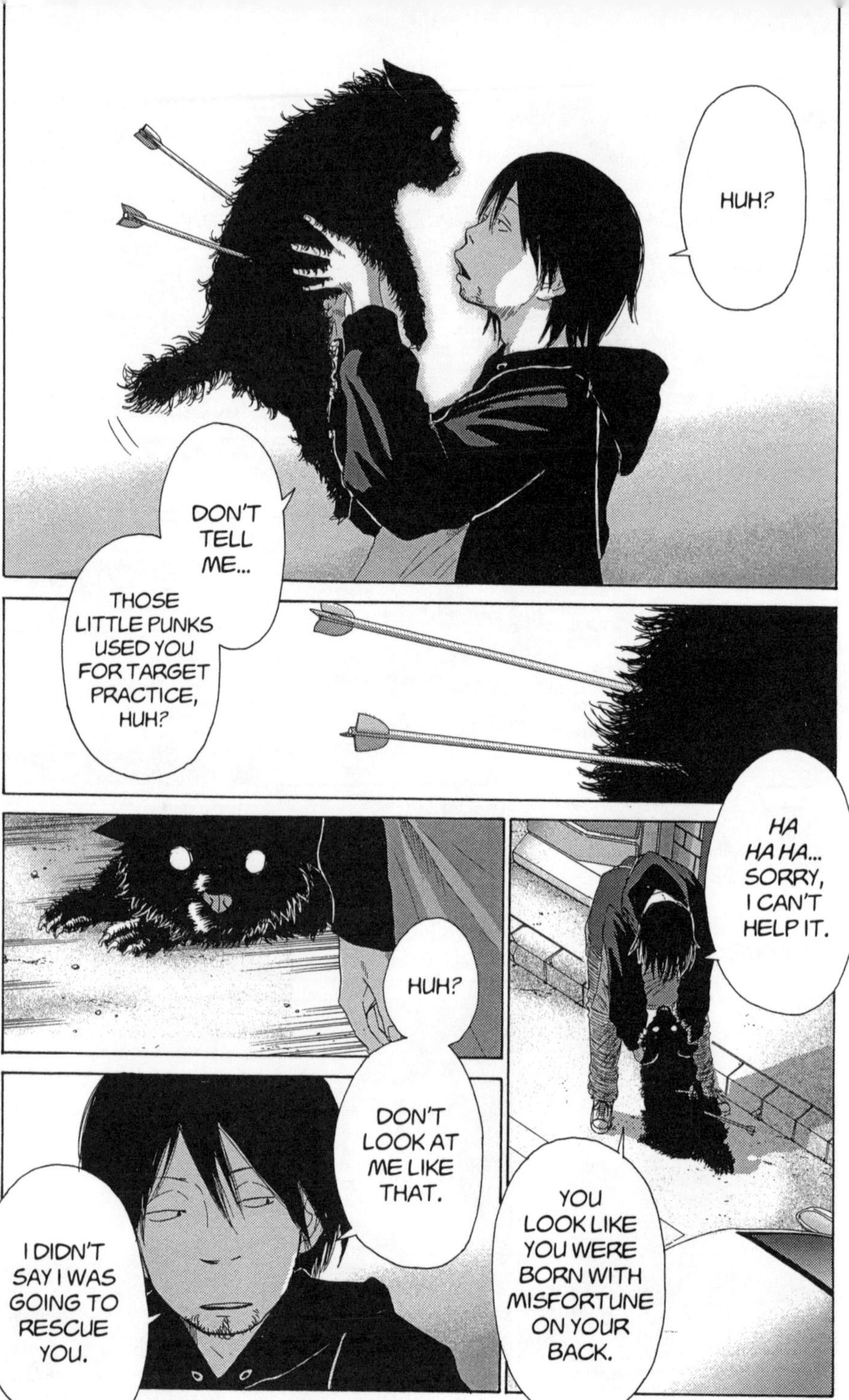
HUH?
DON'T TELL ME...
THOSE LITTLE PUNKS USED YOU FOR TARGET PRACTICE, HUH?
HA HA HA... SORRY, I CAN'T HELP IT.
YOU LOOK LIKE YOU WERE BORN WITH MISFORTUNE ON YOUR BACK.
HUH?
DON'T LOOK AT ME LIKE THAT.
I DIDN'T SAY I WAS GOING TO RESCUE YOU.

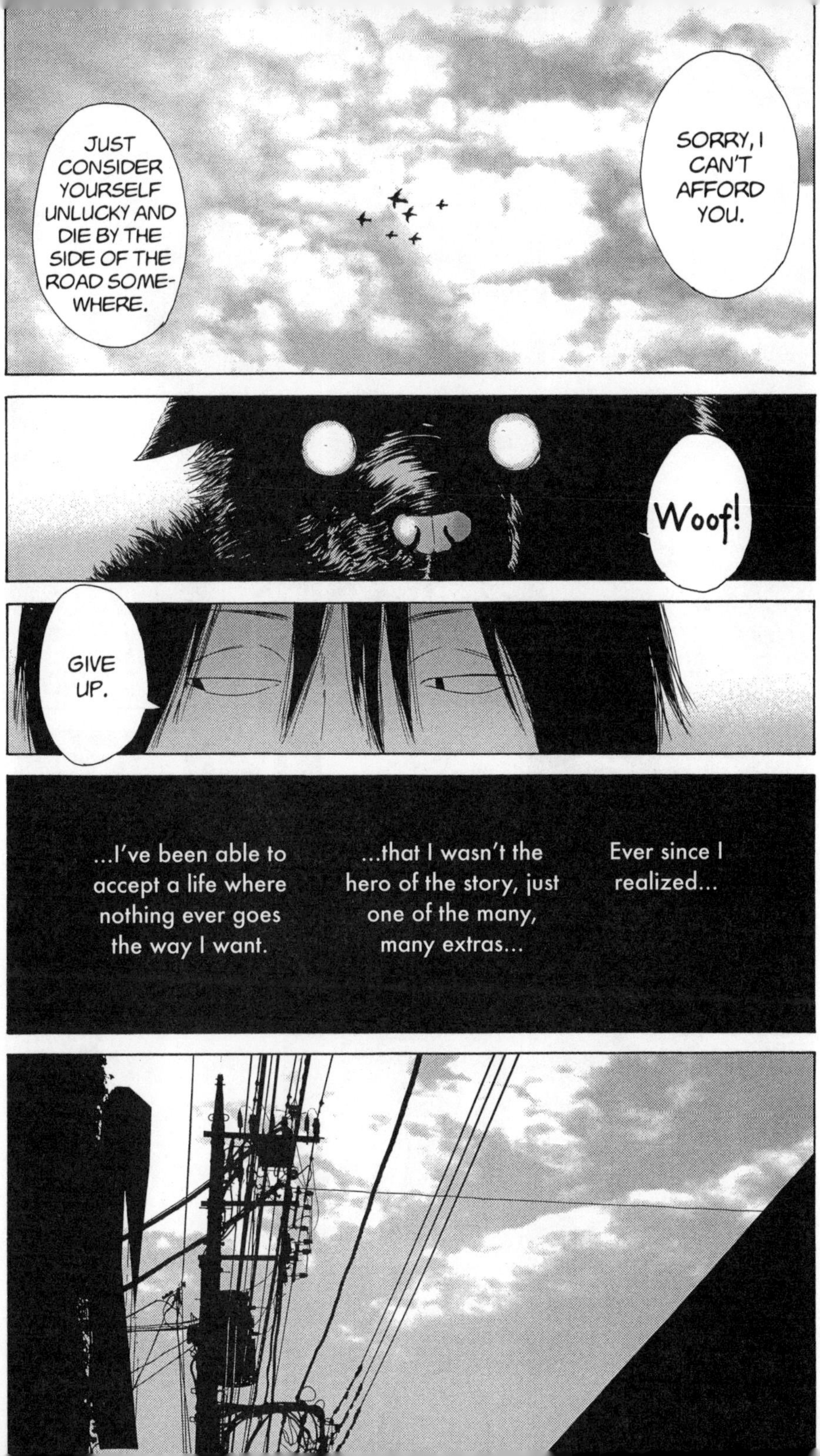
SORRY, I CAN'T AFFORD YOU.
JUST CONSIDER YOURSELF UNLUCKY AND DIE BY THE SIDE OF THE ROAD SOME-WHERE.
Woof!
GIVE UP.
Ever since I realized...
...that I wasn't the hero of the story, just one of the many, many extras...
...I've been able to accept a life where nothing ever goes the way I want.

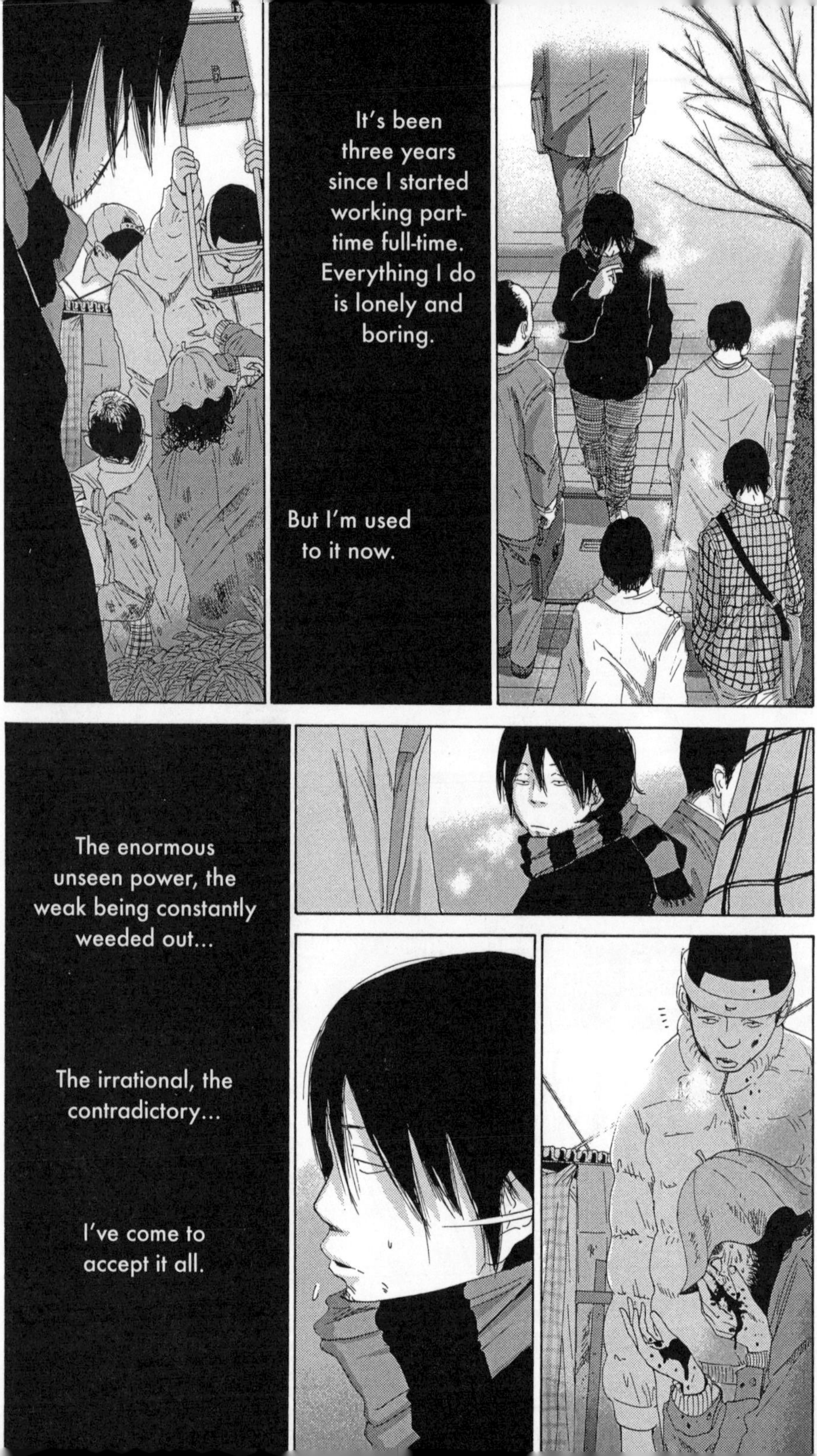
It's been three years since I started working part-time full-time. Everything I do is lonely and boring.
But I'm used to it now.
The enormous unseen power, the weak being constantly weeded out...
The irrational, the contradictory...
I've come to accept it all.

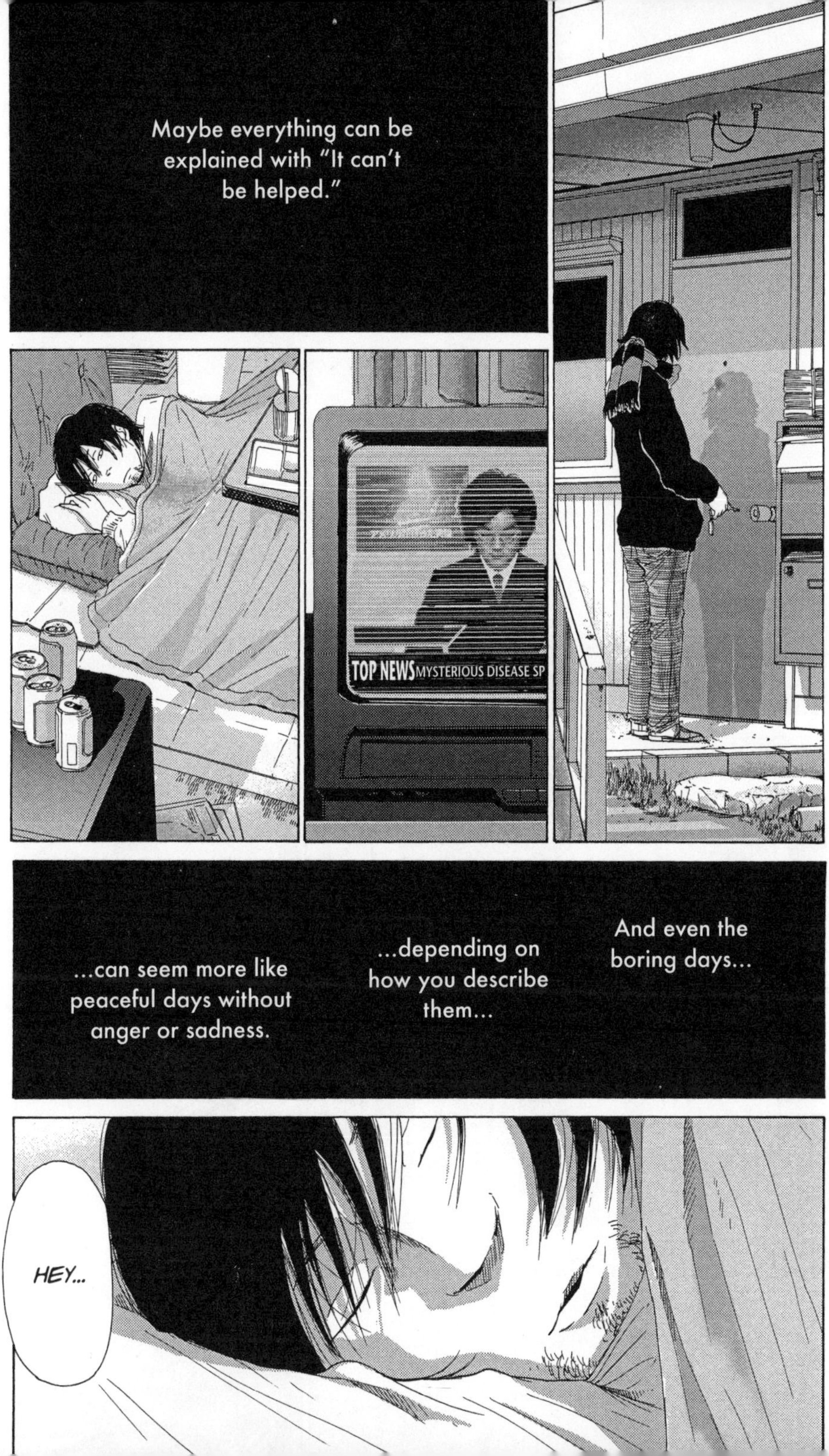
Maybe everything can be explained with "It can't be helped."
TOP NEWS MYSTERIOUS DISEASE SP
And even the boring days...
...depending on how you describe them...
...can seem more like peaceful days without anger or sadness.
HEY...

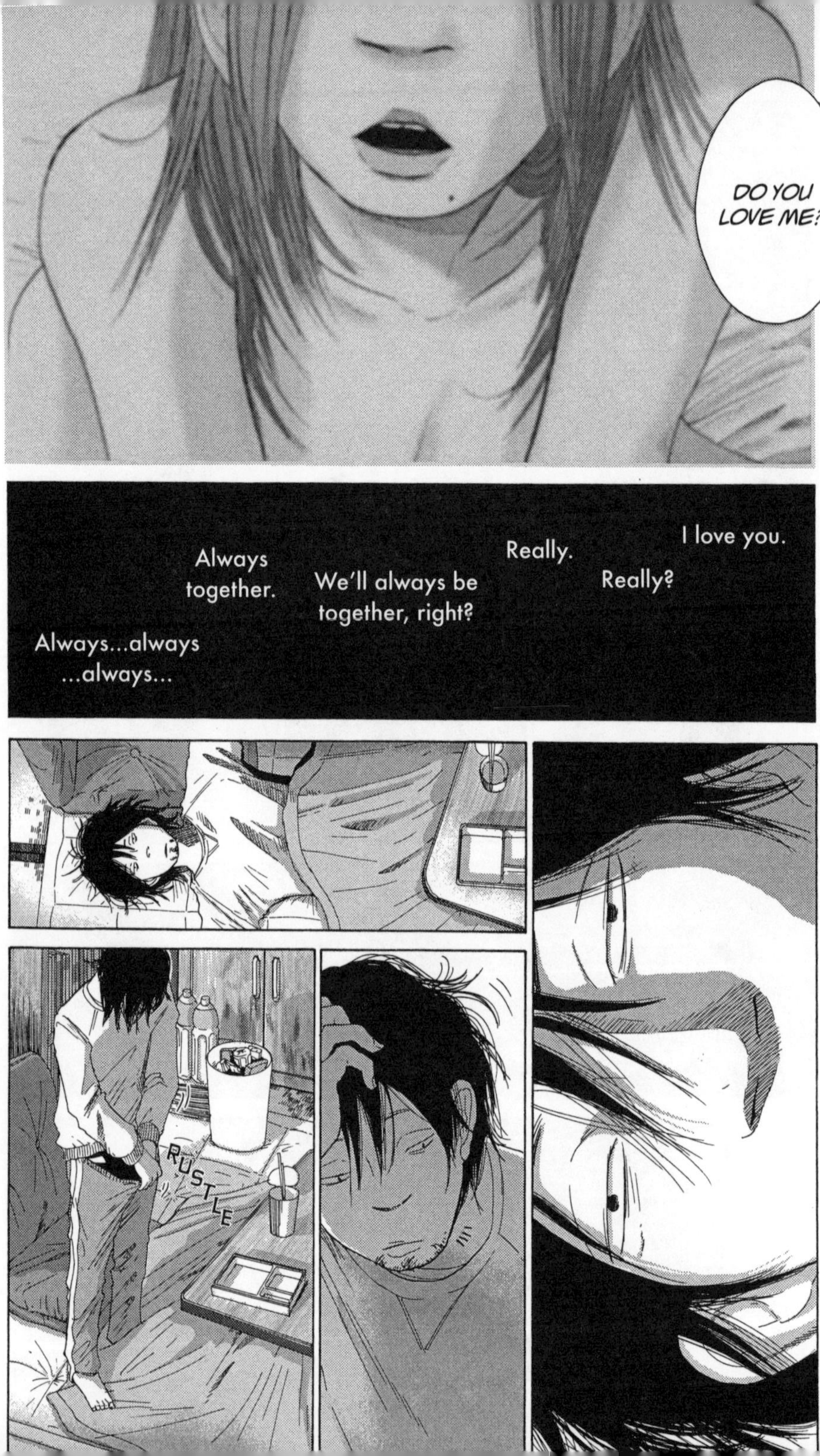
DO YOU LOVE ME?
I love you.
Really?
Really.
We'll always be together, right?
Always together.
Always...always ...always...
RUSTLE

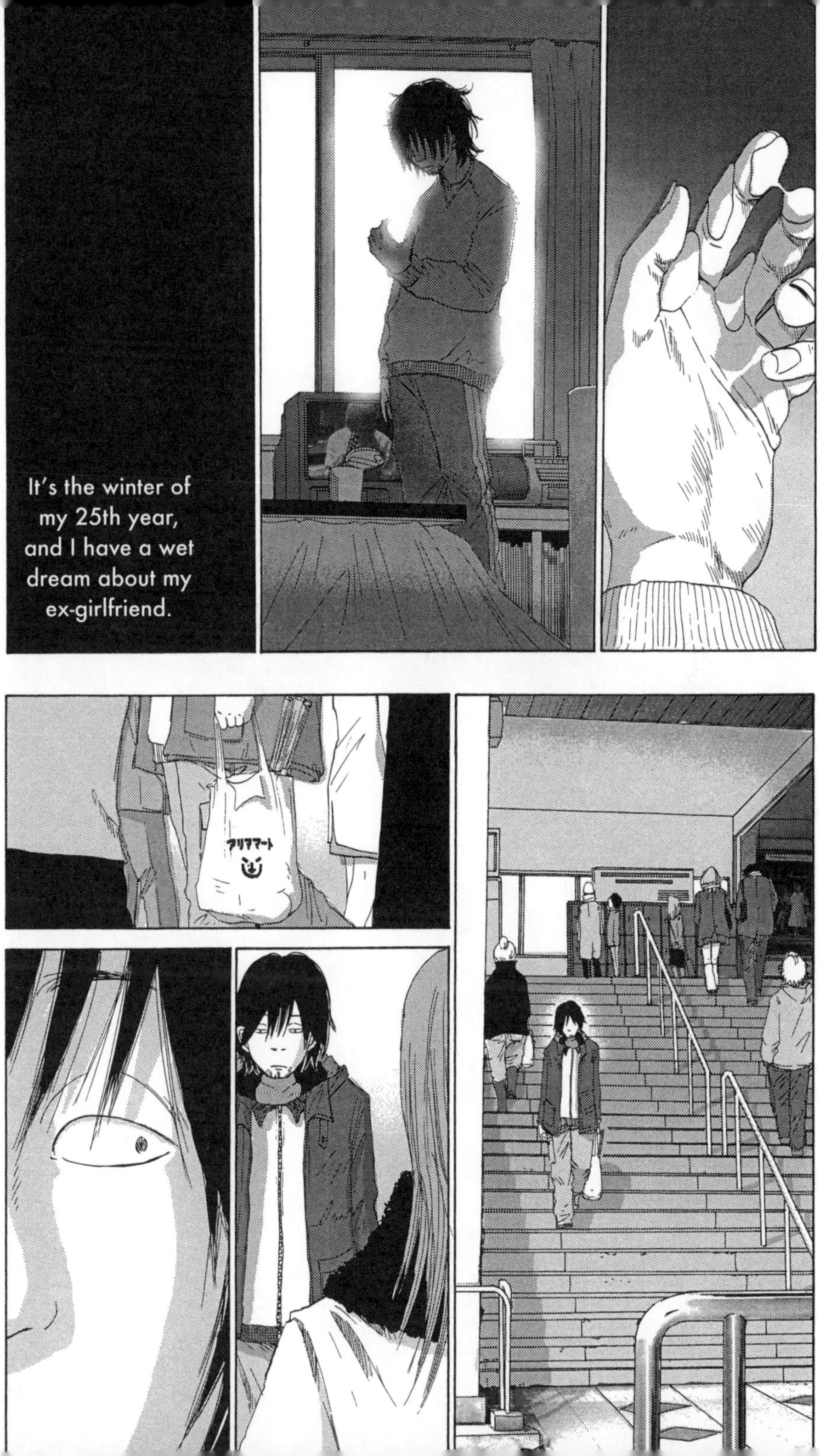
It's the winter of my 25th year, and I have a wet dream about my ex-girlfriend.
アリママート

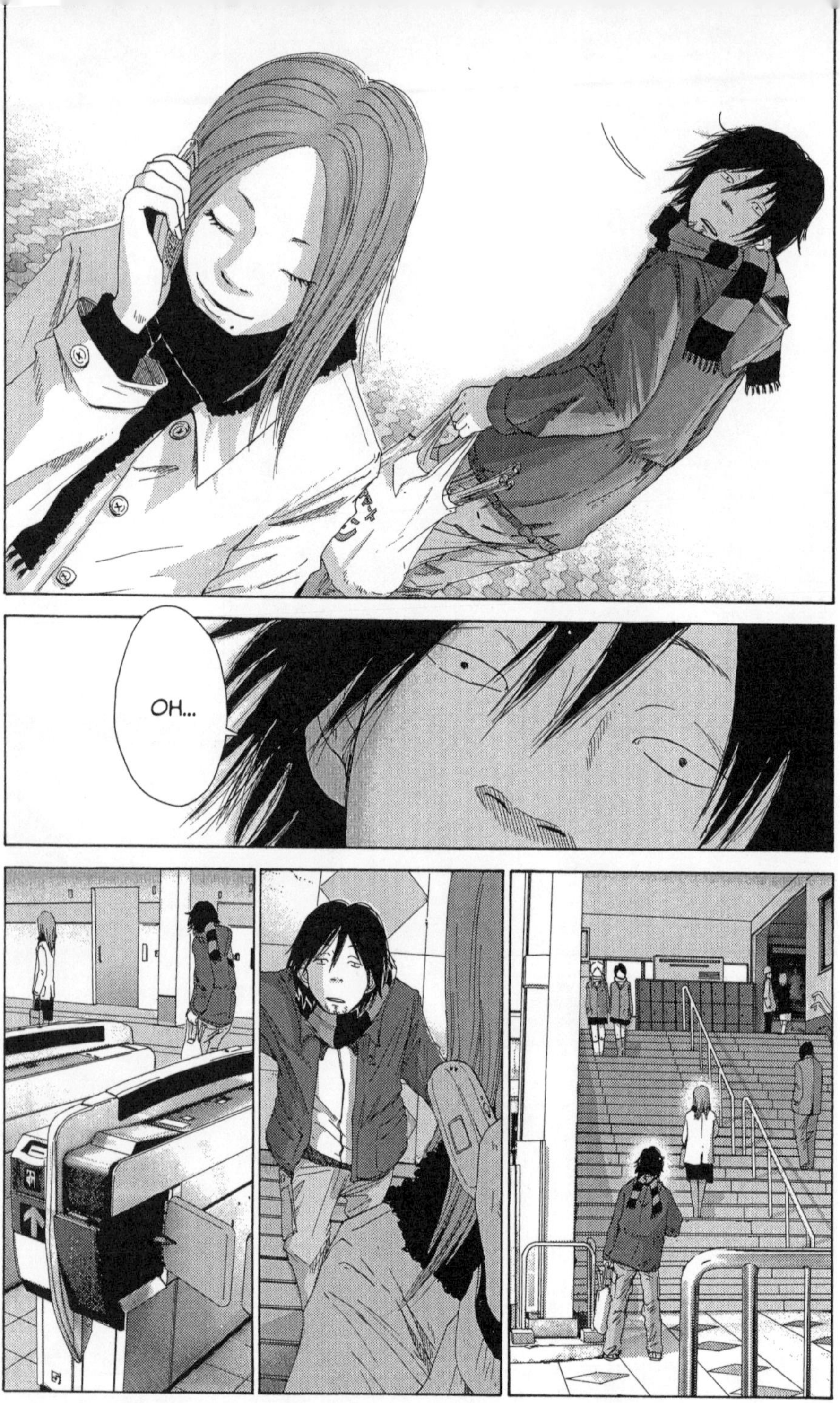
OH...

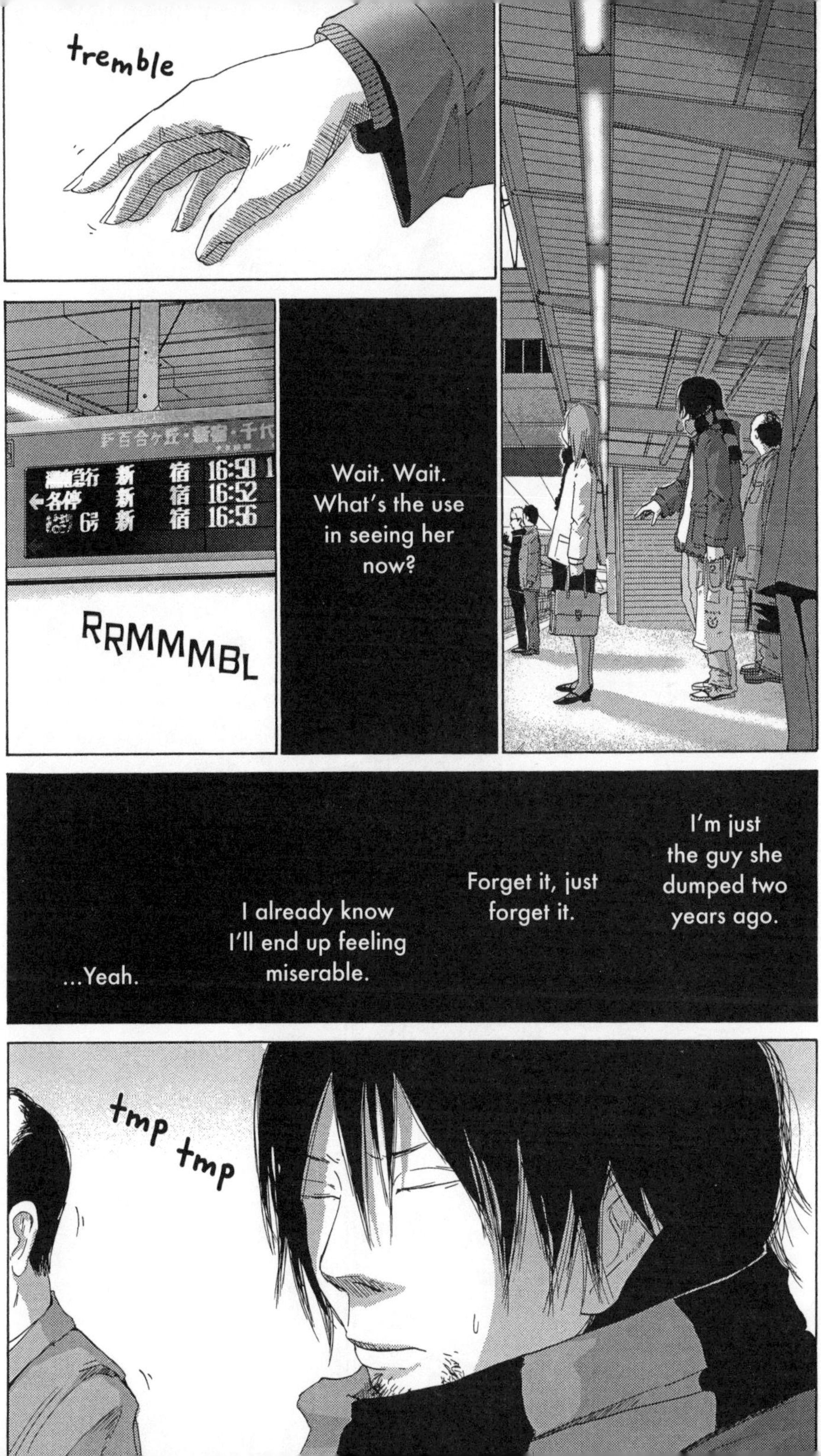

tremble
Wait. Wait. What's the use in seeing her now?
新宿 16:50
各停 新宿 16:52
6号 新宿 16:56
RRMMMBL
I'm just the guy she dumped two years ago.
Forget it, just forget it.
I already know I'll end up feeling miserable.
...Yeah.
tmp tmp

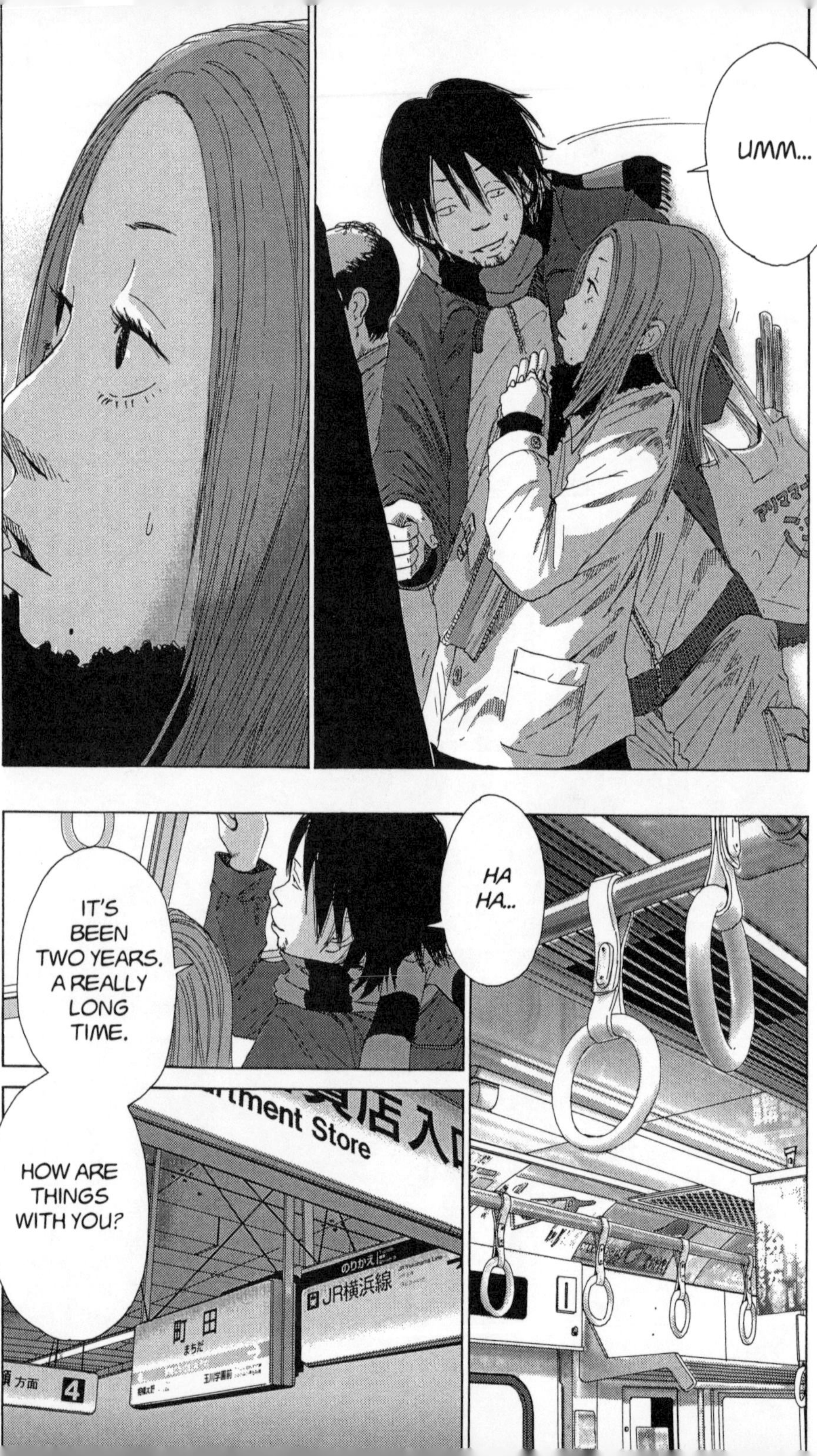
UMM...
HA HA...
IT'S BEEN TWO YEARS. A REALLY LONG TIME.
HOW ARE THINGS WITH YOU?
rtment Store
のりかえ
JR横浜線
町田
まちだ
方面
4

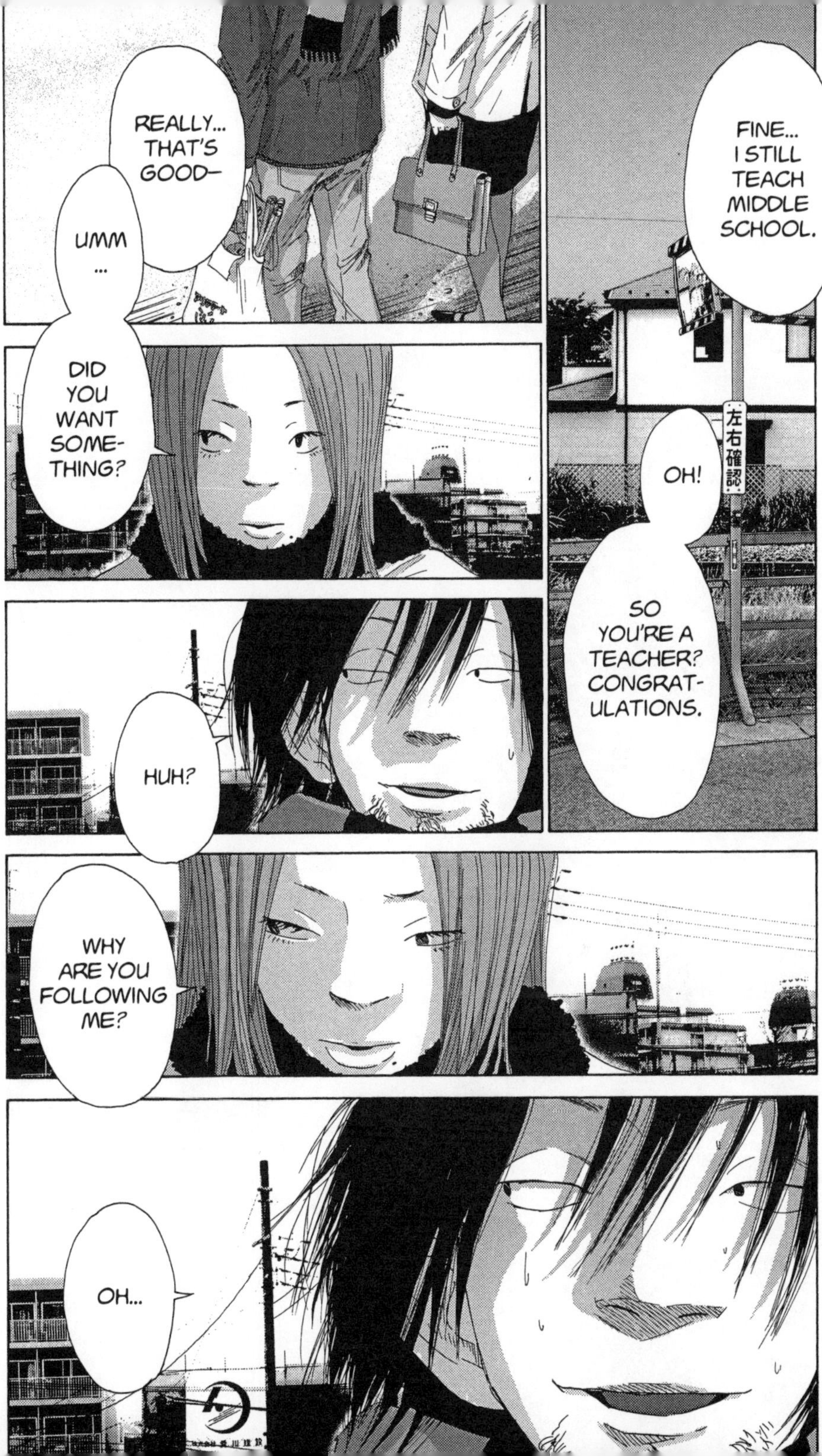
FINE... I STILL TEACH MIDDLE SCHOOL.
左右確認
OH!
SO YOU'RE A TEACHER? CONGRAT-ULATIONS.
REALLY... THAT'S GOOD—
UMM ...
DID YOU WANT SOME-THING?
HUH?
WHY ARE YOU FOLLOWING ME?
OH...

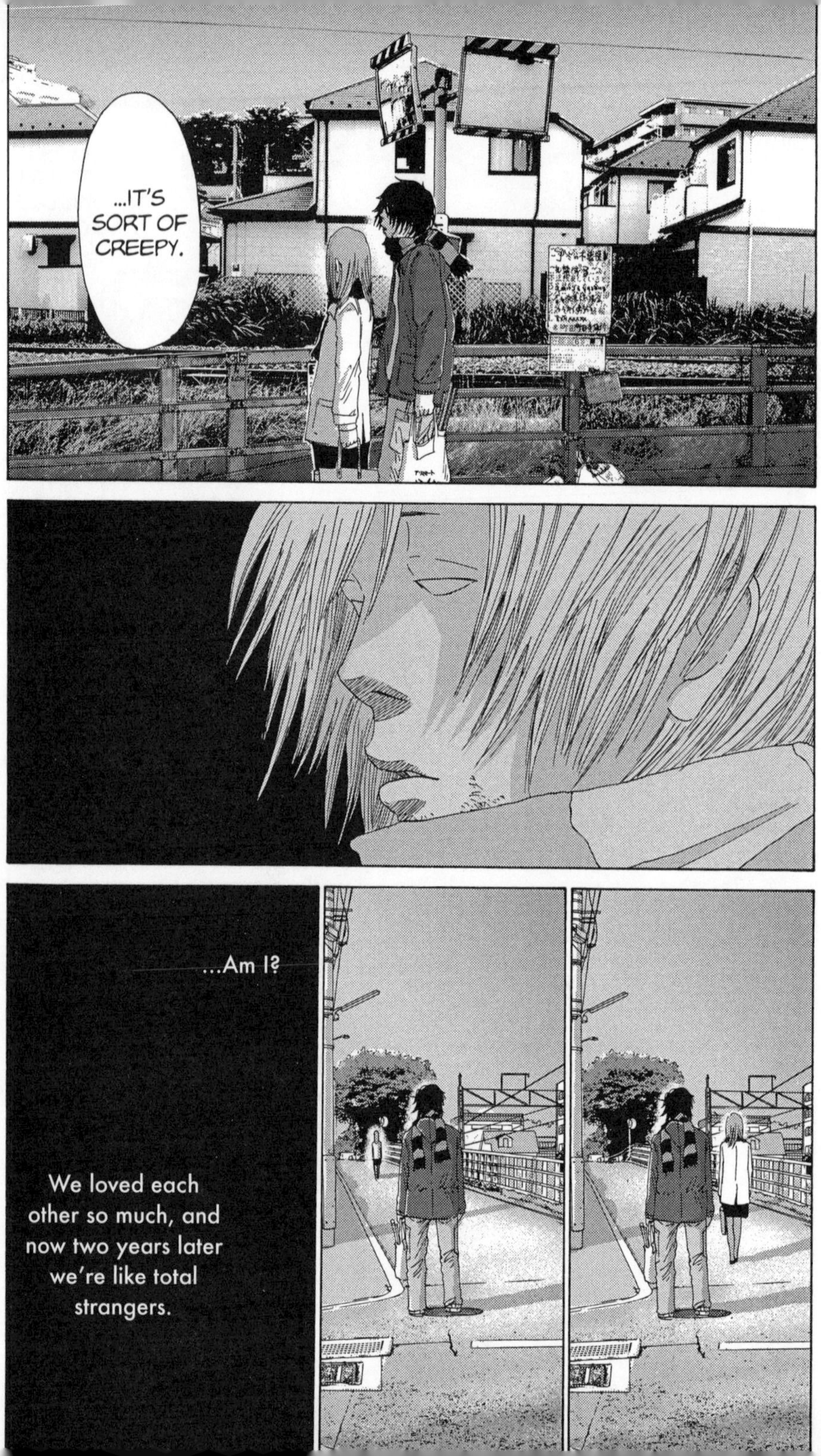
...IT'S SORT OF CREEPY.
...Am I?
We loved each other so much, and now two years later we're like total strangers.

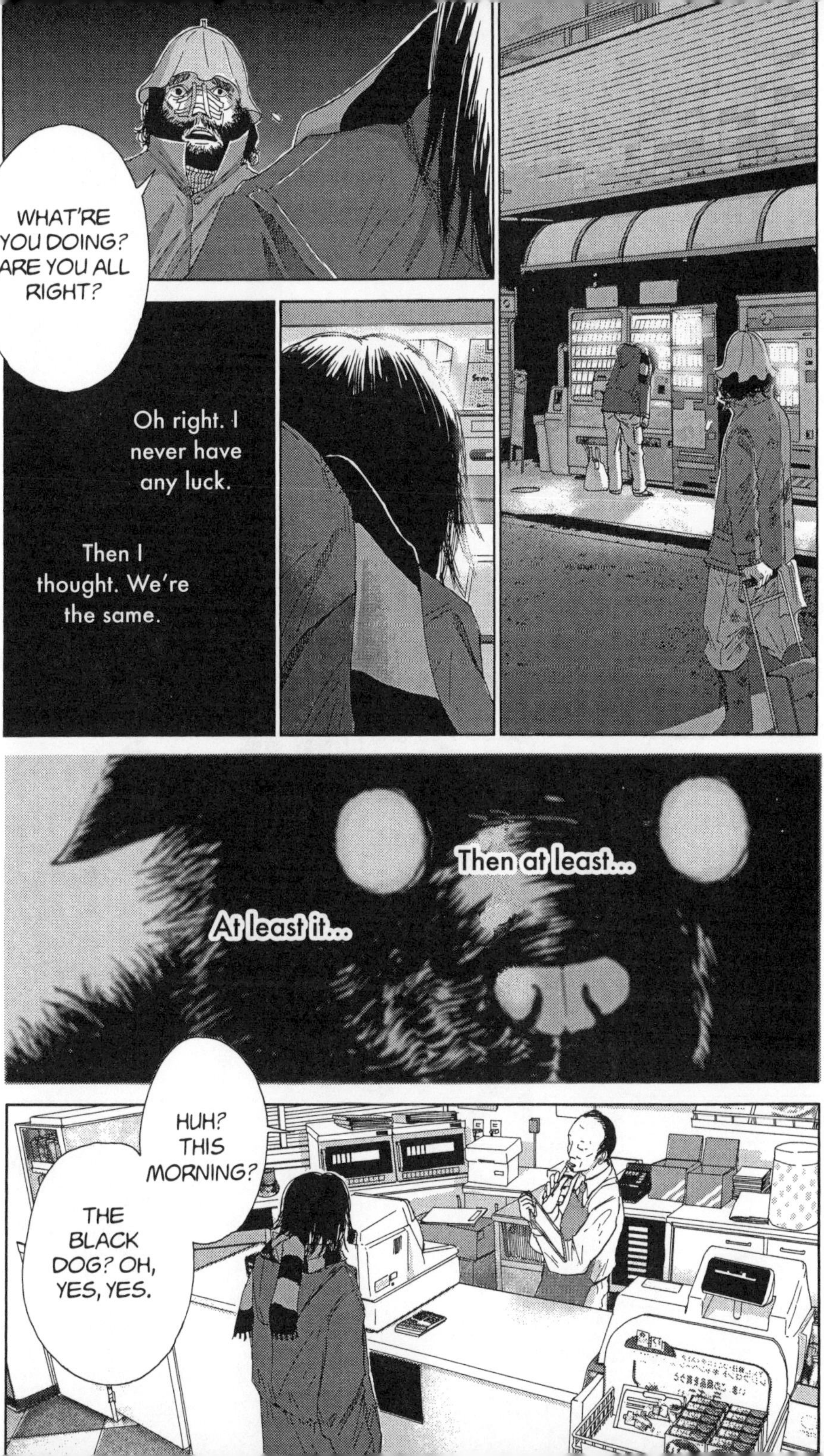
WHAT'RE YOU DOING? ARE YOU ALL RIGHT?
Oh right. I never have any luck.
Then I thought. We're the same.
Then at least...
At least it...
HUH? THIS MORNING?
THE BLACK DOG? OH, YES, YES.

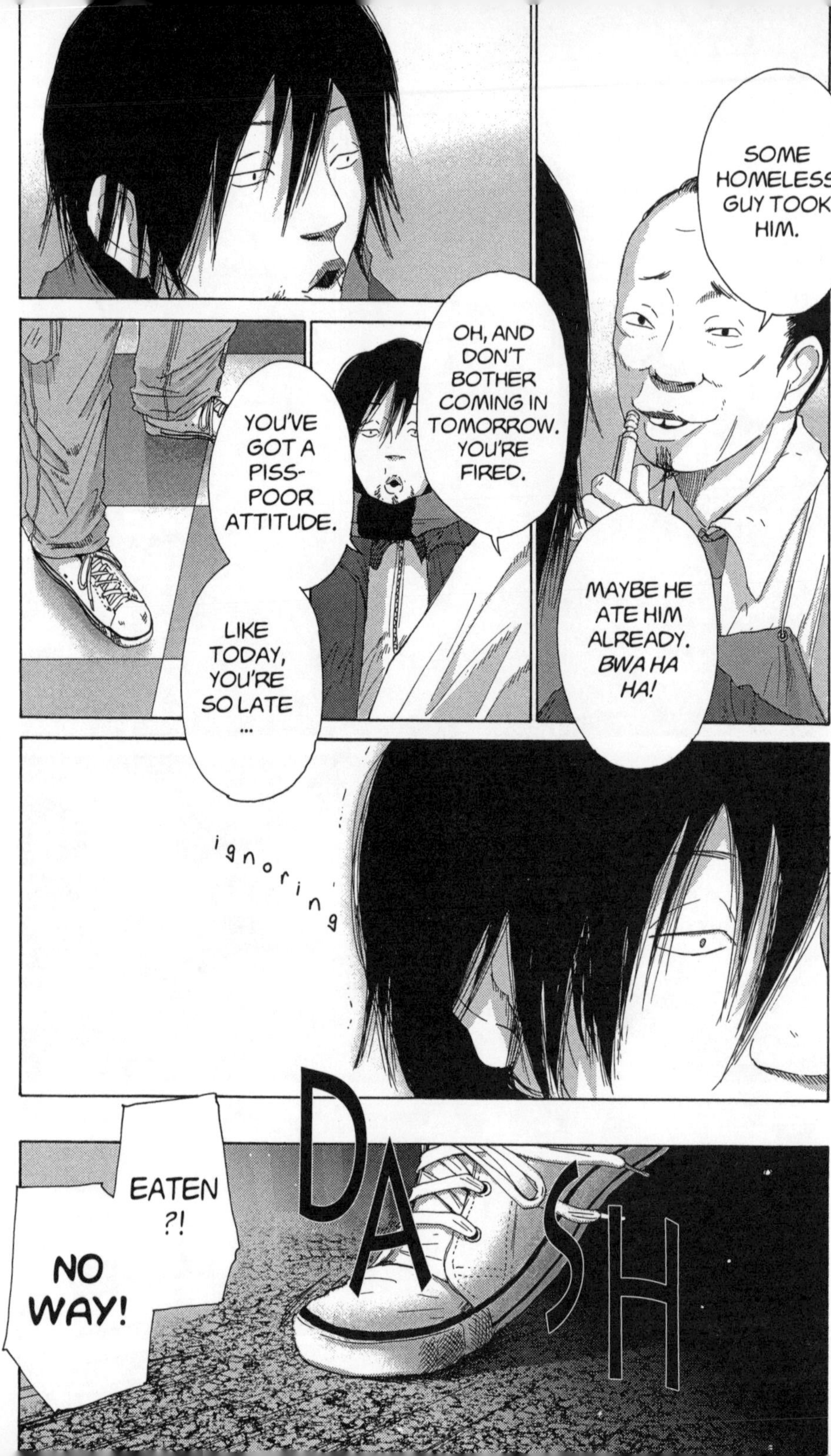
SOME HOMELESS GUY TOOK HIM.
MAYBE HE ATE HIM ALREADY. *BWA HA HA!*
OH, AND DON'T BOTHER COMING IN TOMORROW. YOU'RE FIRED.
YOU'VE GOT A PISS-POOR ATTITUDE.
LIKE TODAY, YOU'RE SO LATE ...
ignoring
DASH
EATEN ?!
NO WAY!

LIVE!

LIVE!

YOU'VE GOTTA LIVE NO MATTER WHAT THE COST!

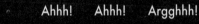

Ahhh!    Ahhh!    Argghhh!

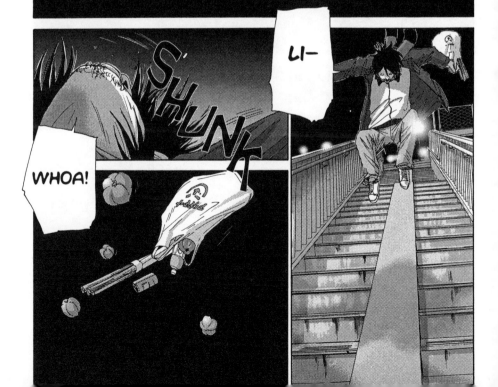

LI—

SHUNK

WHOA!

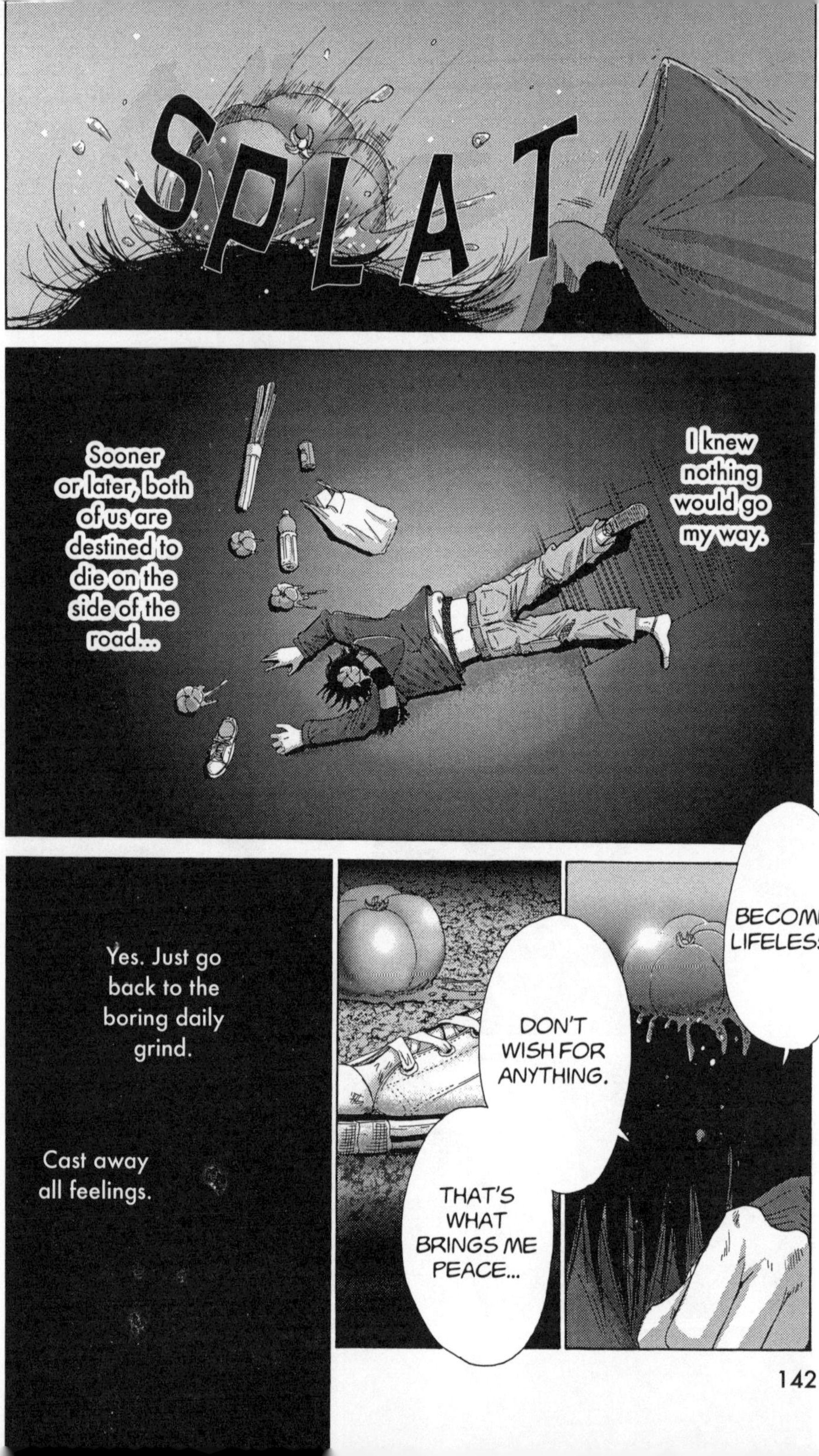
SPLAT
I knew nothing would go my way.
Sooner or later, both of us are destined to die on the side of the road...
BECOME LIFELESS.
DON'T WISH FOR ANYTHING.
THAT'S WHAT BRINGS ME PEACE...
Yes. Just go back to the boring daily grind.
Cast away all feelings.

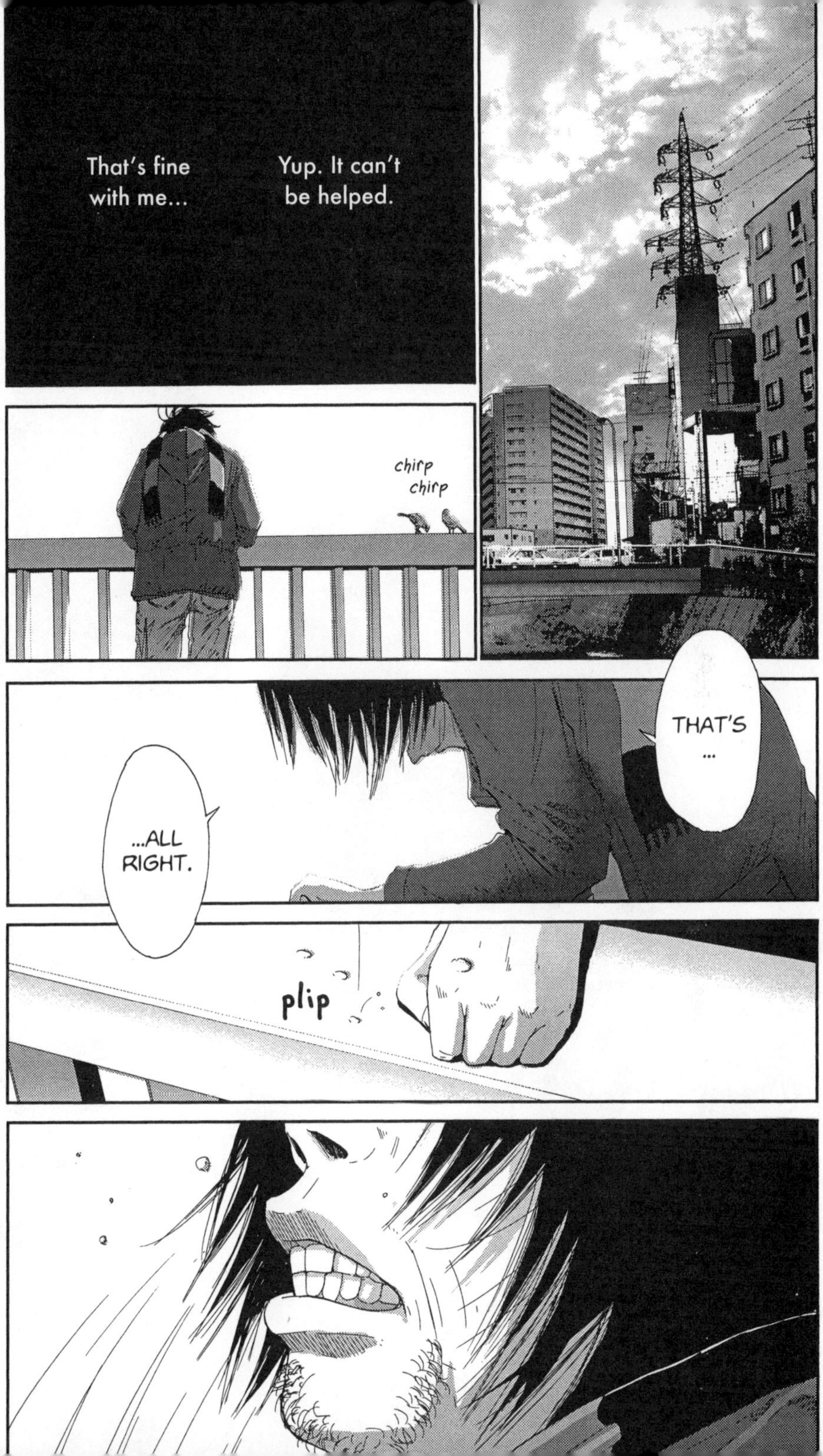
Yup. It can't be helped.
That's fine with me...
chirp chirp
THAT'S...
...ALL RIGHT.
plip

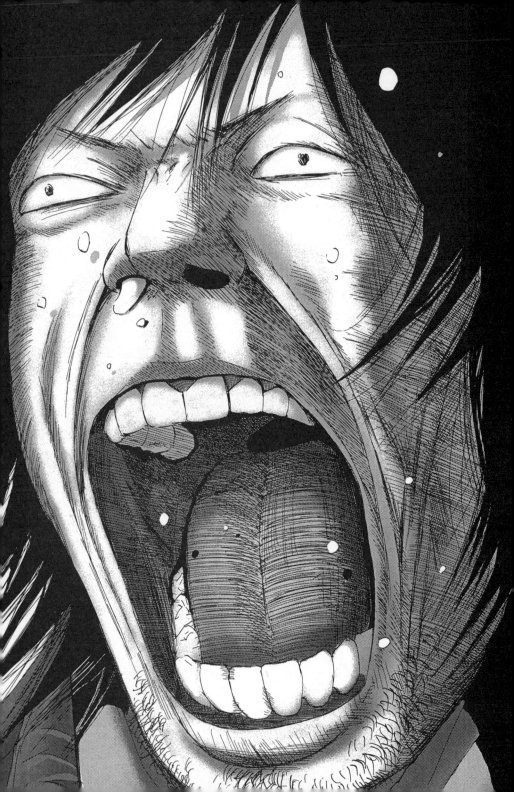

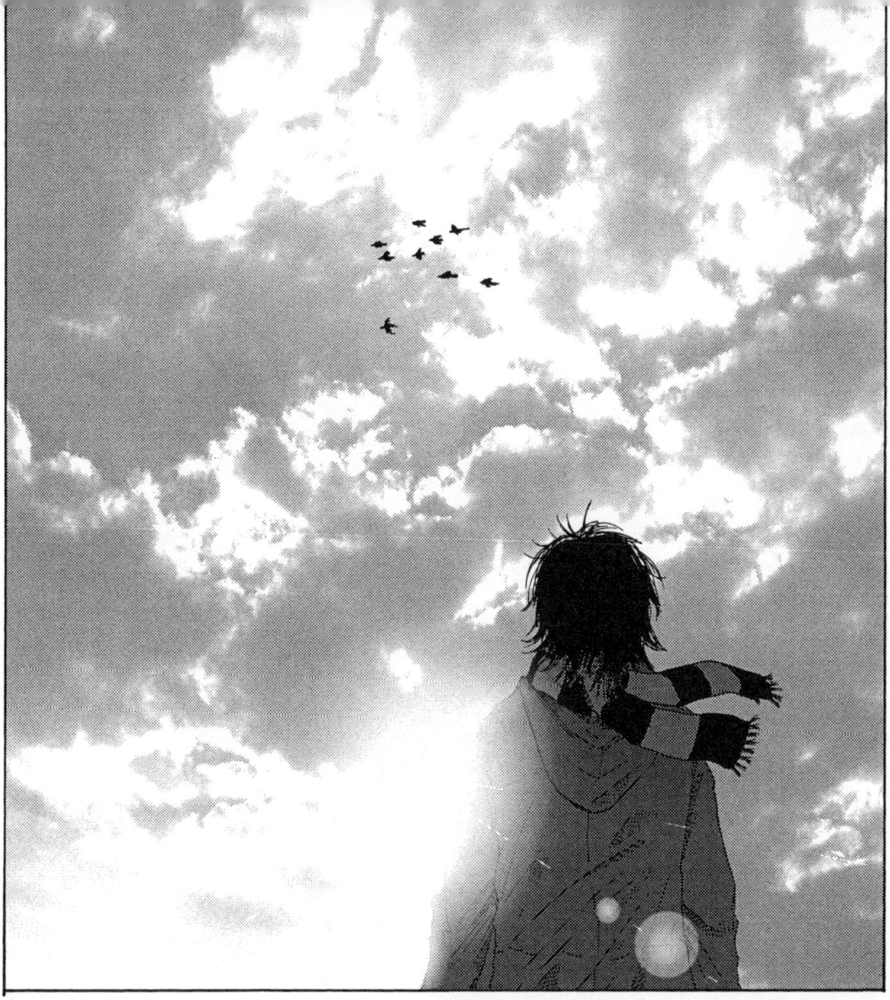

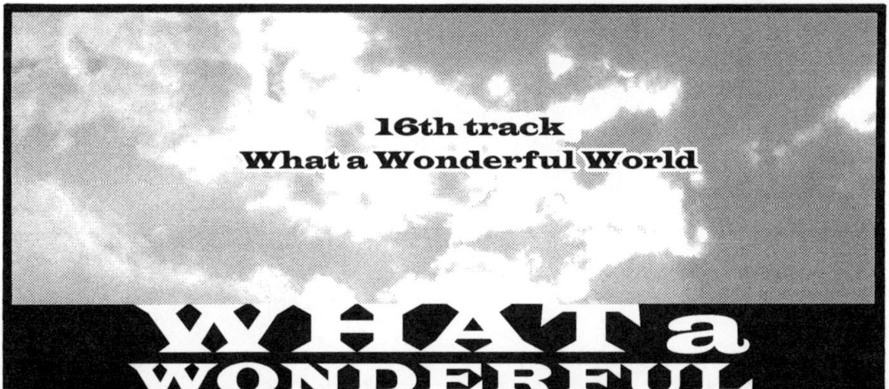
16th track
What a Wonderful World
WHAT a
WONDERFUL
WORLD!

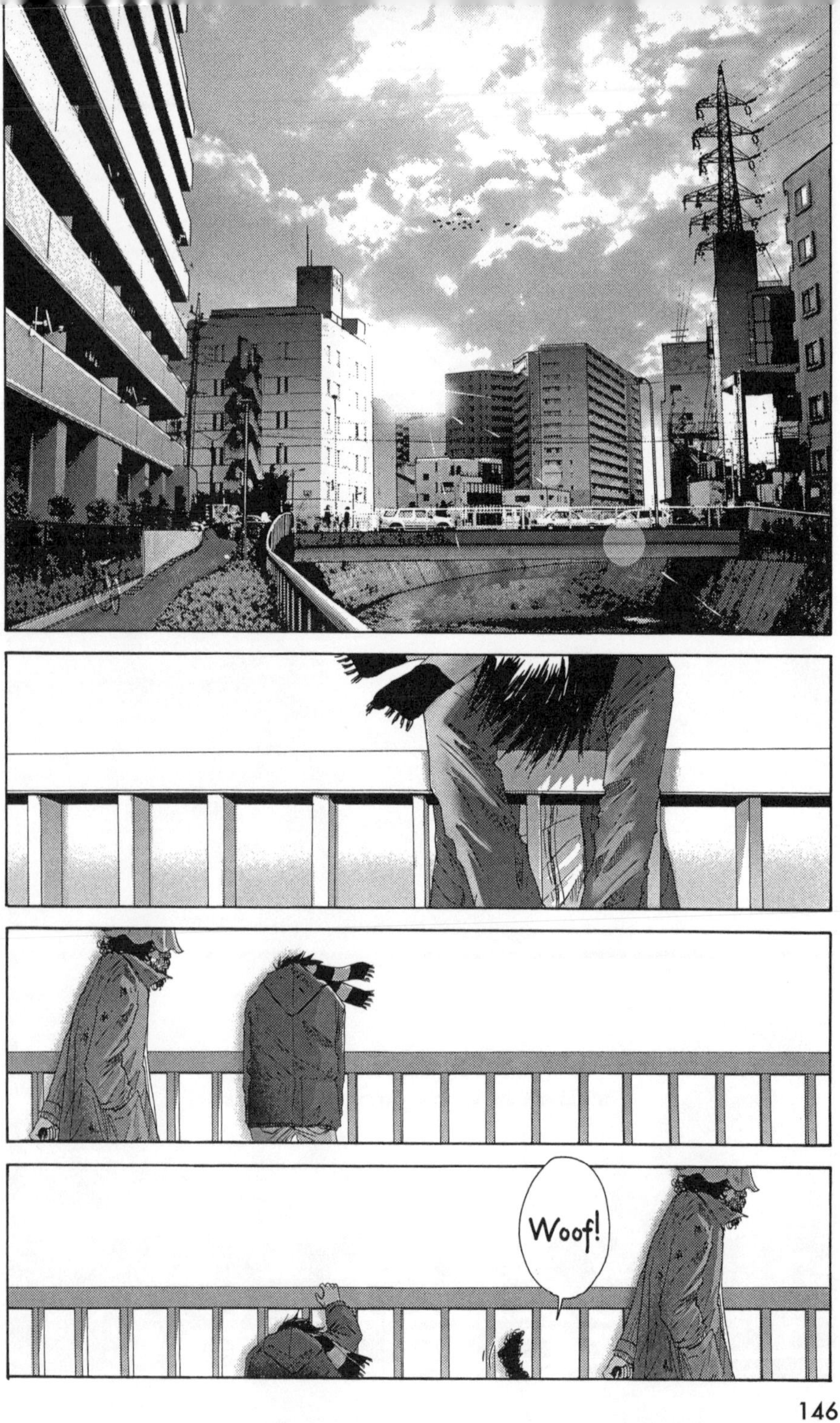
Woof!

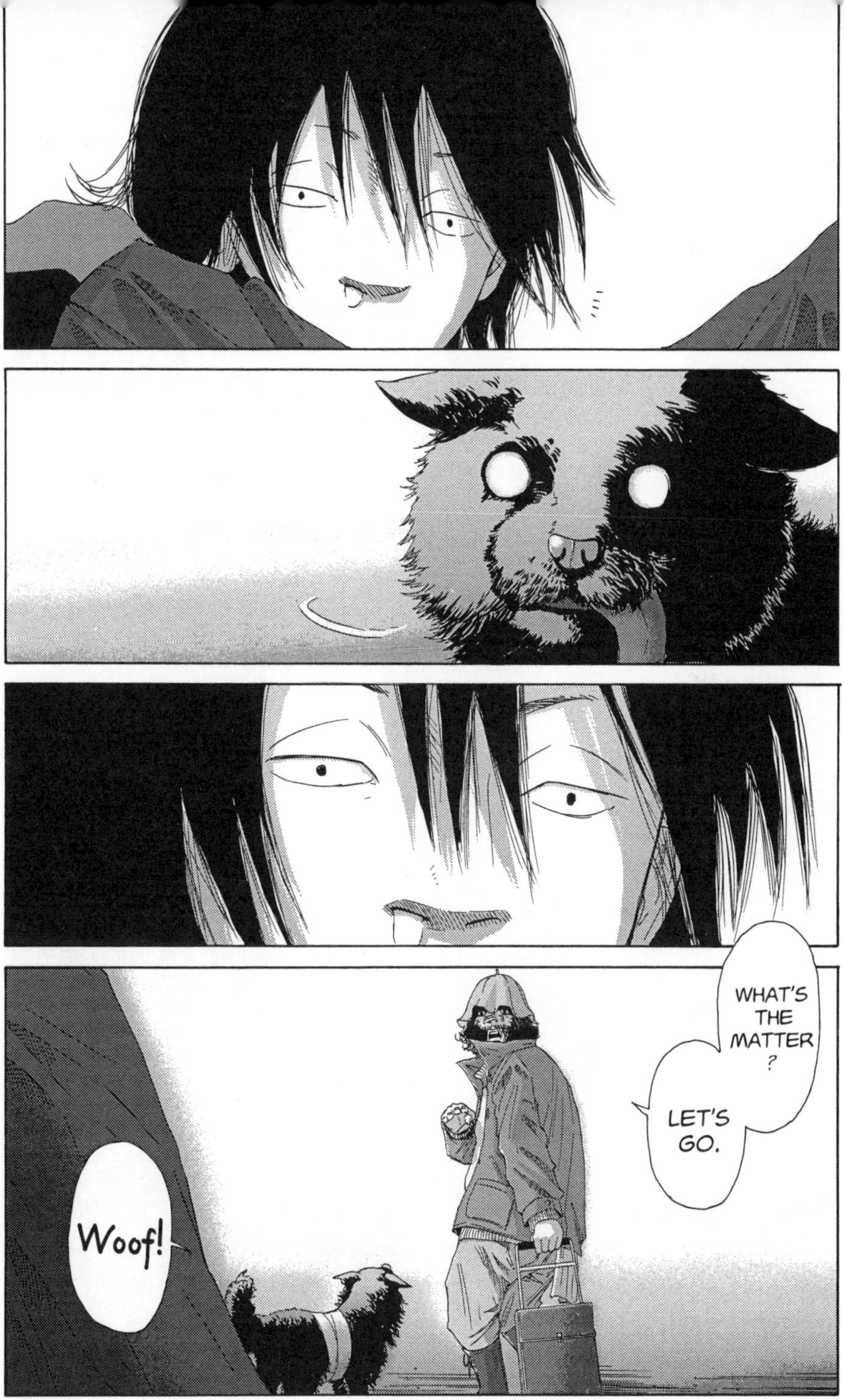
WHAT'S THE MATTER?
LET'S GO.
Woof!

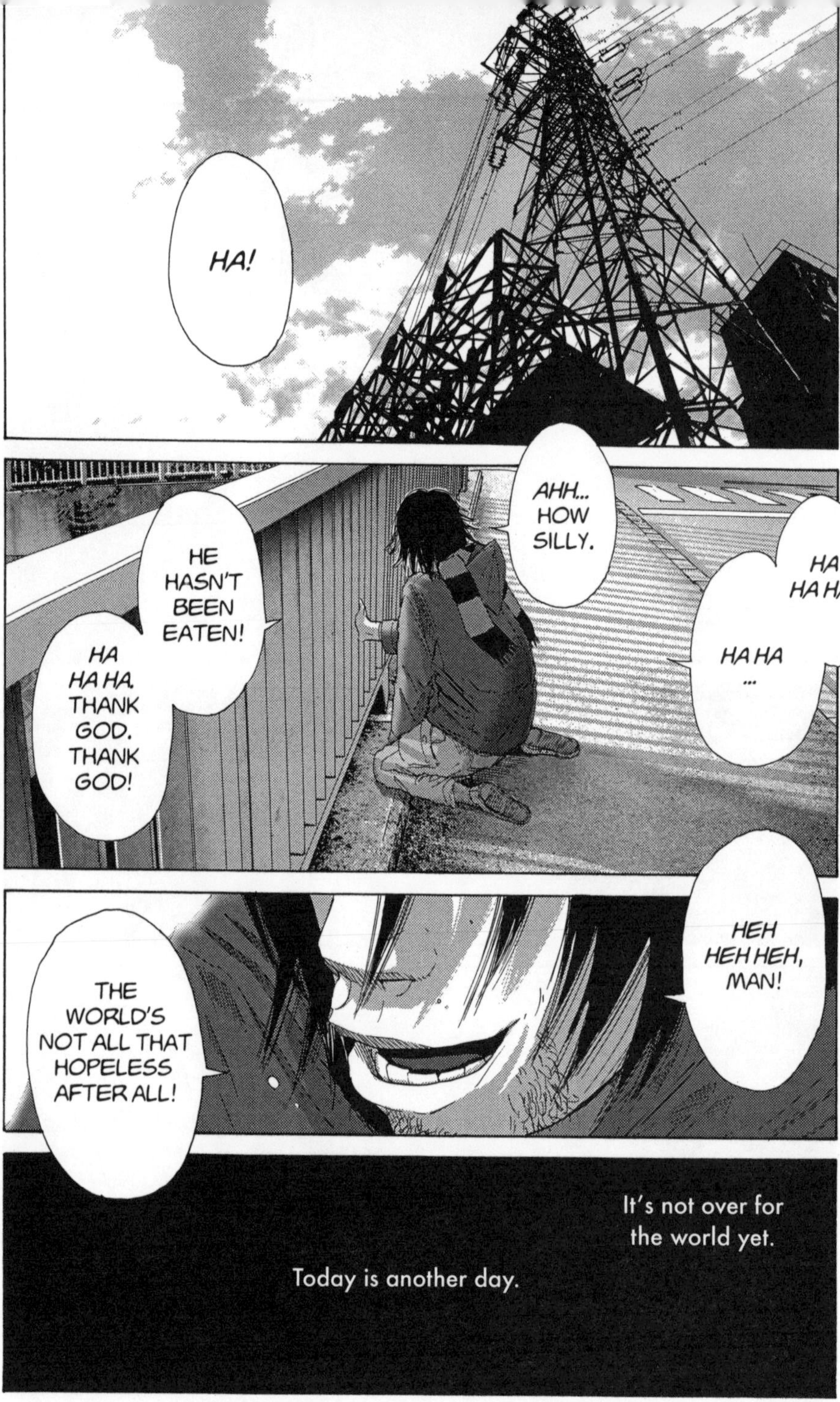
HA!
HA HA HA!
HA HA ...
AHH... HOW SILLY.
HE HASN'T BEEN EATEN!
HA HA HA. THANK GOD. THANK GOD!
HEH HEH HEH, MAN!
THE WORLD'S NOT ALL THAT HOPELESS AFTER ALL!
It's not over for the world yet.
Today is another day.

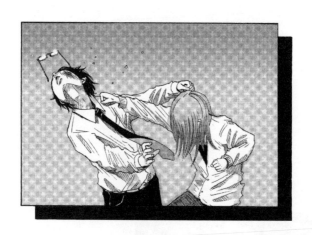

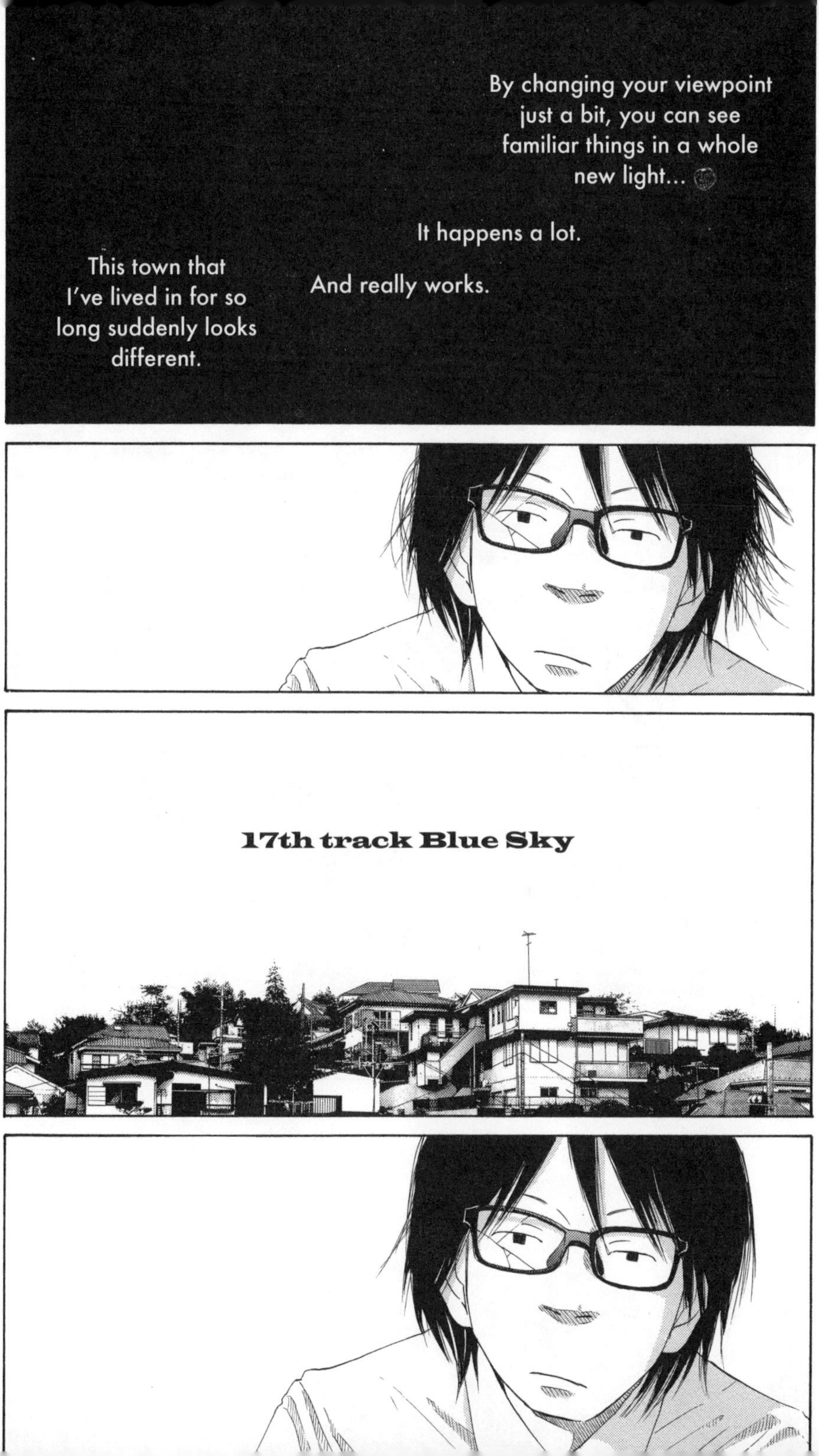
By changing your viewpoint just a bit, you can see familiar things in a whole new light...
It happens a lot.
And really works.
This town that I've lived in for so long suddenly looks different.
17th track Blue Sky

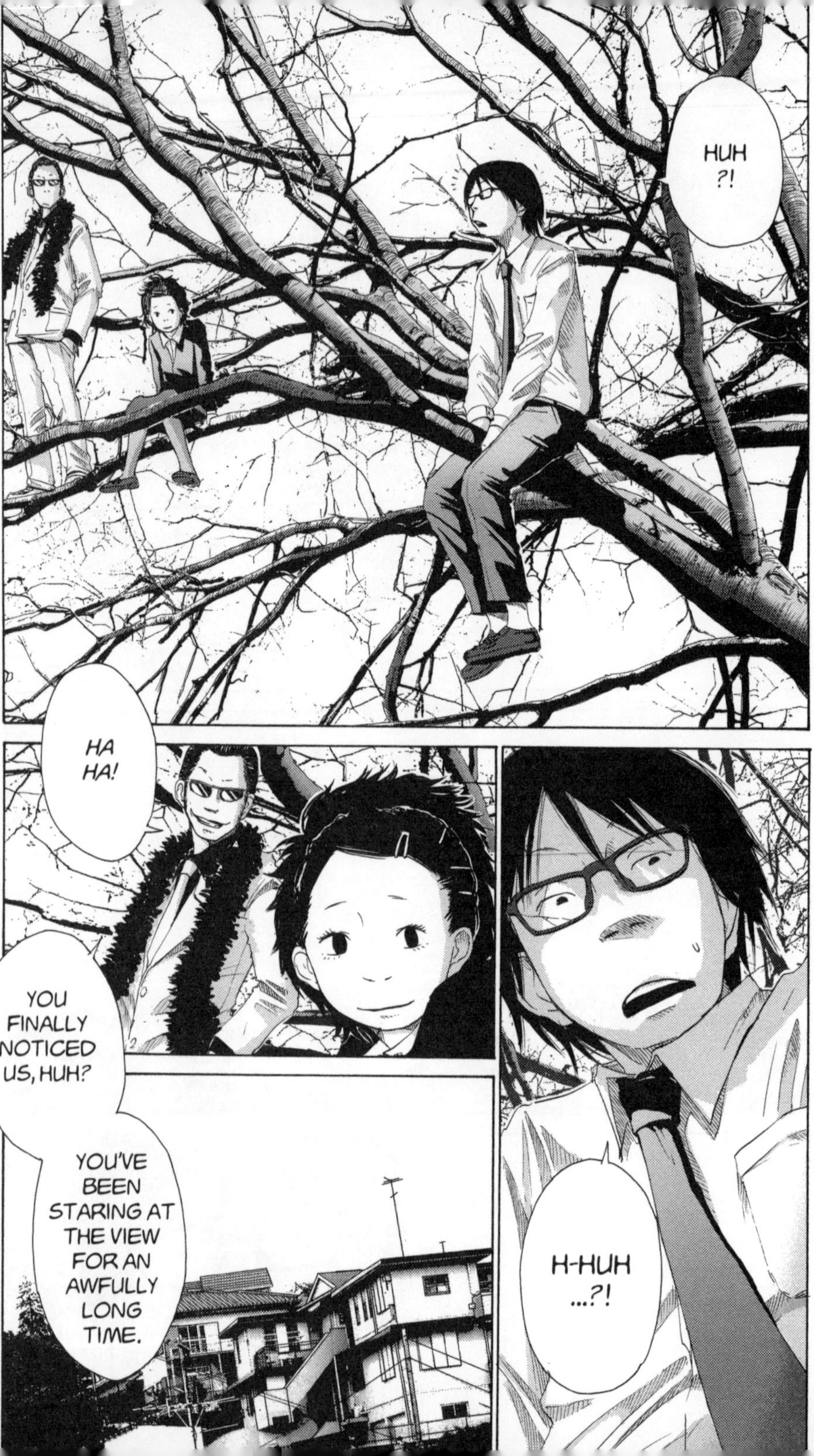
HUH ?!
H-HUH ...?!
HA HA!
YOU FINALLY NOTICED US, HUH?
YOU'VE BEEN STARING AT THE VIEW FOR AN AWFULLY LONG TIME.

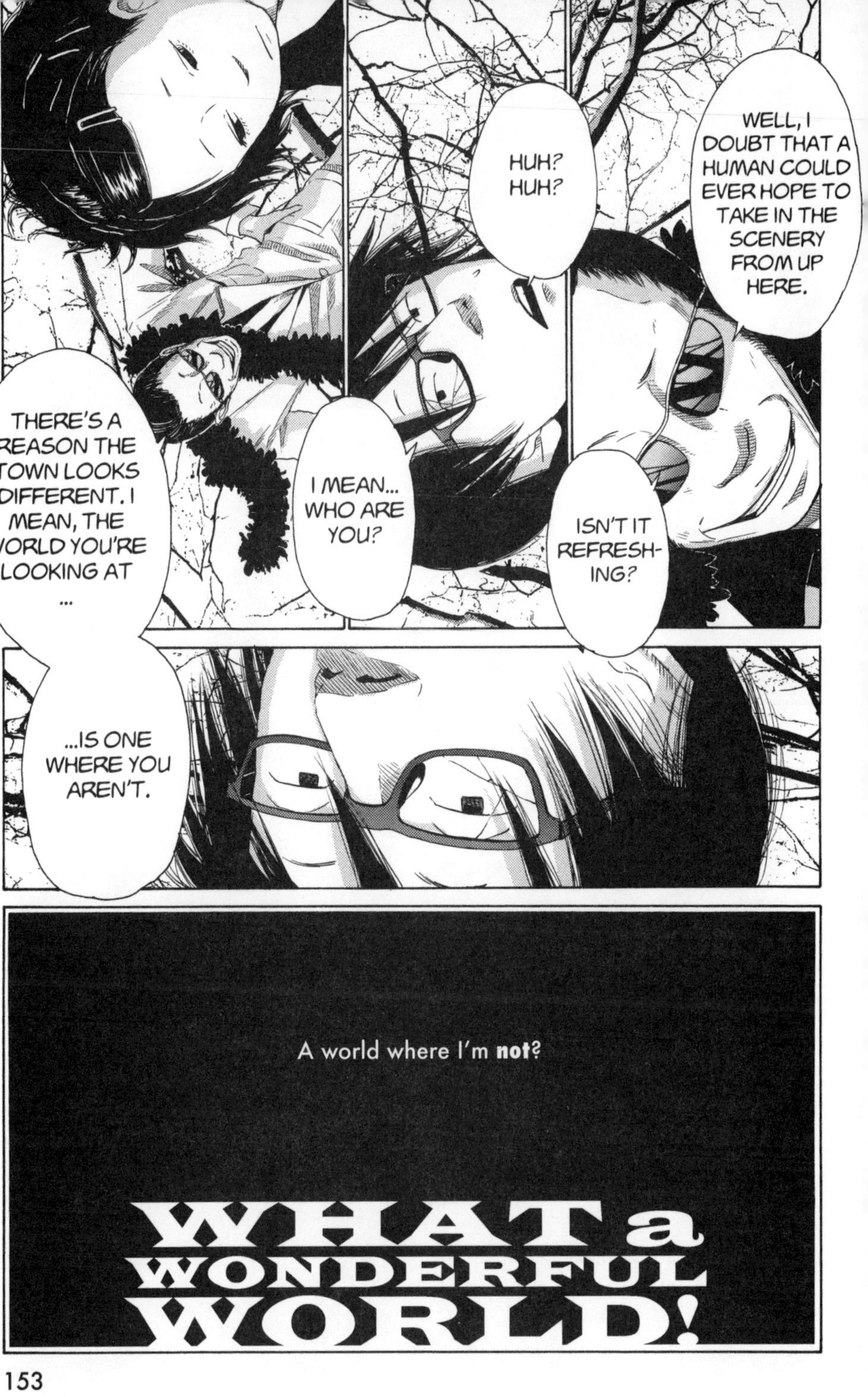
WELL, I DOUBT THAT A HUMAN COULD EVER HOPE TO TAKE IN THE SCENERY FROM UP HERE.
ISN'T IT REFRESHING?
HUH? HUH?
I MEAN... WHO ARE YOU?
THERE'S A REASON THE TOWN LOOKS DIFFERENT. I MEAN, THE WORLD YOU'RE LOOKING AT ...
...IS ONE WHERE YOU AREN'T.

A world where I'm **not**?

# WHAT a WONDERFUL WORLD!

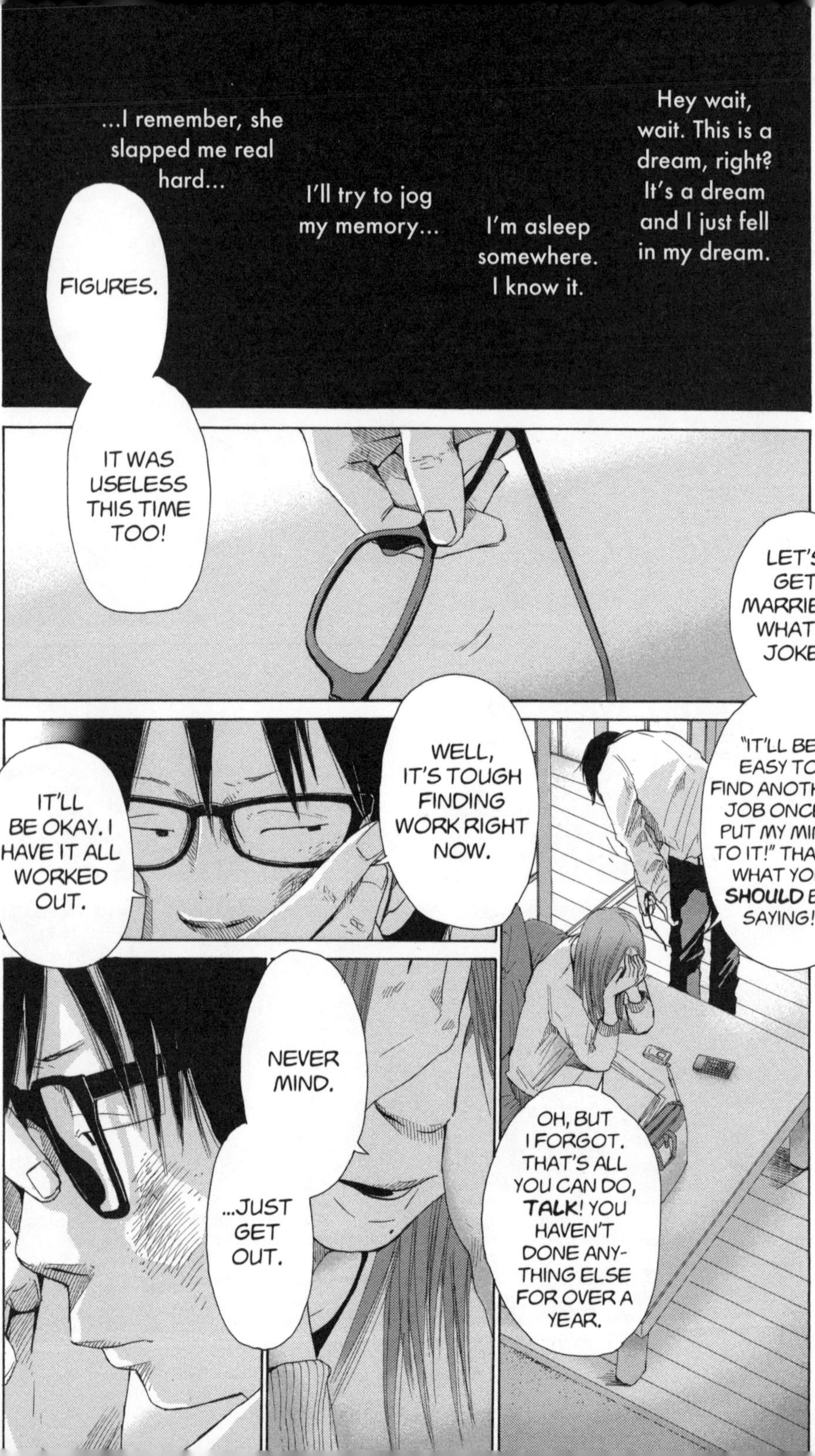
Hey wait, wait. This is a dream, right? It's a dream and I just fell in my dream.
I'm asleep somewhere. I know it.
I'll try to jog my memory...
...I remember, she slapped me real hard...
FIGURES.
LET'S GET MARRIED? WHAT A JOKE!
IT WAS USELESS THIS TIME TOO!
"IT'LL BE EASY TO FIND ANOTHER JOB ONCE I PUT MY MIND TO IT!" THAT'S WHAT YOU **SHOULD** BE SAYING!
OH, BUT I FORGOT. THAT'S ALL YOU CAN DO, **TALK**! YOU HAVEN'T DONE ANYTHING ELSE FOR OVER A YEAR.
WELL, IT'S TOUGH FINDING WORK RIGHT NOW.
IT'LL BE OKAY. I HAVE IT ALL WORKED OUT.
NEVER MIND.
...JUST GET OUT.

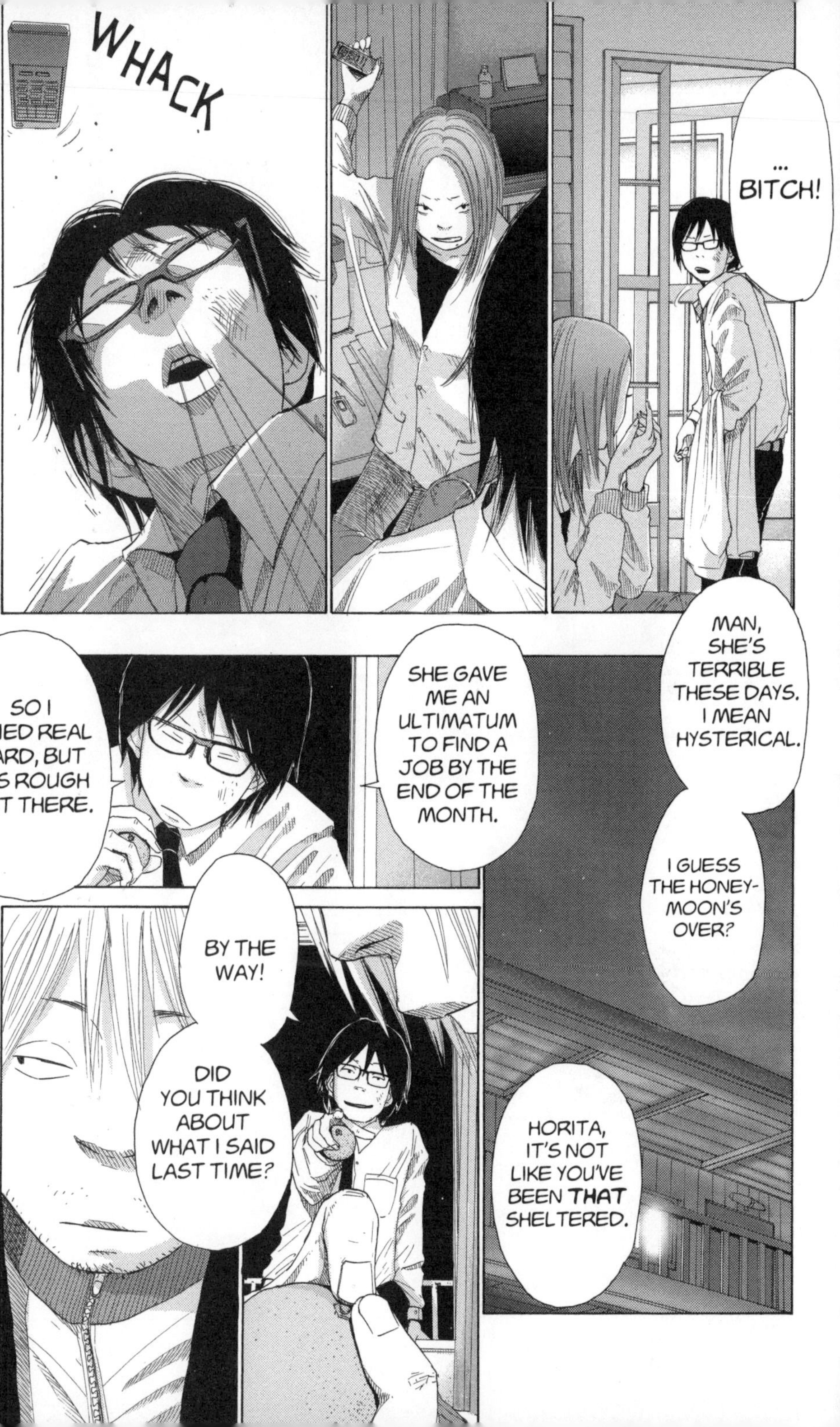
... BITCH!
WHACK
MAN, SHE'S TERRIBLE THESE DAYS. I MEAN HYSTERICAL.
I GUESS THE HONEY-MOON'S OVER?
HORITA, IT'S NOT LIKE YOU'VE BEEN **THAT** SHELTERED.
SHE GAVE ME AN ULTIMATUM TO FIND A JOB BY THE END OF THE MONTH.
SO I TRIED REAL HARD, BUT IT'S ROUGH OUT THERE.
BY THE WAY!
DID YOU THINK ABOUT WHAT I SAID LAST TIME?

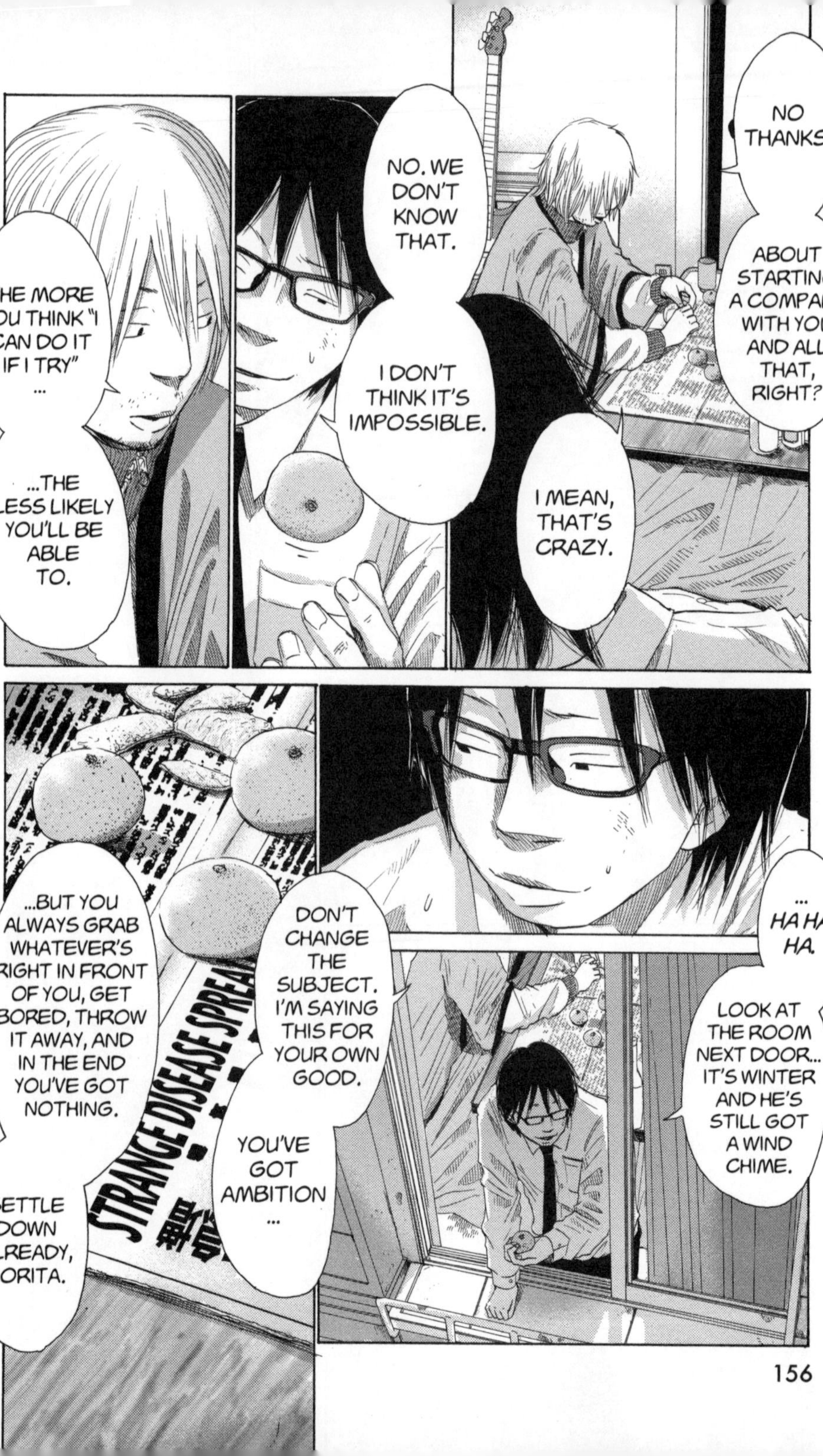
NO THANKS.
ABOUT STARTING A COMPANY WITH YOU AND ALL THAT, RIGHT?
I MEAN, THAT'S CRAZY.
NO. WE DON'T KNOW THAT.
I DON'T THINK IT'S IMPOSSIBLE.
THE MORE YOU THINK "I CAN DO IT IF I TRY" ...
...THE LESS LIKELY YOU'LL BE ABLE TO.
... HA HA HA.
LOOK AT THE ROOM NEXT DOOR... IT'S WINTER AND HE'S STILL GOT A WIND CHIME.
DON'T CHANGE THE SUBJECT. I'M SAYING THIS FOR YOUR OWN GOOD.
YOU'VE GOT AMBITION ...
...BUT YOU ALWAYS GRAB WHATEVER'S RIGHT IN FRONT OF YOU, GET BORED, THROW IT AWAY, AND IN THE END YOU'VE GOT NOTHING.
SETTLE DOWN ALREADY, HORITA.
STRANGE DISEASE SPREA

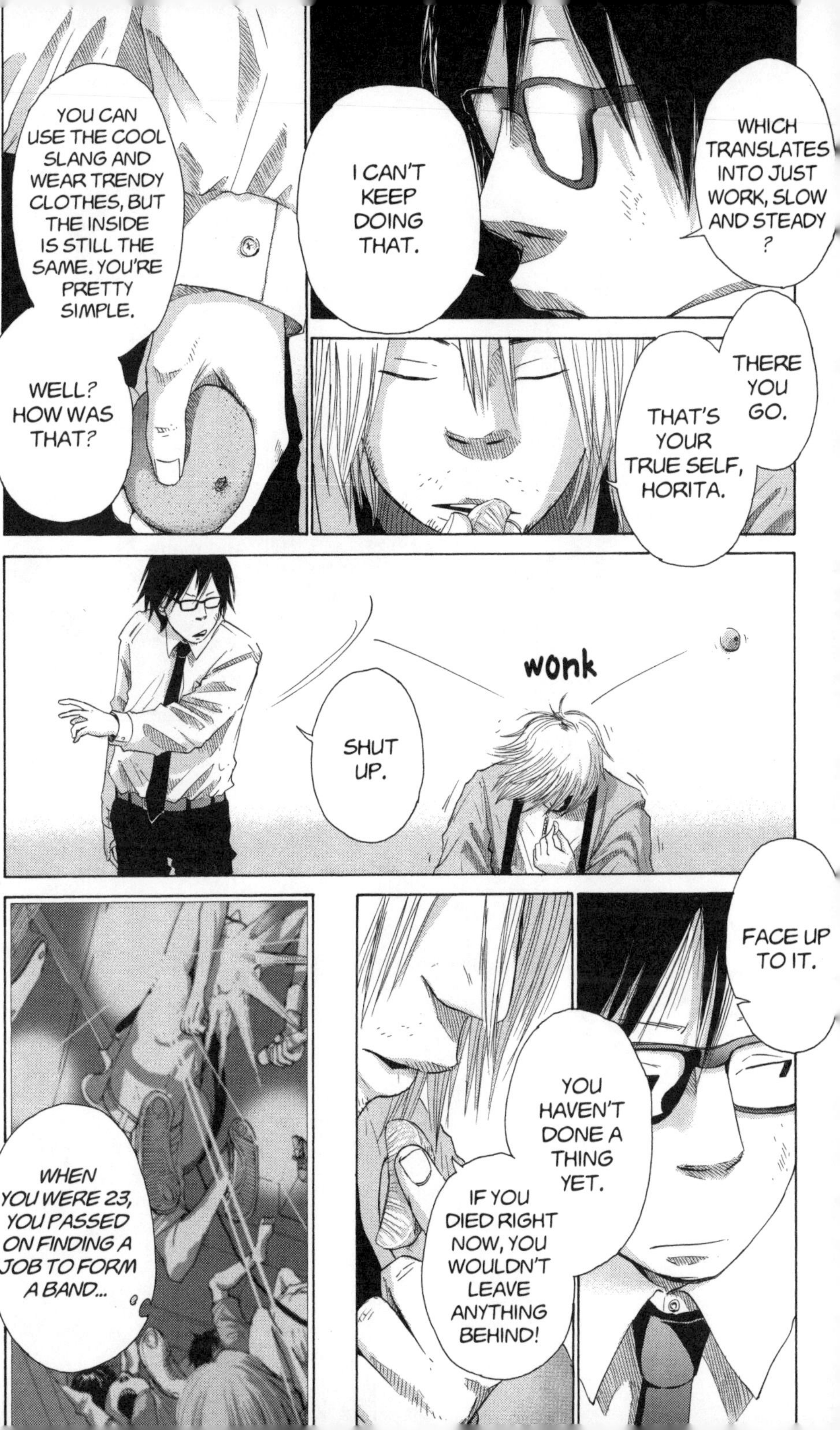
WHICH TRANSLATES INTO JUST WORK, SLOW AND STEADY?
I CAN'T KEEP DOING THAT.
THERE YOU GO.
THAT'S YOUR TRUE SELF, HORITA.
YOU CAN USE THE COOL SLANG AND WEAR TRENDY CLOTHES, BUT THE INSIDE IS STILL THE SAME. YOU'RE PRETTY SIMPLE.
WELL? HOW WAS THAT?
wonk
SHUT UP.
FACE UP TO IT.
YOU HAVEN'T DONE A THING YET.
IF YOU DIED RIGHT NOW, YOU WOULDN'T LEAVE ANYTHING BEHIND!
WHEN YOU WERE 23, YOU PASSED ON FINDING A JOB TO FORM A BAND...

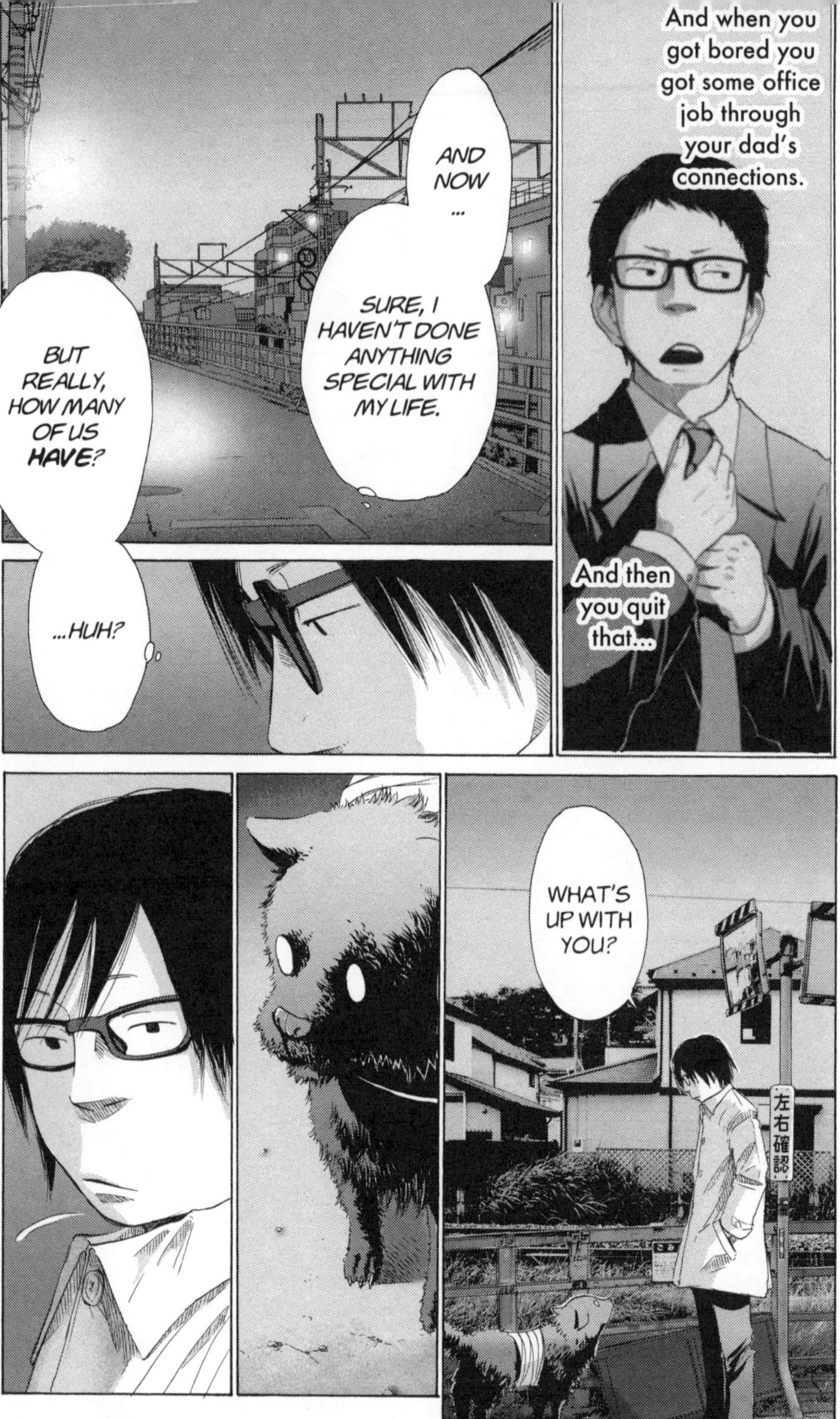
And when you got bored you got some office job through your dad's connections.
And then you quit that...
AND NOW ...
SURE, I HAVEN'T DONE ANYTHING SPECIAL WITH MY LIFE.
BUT REALLY, HOW MANY OF US **HAVE**?
...HUH?
WHAT'S UP WITH YOU?
左右確認

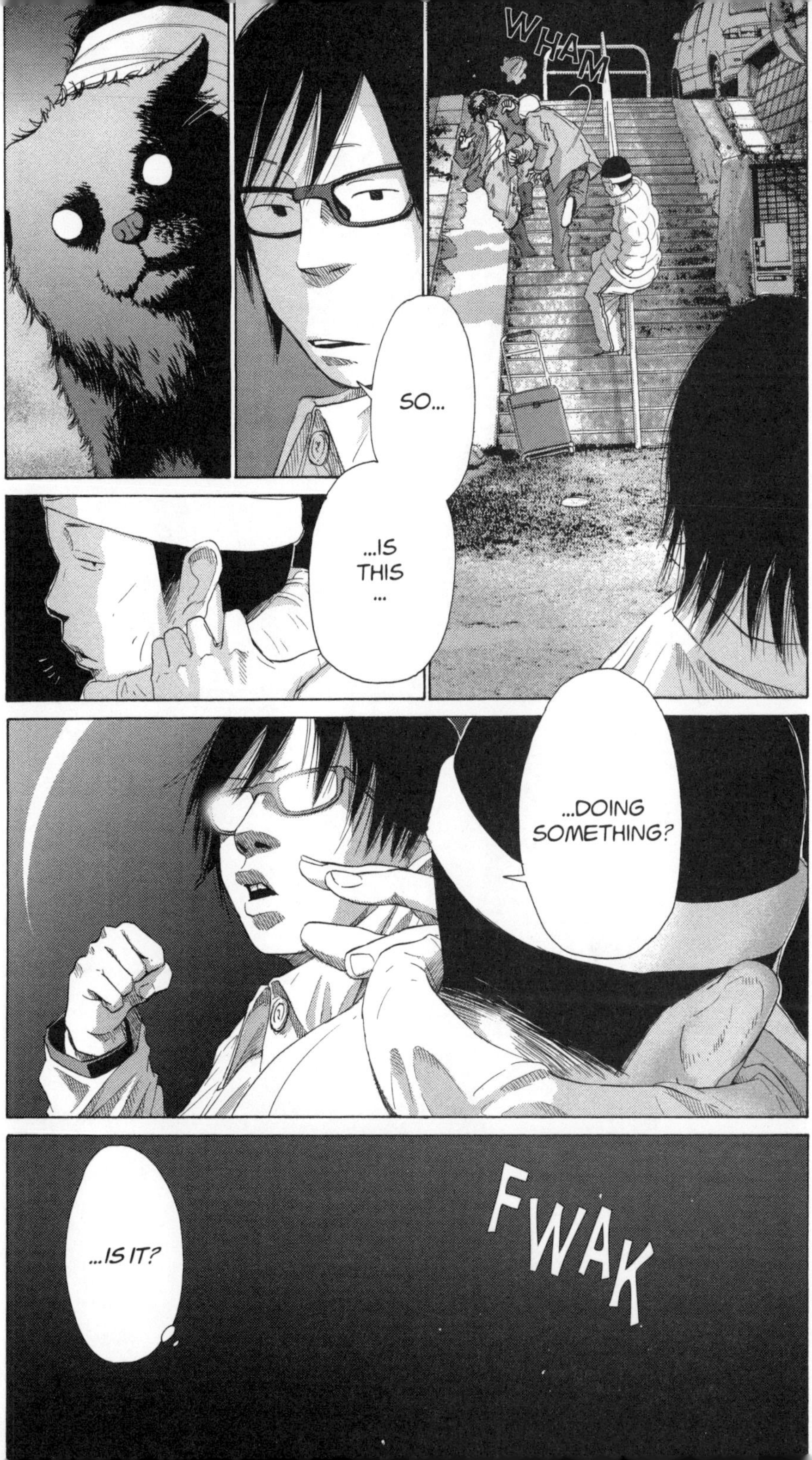
WHAM
SO...
...IS THIS ...
...DOING SOMETHING?
FWAK
...IS IT?

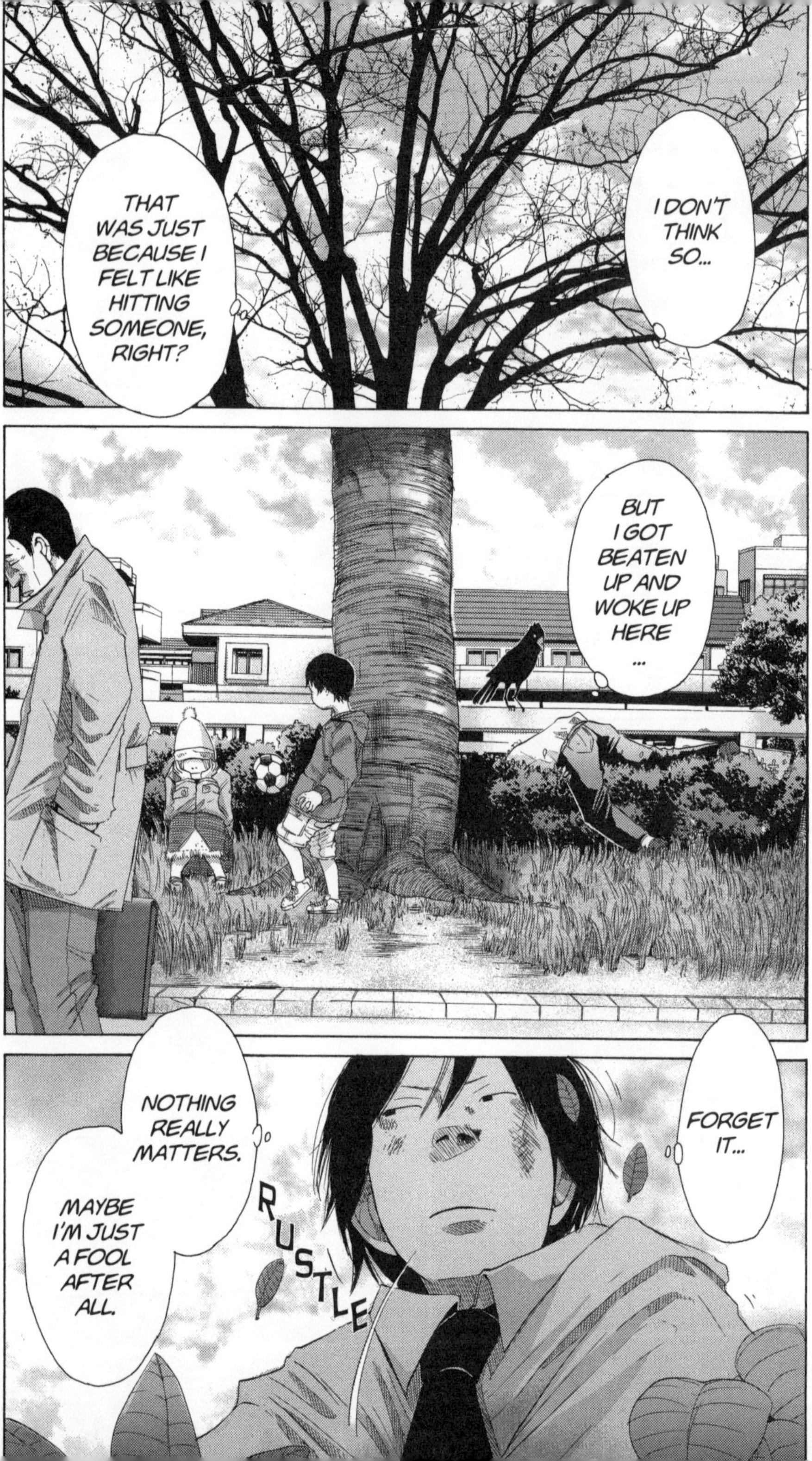
I DON'T THINK SO...
THAT WAS JUST BECAUSE I FELT LIKE HITTING SOMEONE, RIGHT?
BUT I GOT BEATEN UP AND WOKE UP HERE ...
FORGET IT...
NOTHING REALLY MATTERS.
RUSTLE
MAYBE I'M JUST A FOOL AFTER ALL.

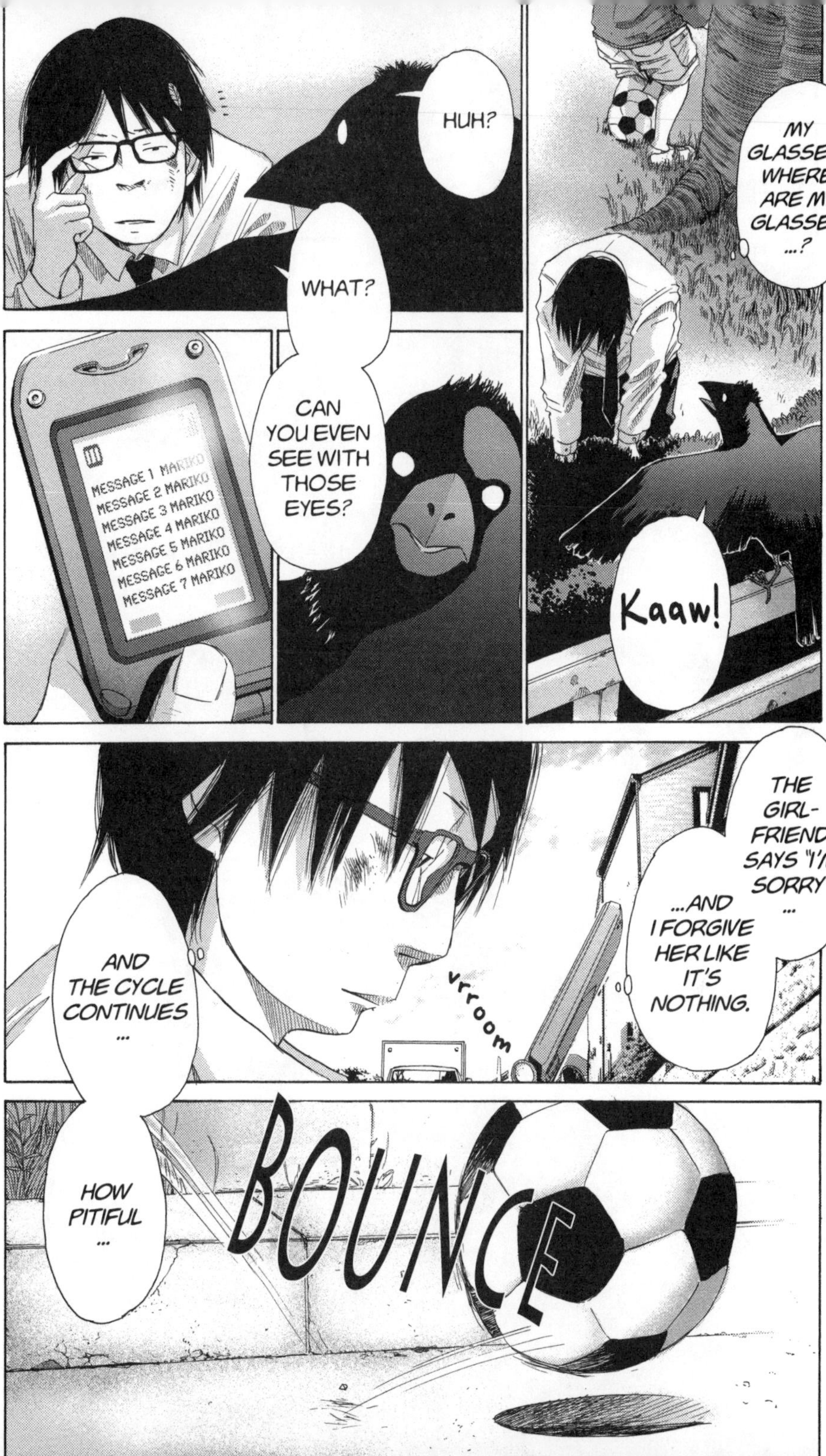
MY GLASSES, WHERE ARE MY GLASSES ...?
Kaaw!
HUH?
WHAT?
CAN YOU EVEN SEE WITH THOSE EYES?
MESSAGE 1 MARIKO
MESSAGE 2 MARIKO
MESSAGE 3 MARIKO
MESSAGE 4 MARIKO
MESSAGE 5 MARIKO
MESSAGE 6 MARIKO
MESSAGE 7 MARIKO
THE GIRL-FRIEND SAYS "I'M SORRY" ...
...AND I FORGIVE HER LIKE IT'S NOTHING.
vrroom
AND THE CYCLE CONTINUES ...
HOW PITIFUL ...
BOUNCE

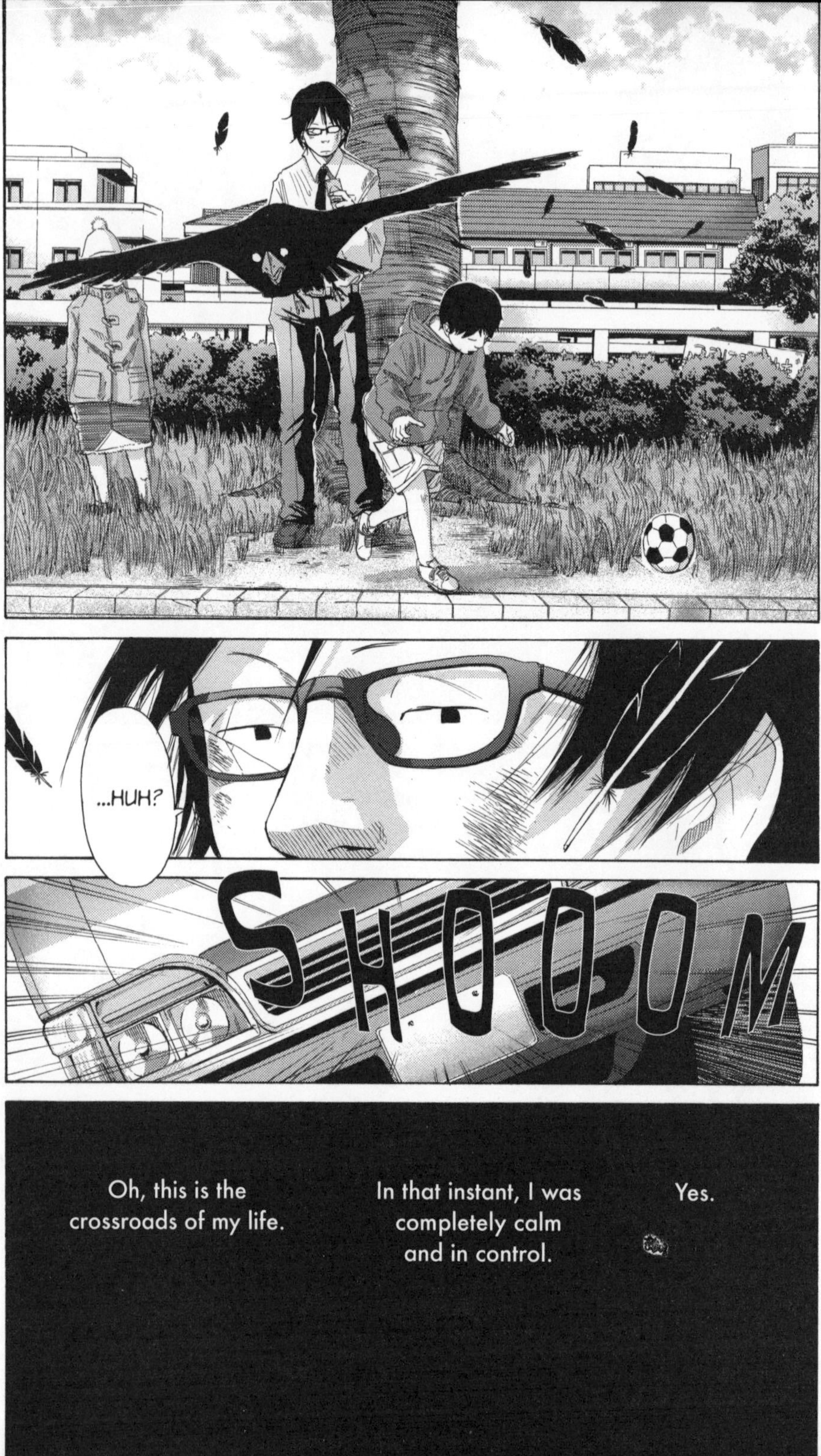
...HUH?
SHOOOM
Yes.
In that instant, I was completely calm and in control.
Oh, this is the crossroads of my life.

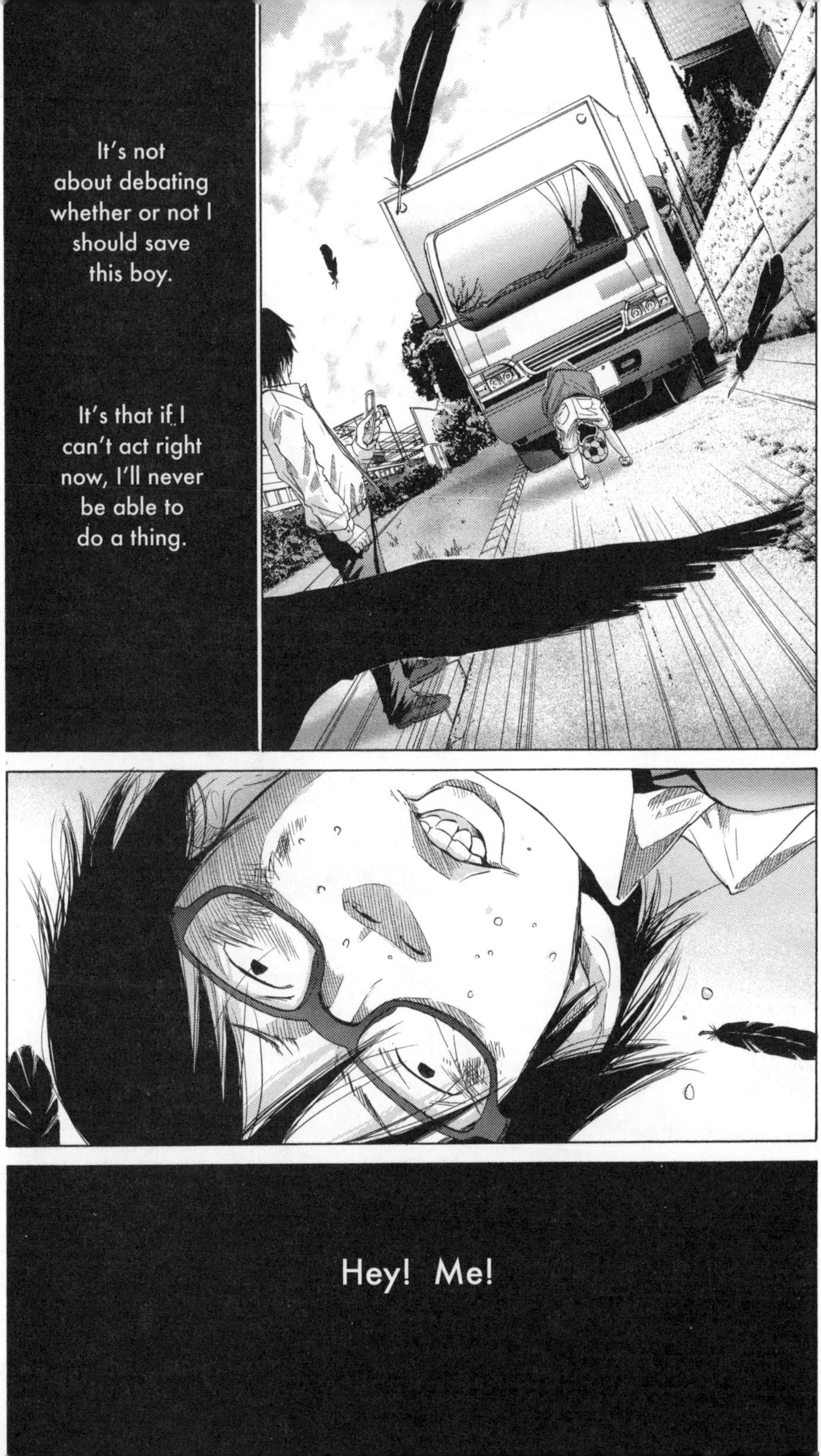
It's not about debating whether or not I should save this boy.
It's that if I can't act right now, I'll never be able to do a thing.
Hey! Me!

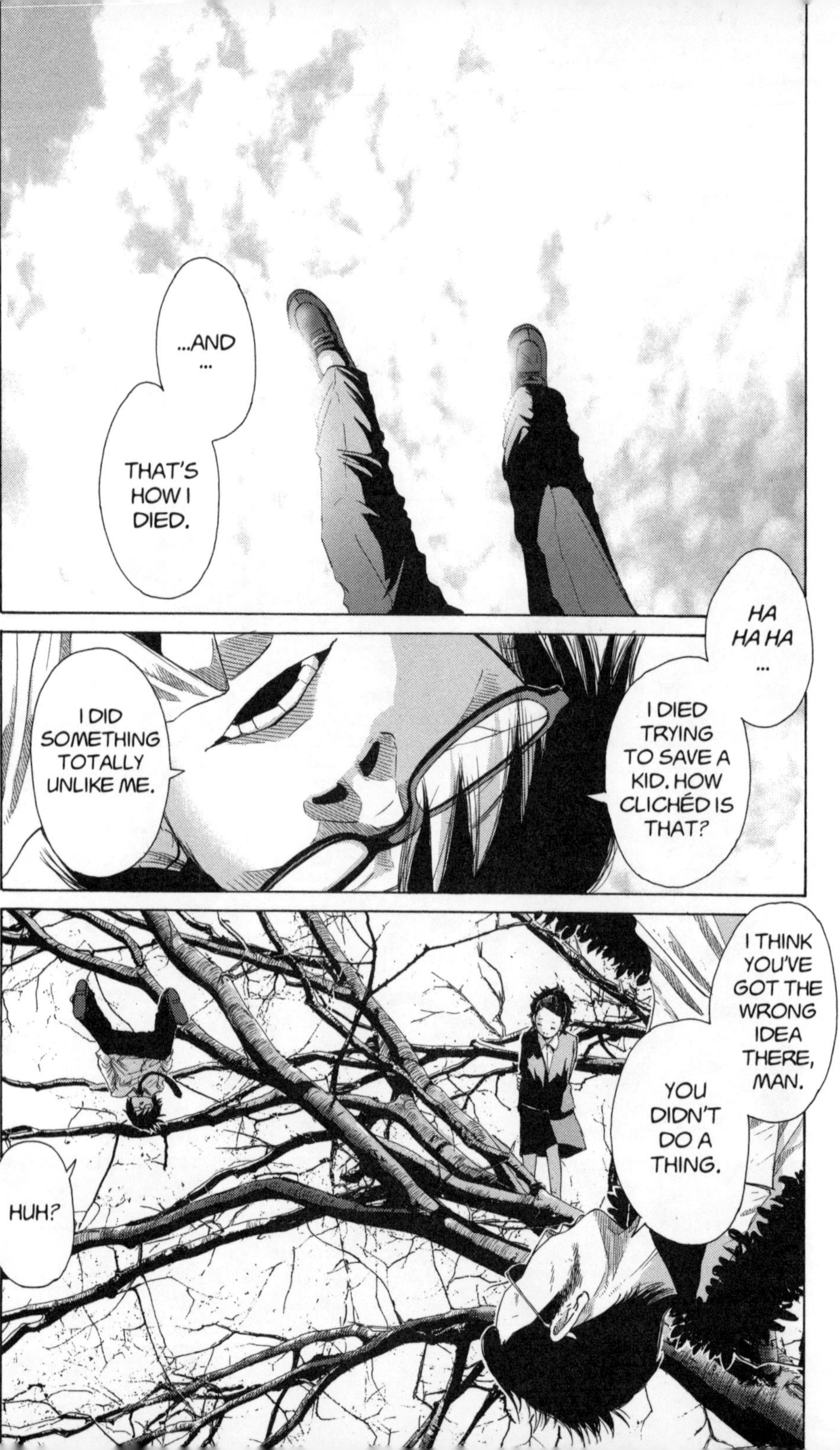
...AND ...
THAT'S HOW I DIED.
HA HA HA ...
I DIED TRYING TO SAVE A KID. HOW CLICHÉD IS THAT?
I DID SOMETHING TOTALLY UNLIKE ME.
I THINK YOU'VE GOT THE WRONG IDEA THERE, MAN.
YOU DIDN'T DO A THING.
HUH?

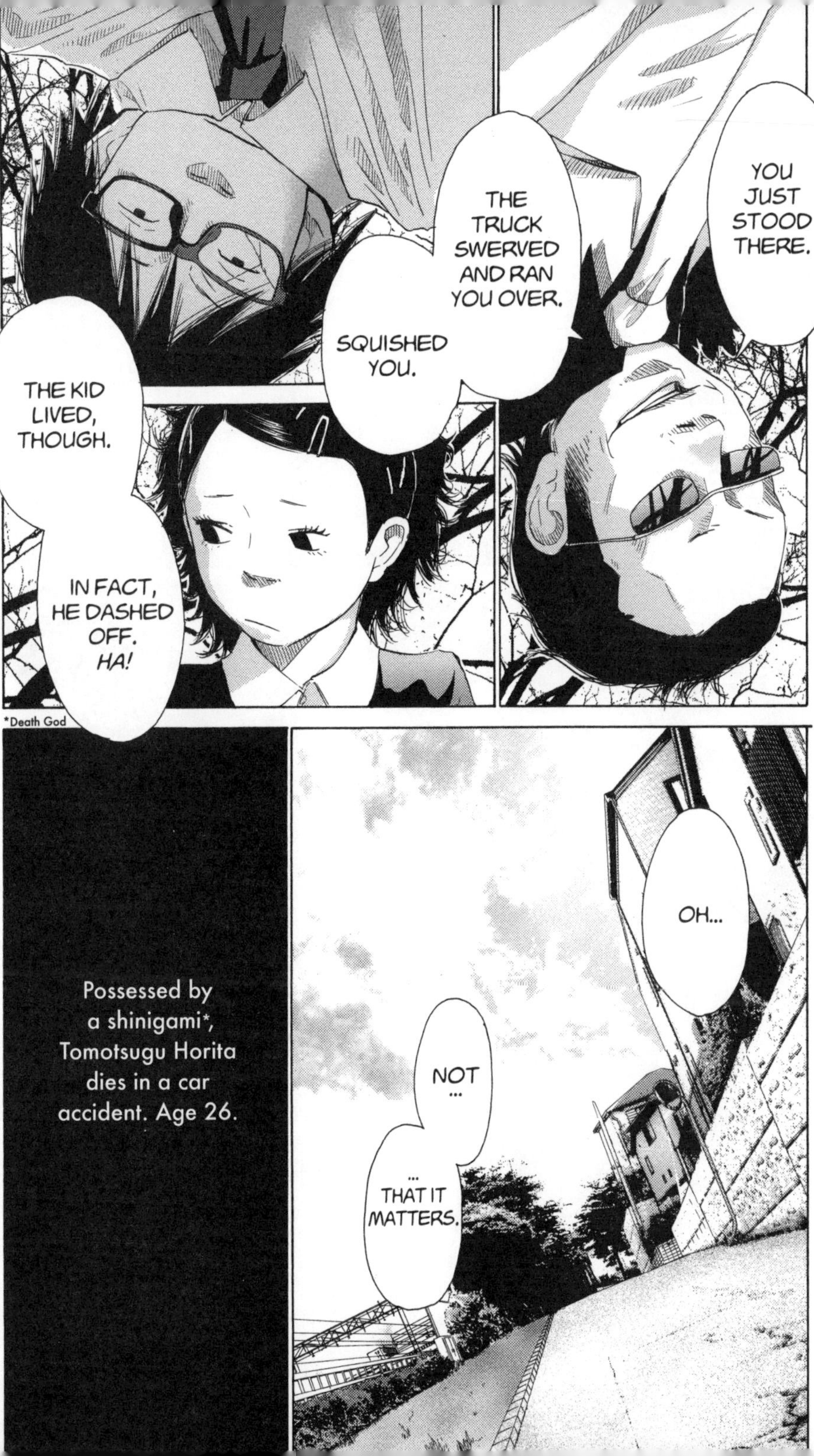
YOU JUST STOOD THERE.
THE TRUCK SWERVED AND RAN YOU OVER.
SQUISHED YOU.
THE KID LIVED, THOUGH.
IN FACT, HE DASHED OFF. HA!
OH...
NOT ...
... THAT IT MATTERS.
Possessed by a shinigami*, Tomotsugu Horita dies in a car accident. Age 26.

*Death God

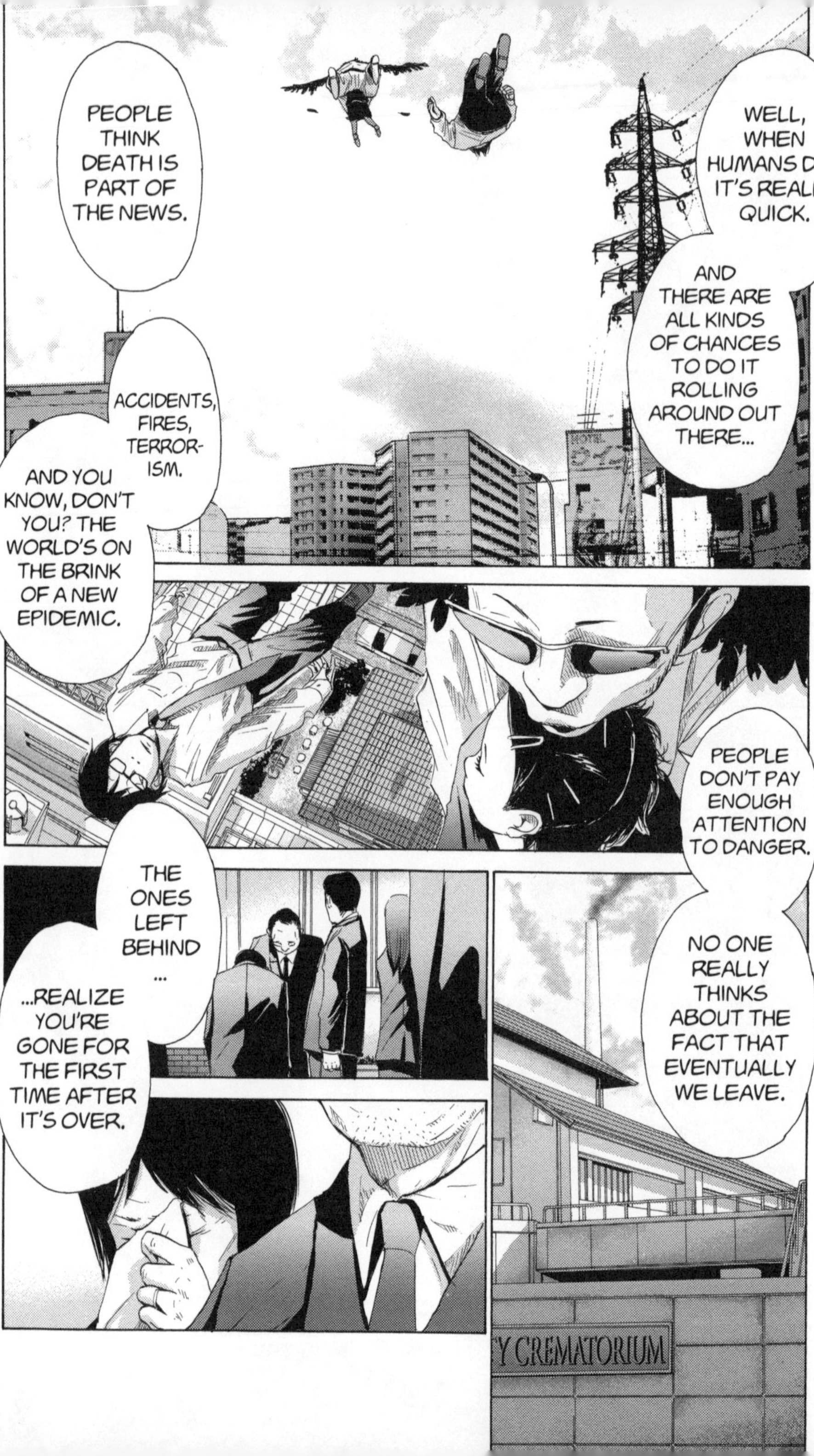
WELL, WHEN HUMANS DIE, IT'S REALLY QUICK.
AND THERE ARE ALL KINDS OF CHANCES TO DO IT ROLLING AROUND OUT THERE...
PEOPLE THINK DEATH IS PART OF THE NEWS.
ACCIDENTS, FIRES, TERRORISM.
AND YOU KNOW, DON'T YOU? THE WORLD'S ON THE BRINK OF A NEW EPIDEMIC.
PEOPLE DON'T PAY ENOUGH ATTENTION TO DANGER.
NO ONE REALLY THINKS ABOUT THE FACT THAT EVENTUALLY WE LEAVE.
Y CREMATORIUM
THE ONES LEFT BEHIND ...
...REALIZE YOU'RE GONE FOR THE FIRST TIME AFTER IT'S OVER.

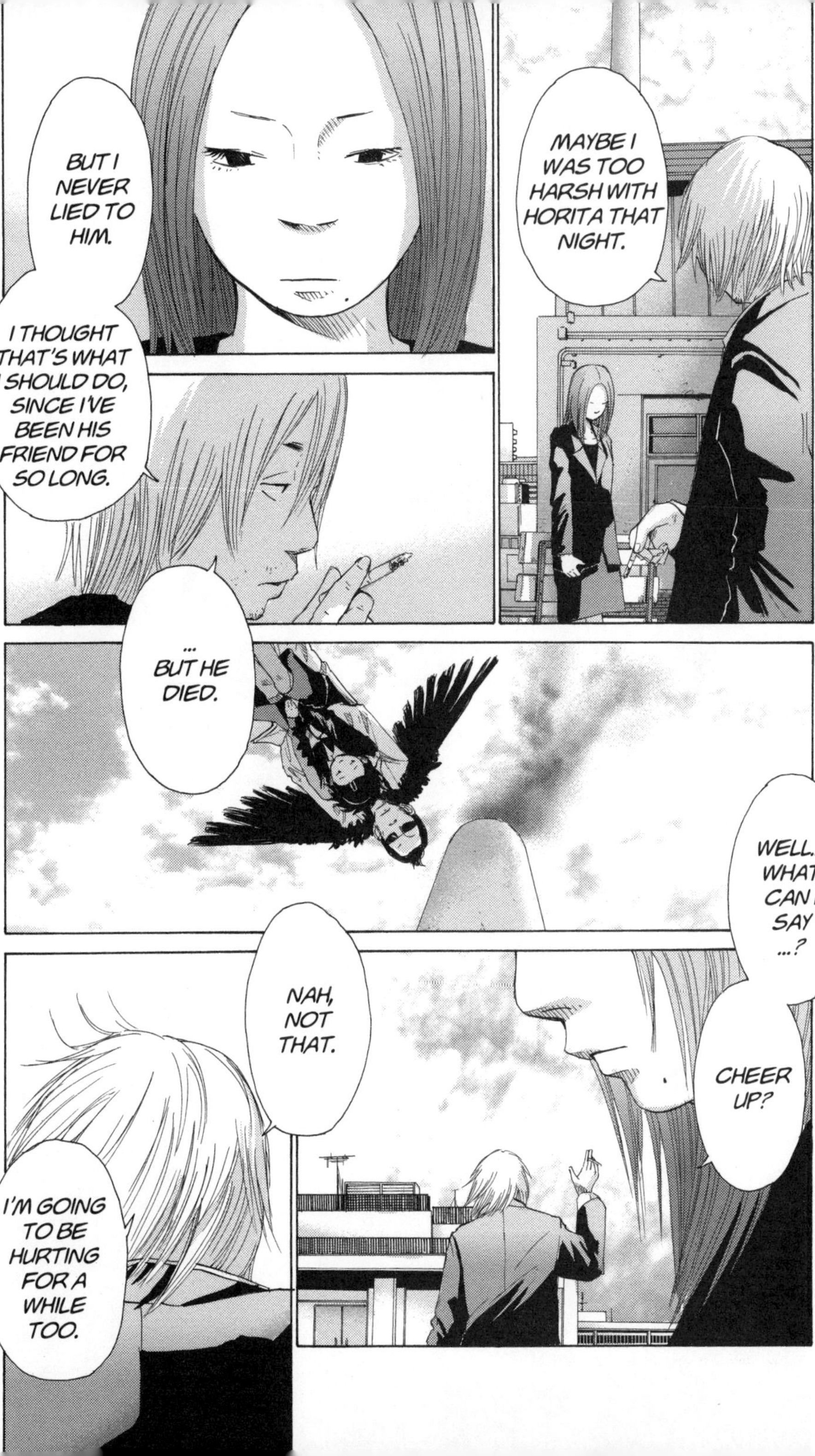
MAYBE I WAS TOO HARSH WITH HORITA THAT NIGHT.
BUT I NEVER LIED TO HIM.
I THOUGHT THAT'S WHAT I SHOULD DO, SINCE I'VE BEEN HIS FRIEND FOR SO LONG.
... BUT HE DIED.
WELL... WHAT CAN I SAY ...?
CHEER UP?
NAH, NOT THAT.
I'M GOING TO BE HURTING FOR A WHILE TOO.

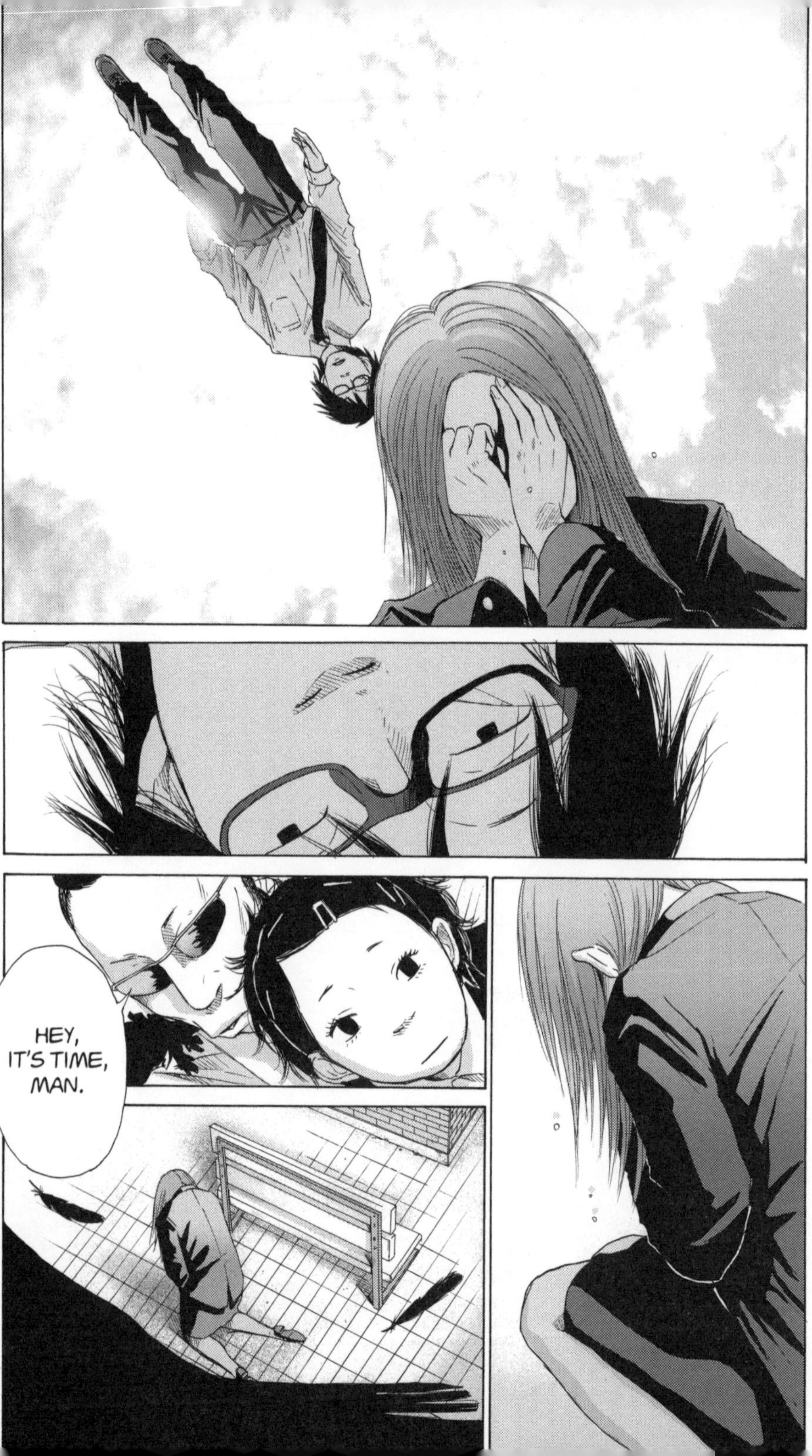
HEY, IT'S TIME, MAN.

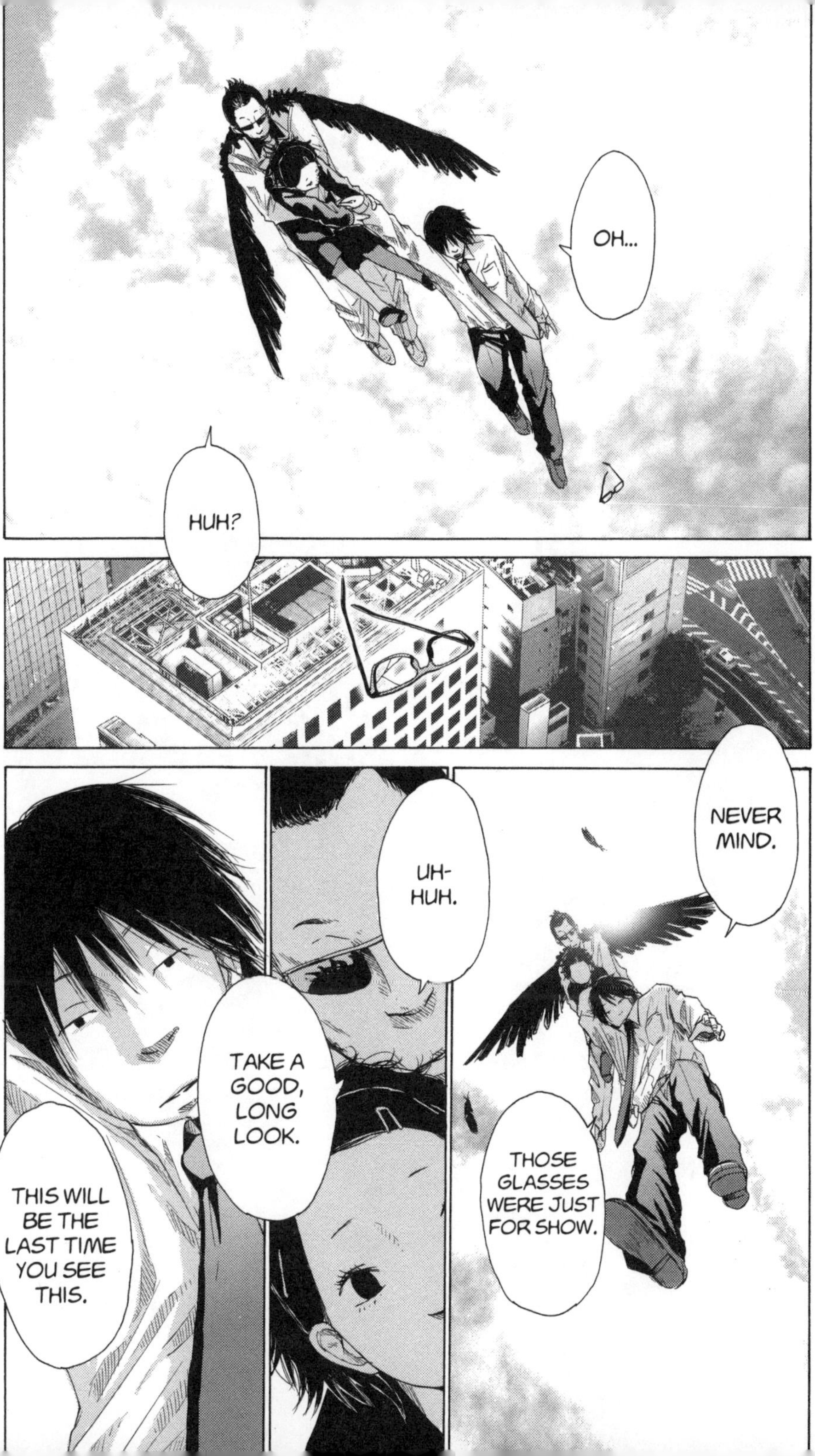
OH...
HUH?
NEVER MIND.
THOSE GLASSES WERE JUST FOR SHOW.
UH-HUH.
TAKE A GOOD, LONG LOOK.
THIS WILL BE THE LAST TIME YOU SEE THIS.

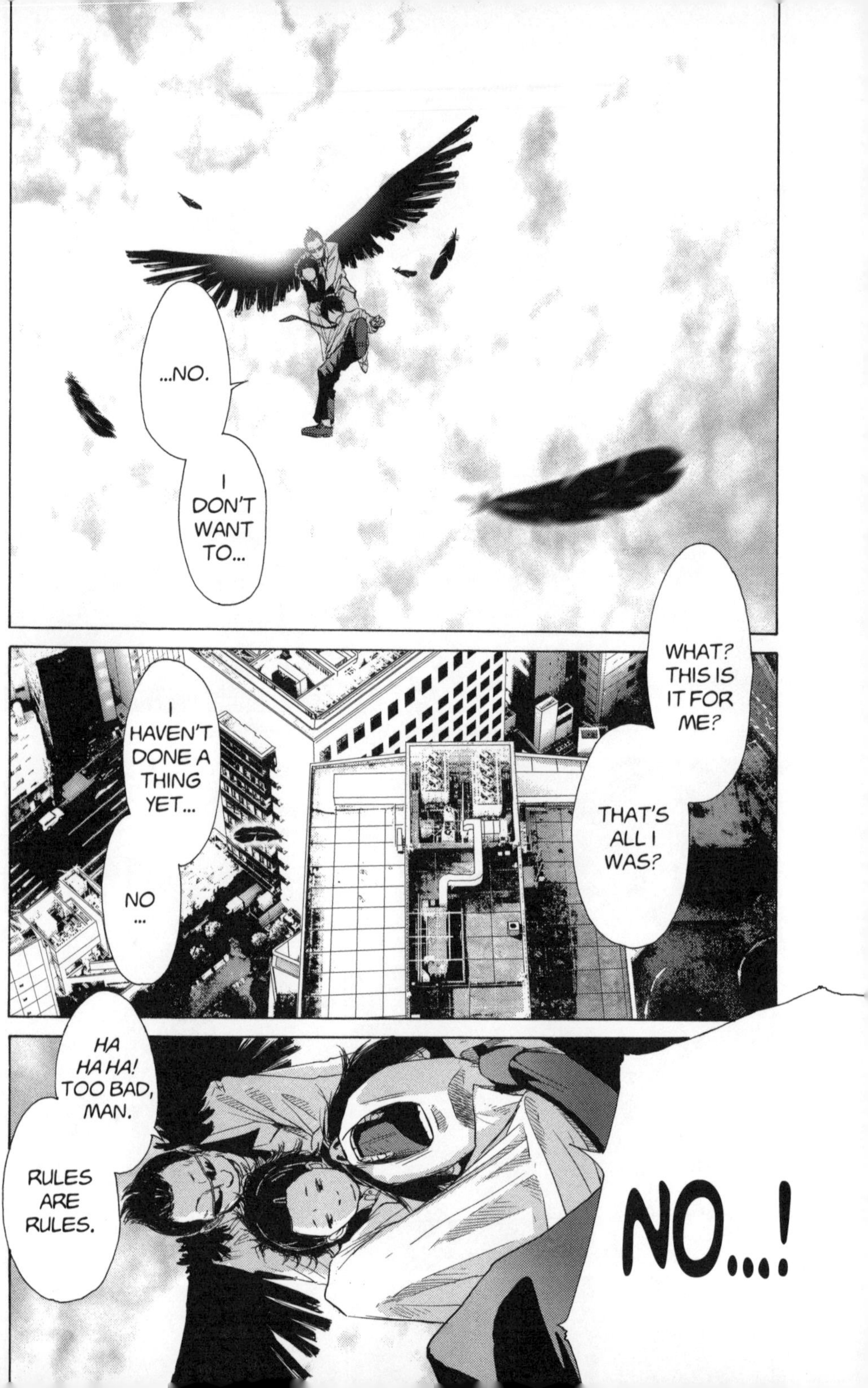
...NO.
I DON'T WANT TO...
WHAT? THIS IS IT FOR ME?
THAT'S ALL I WAS?
I HAVEN'T DONE A THING YET...
NO ...
NO...!
HA HA HA! TOO BAD, MAN.
RULES ARE RULES.

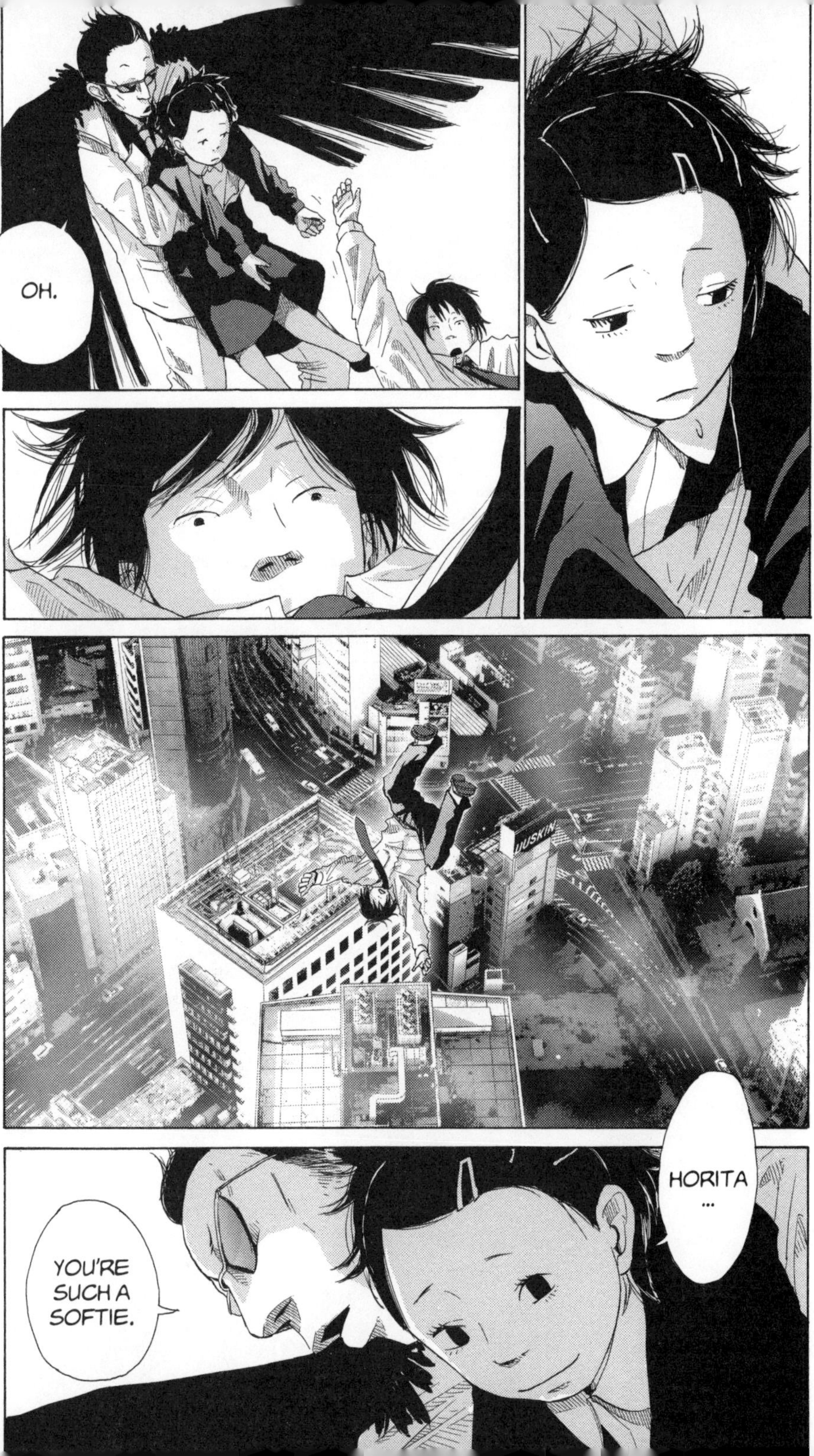
OH.
HORITA ...
YOU'RE SUCH A SOFTIE.

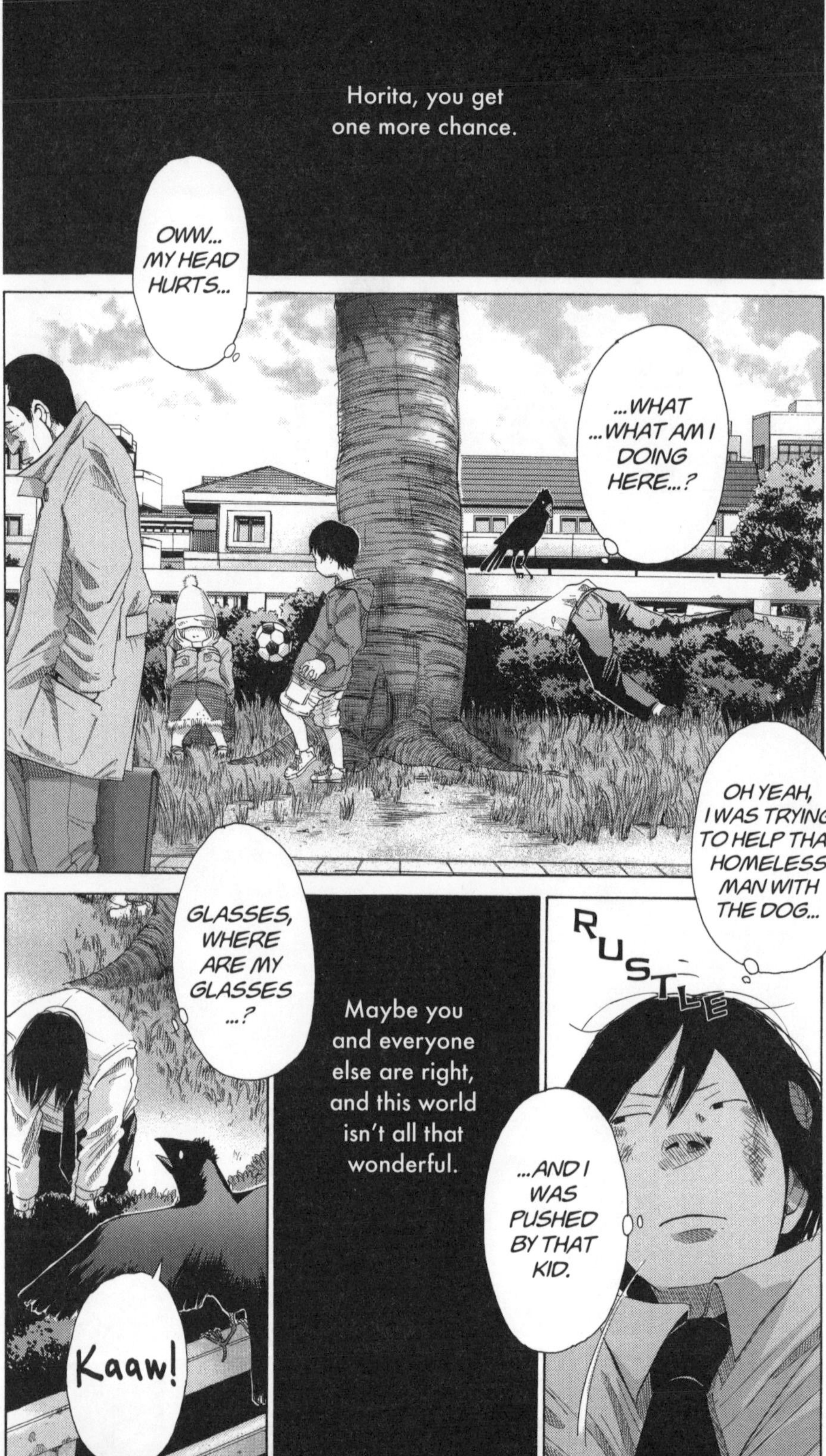
Horita, you get one more chance.
OWW... MY HEAD HURTS...
...WHAT ...WHAT AM I DOING HERE...?
OH YEAH, I WAS TRYING TO HELP THAT HOMELESS MAN WITH THE DOG...
RUSTLE
...AND I WAS PUSHED BY THAT KID.
Maybe you and everyone else are right, and this world isn't all that wonderful.
GLASSES, WHERE ARE MY GLASSES ...?
Kaaw!

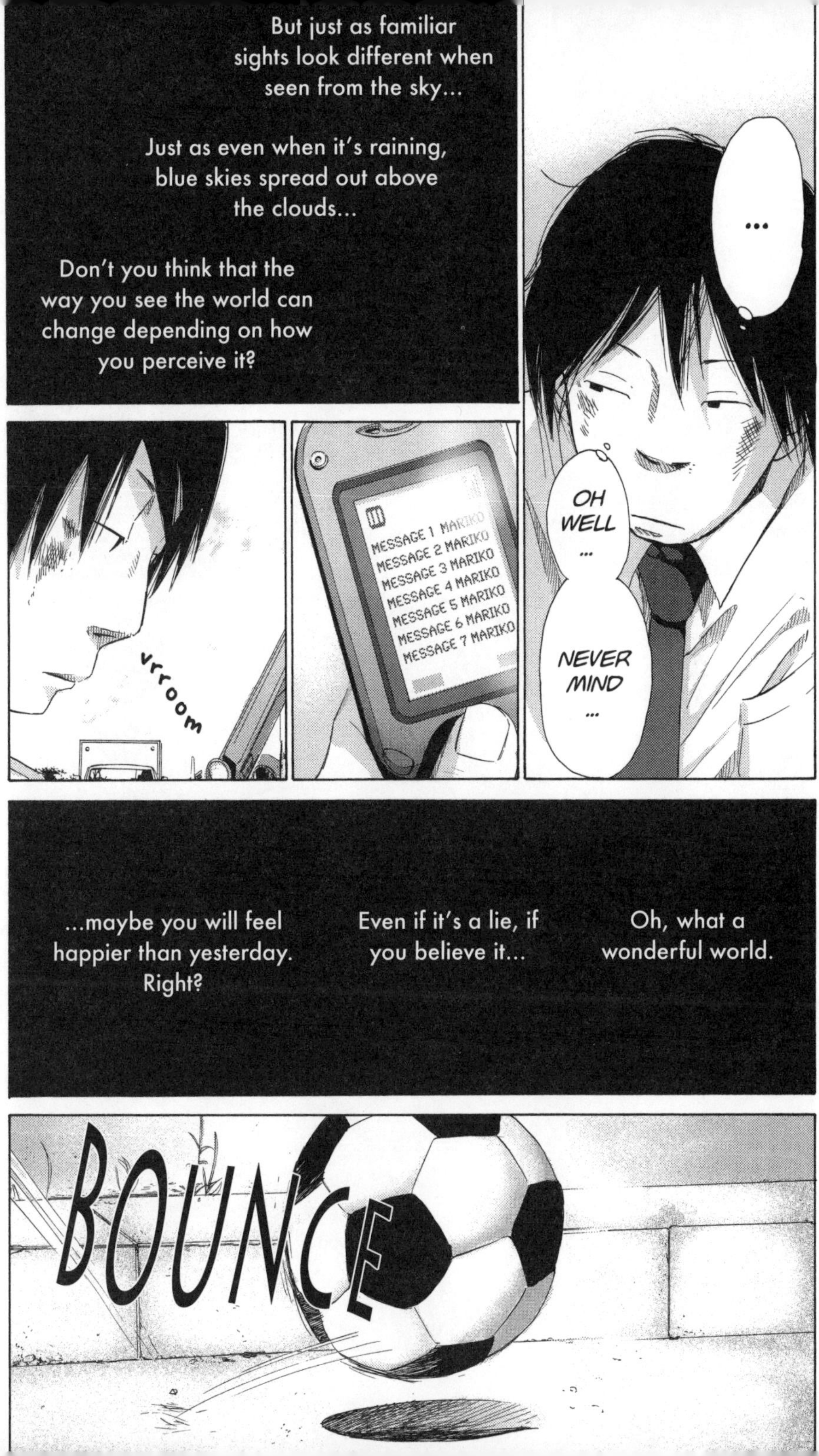
...
OH WELL...
NEVER MIND...
But just as familiar sights look different when seen from the sky...
Just as even when it's raining, blue skies spread out above the clouds...
Don't you think that the way you see the world can change depending on how you perceive it?
MESSAGE 1 MARIKO
MESSAGE 2 MARIKO
MESSAGE 3 MARIKO
MESSAGE 4 MARIKO
MESSAGE 5 MARIKO
MESSAGE 6 MARIKO
MESSAGE 7 MARIKO
vrroom
Oh, what a wonderful world.
Even if it's a lie, if you believe it...
...maybe you will feel happier than yesterday. Right?
BOUNCE

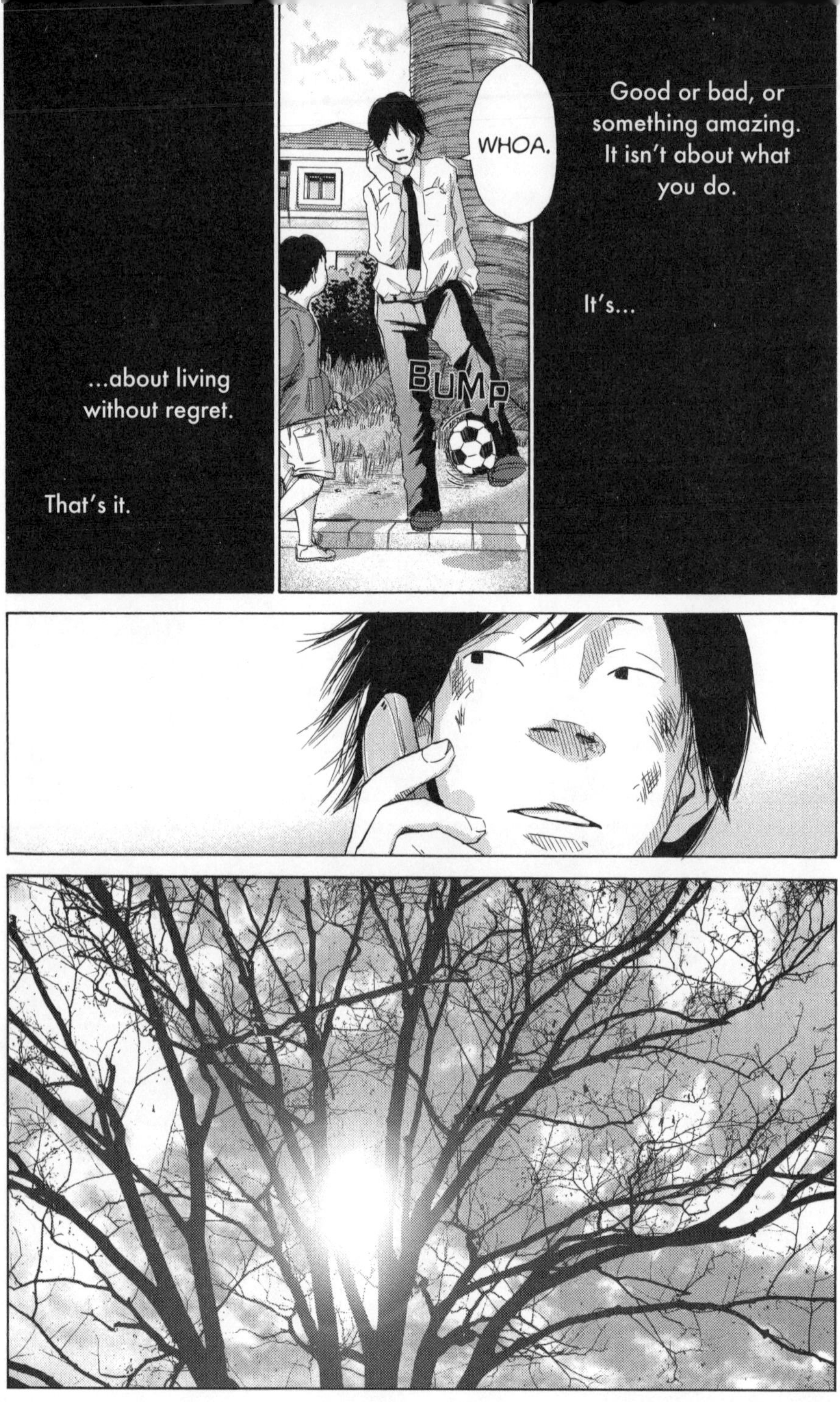
Good or bad, or something amazing. It isn't about what you do.
It's...
WHOA.
BUMP
...about living without regret.
That's it.

# 18th track Spring Breeze

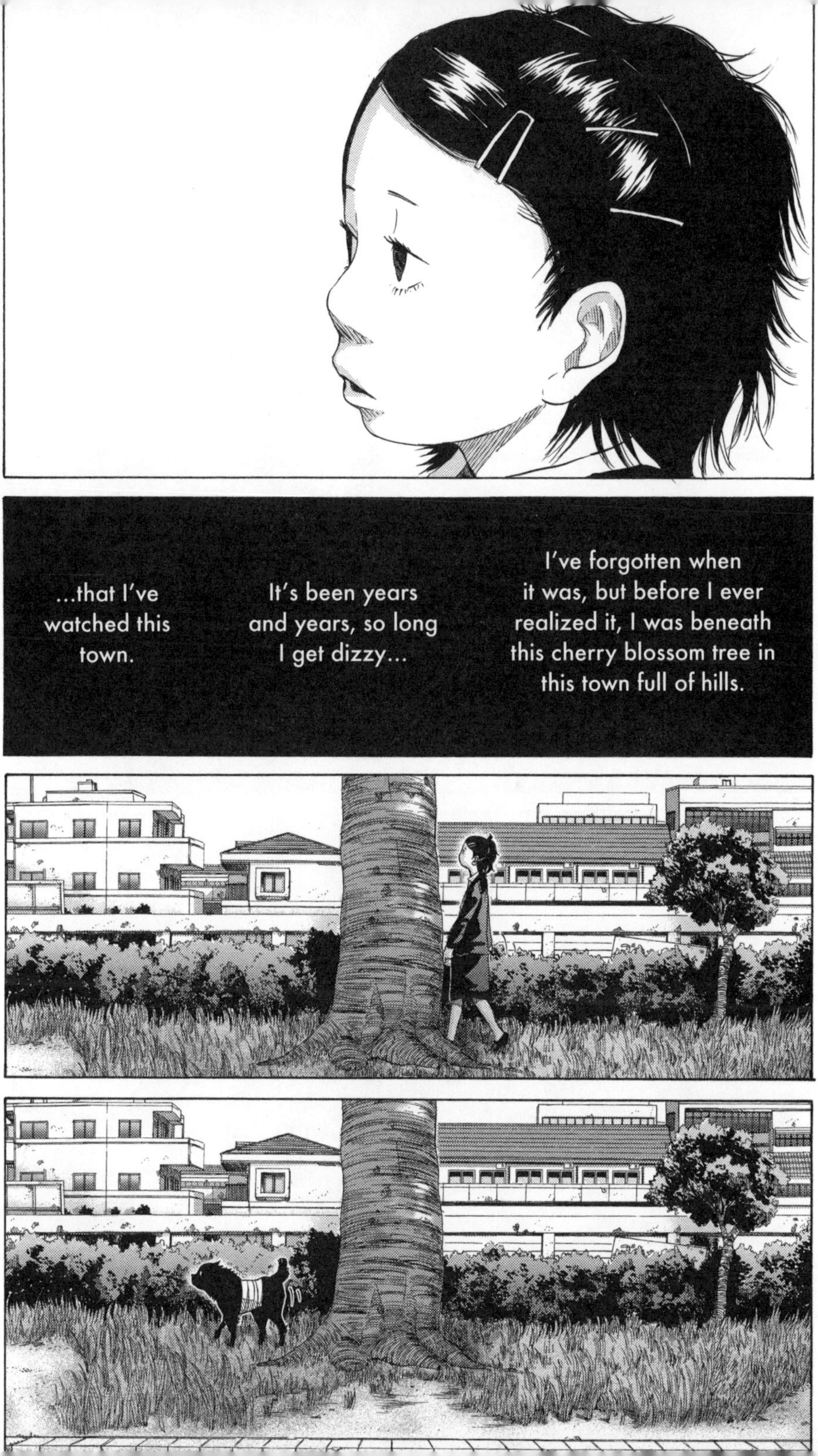
I've forgotten when it was, but before I ever realized it, I was beneath this cherry blossom tree in this town full of hills.
It's been years and years, so long I get dizzy...
...that I've watched this town.

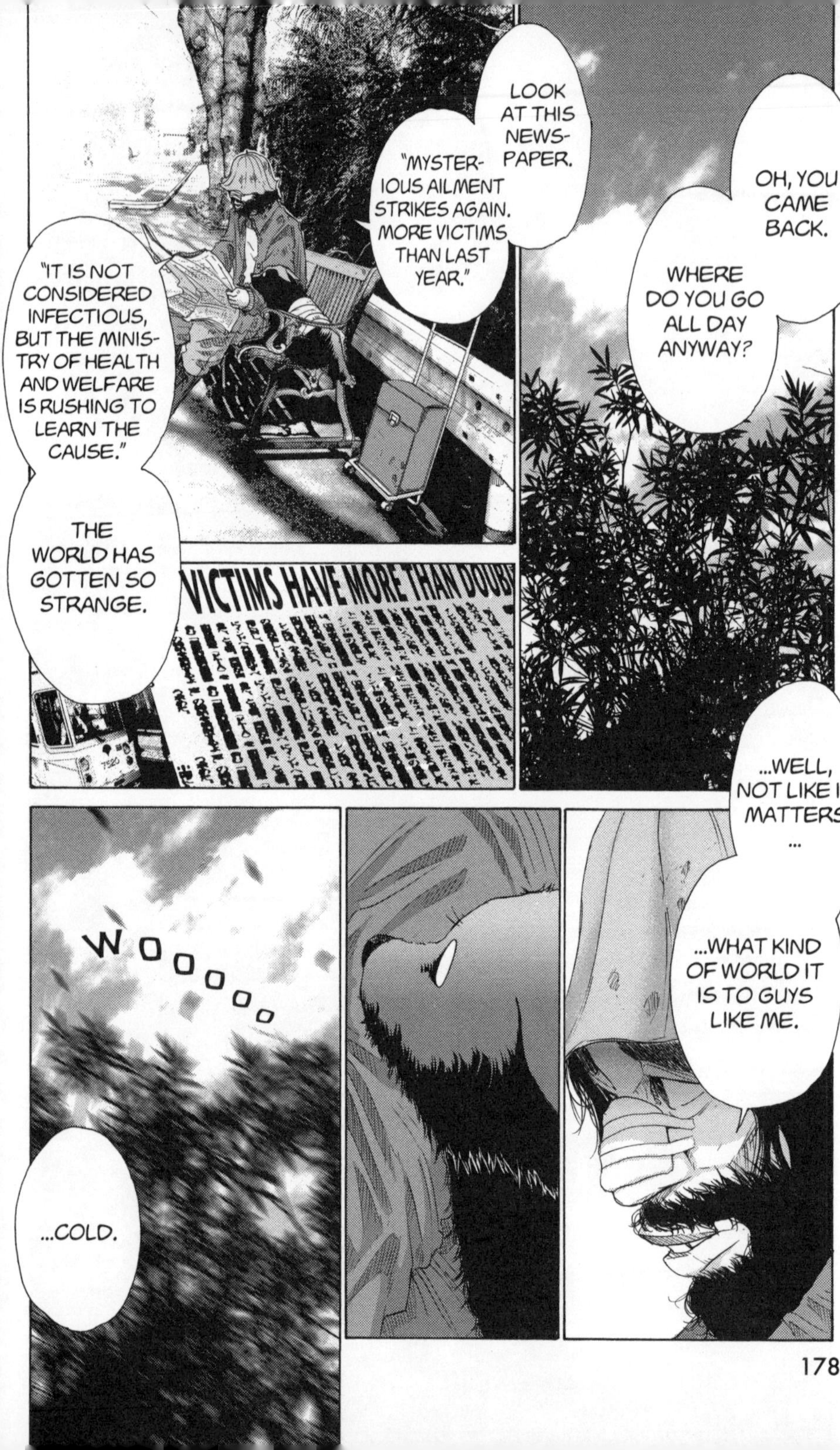
OH, YOU CAME BACK.
WHERE DO YOU GO ALL DAY ANYWAY?
LOOK AT THIS NEWS-PAPER.
"MYSTER-IOUS AILMENT STRIKES AGAIN. MORE VICTIMS THAN LAST YEAR."
"IT IS NOT CONSIDERED INFECTIOUS, BUT THE MINIS-TRY OF HEALTH AND WELFARE IS RUSHING TO LEARN THE CAUSE."
VICTIMS HAVE MORE THAN DOUB
THE WORLD HAS GOTTEN SO STRANGE.
...WELL, NOT LIKE IT MATTERS ...
...WHAT KIND OF WORLD IT IS TO GUYS LIKE ME.
WOOOOOO
...COLD.

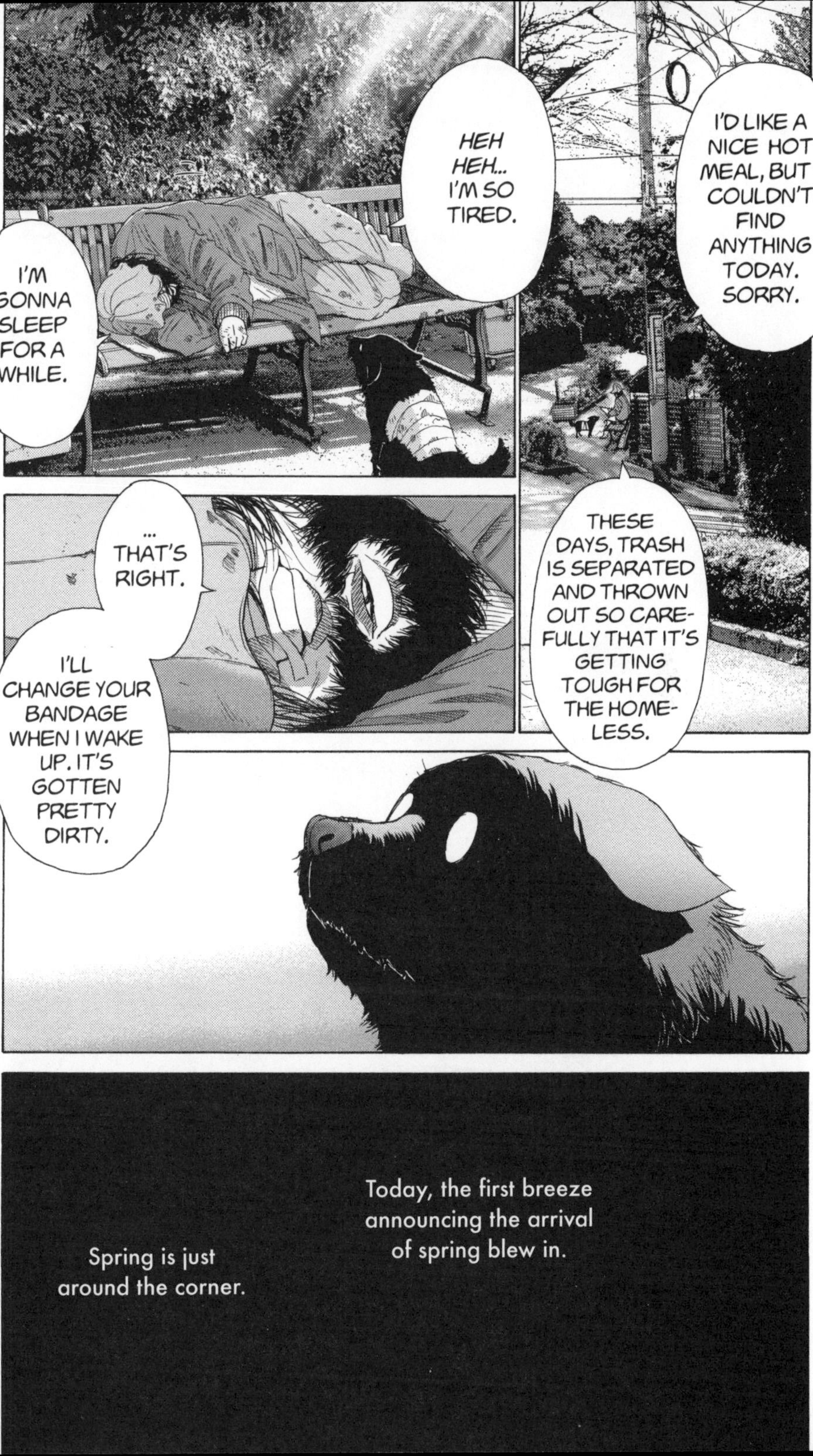
I'D LIKE A NICE HOT MEAL, BUT I COULDN'T FIND ANYTHING TODAY. SORRY.
THESE DAYS, TRASH IS SEPARATED AND THROWN OUT SO CARE-FULLY THAT IT'S GETTING TOUGH FOR THE HOME-LESS.
HEH HEH... I'M SO TIRED.
I'M GONNA SLEEP FOR A WHILE.
... THAT'S RIGHT.
I'LL CHANGE YOUR BANDAGE WHEN I WAKE UP. IT'S GOTTEN PRETTY DIRTY.
Today, the first breeze announcing the arrival of spring blew in.
Spring is just around the corner.

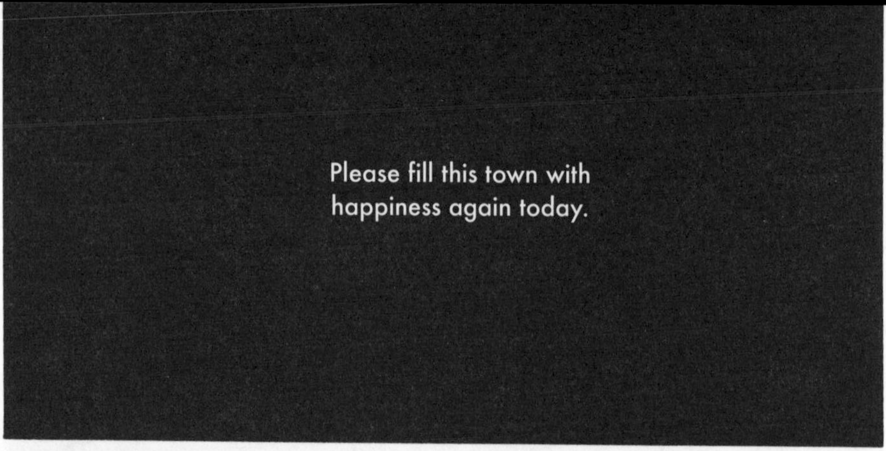
Please fill this town with happiness again today.
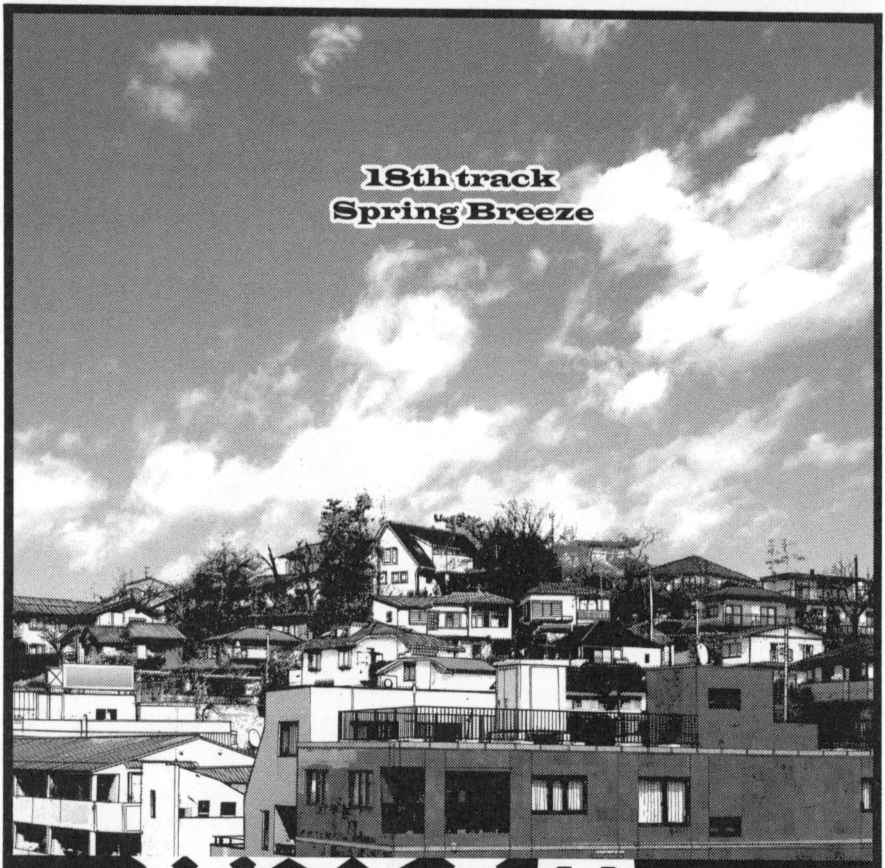
18th track
Spring Breeze
WHAT a WONDERFUL WORLD!

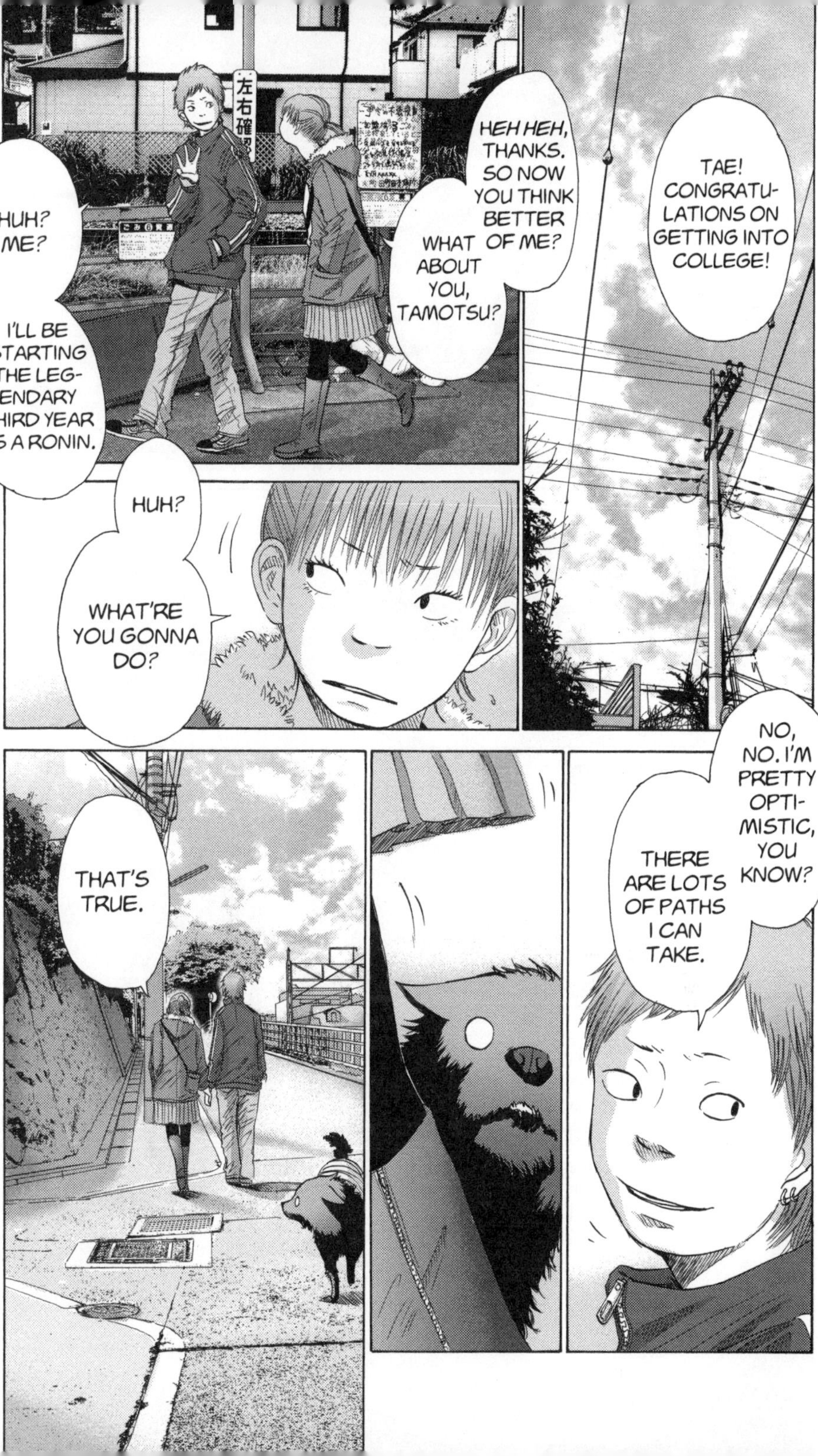
TAE! CONGRATULATIONS ON GETTING INTO COLLEGE!
HEH HEH, THANKS. SO NOW YOU THINK BETTER OF ME?
WHAT ABOUT YOU, TAMOTSU?
左右確認
HUH? ME?
I'LL BE STARTING THE LEGENDARY THIRD YEAR AS A RONIN.
HUH?
WHAT'RE YOU GONNA DO?
NO, NO. I'M PRETTY OPTIMISTIC, YOU KNOW?
THERE ARE LOTS OF PATHS I CAN TAKE.
THAT'S TRUE.

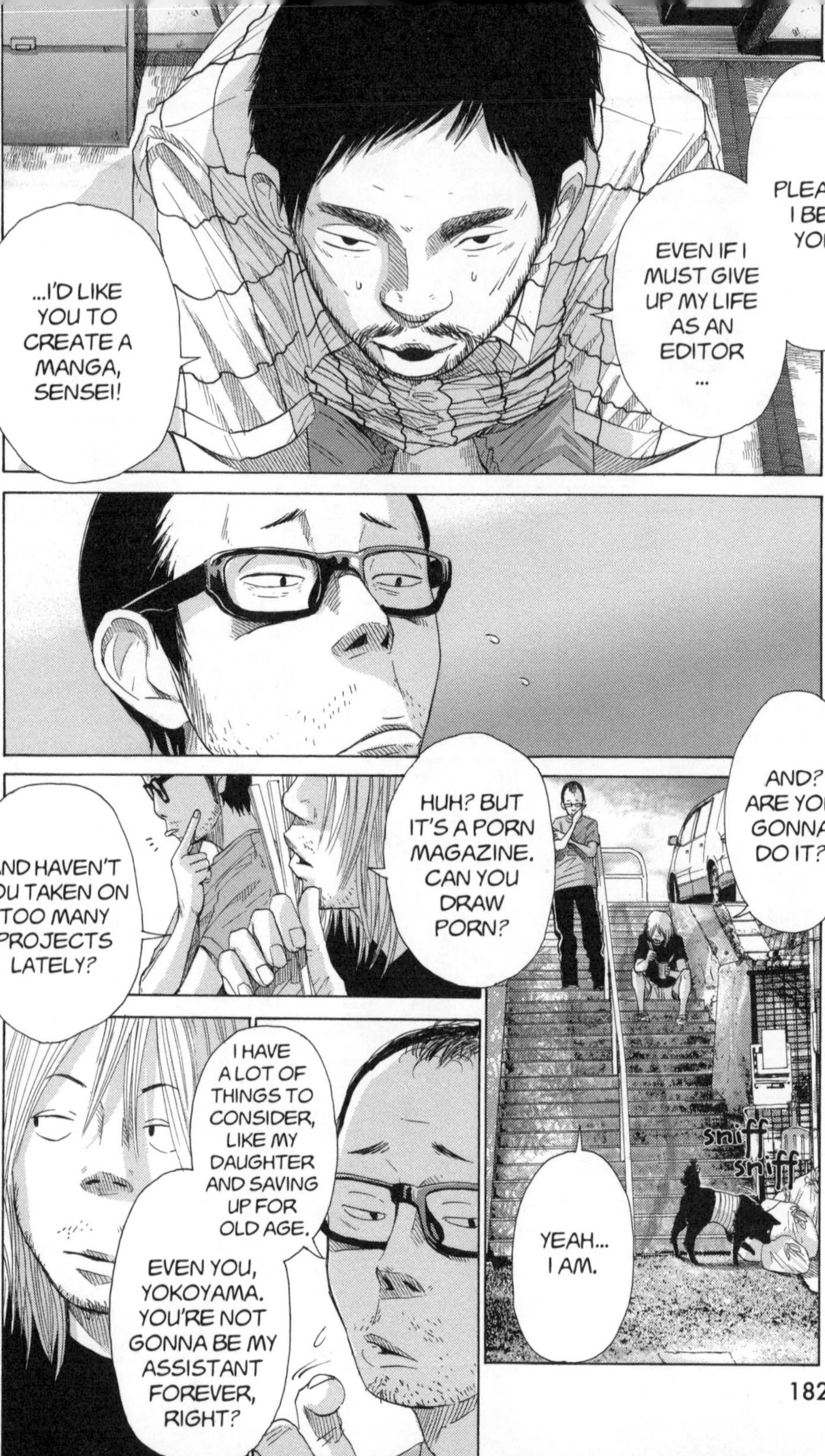
PLEASE, I BEG YOU!
EVEN IF I MUST GIVE UP MY LIFE AS AN EDITOR ...
...I'D LIKE YOU TO CREATE A MANGA, SENSEI!
AND? ARE YOU GONNA DO IT?
sniff sniff
YEAH... I AM.
HUH? BUT IT'S A PORN MAGAZINE. CAN YOU DRAW PORN?
AND HAVEN'T YOU TAKEN ON TOO MANY PROJECTS LATELY?
I HAVE A LOT OF THINGS TO CONSIDER, LIKE MY DAUGHTER AND SAVING UP FOR OLD AGE.
EVEN YOU, YOKOYAMA. YOU'RE NOT GONNA BE MY ASSISTANT FOREVER, RIGHT?

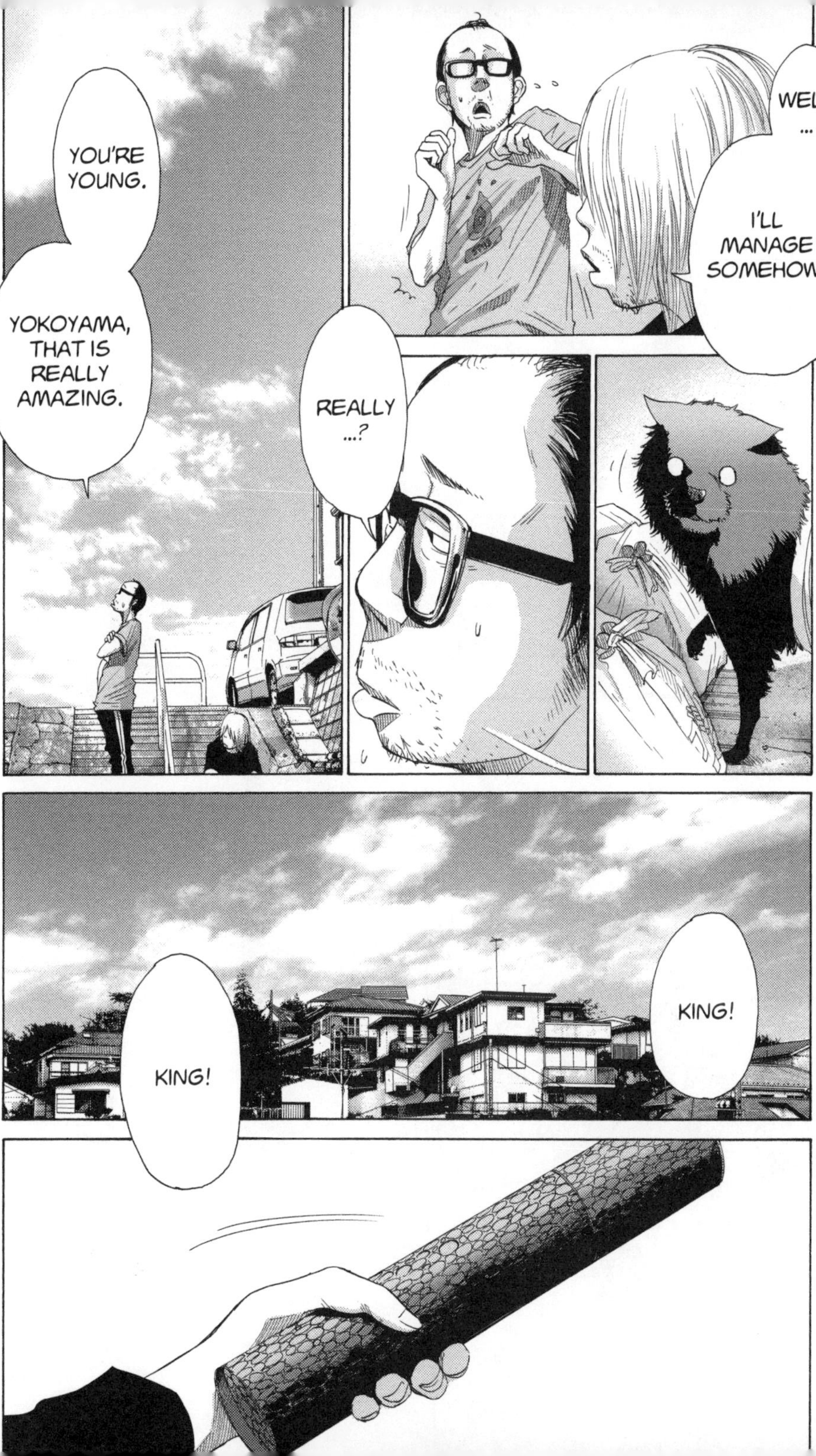
WELL ...
I'LL MANAGE SOMEHOW.
REALLY ...?
YOU'RE YOUNG.
YOKOYAMA, THAT IS REALLY AMAZING.
KING!
KING!

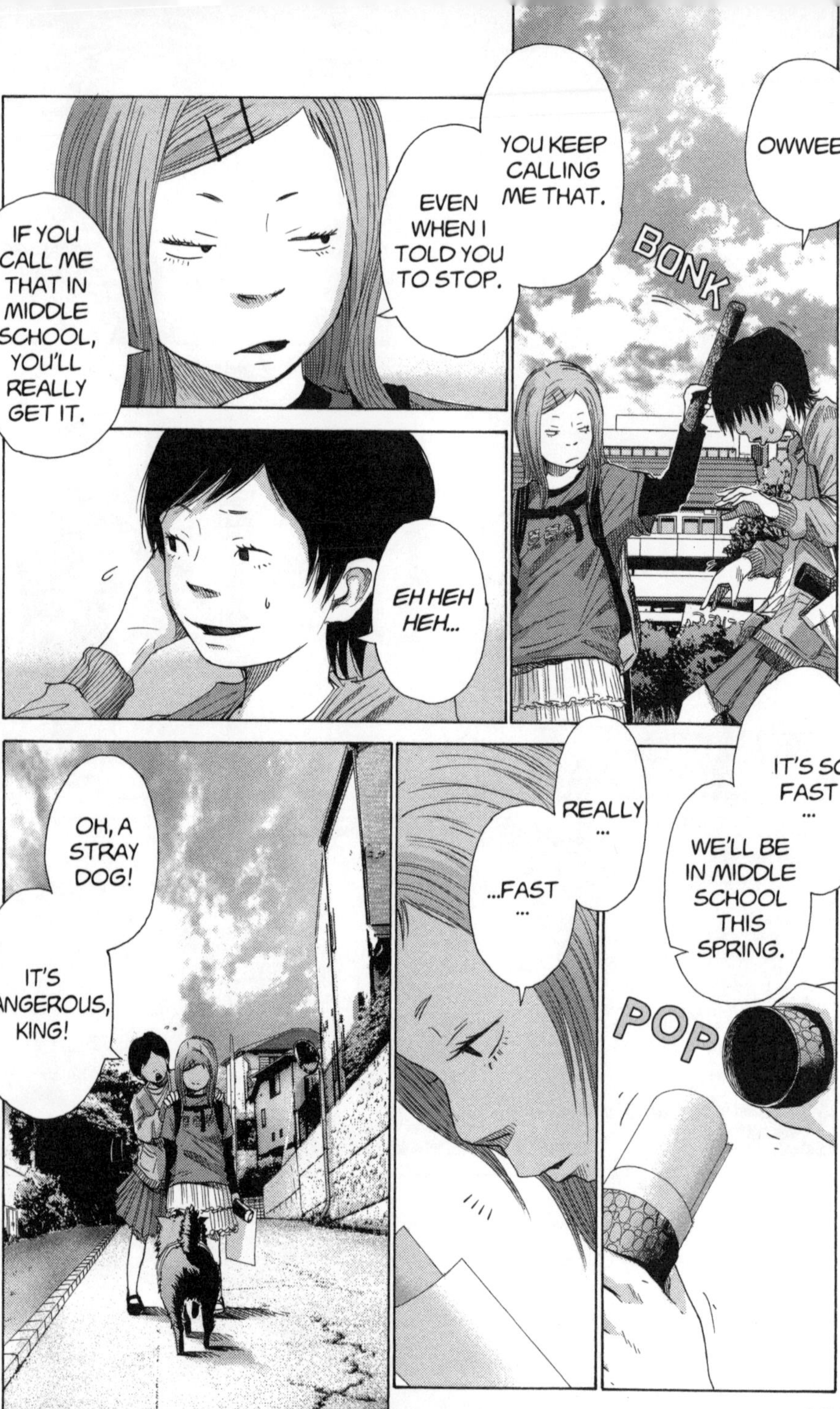
OWWEE.
BONK
YOU KEEP CALLING ME THAT.
EVEN WHEN I TOLD YOU TO STOP.
IF YOU CALL ME THAT IN MIDDLE SCHOOL, YOU'LL REALLY GET IT.
EH HEH HEH...
POP
IT'S SO FAST ...
WE'LL BE IN MIDDLE SCHOOL THIS SPRING.
REALLY ...
...FAST ...
OH, A STRAY DOG!
IT'S DANGEROUS, KING!

HA HA.

IT'S SO CUTE.

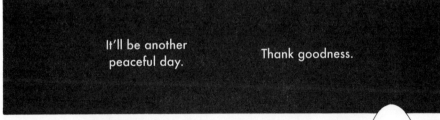

It'll be another peaceful day.

Thank goodness.

DAMN.

I FORGOT TO ASK FOR GINGER.

HUH? IT'S OKAY.

NO, NO, NO. I'LL RUSH BACK AND GET SOME!

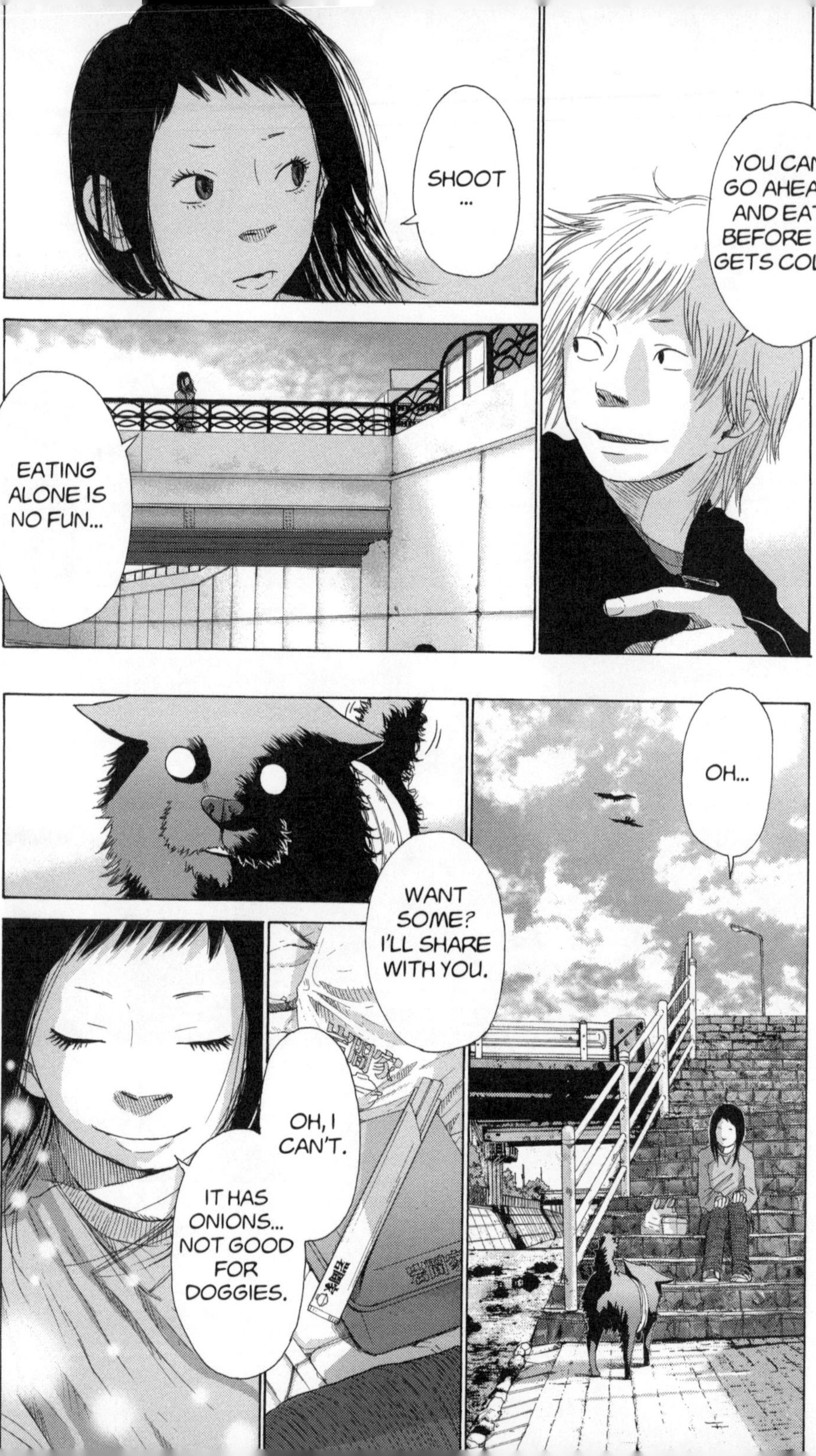
YOU CAN GO AHEAD AND EAT BEFORE IT GETS COLD.
SHOOT ...
EATING ALONE IS NO FUN...
OH...
WANT SOME? I'LL SHARE WITH YOU.
OH, I CAN'T.
IT HAS ONIONS... NOT GOOD FOR DOGGIES.

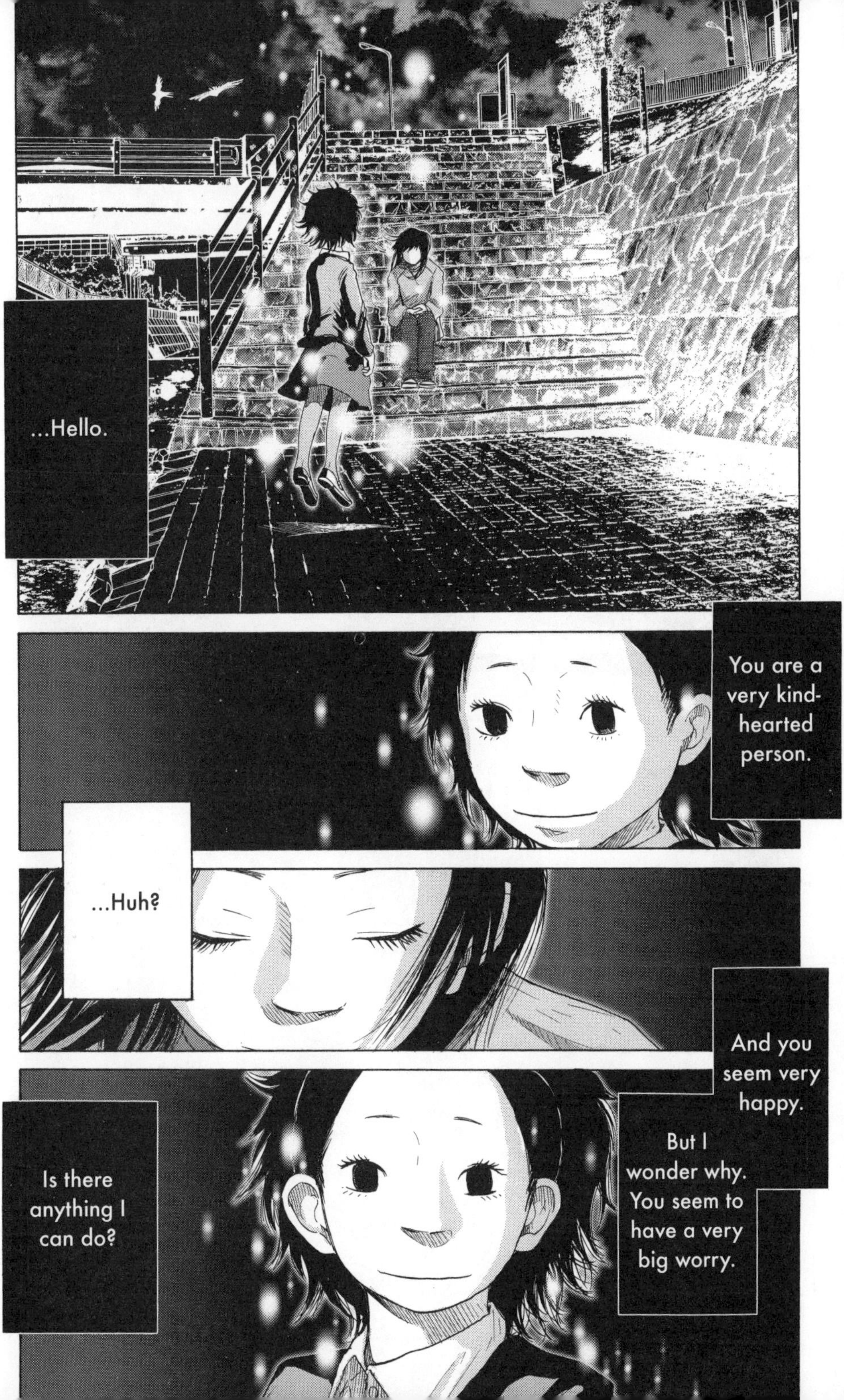
...Hello.
You are a very kind-hearted person.
...Huh?
And you seem very happy.
But I wonder why. You seem to have a very big worry.
Is there anything I can do?

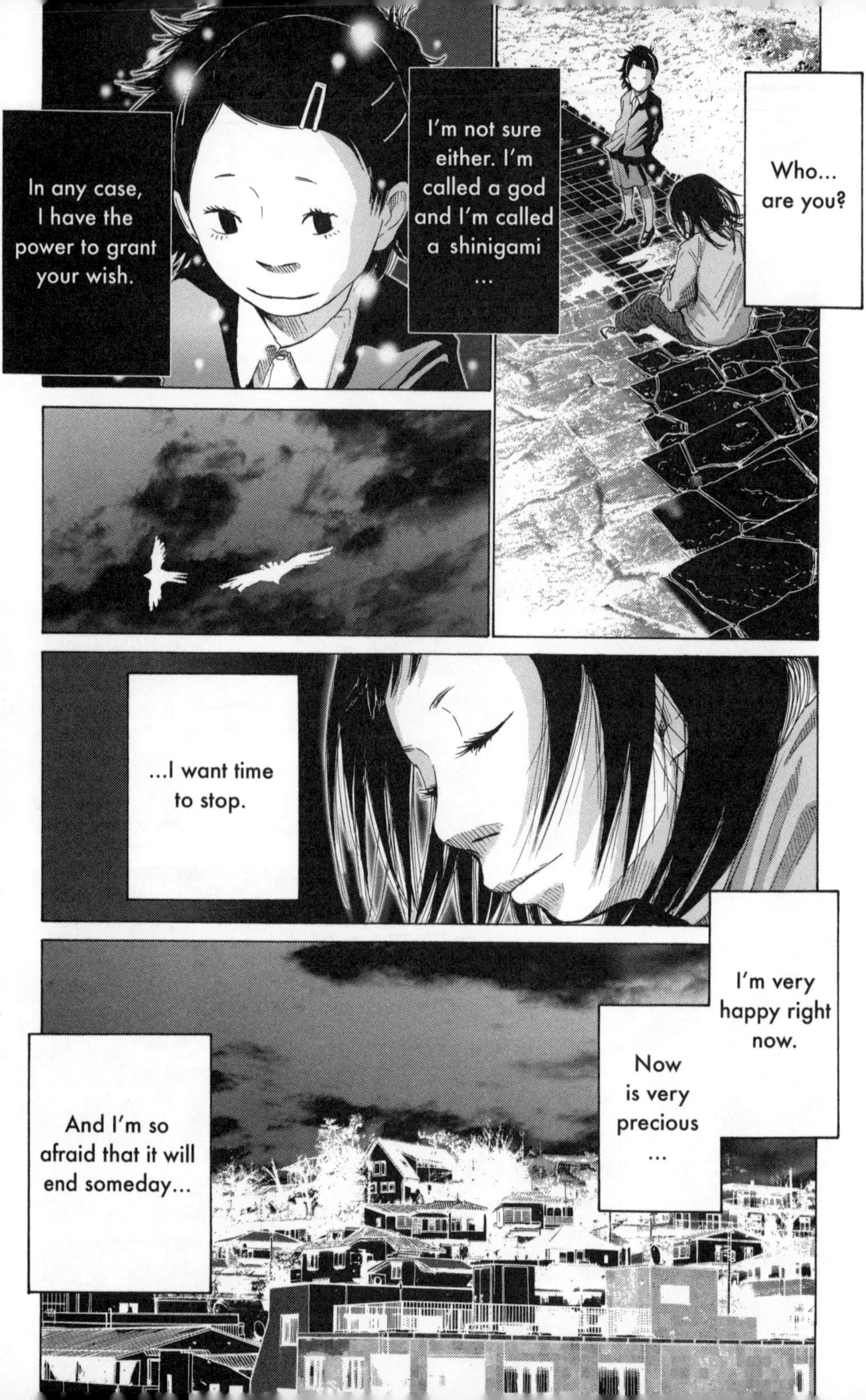
Who... are you?
I'm not sure either. I'm called a god and I'm called a shinigami ...
In any case, I have the power to grant your wish.
...I want time to stop.
I'm very happy right now.
Now is very precious ...
And I'm so afraid that it will end someday...

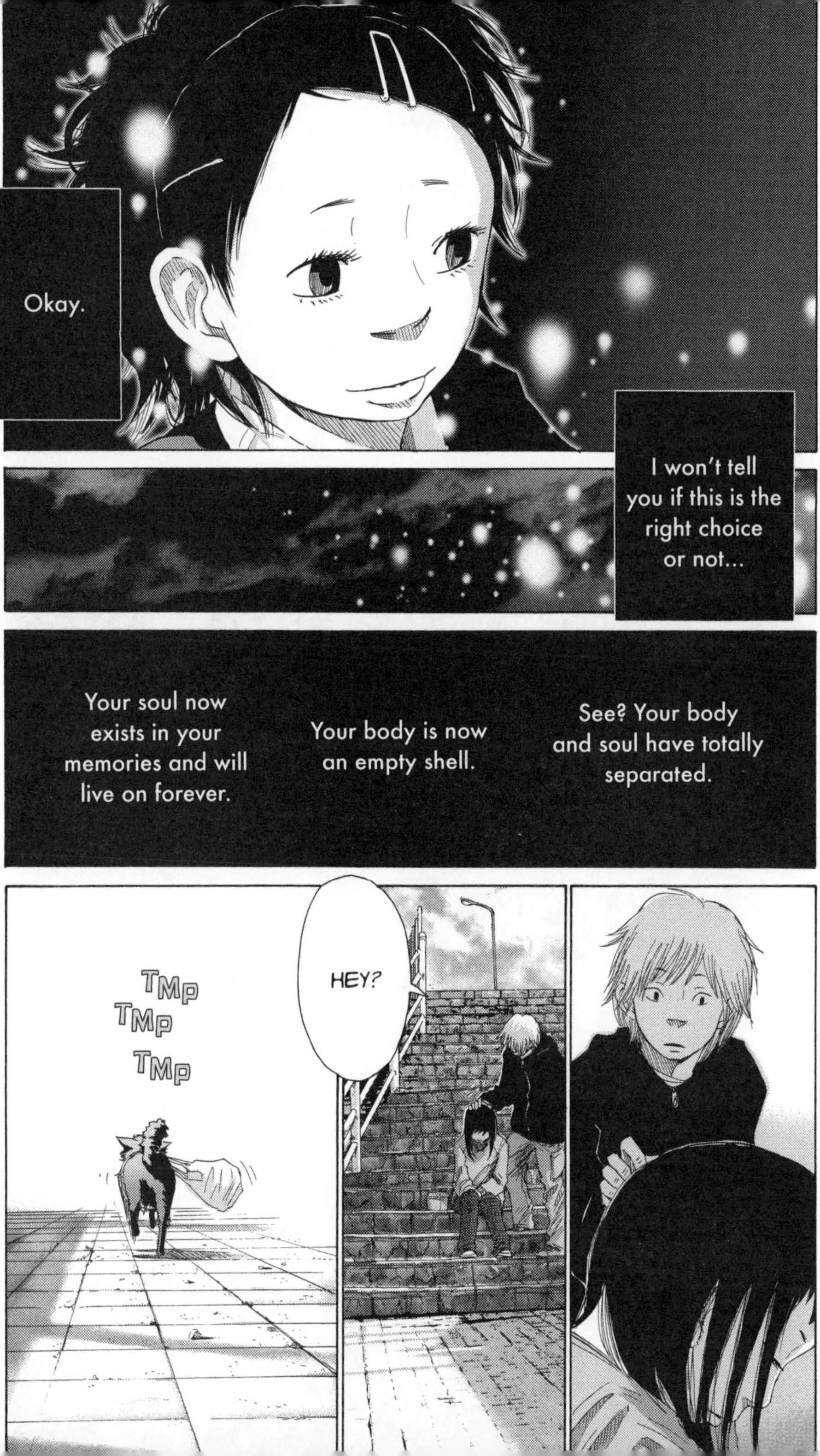
Okay.
I won't tell you if this is the right choice or not...
See? Your body and soul have totally separated.
Your body is now an empty shell.
Your soul now exists in your memories and will live on forever.
HEY?
TMP
TMP
TMP

In the center of this town of hills, there is a giant, giant cherry tree...

...and until today, it has blossomed many times and its flowers have fallen many times.

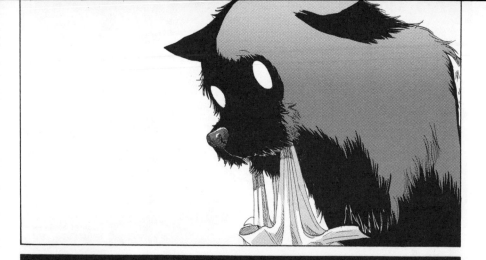

Humans and trees have essentially been born to follow this destiny.

Time always flows in the same direction.

Perhaps it's cruel.

But...

If we fear tomorrow because of that...

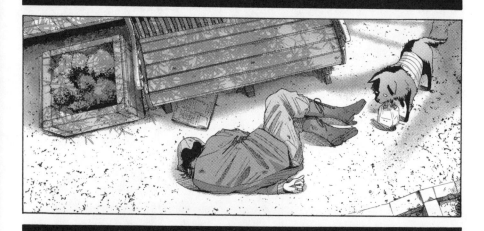

...we'll never get anything done today.

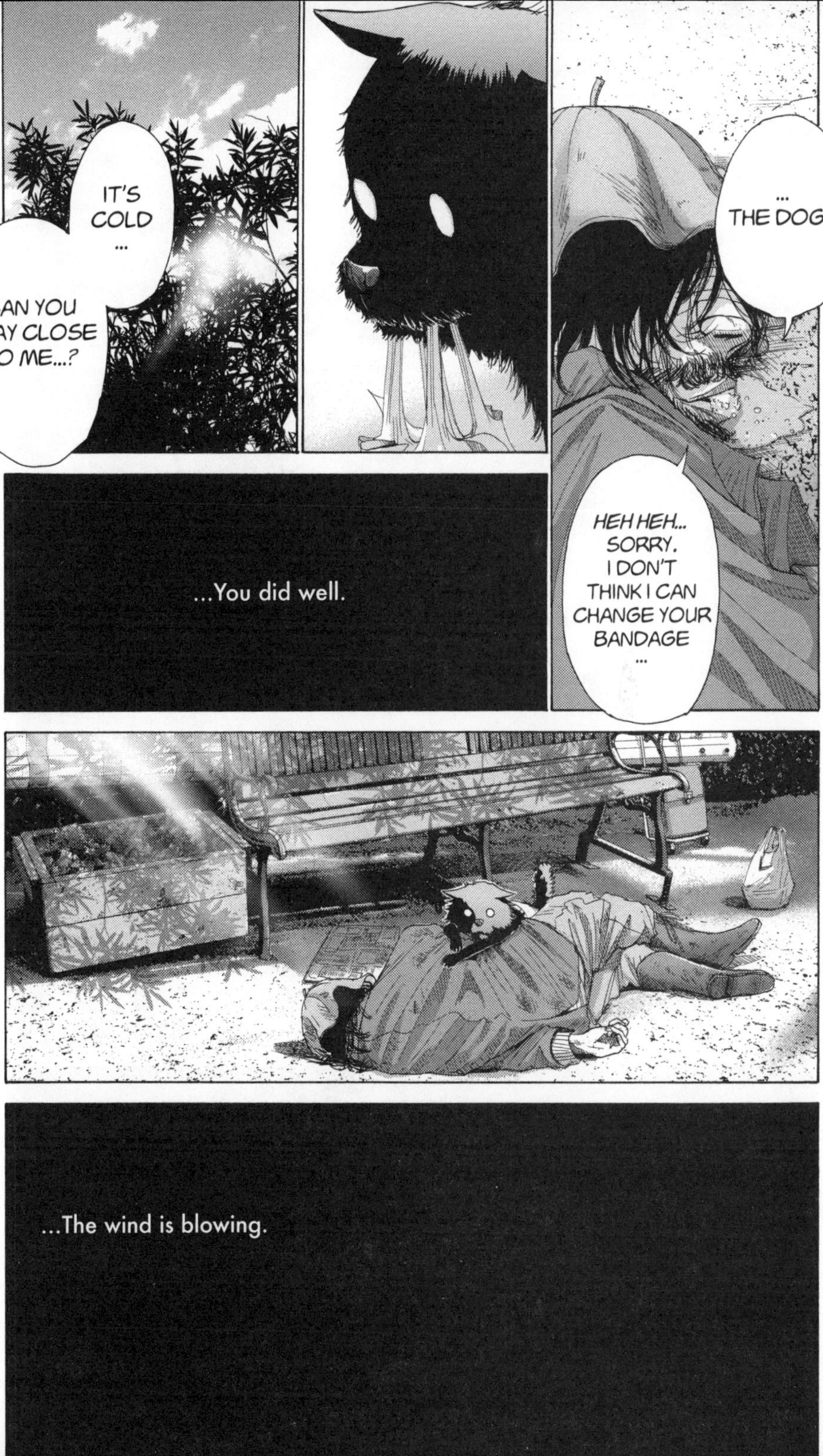
... THE DOG?
HEH HEH... SORRY. I DON'T THINK I CAN CHANGE YOUR BANDAGE ...
IT'S COLD ...
CAN YOU STAY CLOSE TO ME...?
...You did well.
...The wind is blowing.

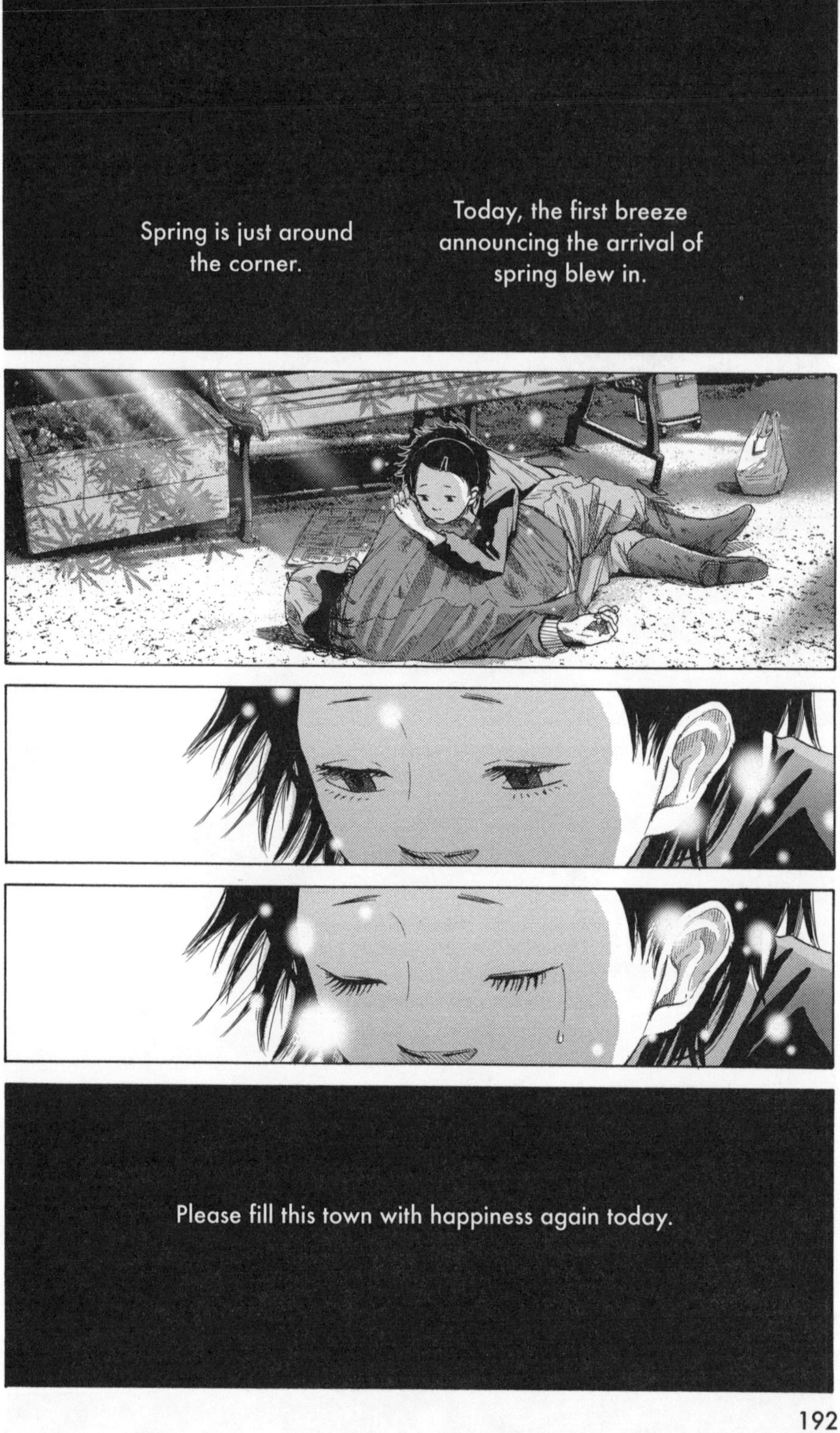
Today, the first breeze announcing the arrival of spring blew in.
Spring is just around the corner.
Please fill this town with happiness again today.

This wind chime hangs there all year long.

More than anything, it goes to show that I have a pretty pathetic sense of seasons.

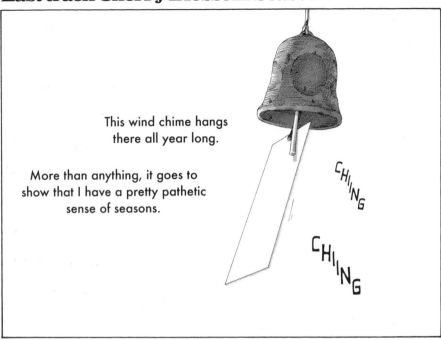

CHIING

CHIING

voosh

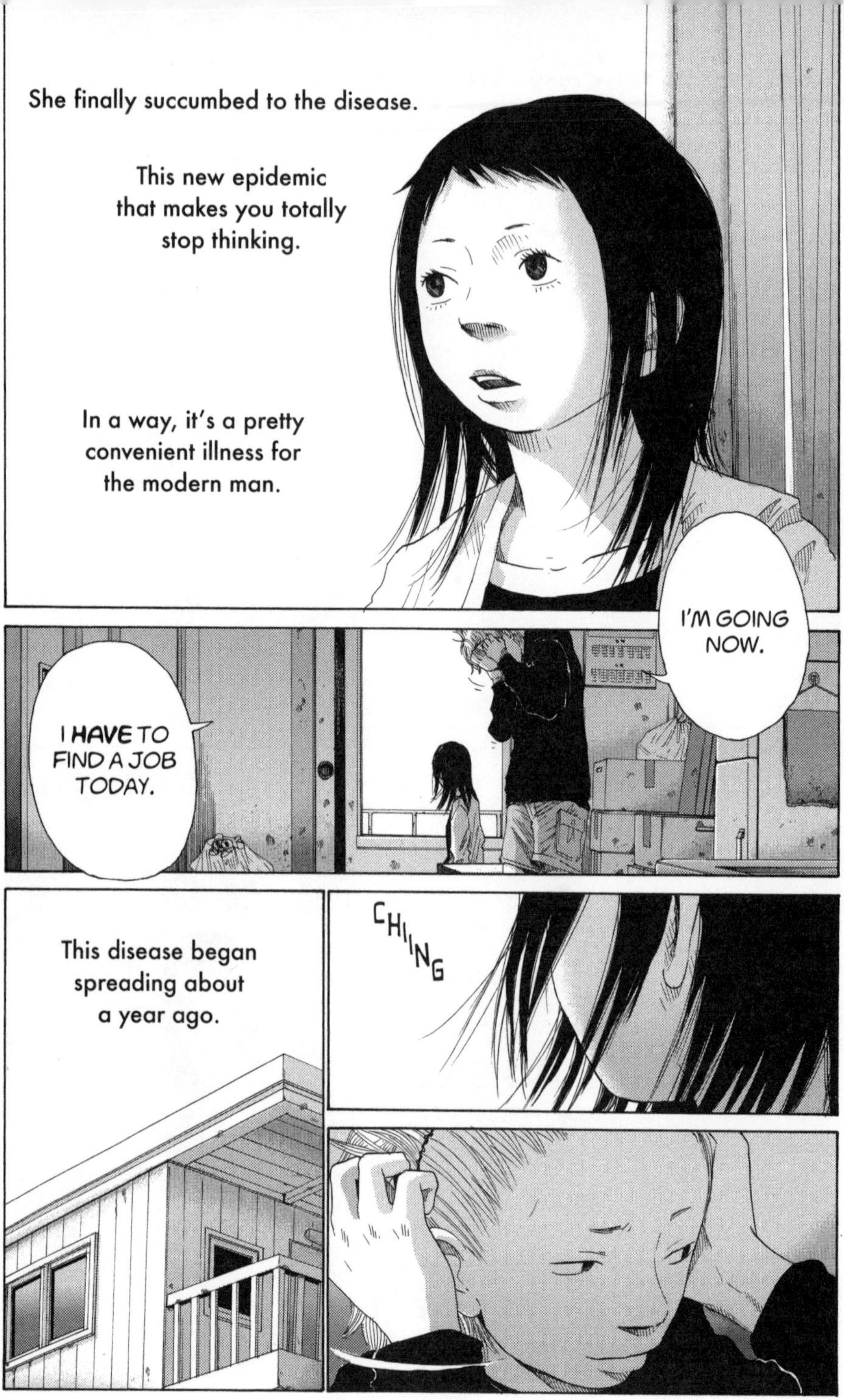
She finally succumbed to the disease.
This new epidemic that makes you totally stop thinking.
In a way, it's a pretty convenient illness for the modern man.
I'M GOING NOW.
I HAVE TO FIND A JOB TODAY.
CHIIING
This disease began spreading about a year ago.

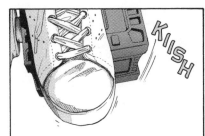

They still don't know the cause or the cure.
KIISH
And one month ago...
...she became like a remote-controlled doll.
Last track Cherry Blossom Season
左右確認
WHAT a WONDERFUL WORLD!

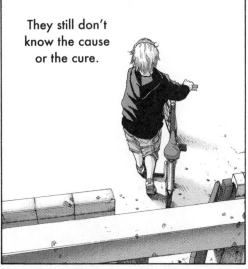

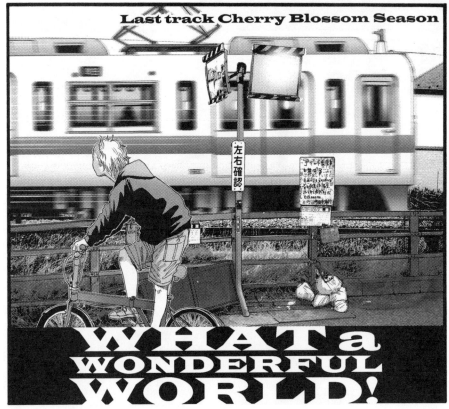

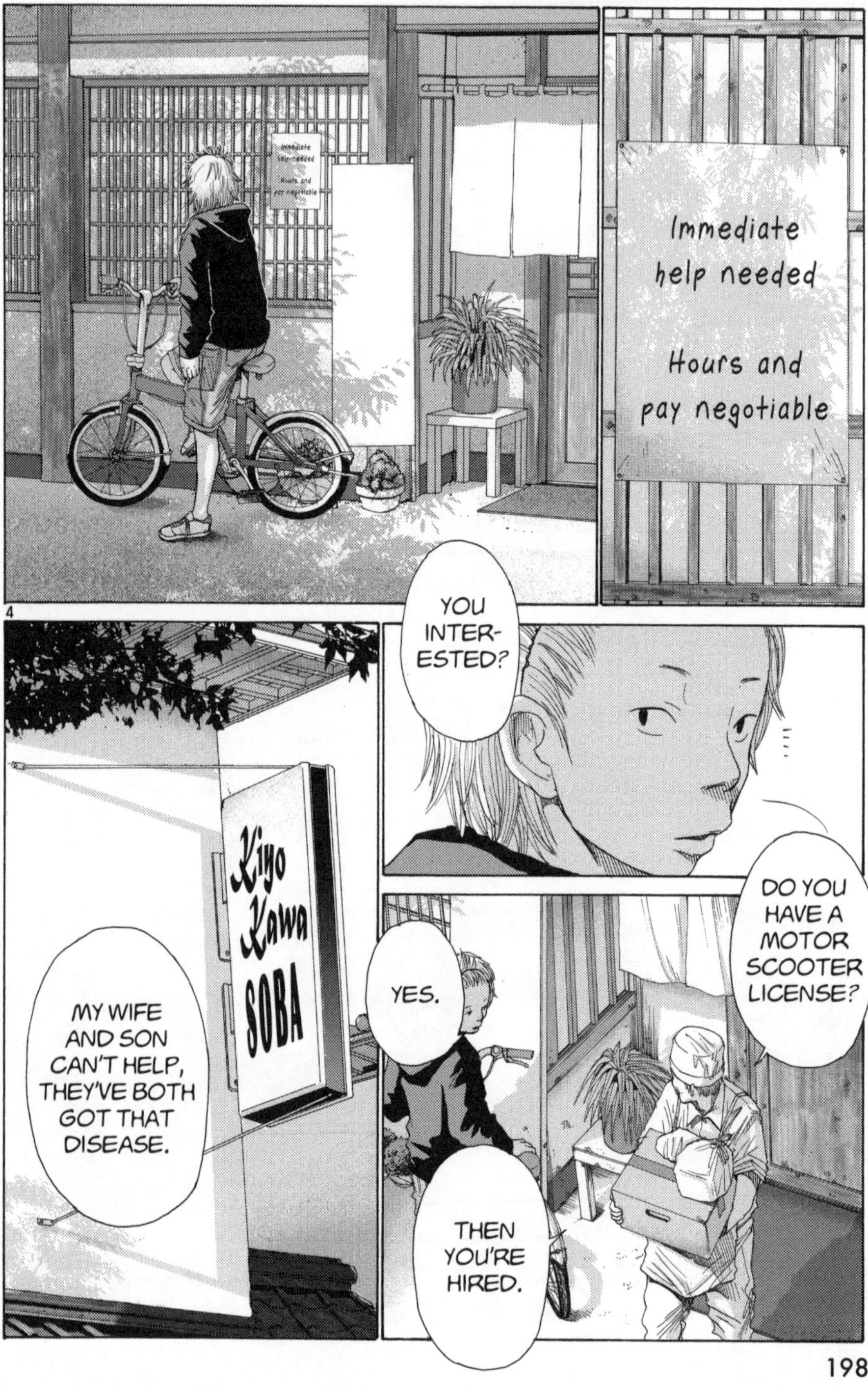
Immediate help needed
Hours and pay negotiable
YOU INTER-ESTED?
DO YOU HAVE A MOTOR SCOOTER LICENSE?
YES.
THEN YOU'RE HIRED.
Kiyo Kawa SOBA
MY WIFE AND SON CAN'T HELP, THEY'VE BOTH GOT THAT DISEASE.

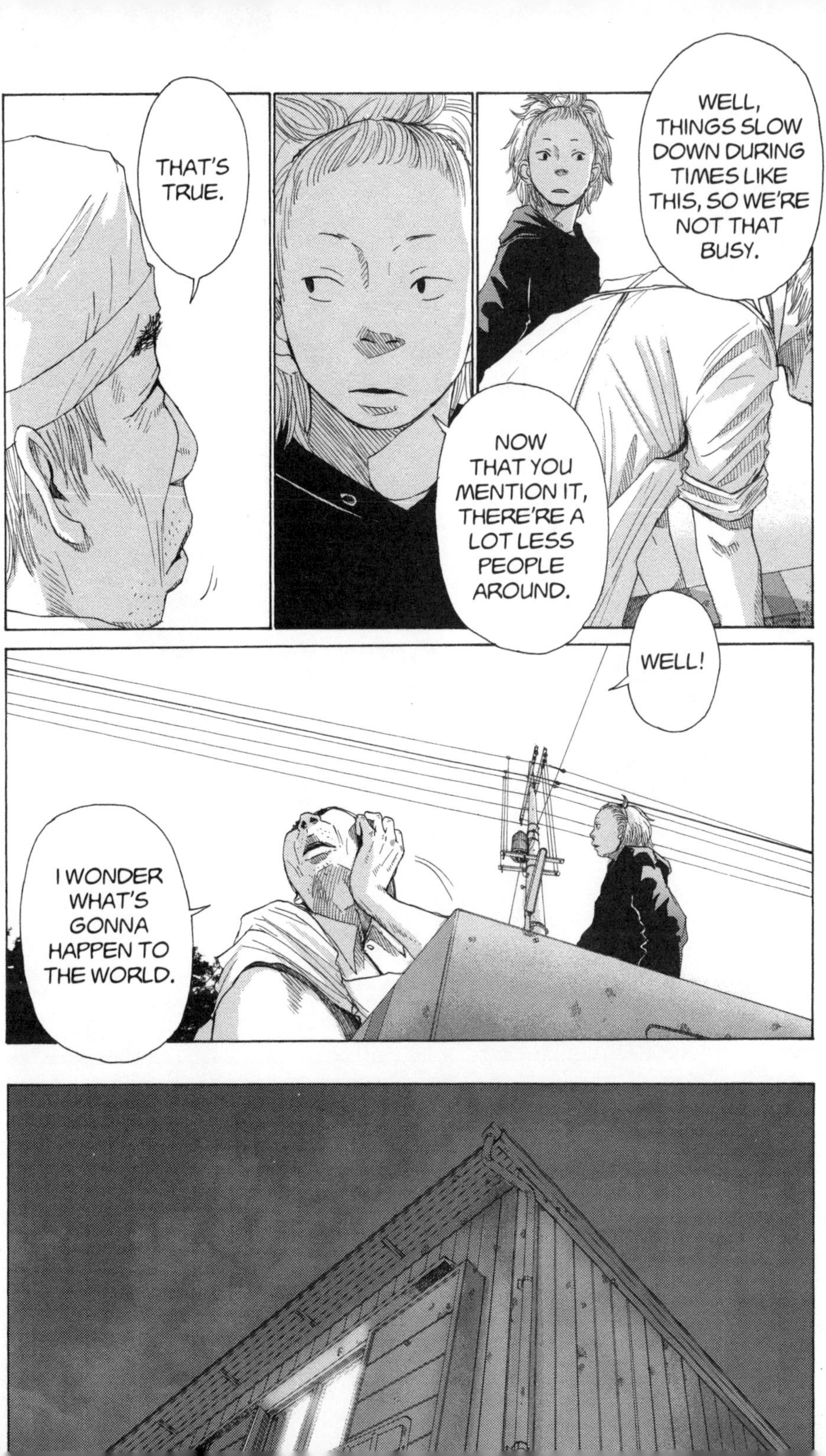
WELL, THINGS SLOW DOWN DURING TIMES LIKE THIS, SO WE'RE NOT THAT BUSY.
NOW THAT YOU MENTION IT, THERE'RE A LOT LESS PEOPLE AROUND.
THAT'S TRUE.
WELL!
I WONDER WHAT'S GONNA HAPPEN TO THE WORLD.

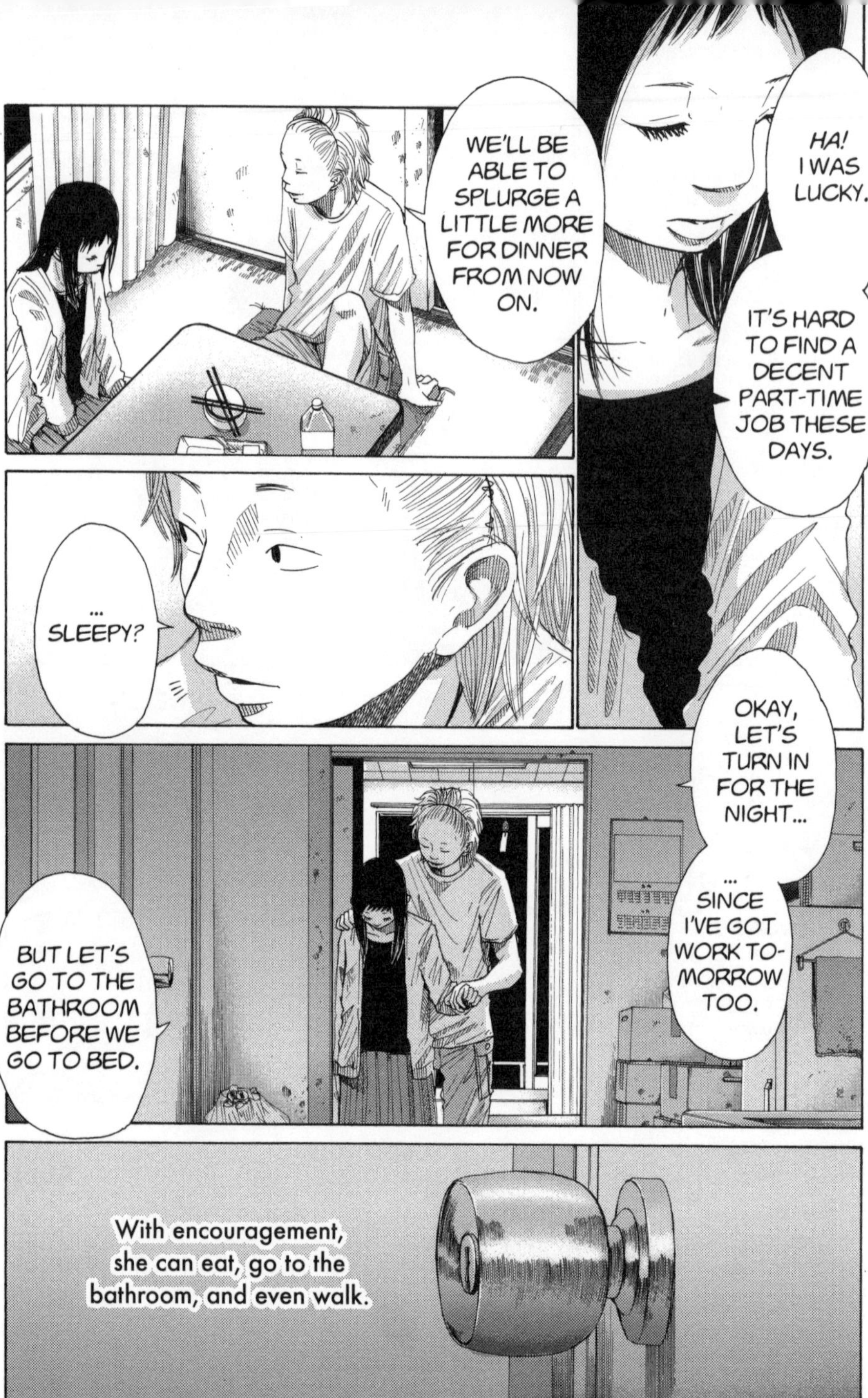
HA! I WAS LUCKY.
IT'S HARD TO FIND A DECENT PART-TIME JOB THESE DAYS.
WE'LL BE ABLE TO SPLURGE A LITTLE MORE FOR DINNER FROM NOW ON.
... SLEEPY?
OKAY, LET'S TURN IN FOR THE NIGHT...
... SINCE I'VE GOT WORK TO-MORROW TOO.
BUT LET'S GO TO THE BATHROOM BEFORE WE GO TO BED.
With encouragement, she can eat, go to the bathroom, and even walk.

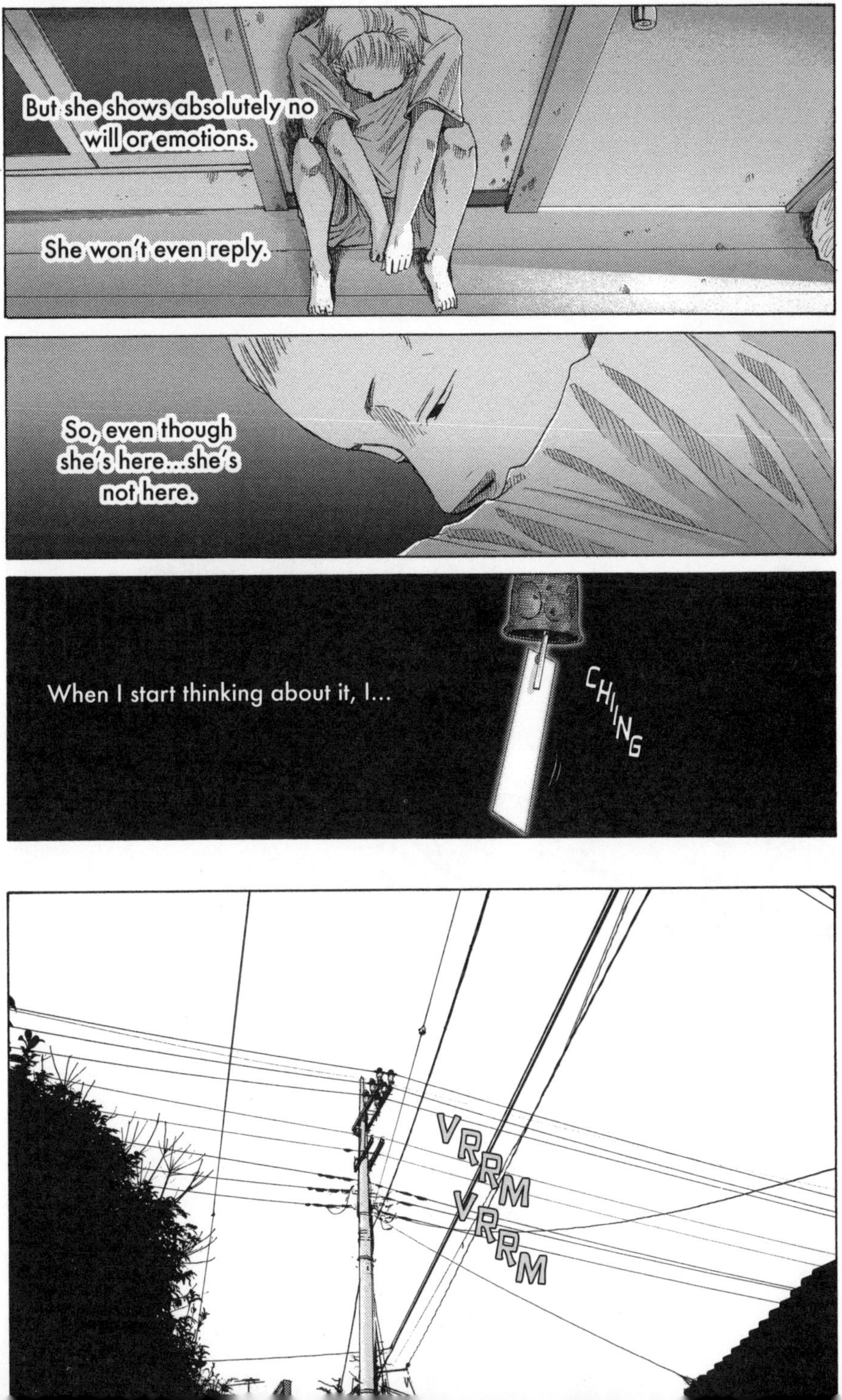
But she shows absolutely no will or emotions.
She won't even reply.
So, even though she's here...she's not here.
CHING
When I start thinking about it, I...
VRRM VRRRM

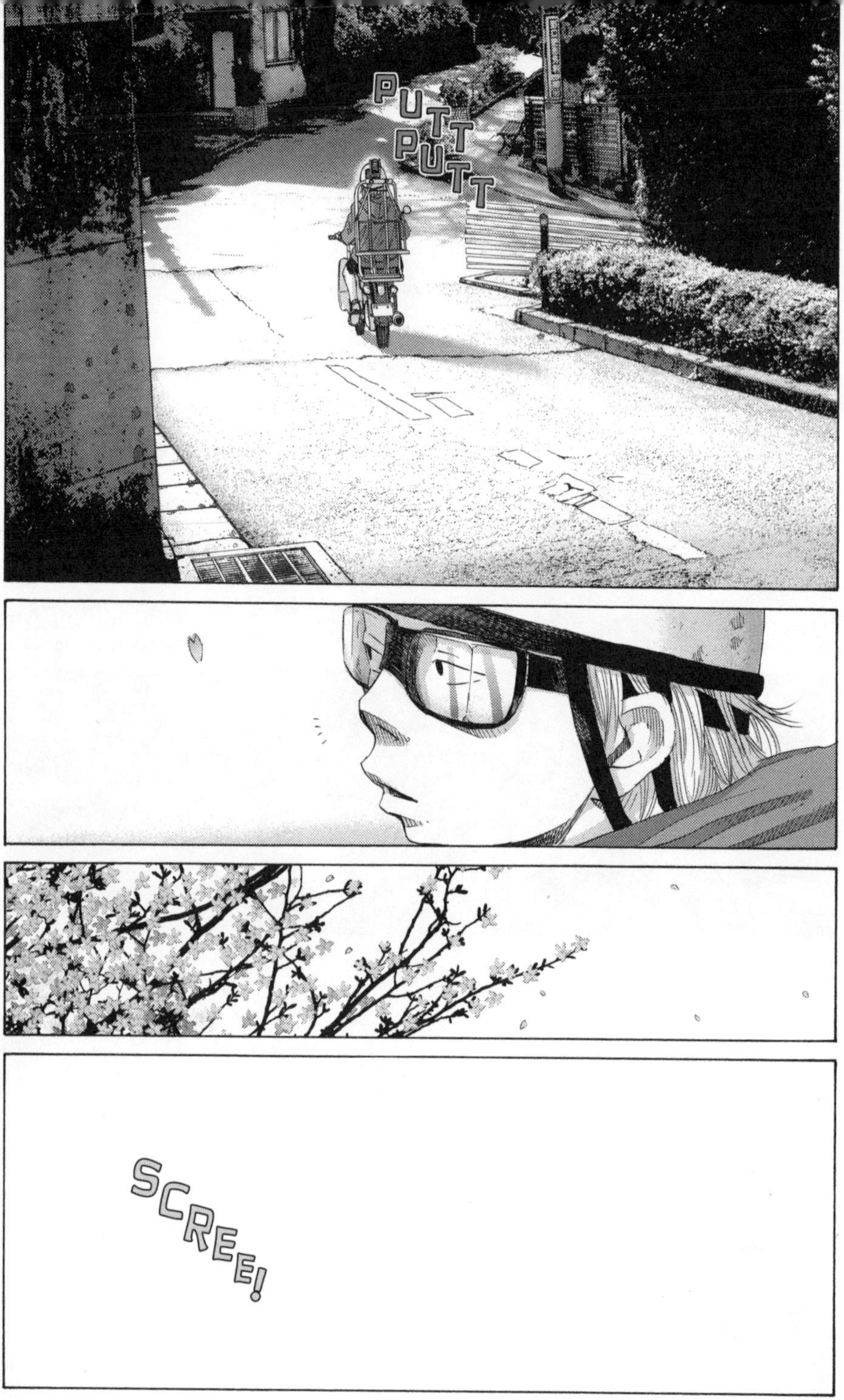
PUTT PUTT
SCREE!

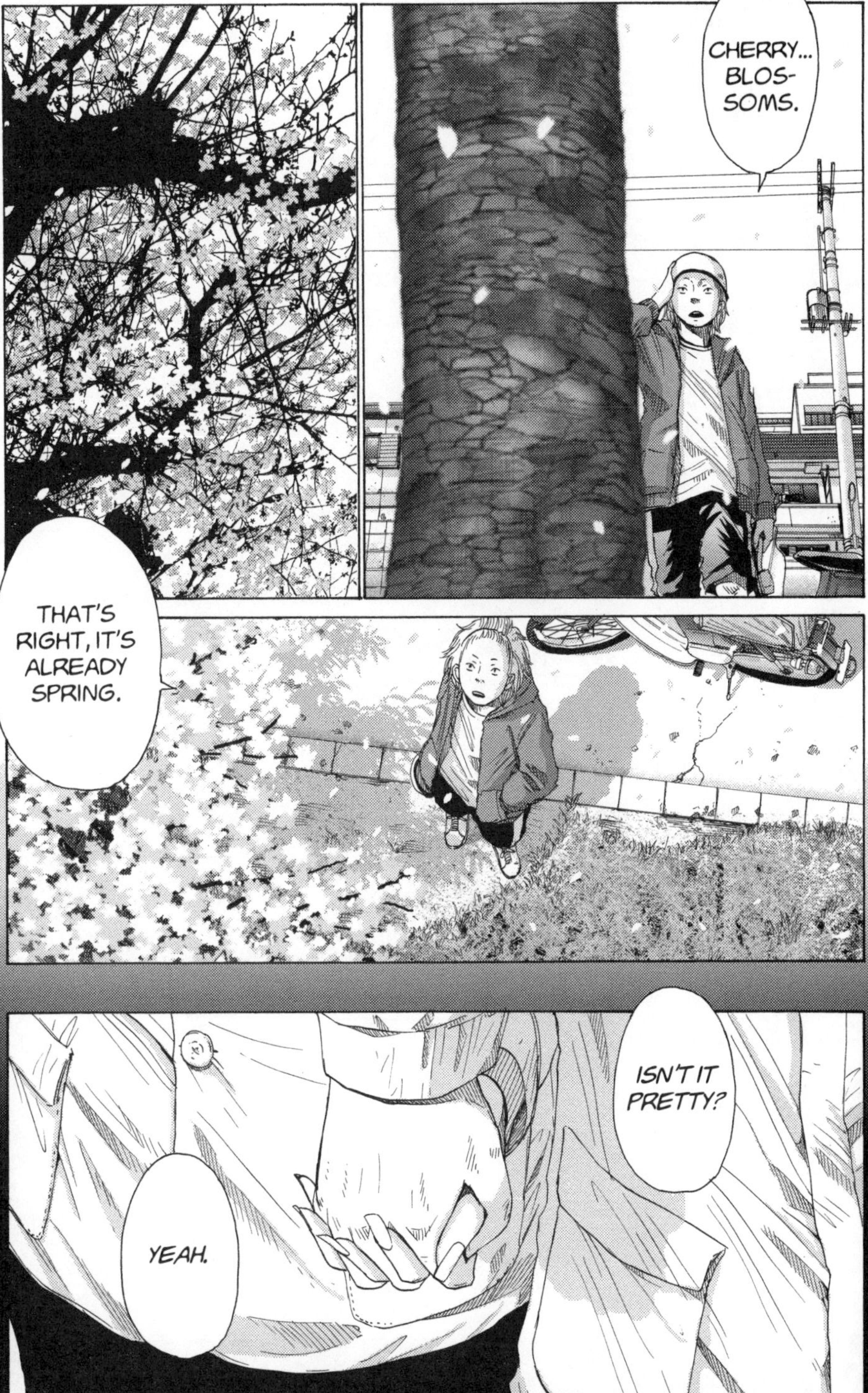
CHERRY... BLOS-SOMS.
THAT'S RIGHT, IT'S ALREADY SPRING.
ISN'T IT PRETTY?
YEAH.

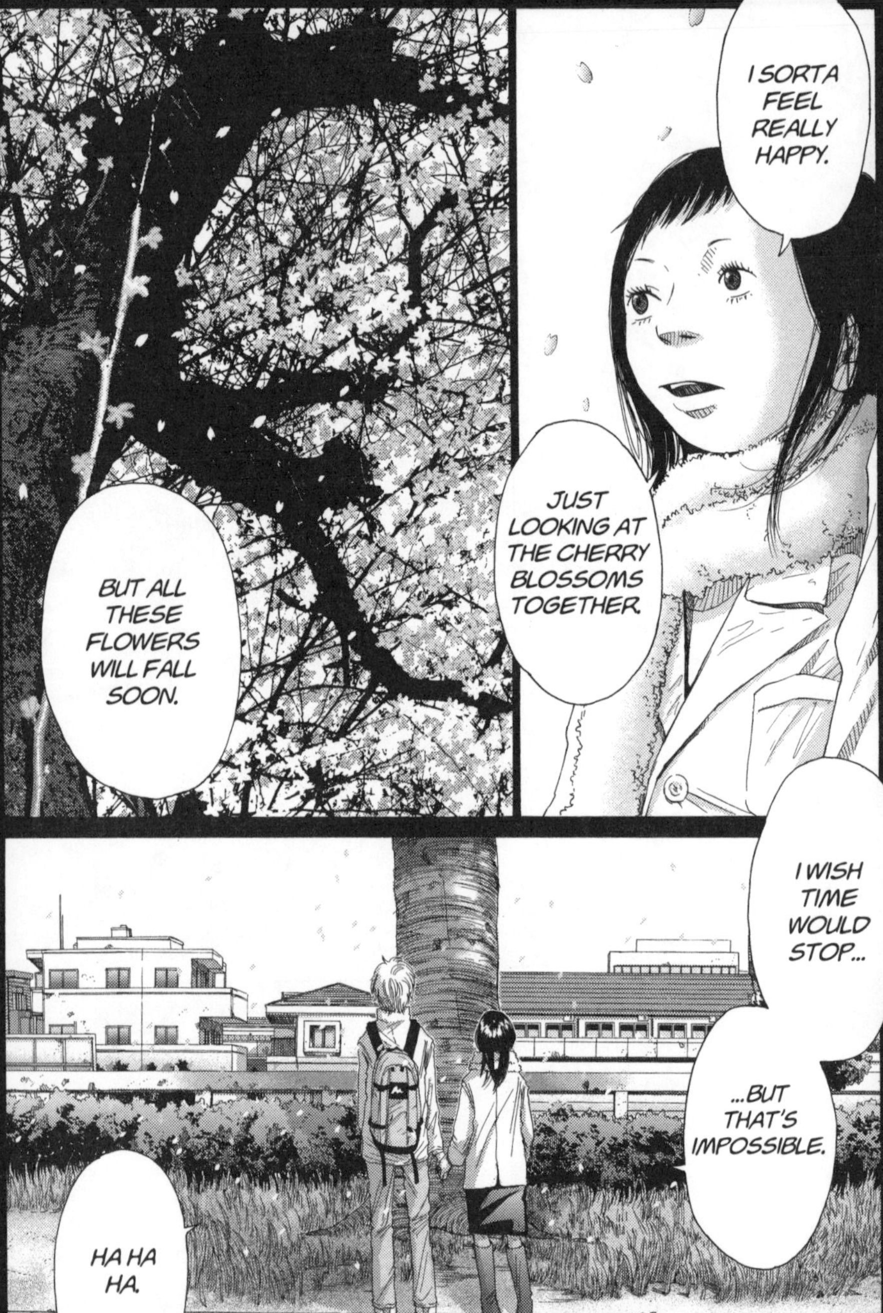
I SORTA FEEL REALLY HAPPY.
JUST LOOKING AT THE CHERRY BLOSSOMS TOGETHER.
BUT ALL THESE FLOWERS WILL FALL SOON.
I WISH TIME WOULD STOP...
...BUT THAT'S IMPOSSIBLE.
HA HA HA.

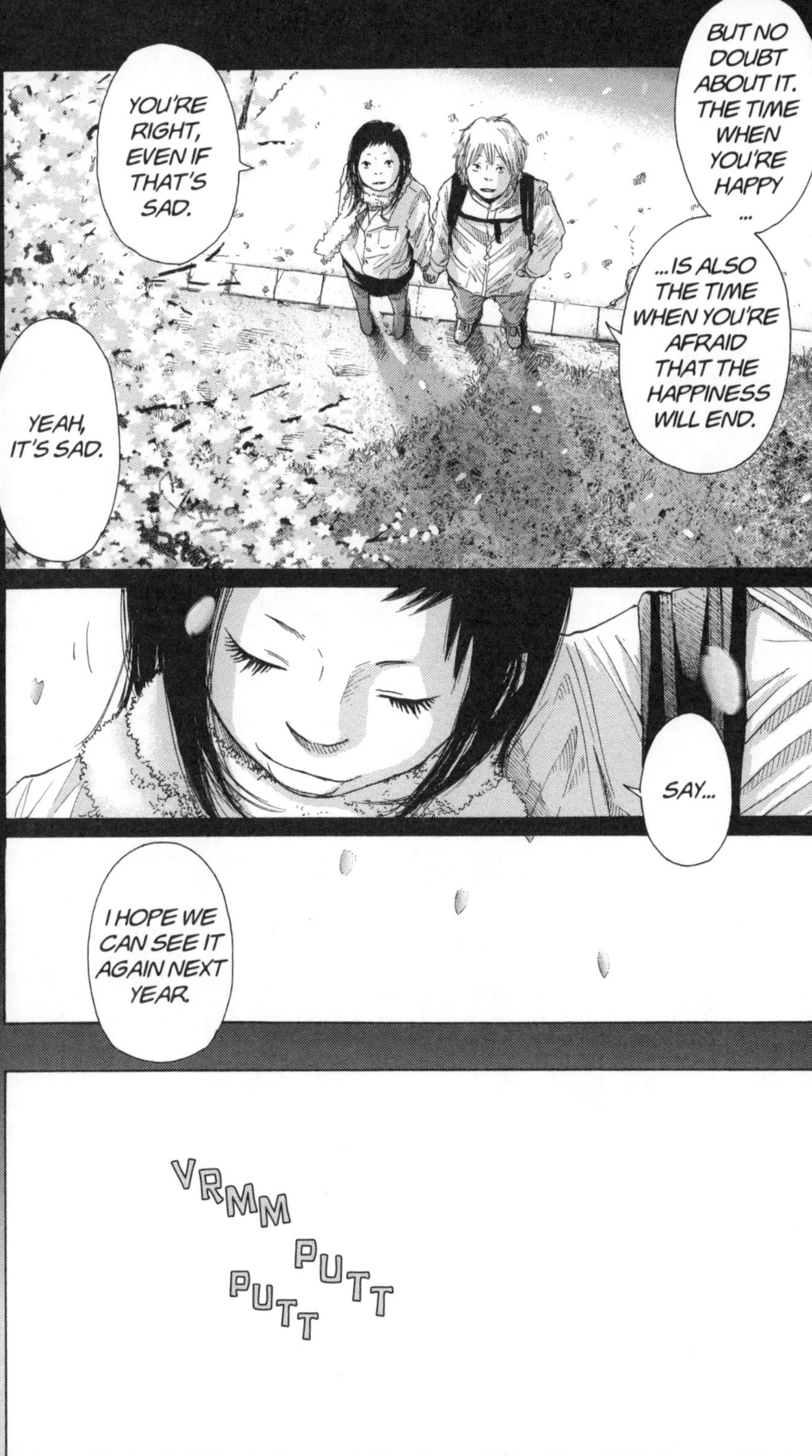
BUT NO DOUBT ABOUT IT. THE TIME WHEN YOU'RE HAPPY ...
...IS ALSO THE TIME WHEN YOU'RE AFRAID THAT THE HAPPINESS WILL END.
YOU'RE RIGHT, EVEN IF THAT'S SAD.
YEAH, IT'S SAD.
SAY...
I HOPE WE CAN SEE IT AGAIN NEXT YEAR.
VRMM
PUTT PUTT

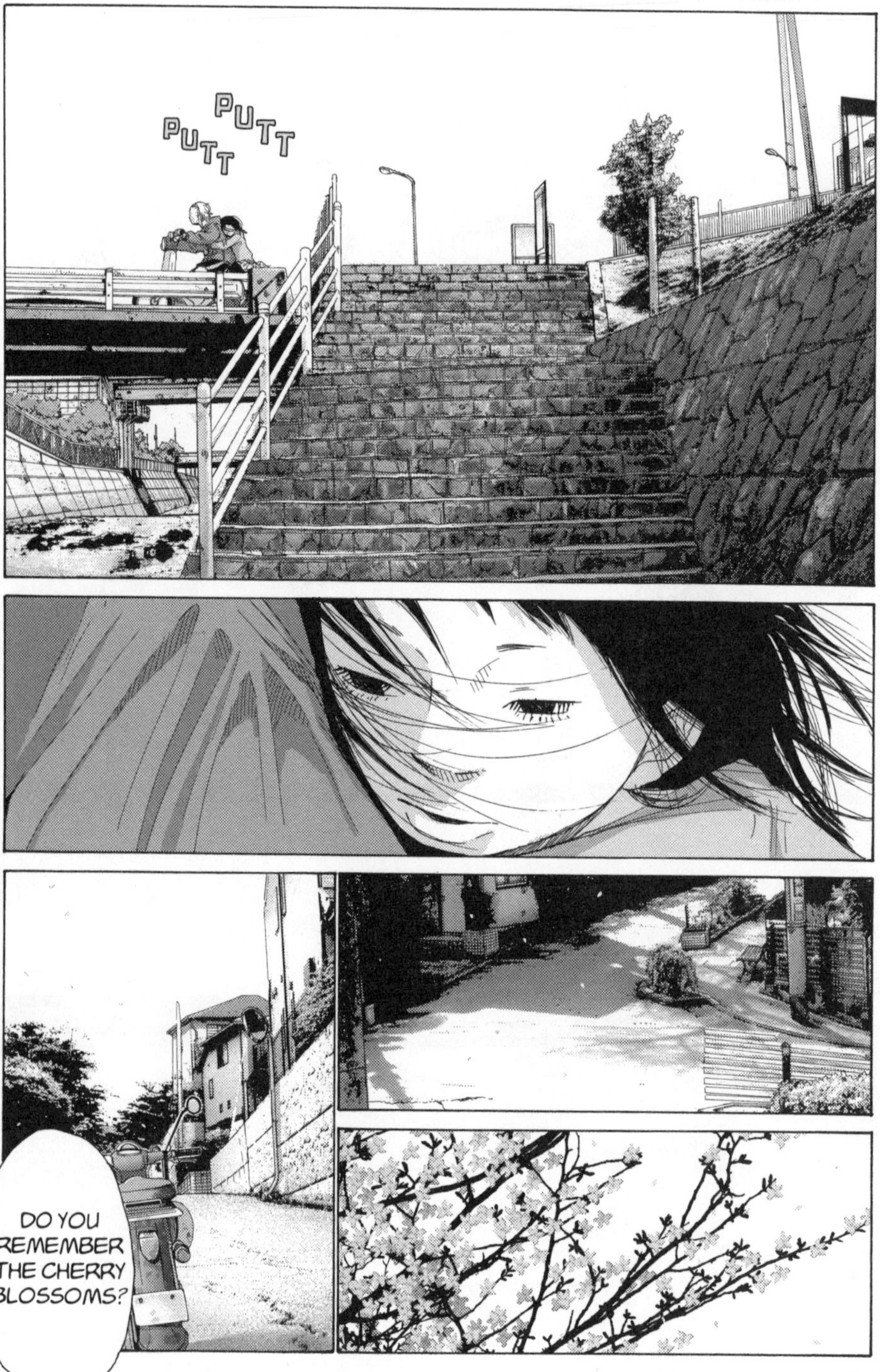
PUTT
PUTT
DO YOU REMEMBER THE CHERRY BLOSSOMS?

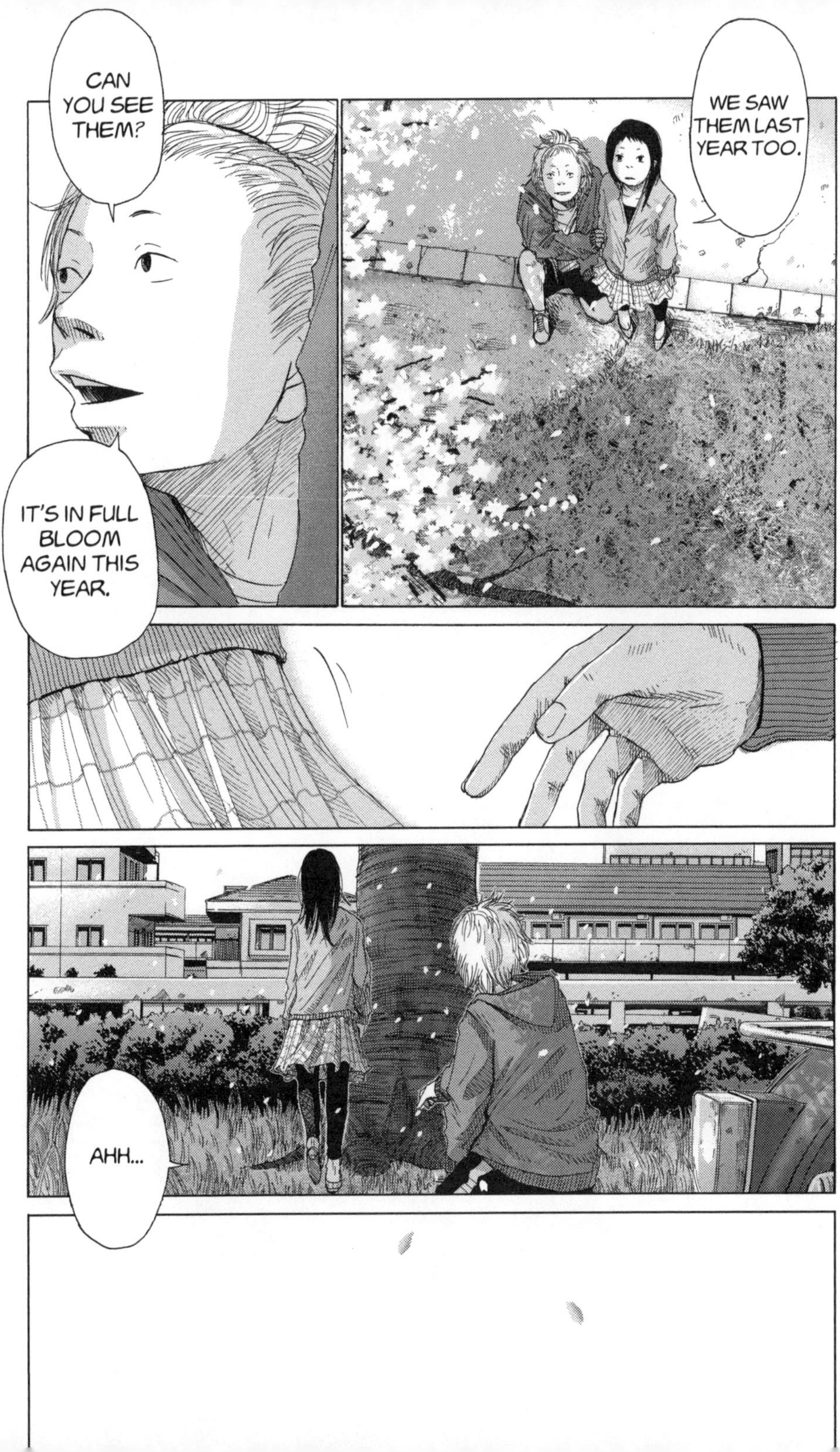
WE SAW THEM LAST YEAR TOO.
CAN YOU SEE THEM?
IT'S IN FULL BLOOM AGAIN THIS YEAR.
AHH...

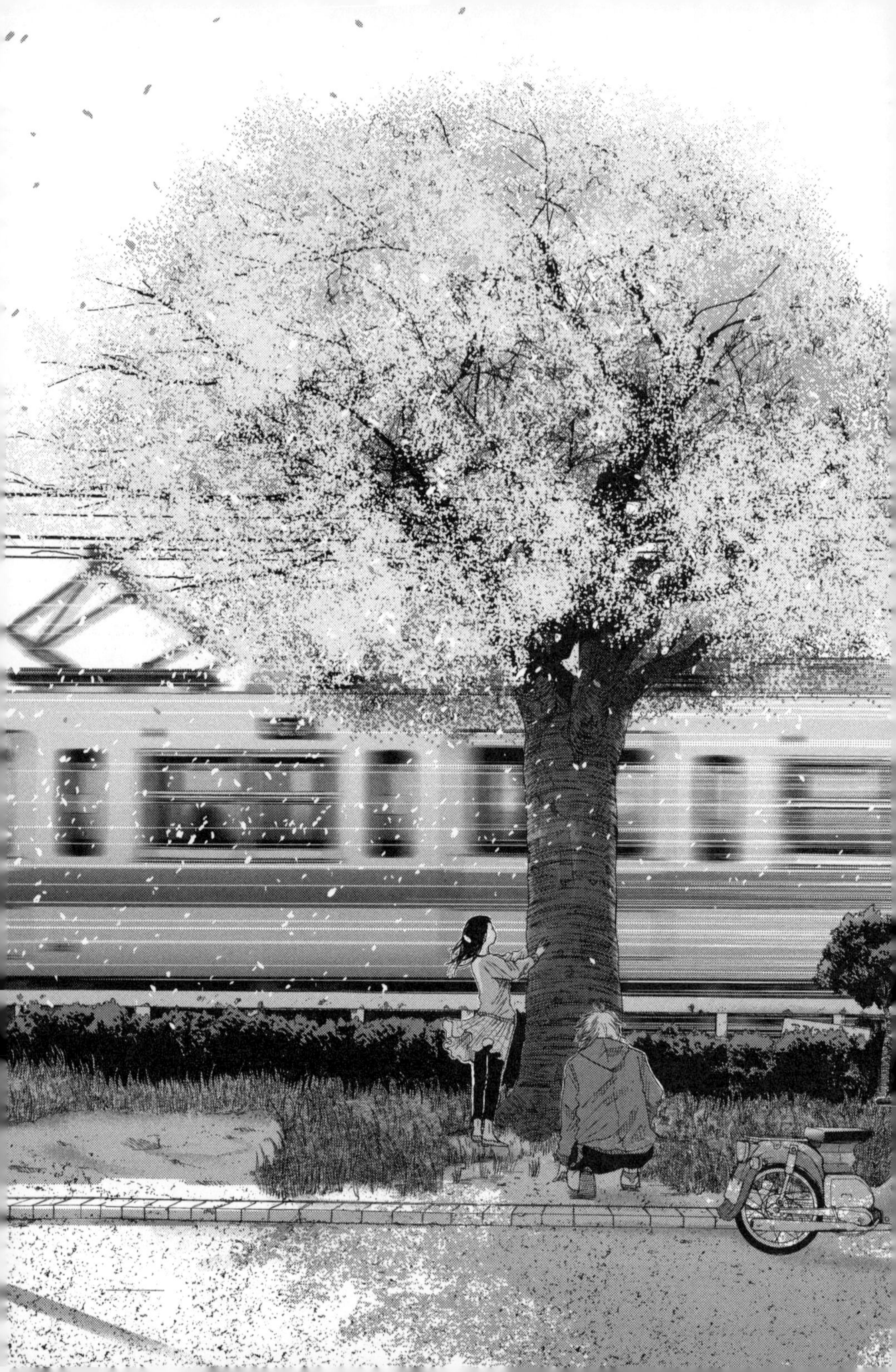

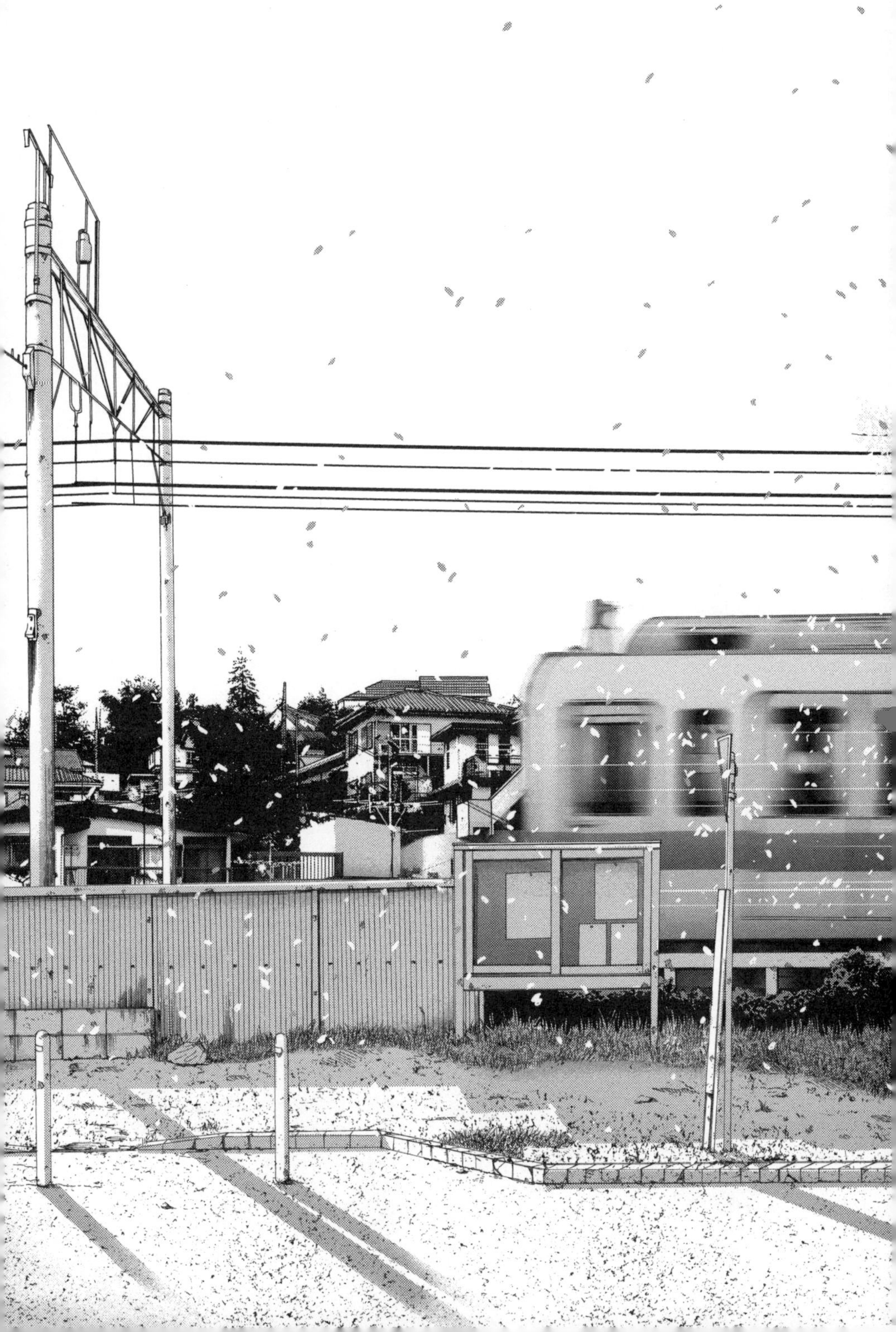

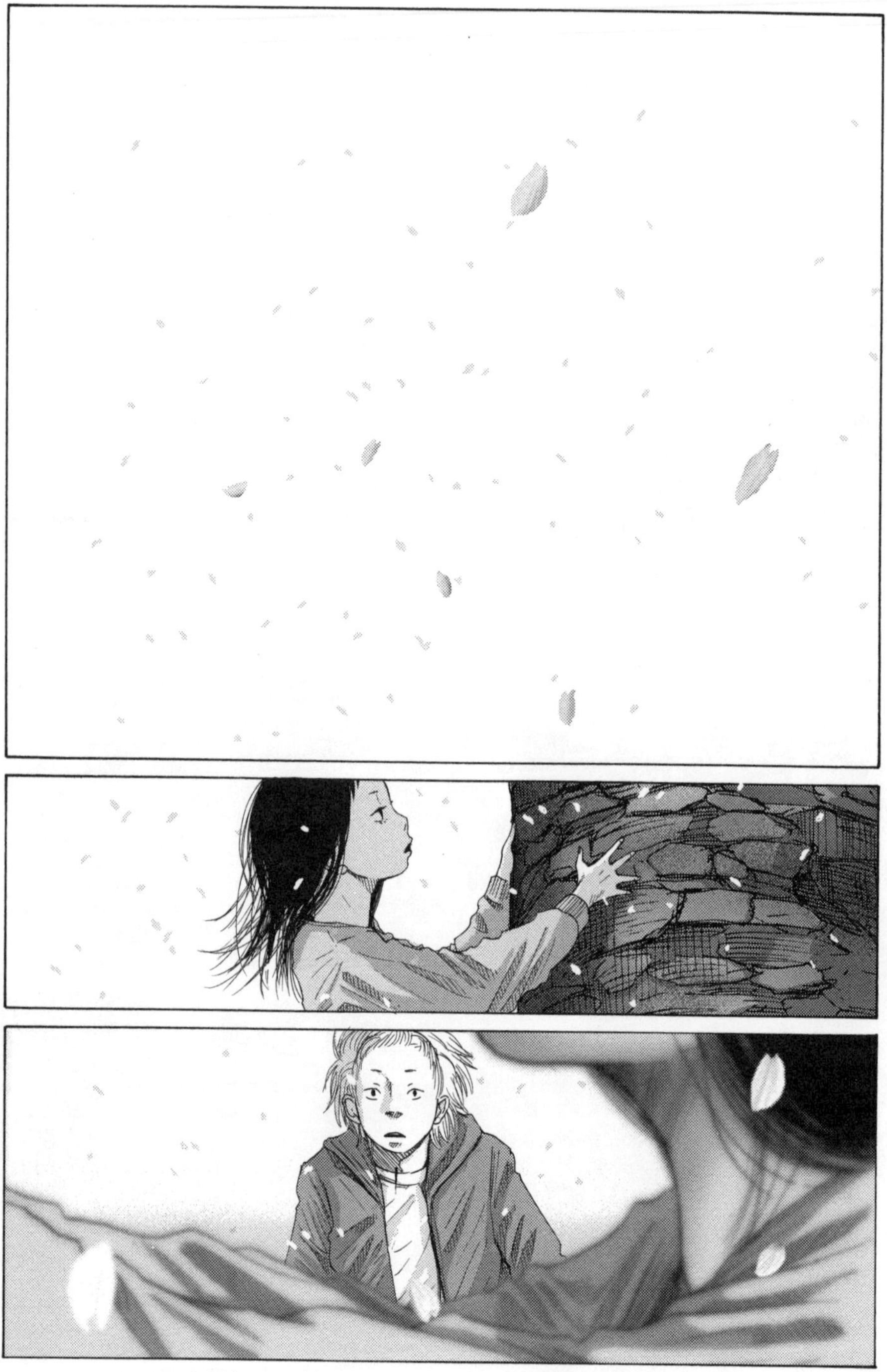

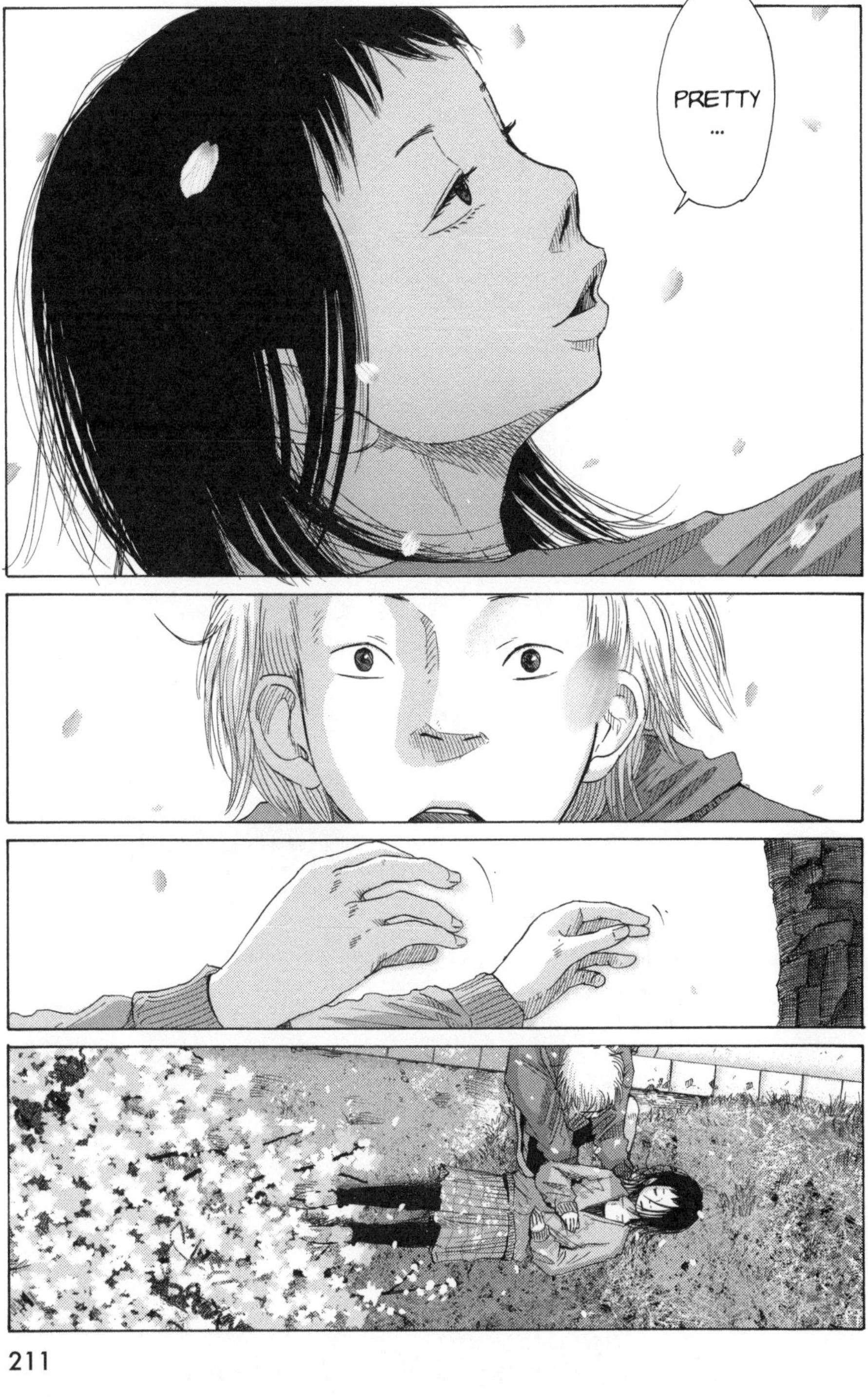
PRETTY
...

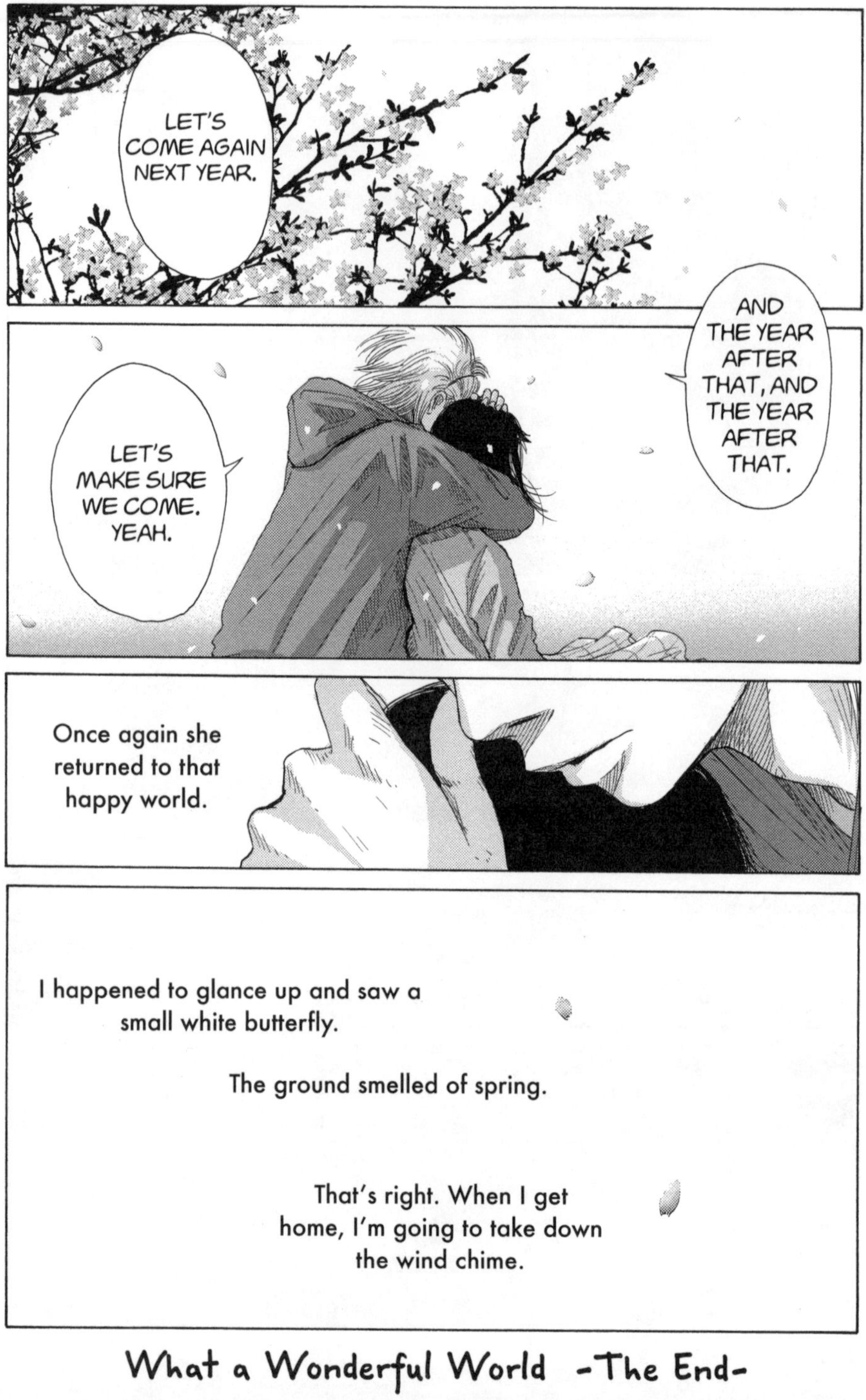
LET'S COME AGAIN NEXT YEAR.
AND THE YEAR AFTER THAT, AND THE YEAR AFTER THAT.
LET'S MAKE SURE WE COME. YEAH.
Once again she returned to that happy world.
I happened to glance up and saw a small white butterfly.
The ground smelled of spring.
That's right. When I get home, I'm going to take down the wind chime.

What a Wonderful World -The End-

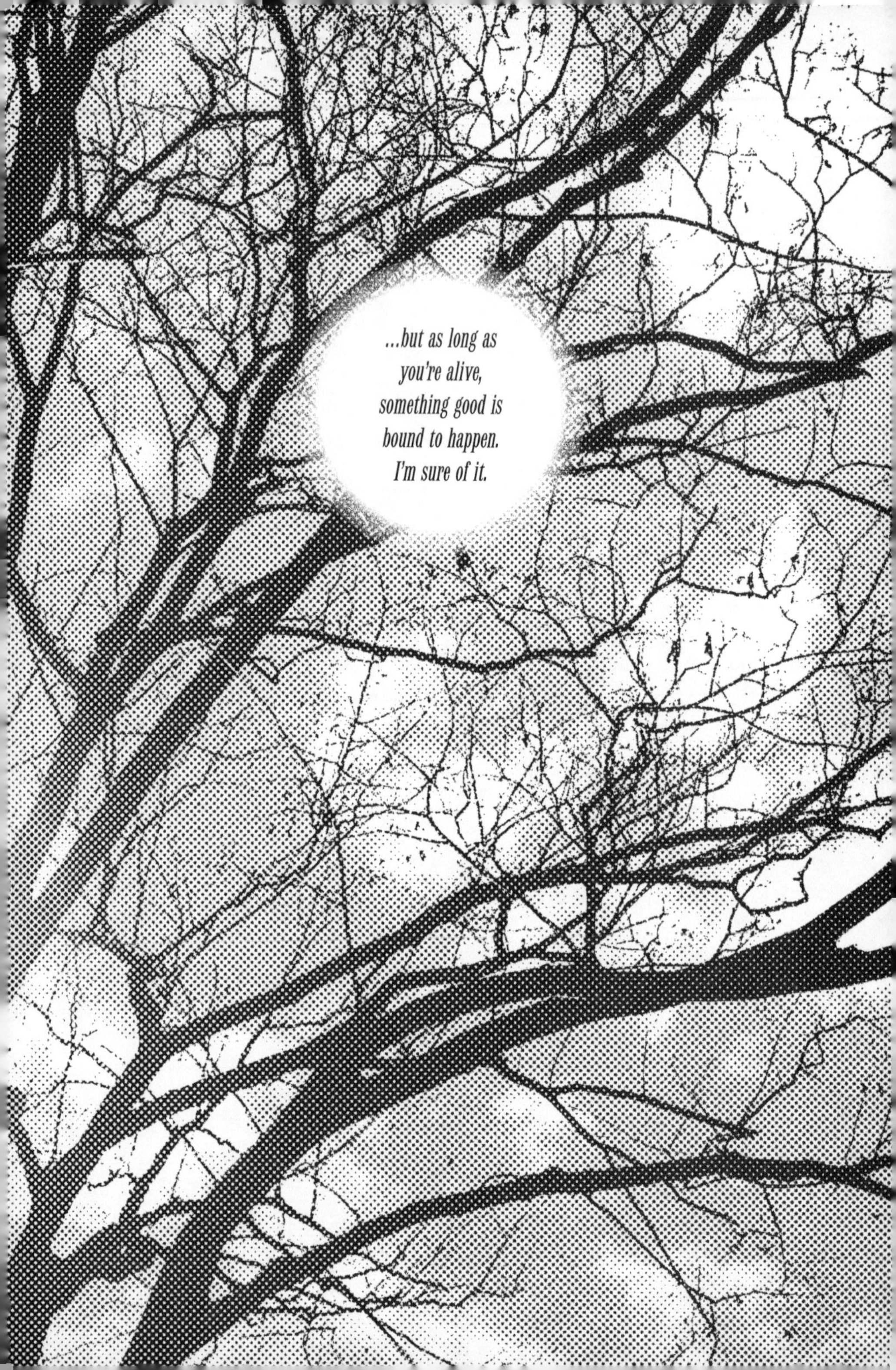
...but as long as you're alive, something good is bound to happen. I'm sure of it.

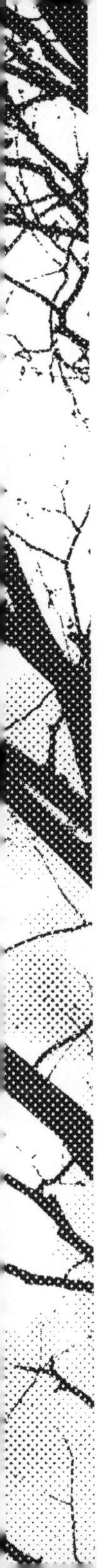

What a Wonderful World! 2

VIZ Signature Edition

Story and Art by Inio Asano


Original Japanese edition "SUBARASHII SEKAI"
published by SHOGAKUKAN Inc.

Translation/JN Productions
Touch-up Art & Lettering/Joanna Estep
Design/Frances O. Liddell
Editor/Pancha Diaz



Printed in the U.S.A.

Published by VIZ Media, LLC
P.O. Box 77010
San Francisco, CA 94107

10 9 8 7 6 5 4 3
First printing, October 2009
Third printing, December 2017

www.viz.com www.vizsignature.com



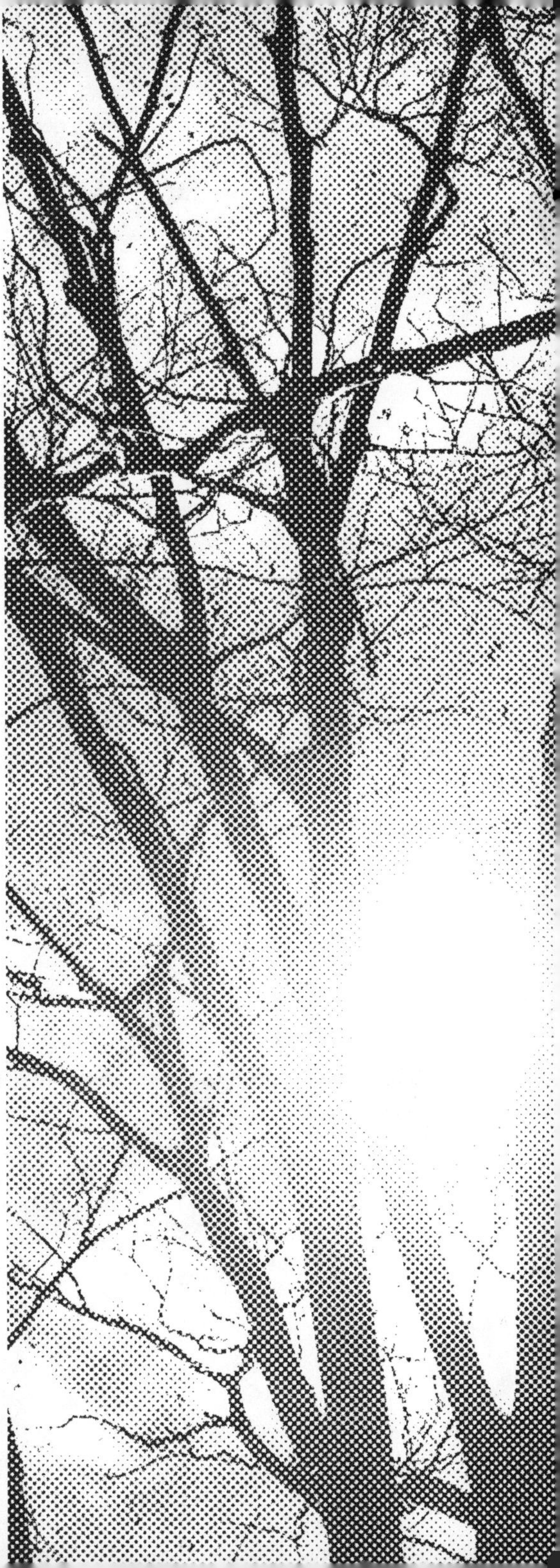

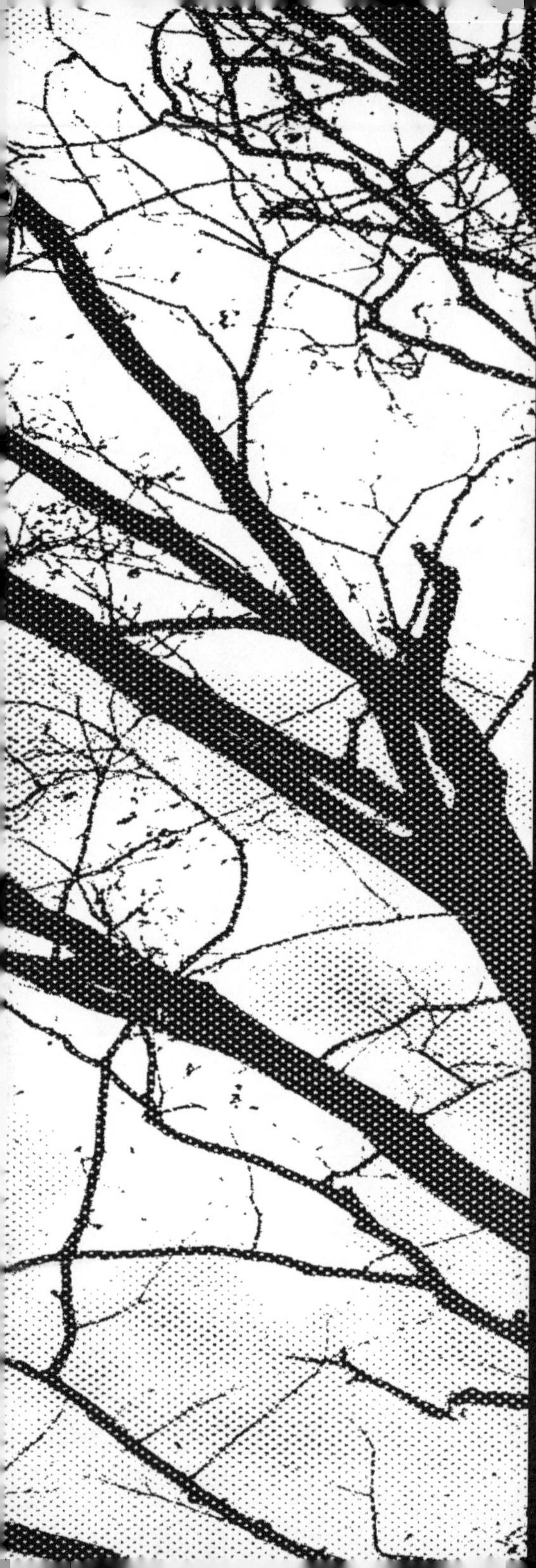

## this is the last page.

*What a Wonderful World!* has been printed in the original Japanese format in order to preserve the orientation of the original artwork.